*Quick*notes

THE

DICTIONARY
OF
BIBLE NAMES

THE
DICTIONARY
OF
BIBLE NAMES

PAMELA McQUADE

with Paul Kent

BARBOUR
PUBLISHING

© 2009 by Barbour Publishing, Inc.

ISBN 978-1-60260-480-3

All scripture quotations are taken from the King James Version of the Bible.

Cover image © P Deliss/Godong/Corbris

Published by Barbour Publishing, Inc., P.O. Box 719, Uhrichsville, Ohio 44683, www.barbourbooks.com.

Our mission is to publish and distribute inspirational products offering exceptional value and biblical encouragement to the masses.

 Member of the
Evangelical Christian
Publishers Association

Printed in the United States of America

We have based this *Dictionary of Bible Names* on the King James Version of the Bible and *Strong's Expanded Exhaustive Concordance of the Bible* (Nashville/Thomas Nelson, 2001). The King James Version is the standard text for many Christians, and James Strong based his widely used concordance on it—so instead of reworking our entire volume to another, perhaps passing, translation, we have used these favorite and familiar volumes as the starting place for our work.

For the 2,026 proper names in scripture, covering some 3,400 people, the *Dictionary of Bible Names* provides readers with concise information in the following categories:

- **Number of Times Mentioned**—providing the number of times the name is found in the King James Version.

- **Number of Men and Number of Women**—since, as today, some names can be used by both men and women, the number of references for each gender has also been included.

- **Genealogy of Jesus**—when scripture indicates that a person was part of Jesus' family tree, it is shown by a crown graphic, as well as separate scripture references.

- **Meaning**—where possible, a name translation based on Strong's Hebrew and Aramaic Dictionary and The New Strong's Expanded Dictionary of the Words in the Greek New Testament is provided.

- **Biography**—an outline of each person's history. For those mentioned only once or twice, this information is necessarily brief. More prominent individuals receive proportionately longer entries.

- **References**—including the first (or only) time the name appears in scripture and the last. Where many references describe one person, some key references for that biography have also been provided.

Where a person had more than one name or where scripture provides us with variations of the name, alternative names or spellings are listed at the end of the biography section. For example, Jashub's biography includes the information "Same as Job (1)," referring readers to the first listing for the name Job. Please note that we have not included titles or the names of spirit beings in this dictionary.

In a few cases, readers will find differences here from what is shown in *Strong's*. One man, working manually on such a large project, was bound, perhaps, to make some minor errors. On top of that, scholarship through the ages has given us varying answers to questions about confusing references. Scholars of any age may differ on whether, for example, a person mentioned in one of the biblical name lists is the same as one mentioned in another place. Where a name is listed multiple times and references are not clear, we have made use of existing scholarship to determine one logical solution.

For the many hundreds of people recorded in scripture, this *Dictionary of Bible Names* will provide the concise information you need to quickly understand each individual's background, prominence, and contribution to history. We hope it will spur you on to further study of scripture.

-A-

AARON   350
Meaning uncertain

The older brother of Moses, Aaron was called into God's service when Moses balked at confronting Pharaoh about his enslavement of the people of Israel. "I know that he can speak well," God said of Aaron (Exodus 4:14). He became God's spokesman and supported Moses' leadership for nearly forty years. He was the first priest of Israel and headed a familial line of priests that continued for more than a thousand years. But Aaron made three memorable mistakes: He created a golden calf idol for the people of Israel when Moses stayed long on Mount Sinai receiving God's Ten Commandments (Exodus 32)—starting a cycle of idolatry that would plague the Israelites for centuries. He and his sister, Miriam, complained about Moses' Ethiopian wife—and Miriam contracted a temporary case of leprosy as punishment (Numbers 12). And Aaron and Moses both incurred God's judgment—banishment from the Promised Land—when they disobeyed the Lord by striking, rather than speaking to, a rock to provide miraculous water for the people at Kadesh (Numbers 20). Aaron died at age 123 on Mount Hor (Number 33:39), with his brother at his side.

FIRST REFERENCE
EXODUS 4:14
LAST REFERENCE
HEBREWS 9:4
KEY REFERENCES
EXODUS 4:30; 32:2–4; LEVITICUS 9:7

ABAGTHA   I

One of seven eunuchs serving the Persian king Ahasuerus in Esther's time.

ONLY REFERENCE
ESTHER 1:10

ABDA   2
Work

1) Father of King Solomon's official over forced labor, Adoniram.

ONLY REFERENCE
I KINGS 4:6

2) A Levite worship leader in Jerusalem after the Babylonian Exile.

ONLY REFERENCE
NEHEMIAH 11:17

ABDEEL   I
Serving God

Father of Shelemiah, an official under Judah's king Jehoiakim.

ONLY REFERENCE
JEREMIAH 36:26

ABDI 3

Serviceable

1) A Levite, father of temple servant Kish of King Hezekiah's day.

FIRST REFERENCE
I CHRONICLES 6:44
LAST REFERENCE
2 CHRONICLES 29:12

2) An exiled Israelite who married a "strange" (foreign) woman.

ONLY REFERENCE
EZRA 10:26

ABDIEL I

Servant of God

A descendant of Abraham through Jacob's son Gad.

ONLY REFERENCE
I CHRONICLES 5:15

ABDON 6

Servitude

1) The twelfth judge of Israel who led the nation for eight years. He was known for having forty sons and thirty nephews who each rode a donkey.

FIRST REFERENCE
JUDGES 12:13
LAST REFERENCE
JUDGES 12:15

2) A descendant of Abraham through Jacob's son Benjamin.

ONLY REFERENCE
I CHRONICLES 8:23

3) Another descendant of Abraham through Jacob's son Benjamin.

FIRST REFERENCE
I CHRONICLES 8:30
LAST REFERENCE
I CHRONICLES 9:36

4) One of five men sent by King Josiah to ask God's prophetess Huldah what to do about the "book of the law" recently discovered in the temple.

ONLY REFERENCE
2 CHRONICLES 34:20

ABED-NEGO 15

The Babylonian name for Azariah, one of Daniel's companions in exile. Daniel had King Nebuchadnezzar make Abed-nego a ruler in Babylon. When some Chaldeans accused Abed-nego and his fellow Jews and corulers, Shadrach and Meshach, of not worshipping the king's golden idol, the three faithful Jews were thrown into a furnace. God protected His men, who were not even singed. The king recognized the power of their God and promoted them in his service.

FIRST REFERENCE
DANIEL 1:7
LAST REFERENCE
DANIEL 3:30
KEY REFERENCE
DANIEL 3:16–18

ABEL 12

Emptiness or vanity

Humanity's fourth member, the second son of Adam and Eve, Abel was murdered by his jealous brother, Cain. The shepherd Abel's meat offering pleased God more than Cain's "fruit of the ground." When God asked Cain the whereabouts of his murdered brother, Cain replied, "I know not: Am I my brother's keeper?" (Genesis 4:9). Jesus called Abel "righteous" in His denunciation of the scribes and Pharisees for persecuting the prophets.

FIRST REFERENCE
GENESIS 4:2
LAST REFERENCE
HEBREWS 12:24
KEY REFERENCE
GENESIS 4:4

ABI

Fatherly

Daughter of Zachariah and mother of Judah's good king Hezekiah.

ONLY REFERENCE
2 KINGS 18:2

ABIA 4 2

Worshipper of God

1) Grandson of King Solomon and son of King Rehoboam. He inherited the throne of Judah. Same as Abijah (3).

FIRST REFERENCE
I CHRONICLES 3:10
LAST REFERENCE
MATTHEW 1:7
GENEALOGY OF JESUS
MATTHEW 1:7

2) A priest who headed a division of priests at the time of Jesus' birth.

ONLY REFERENCE
LUKE 1:5

ABIAH 4

Worshipper of God

1) The second son of the prophet Samuel. Abiah and his brother, Joel, served as judges in Beersheba, but their poor character caused Israel's leaders to ask Samuel for a king to rule over them.

FIRST REFERENCE
I SAMUEL 8:2
LAST REFERENCE
I CHRONICLES 6:28

2) Wife of Hezron, a descendant of Abraham through Jacob's son Judah.

ONLY REFERENCE
I CHRONICLES 2:24

3) A descendant of Abraham through Jacob's son Benjamin.

ONLY REFERENCE
I CHRONICLES 7:8

ABI-ALBON I

Father of strength

One of King David's warriors known as the "mighty men."

ONLY REFERENCE
2 SAMUEL 23:31

ABIASAPH I

Gatherer

A descendant of Abraham through Jacob's son Levi.

ONLY REFERENCE
EXODUS 6:24

ABIATHAR 31
Father of abundance

The only priest of Nob who escaped when King Saul killed this enclave of priests because they supported David. He became one of David's trusted counselors and the high priest of Israel. But at the end of David's life, Abiathar supported David's son Adonijah as king and drew King Solomon's displeasure down on him. He was banished to his home, though he kept the title of high priest.

FIRST REFERENCE
I SAMUEL 22:20
LAST REFERENCE
MARK 2:26
KEY REFERENCES
I SAMUEL 22:21–22; I KINGS 1:7

ABIDA 1
Knowing

A descendant of Abraham through his second wife, Keturah. Same as Abidah.

ONLY REFERENCE
I CHRONICLES 1:33

ABIDAH 1
Knowing

A descendant of Abraham through his second wife, Keturah. Same as Abida.

ONLY REFERENCE
GENESIS 25:4

ABIDAN 5
Judge

A prince of Benjamin who helped Moses take a census of his tribe.

FIRST REFERENCE
NUMBERS 1:11
LAST REFERENCE
NUMBERS 10:24

ABIEL 3
Possessor of God

1) Grandfather of Israel's king Saul and Saul's army commander, Abner.

FIRST REFERENCE
I SAMUEL 9:1
LAST REFERENCE
I SAMUEL 14:51

2) One of King David's valiant warriors.

ONLY REFERENCE
I CHRONICLES 11:32

ABIEZER 7
Helpful

1) A descendant of Abraham through Joseph's son Manasseh.

FIRST REFERENCE
JOSHUA 17:2
LAST REFERENCE
I CHRONICLES 7:18

2) A commander in King David's army overseeing twenty-four thousand men in the ninth month of each year.

FIRST REFERENCE
2 SAMUEL 23:27
LAST REFERENCE
I CHRONICLES 27:12

ABIGAIL   17

Source of joy

1) A wife of King David. She provided food for David and his men after her first husband, Nabal, refused to help these warriors who defended his land from harm while King Saul and David fought. Nabal died following his wife's telling him what she had done. Because David appreciated Abigail, he married her.

FIRST REFERENCE
I SAMUEL 25:3
LAST REFERENCE
I CHRONICLES 3:1

2) Mother of Amasa, whom Absalom made captain of his army, and aunt of David's commander, Joab.

FIRST REFERENCE
2 SAMUEL 17:25
LAST REFERENCE
I CHRONICLES 2:17

ABIHAIL   6

Possessor of might

1) Forefather of a Levitical family that had responsibility for parts of the tabernacle.

ONLY REFERENCE
NUMBERS 3:35

2) Wife of Abishur, a descendant of Abraham through Jacob's son Judah.

ONLY REFERENCE
I CHRONICLES 2:29

3) A descendant of Abraham through Jacob's son Gad.

ONLY REFERENCE
I CHRONICLES 5:14

4) One of the wives of King Rehoboam of Judah.

ONLY REFERENCE
2 CHRONICLES 11:18

5) The father of Queen Esther, who married the Persian king Ahasuerus.

FIRST REFERENCE
ESTHER 2:15
LAST REFERENCE
ESTHER 9:29

ABIHU   12

Worshipper of God

A son of Aaron who, along with his brother Nadab, offered strange fire before the Lord. God sent fire from His presence to consume them, and they died. He had no children.

FIRST REFERENCE
EXODUS 6:23
LAST REFERENCE
I CHRONICLES 24:2
KEY REFERENCE
LEVITICUS 10:1

ABIHUD   1

Possessor of renown

A descendant of Abraham through Jacob's son Benjamin.

ONLY REFERENCE
I CHRONICLES 8:3

ABIJAH   20

Worshipper of God

1) A son of King Jeroboam of Israel who died in childhood.

ONLY REFERENCE
I KINGS 14:1

2) One of twenty-four priests in David's time who was chosen by lot to serve in the tabernacle.

3) A son of King Rehoboam of Judah. He inherited the throne from his father and went to war against Jeroboam of Israel, claiming that God had given Israel to David and his heirs. Triumphant because his troops called on the Lord in desperation, he gained some cities from Israel and "waxed mighty" (2 Chronicles 13:21). Same as Abia (1).

FIRST REFERENCE
2 CHRONICLES 11:20
LAST REFERENCE
2 CHRONICLES 14:1
KEY REFERENCE
2 CHRONICLES 13:1–5

4) Mother of Judah's good king Hezekiah.

ONLY REFERENCE
2 CHRONICLES 29:1

5) A priest who renewed the covenant under Nehemiah.

ONLY REFERENCE
NEHEMIAH 10:7

6) An exiled priest who returned to Judah under Zerubbabel.

FIRST REFERENCE
NEHEMIAH 12:4
LAST REFERENCE
NEHEMIAH 12:17

ABIJAM 5

Seaman

Son of Rehoboam, king of Judah. He inherited his father's throne and did evil for the three years of his reign, during which he fought with King Jeroboam of Israel.

FIRST REFERENCE
I KINGS 14:31
LAST REFERENCE
I KINGS 15:8

ABIMAEL 2

Father of Mael

A descendant of Noah through Noah's son Shem.

FIRST REFERENCE
GENESIS 10:28
LAST REFERENCE
I CHRONICLES 1:22

ABIMELECH 66

Father of the king

1) The Philistine king of Gerar who took Abraham's wife, Sarah, as his concubine because Abraham introduced her as his sister. God warned Abimelech, and the king returned Sarah to her husband. Later Abraham made a covenant with Abimelech. Isaac repeated his father, Abraham's, lie when he moved to Gerar during a famine, but the king discovered it and protected him and his wife, Rebekah. God so blessed Isaac that Abimelech asked him and his family to leave. But eventually the two made a covenant.

FIRST REFERENCE
GENESIS 20:2
LAST REFERENCE
GENESIS 26:26
KEY REFERENCES
GENESIS 20:3–18; 26:8–11

2) A son of Gideon, by his concubine. He killed all but one of his brothers and was made king

of Shechem. But three years later the Shechemites rebelled, and he destroyed the city. He moved on to attack Thebez, and there he was killed when a woman dropped part of a millstone on his head.

FIRST REFERENCE
JUDGES 8:31
LAST REFERENCE
2 SAMUEL 11:21
KEY REFERENCES
JUDGES 9:5–6, 45, 50–53

3) One of the chief priests serving in the government of King David.

ONLY REFERENCE
1 CHRONICLES 18:16

ABINADAB 13

Liberal or generous

1) A Levite who lived in Gibeah and housed the ark of the covenant for twenty years.

FIRST REFERENCE
1 SAMUEL 7:1
LAST REFERENCE
1 CHRONICLES 13:7

2) Second son of Jesse and an older brother of King David.

FIRST REFERENCE
1 SAMUEL 16:8
LAST REFERENCE
1 CHRONICLES 2:13

3) One of three sons of Israel's king Saul. Abinadab and his brothers died with Saul in a battle against the Philistines on Mount Gilboa (1 Samuel 31:1–2). Same as Ishui.

FIRST REFERENCE
1 SAMUEL 31:2
LAST REFERENCE
1 CHRONICLES 10:2

4) Father of one of King Solomon's commissary officers, who married the king's daughter Taphath.

ONLY REFERENCE
1 KINGS 4:11

ABINOAM 4

Gracious

Father of Barak, who led Israel's army under Deborah.

FIRST REFERENCE
JUDGES 4:6
LAST REFERENCE
JUDGES 5:12

ABIRAM 11

Lofty

1) One of the Reubenites who, with Korah the Levite, conspired against Moses. Because they wrongly claimed that all of Israel was holy, God had the earth swallow the rebellious Reubenites.

FIRST REFERENCE
NUMBERS 16:1
LAST REFERENCE
PSALM 106:17

2) The son of Hiel, who rebuilt Jericho. Abiram died as his father built the foundations of the city.

ONLY REFERENCE
1 KINGS 16:34

ABISHAG 5

Blundering

A beautiful young woman called to serve the dying King David by lying with him to keep him warm. After David died, his son Adonijah wanted to marry Abishag, but he was put to death by his half brother Solomon,

13

who feared Adonijah was trying to usurp the kingship.

FIRST REFERENCE
1 KINGS 1:3
LAST REFERENCE
1 KINGS 2:22

ABISHAI 25

Generous

The brother of David's commander, Joab, Abishai accompanied David to Saul's camp on a spying mission in which David chose to spare the king's life. Abishai became a military leader under his brother and supported David in his fight with Absalom. He killed the Philistine Ishbibenob, who sought to kill David, and became a respected captain of the king's troops.

FIRST REFERENCE
1 SAMUEL 26:6
LAST REFERENCE
1 CHRONICLES 19:15
KEY REFERENCE
1 SAMUEL 26:6–12

ABISHALOM 2

Friendly

Grandfather of King Abijam of Judah.

FIRST REFERENCE
1 KINGS 15:2
LAST REFERENCE
1 KINGS 15:10

ABISHUA 5

Prosperous

1) A descendant of Abraham through Jacob's son Levi and a priest through the line of Aaron.

FIRST REFERENCE
1 CHRONICLES 6:4
LAST REFERENCE
EZRA 7:5

2) A descendant of Abraham through Jacob's son Benjamin.

ONLY REFERENCE
1 CHRONICLES 8:4

ABISHUR 2

Mason

A descendant of Abraham through Jacob's son Judah.

FIRST REFERENCE
1 CHRONICLES 2:28
LAST REFERENCE
1 CHRONICLES 2:29

ABITAL 2

Fresh

A wife of King David; mother of David's son Shephatiah.

FIRST REFERENCE
2 SAMUEL 3:4
LAST REFERENCE
1 CHRONICLES 3:3

ABITUB 1

Good

A descendant of Abraham through Jacob's son Benjamin.

ONLY REFERENCE
1 CHRONICLES 8:11

ABIUD 2 ♛ 👤

My father is majesty

A descendant of Abraham through Isaac's line.

ONLY REFERENCE
MATTHEW 1:13
GENEALOGY OF JESUS
MATTHEW 1:13

ABNER 63 👤

Enlightening

The son of Ner, Abner was the uncle of King Saul of Israel and captain of his army. David confronted Abner for not protecting Saul when David crept into Israel's camp and removed Saul's spear and water jar. After Saul's death, Abner declared Saul's son Ishbosheth king of Israel. When Ishbosheth wrongly accused Abner of taking one of his father's concubines, Abner went over to David's side and began encouraging all Israel to support him as king. David's commander, Joab, objected to David's accepting Abner as a friend, because Abner had killed the commander's brother Asahel. After Joab and his brother Abishai killed Abner, David mourned at his funeral. Solomon declared that Abner was more righteous than his killer (1 Kings 2:32).

FIRST REFERENCE
I SAMUEL 14:50
LAST REFERENCE
I CHRONICLES 27:21
KEY REFERENCE
2 SAMUEL 3:12

ABRAHAM 250 👤

Father of a multitude

A new name for Abram, whom God called out of Ur of the Chaldees and into the Promised Land. This new name was a symbol of the covenant between God and Abraham. The Lord promised to build a nation through Abraham and his wife, Sarai (whom he renamed Sarah), though she was too old to have children. God refused to accept Ishmael, son of Abraham and Sarah's maid, Hagar, as the child of promise.

In time, God gave Sarah and Abraham a son, Isaac, who would found the nation God promised. When God asked Abraham to sacrifice his son on an altar, Abraham took Isaac and set out toward Moriah. There he prepared the altar and laid his son on it. But the angel of the Lord intervened, and God gave Abraham a ram to sacrifice in Isaac's place. God knew the depth of Abraham's faith from his willingness to sacrifice his son. He promised to bless Abraham and his seed.

In his old age, after Sarah's death, Abraham arranged a marriage for Isaac, ensuring God's promise. Then the old man married Keturah. But her sons and the sons of his concubines were not to disturb Isaac's inheritance. Abraham gave them gifts and sent them away from his land.

Abraham lived to be 175. He was buried with Sarah in the cave of Machpelah, in Hebron. Same as Abram

FIRST REFERENCE
GENESIS 17:5
LAST REFERENCE
I PETER 3:6
KEY REFERENCES
GENESIS 17:2–8; 22:8

ABRAM 58

High father

A man from Ur of the Chaldees, married to Sarai. God called him to the Promised Land and promised to bless him. At age seventy-five, Abram left with Sarai, his nephew Lot, and all their goods and servants. As he entered Canaan, God promised to give the land to Abram and his descendants.

God blessed Abram. When his flocks and Lot's were too large, they separated, and Lot headed for the area around Sodom. When Lot ran into trouble there, Abram prayed for him and rescued him, and God removed his family from the wicked city.

God promised Abram a son, but he and Sarai waited many years. Sarai gave him her maid, Hagar, to bear him a child, but the promised child did not come. When Abram was ninety years old, God made a covenant with

him and changed his name to Abraham. Same as Abraham.

FIRST REFERENCE
GENESIS 11:26
LAST REFERENCE
NEHEMIAH 9:7
KEY REFERENCES
GENESIS 12:1–4; 17:1–5

ABSALOM 102

Friendly

King David's son by his wife Maacah. When Absalom's sister Tamar was raped by their brother Amnon, Absalom hated him and commanded his servants to kill Amnon. When this was accomplished, Absalom fled Jerusalem for three years.

Joab, the head of David's army, tried to reconcile father and son. Though David allowed Absalom to return to Jerusalem, he would not see him. But as David ignored him, Absalom won over the hearts of Israel's people. David's counselor Ahithophel went over to Absalom's side.

When David left Jerusalem, Absalom took over the city and a battle began in the wood of Ephraim. As Absalom rode under an oak tree, he was caught in it and his mule ran out from under him.

Joab heard of this, went to Absalom, and thrust three spears into his heart. Yet Absalom lived, so Joab's armor bearers killed him and threw his body into a pit. They covered his body with a pile of stones, and the battle ended.

FIRST REFERENCE
2 SAMUEL 3:3
LAST REFERENCE
2 CHRONICLES 11:21
KEY REFERENCES
2 SAMUEL 13:22; 15:10; 18:9

ACHAICUS

A Corinthian Christian who visited the apostle Paul in Ephesus and "refreshed [Paul's] spirit."

ONLY REFERENCE
I CORINTHIANS 16:17

ACHAN

Troublesome

An Israelite who ignored Joshua's command that nothing in Jericho should live or be taken from the city. He stole a mantle, 200 shekels of silver, and 50 shekels of gold and hid them under his tent. Because of his sin, Israel could not stand at the first battle of Ai. When Joshua discovered Achan's sin, he asked, "Why has thou troubled us?" and promised that the Lord would trouble Achan that day (Joshua 7:25). The sinner and his family were taken to the Valley of Achor and stoned.

FIRST REFERENCE
JOSHUA 7:1
LAST REFERENCE
JOSHUA 22:20

ACHAR

Troublesome

A variant spelling of Achan, "the troubler of Israel."

ONLY REFERENCE
I CHRONICLES 2:7

ACHAZ

A descendant of Abraham through Isaac; forebear of Jesus' earthly father, Joseph. Same as Ahaz.

ONLY REFERENCE
MATTHEW 1:9
GENEALOGY OF JESUS
MATTHEW 1:9

ACHBOR

1) Father of a king of Edom, "before there reigned any king over the children of Israel" (Genesis 36:31).

FIRST REFERENCE
GENESIS 36:38
LAST REFERENCE
I CHRONICLES 1:49

2) One of the men who was sent to consult Huldah the prophetess, after Josiah discovered the book of the law.

FIRST REFERENCE
2 KINGS 22:12
LAST REFERENCE
2 KINGS 22:14

3) Father of Elnathan, who was sent by King Jehoiakim of Judah to bring the prophet Urijah back from Egypt. With the other princes of Judah, the scribe Baruch read Jeremiah's prophecies to him.

FIRST REFERENCE
JEREMIAH 26:22
LAST REFERENCE
JEREMIAH 36:12

ACHIM 2

A descendant of Abraham through Isaac; forebear of Jesus' earthly father, Joseph.

ONLY REFERENCE
MATTHEW 1:14
GENEALOGY OF JESUS
LUKE 3:25

ACHISH 21

1) The Philistine king of Gath before whom David, who feared him, pretended madness. Later David sought refuge in Achish's land and received the town of Ziklag from him. Though Achish wanted David to fight with him against Israel, when the king's troops objected, he sent David home.

FIRST REFERENCE
I SAMUEL 21:10
LAST REFERENCE
I SAMUEL 29:9
KEY REFERENCES
I SAMUEL 21:10–15; 29:6–7

2) Another king of Gath, in the time of Solomon. Two runaway servants of Shimei came to him.

FIRST REFERENCE
I KINGS 2:39
LAST REFERENCE
I KINGS 2:40

ACHSA 1

Anklet

Daughter of Caleb, a descendant of Abraham through Jacob's son Judah. Same as Achsah.

ONLY REFERENCE
I CHRONICLES 2:49

ACHSAH 4

Anklet

Caleb's daughter, whom he promised in marriage to the man who could capture the city of Kirjathsepher. His brother Othniel captured the city and won Achsah as his wife. Afterward Caleb gave her land that held springs, since the lands of her dowry were dry. Same as Achsa.

FIRST REFERENCE
JOSHUA 15:16
LAST REFERENCE
JUDGES 1:13

ADAH 8

Ornament

1) A wife of Lamech, the first man in scripture to have two wives. Her son was named Jabal.

FIRST REFERENCE
GENESIS 4:19
LAST REFERENCE
GENESIS 4:23

2) A wife of Esau, "of the daughters of Canaan." Same as Bashemath (2).

FIRST REFERENCE
GENESIS 36:2
LAST REFERENCE
GENESIS 36:16

ADAIAH 9

God has adorned

1) Grandfather of King Josiah of Judah, on his mother's side.

ONLY REFERENCE
2 KINGS 22:1

2) A descendant of Abraham through Jacob's son Levi.

3) A descendant of Abraham through Jacob's son Benjamin.

4) A Levite who returned to Jerusalem following the Babylonian captivity.

5) Forefather of Maaseiah, captain of hundreds for the priest Jehoiada, who crowned Joash king of Judah.

6) An exiled Israelite who married a "strange" (foreign) woman.

7) Another exiled Israelite who married a foreign woman.

8) Ancestor of a man of the tribe of Judah who was chosen by lot to resettle Jerusalem after returning from the Babylonian Exile.

9) A Levite who settled in Jerusalem following the Babylonian Exile and worked in the temple.

ADALIA 1

One of ten sons of Haman, the villain of the story of Esther.

ADAM 30
Ruddy

The first man, who was created by God to have dominion over the earth. Adam's first act was to name the animals; then God created Adam's wife, Eve, as "a help meet for him" (Genesis 2:18). God gave this couple the beautiful Garden of Eden to care for. There Satan, in the form of a serpent, tempted Eve. Though God had banned them from eating the fruit of the tree of the knowledge of good and evil, under Satan's influence Eve picked it, ate it, and offered it to Adam, who also ate. Aware of their sin, they attempted to avoid God. He banned them from the garden and cursed the earth's ground so Adam would have to work hard to grow food. As a result of their sin, they would die. Following their banishment, the couple had two children, Cain and Abel. When Cain killed his brother, God gave Adam another son, Seth. Adam lived to be 930.

FIRST REFERENCE
GENESIS 2:19
LAST REFERENCE
JUDE 1:4
KEY REFERENCES
GENESIS 2:7, 21–23; 3:6

ADBEEL   2
Disciplined of God

A descendant of Abraham through Ishmael, who was Abraham's son with his surrogate wife, Hagar.

FIRST REFERENCE
GENESIS 25:13
LAST REFERENCE
I CHRONICLES 1:29

ADDAR   I
Ample

A descendant of Abraham through Jacob's son Benjamin.

ONLY REFERENCE
I CHRONICLES 8:3

ADDI   I
A descendant of Abraham through Isaac; forebear of Jesus' earthly father, Joseph.

ONLY REFERENCE
LUKE 3:28
GENEALOGY OF JESUS
LUKE 3:28

ADER   I
An arrangement

A descendant of Abraham through Jacob's son Benjamin.

ONLY REFERENCE
I CHRONICLES 8:15

ADIEL   3
Ornament of God

1) A descendant of Abraham through Jacob's son Simeon.

ONLY REFERENCE
I CHRONICLES 4:36

2) Forefather of a Babylonian exile from the tribe of Levi who resettled Jerusalem.

ONLY REFERENCE
I CHRONICLES 9:12

3) Father of King David's treasurer Azmaveth.

ONLY REFERENCE
I CHRONICLES 27:25

ADIN   4
Voluptuous

1) Forefather of an exiled family that returned to Judah under Zerubbabel.

FIRST REFERENCE
EZRA 2:15
LAST REFERENCE
NEHEMIAH 7:20

2) A Jewish leader who renewed the covenant under Nehemiah.

ONLY REFERENCE
NEHEMIAH 10:16

3) Forefather of a Jewish exile who returned from Babylon to Judah under Ezra.

ONLY REFERENCE
EZRA 8:6

ADINA   I
Effeminacy

One of King David's valiant warriors.

ONLY REFERENCE
I CHRONICLES 11:42

ADINO 1

Slender

One of King David's warriors known as the "mighty men."

ONLY REFERENCE
2 SAMUEL 23:8

ADLAI 1

Father of King David's chief shepherd over herds in the valleys.

ONLY REFERENCE
1 CHRONICLES 27:29

ADMATHA 1

One of seven Persian princes serving under King Ahasuerus.

ONLY REFERENCE
ESTHER 1:14

ADNA 2

Pleasure

1) An exiled Israelite who married a "strange" (foreign) woman.

ONLY REFERENCE
EZRA 10:30

2) Forefather of a priest who returned to Jerusalem under Zerubbabel.

ONLY REFERENCE
NEHEMIAH 12:15

ADNAH 2

Pleasure

1) A captain in David's army.

ONLY REFERENCE
1 CHRONICLES 12:20

2) A commander in King Jehoshaphat's army.

ONLY REFERENCE
2 CHRONICLES 17:14

ADONI-BEZEK 3

Lord of Bezek

The ruler of a Canaanite city who ran from the army of Judah during its cleansing of the Promised Land. When soldiers caught Adoni-bezek, they cut off his thumbs and big toes, as he had previously done to seventy kings he had conquered. He died in captivity in Jerusalem.

FIRST REFERENCE
JUDGES 1:5
LAST REFERENCE
JUDGES 1:7

ADONIJAH 26

Worshipper of God

1) A son of King David, born in Hebron. When David was old, Adonijah attempted to take the throne, though David had promised it to Solomon. Nathan the prophet and Bath-sheba, Solomon's mother, reported this to David, who immediately had Solomon anointed king. When Adonijah heard this, he went to the temple and grasped the horns of the altar, in fear of his life. Solomon promised he would not be killed if he showed himself a worthy man. But when Adonijah wanted David's concubine Abishag as his wife, Solomon saw it as another threat to his throne and had Adonijah executed.

FIRST REFERENCE
2 SAMUEL 3:4
LAST REFERENCE
1 CHRONICLES 3:2
KEY REFERENCES
1 KINGS 1:5, 50

2) A Levite sent by King Jehoshaphat to teach the law of the Lord throughout the nation of Judah.

ONLY REFERENCE
2 CHRONICLES 17:8

3) A Jewish leader who renewed the covenant under Nehemiah.

ONLY REFERENCE
NEHEMIAH 10:16

ADONIKAM 3

High

Forefather of a Jewish exile who returned from Babylon to Judah under Zerubbabel.

FIRST REFERENCE
EZRA 2:13
LAST REFERENCE
NEHEMIAH 7:18

ADONIRAM 2

Lord of height

King Solomon's official over forced labor for building the temple.

FIRST REFERENCE
I KINGS 4:6
LAST REFERENCE
I KINGS 5:14

ADONI-ZEDEC 2

Lord of justice

A pagan king of Jerusalem during Joshua's conquest of the Promised Land, Adoni-zedec allied with four other rulers to attack Gibeon, which had deceptively made a peace treaty with the Israelites. Joshua's soldiers defeated the five armies, and Joshua executed the allied kings.

FIRST REFERENCE
JOSHUA 10:1
LAST REFERENCE
JOSHUA 10:3

ADORAM 2

Lord of height

1) King David's official over forced labor.

ONLY REFERENCE
2 SAMUEL 20:24

2) An official over forced labor under Judah's king Rehoboam (son of Solomon). Adoram was stoned to death by rebellious Israelites, who seceded to form their own northern kingdom.

ONLY REFERENCE
I KINGS 12:18

ADRAMMELECH 2

Splendor of the king

Son of the Assyrian king Sennacherib, who, with his brother Sharezer, killed his father with a sword. After the assassination, Adrammelech fled to Armenia.

FIRST REFERENCE
2 KINGS 19:37
LAST REFERENCE
ISAIAH 7:38

ADRIEL 2

Flock of God

The man who married Saul's daughter Merab, who had been promised to David.

FIRST REFERENCE
I SAMUEL 18:19
LAST REFERENCE
2 SAMUEL 21:8

AENEAS 2

A lame man of Lydda healed by the apostle Peter after spending eight years in his sickbed. His healing turned many people to the Lord.

FIRST REFERENCE
ACTS 9:33
LAST REFERENCE
ACTS 9:34

AGABUS 2
Locust

An early Christian prophet from Jerusalem who made two recorded predictions: that a famine would affect the region of Judea and that the apostle Paul would be bound and delivered "into the hands of the Gentiles" (Acts 21:11).

FIRST REFERENCE
ACTS 11:28
LAST REFERENCE
ACTS 21:10

AGAG 8
Flame

1) A king mentioned by Balaam in his prophecy concerning God's blessing on Israel.
ONLY REFERENCE
NUMBERS 24:7

2) A king of the Amalekites whom King Saul of Israel spared in defiance of God's command. Obeying God, the prophet Samuel killed Agag.

FIRST REFERENCE
1 SAMUEL 15:8
LAST REFERENCE
1 SAMUEL 15:33

AGAR 2

Greek form of the name *Hagar*, used in the New Testament.

FIRST REFERENCE
GALATIANS 4:24
LAST REFERENCE
GALATIANS 4:25

AGEE 1

Father of one of King David's "mighty men," Shammah.

ONLY REFERENCE
2 SAMUEL 23:11

AGRIPPA 12
Wild horse tamer

Herod Agrippa II, great-grandson of Herod the Great. He became king of the tetrarchy of Philip and Lysanias. Porcius Festus asked for his advice on Paul's legal case, so he heard Paul's testimony, which almost persuaded him to become a Christian. Same as Herod (4).

FIRST REFERENCE
ACTS 25:13
LAST REFERENCE
ACTS 26:32
KEY REFERENCE
ACTS 26:28

AGUR 1
Gathered

A little-known biblical writer who penned the thirtieth chapter of Proverbs.

ONLY REFERENCE
PROVERBS 30:1

AHAB 94
Friend of his father

1) A king of Israel, Ahab did great evil. He married Jezebel, daughter of the king of Zidon, and fell into Baal worship. God sent Israel a drought that only the prophet Elijah could break. The nation suffered for three years, until Elijah returned and challenged Israel to follow God. He proved that God was Lord in a showdown with the prophets of Baal, before killing them and ending the drought.

Ahab coveted the vineyard of his subject Naboth, who refused to sell his inheritance to him. While the king sulked, Jezebel plotted to kill Naboth and get the land. Because Ahab humbled himself before God, the Lord promised to bring evil in his son's life instead of visiting it on Ahab. He was killed in a battle with Syria.

> FIRST REFERENCE
> I KINGS 16:28
> LAST REFERENCE
> MICAH 6:16
> KEY REFERENCE
> I KINGS 16:29–30

2) A false prophet who claimed God would not deliver Judah into King Nebuchadnezzar's hand.

> FIRST REFERENCE
> JEREMIAH 29:21
> LAST REFERENCE
> JEREMIAH 29:22

AHARAH I
After his brother

A descendant of Abraham through Jacob's son Benjamin. Aharah was Benjamin's third son.

> ONLY REFERENCE
> I CHRONICLES 8:1

AHARHEL I
Safe

A descendant of Abraham through Jacob's son Judah.

> ONLY REFERENCE
> I CHRONICLES 4:8

AHASAI I
Seizer

Forefather of an exiled Israelite family.

> ONLY REFERENCE
> NEHEMIAH 11:13

AHASBAI I

Father of one of King David's "mighty men," Eliphelet.

> ONLY REFERENCE
> 2 SAMUEL 23:34

AHASUERUS 31

1) A Persian king who received accusations against the inhabitants of Judah and Jerusalem.

> ONLY REFERENCE
> EZRA 4:6

2) A king of Media and the father of Darius the Mede, who would become king of the Chaldeans.

3) A Persian king who reigned over an empire that ran from India to Ethiopia. When his queen Vashti displeased him, Ahasuerus ordered the beautiful women of his kingdom to be gathered at the palace so he could choose a new wife. In this way he met the Jewess Esther, loved her, and made her his queen.

Not knowing that Esther was Jewish, Ahasuerus listened to his counselor, wicked Haman, who wanted to destroy the Jews. Hearing only Haman's false information, the king gave Haman permission to eradicate what he saw as a dangerous people. When Esther heard this, she came before the king and invited both men to a banquet. That night Ahasuerus discovered the faithfulness of Esther's cousin, Mordecai, who had reported a plot against the king. Ahasuerus commanded Haman to honor this Jew whom the counselor hated and had planned to kill.

On the second day of her banquet, Esther divulged Haman's plot to harm her people. Angered, the king had Haman hanged on the gallows he had built for Mordecai. Esther gave Mordecai Haman's household, and the king made Mordecai a royal advisor. Since his original law could not be changed, Ahasuerus had Mordecai write a new law that allowed the Jews to protect themselves from the attack Haman had planned.

FIRST REFERENCE
ESTHER 1:1
LAST REFERENCE
ESTHER 10:3
KEY REFERENCES
ESTHER 1:1; 7:5–10

AHAZ 42

Possessor

1) A king of Judah who became deeply involved in paganism. God sent the kings of Syria and Israel against Judah in punishment, and Ahaz was unsuccessful in fighting off his enemies. Many people of Judah were captured and carried off. Ahaz sent to Tiglath-pileser, king of Assyria, for help, offering the temple silver and gold and the treasures of his own household to the pagan king as a gift. The Assyrian army responded by attacking Damascus, but was not otherwise helpful. When Ahaz joined the Assyrian king in Damascus, he saw and admired a pagan altar. He had it copied. When he returned to Jerusalem, he had the altars of the Lord moved and commanded Urijah the priest to use this pagan altar for worship.

Isaiah had prophesied the sign of Immanuel, "God with us," but because God did not rescue him, Ahaz became increasingly involved in paganism. He destroyed the temple vessels and closed the building to worship. Instead he built pagan temples throughout Jerusalem and established altars on high places near other cities. When he died, he was not buried with the other kings of Israel.

FIRST REFERENCE
2 KINGS 15:38
LAST REFERENCE
MICAH 1:1
KEY REFERENCES
2 CHRONICLES 28:1–5; ISAIAH 7:11–14

2) A descendant of Abraham through Jacob's son Benjamin, in the line of King Saul and his son Jonathan.

FIRST REFERENCE
1 CHRONICLES 8:35
LAST REFERENCE
1 CHRONICLES 9:42

AHAZIAH 37
God has seized

1) A king of Israel and the son of Ahab. He reigned for two years and walked in the pagan ways of his parents. When he fell through a lattice in his chamber and was badly hurt, he sought help from the pagan god Baalzebub. God sent Elijah to the king's messenger, asking if there was no God in Israel. Twice Ahaziah sent soldiers to Elijah to demand that he come to the king. Twice Elijah called fire down on them. When a third captain came more humbly, Elijah went to the king and prophesied that he would die.

FIRST REFERENCE
1 KINGS 22:40
LAST REFERENCE
2 CHRONICLES 20:37
KEY REFERENCE
1 KINGS 22:40–51

2) A king of Judah, son of Joram and Athaliah. Following the advice of bad counselors, he joined with Joram, king of Israel, to fight against the Syrians. When Joram was wounded, Israel's king went to Jezreel, where the king of Judah visited him. There Jehu killed Joram and sent his men on to Samaria, after Ahaziah. Ahaziah died of his wounds in Megiddo.

FIRST REFERENCE
2 KINGS 8:24
LAST REFERENCE
2 CHRONICLES 22:11
KEY REFERENCE
2 CHRONICLES 22:2–4

AHBAN 1
Possessor of understanding

A descendant of Abraham through Jacob's son Judah.

ONLY REFERENCE
1 CHRONICLES 2:29

AHER 1
Hinder

A descendant of Abraham through Jacob's son Benjamin.

ONLY REFERENCE
1 CHRONICLES 7:12

AHI 2
Brotherly

1) A descendant of Abraham through Jacob's son Gad.

ONLY REFERENCE
I CHRONICLES 5:15

2) A descendant of Abraham through Jacob's son Asher.

ONLY REFERENCE
I CHRONICLES 7:34

AHIAH 4
Worshipper of God

1) "The Lord's priest in Shiloh" who was with King Saul at Gibeah when Jonathan and his armor bearer together conquered the Philistines.

FIRST REFERENCE
I SAMUEL 14:3
LAST REFERENCE
I SAMUEL 14:18

2) A scribe serving under King Solomon.

ONLY REFERENCE
I KINGS 4:3

3) A son of Ehud who moved to Manahath.

ONLY REFERENCE
I CHRONICLES 8:7

AHIAM 2
Uncle

One of King David's valiant warriors.

FIRST REFERENCE
2 SAMUEL 23:33
LAST REFERENCE
I CHRONICLES 11:35

AHIAN 1
Brotherly

A descendant of Abraham through Joseph's son Manasseh.

ONLY REFERENCE
I CHRONICLES 7:19

AHIEZER 6
Brother of help

1) A man of the tribe of Dan who helped Aaron number the Israelites. God made him captain of his tribe.

FIRST REFERENCE
NUMBERS 1:12
LAST REFERENCE
NUMBERS 10:25

2) A "mighty man" who supported the future king David during his conflict with Saul.

ONLY REFERENCE
I CHRONICLES 12:3

AHIHUD 2
Possessor of renown, mysterious

1) A prince of the tribe of Asher when the Israelites entered the Promised Land.

ONLY REFERENCE
NUMBERS 34:27

2) A descendant of Abraham through Jacob's son Benjamin.

ONLY REFERENCE
I CHRONICLES 8:7

AHIJAH   20
Worshipper of God

1) A prophet who prophesied the division of Israel into the countries of Israel and Judah. He promised Jeroboam that he would rule Israel. After the king disobeyed God, Ahijah prophesied the death of Jeroboam's son and Jeroboam's destruction.

> **FIRST REFERENCE**
> I KINGS 11:29
> **LAST REFERENCE**
> 2 CHRONICLES 10:15

2) A descendant of Issachar. His son Baasha conspired against King Nadab of Israel.

> **FIRST REFERENCE**
> I KINGS 15:27
> **LAST REFERENCE**
> 2 KINGS 9:9

3) A descendant of Abraham through Jacob's son Judah.

> **ONLY REFERENCE**
> I CHRONICLES 2:25

4) One of King David's valiant warriors.

> **ONLY REFERENCE**
> I CHRONICLES 11:36

5) A Levite assigned to the treasury during King David's reign.

> **ONLY REFERENCE**
> I CHRONICLES 26:20

6) A Jewish leader who renewed the covenant under Nehemiah.

> **ONLY REFERENCE**
> NEHEMIAH 10:26

AHIKAM   20
High

One of the men who was sent to consult Huldah the prophetess after King Josiah rediscovered the book of the law. Ahikam supported Jeremiah, protecting him from death, when his prophecies became unpopular. When Jeremiah was released from prison, he was given into the care of Ahikam's son Gedaliah.

> **FIRST REFERENCE**
> 2 KINGS 22:12
> **LAST REFERENCE**
> JEREMIAH 43:6
> **KEY REFERENCE**
> 2 KINGS 22:12–14

AHILUD   5
Brother of one born

Father of Jehoshaphat. His son served as King David's recorder.

> **FIRST REFERENCE**
> 2 SAMUEL 8:16
> **LAST REFERENCE**
> I CHRONICLES 18:15

AHIMAAZ   15
Brother of anger

1) Father of King Saul's wife Ahinoam.

> **ONLY REFERENCE**
> I SAMUEL 14:50

2) Son of the priest Zadok. When Absalom forced David from his throne, Ahimaaz carried messages to David from his spy, Hushai the Archite. He also brought King David the news of his troops' victory over Absalom.

FIRST REFERENCE
2 SAMUEL 15:27
LAST REFERENCE
1 CHRONICLES 6:53

3) One of King Solomon's twelve officials over provisions. Ahimaaz married Solomon's daughter Basmath.

ONLY REFERENCE
1 KINGS 4:15

AHIMAN 4
Gift

1) One of the gigantic children of Anak who was killed after Joshua's death, as Judah battled against the Canaanites.

FIRST REFERENCE
NUMBERS 13:22
LAST REFERENCE
JUDGES 1:10

2) A Jewish exile from the tribe of Levi who resettled Jerusalem.

ONLY REFERENCE
1 CHRONICLES 9:17

AHIMELECH 16
Brother of the king

1) The priest of Nob who gave David the hallowed bread to feed his men, when David was fleeing from Saul. When King Saul discovered this, he had all the men in Ahimelech's priestly enclave killed, except the priest's son Abiathar, who escaped.

FIRST REFERENCE
1 SAMUEL 21:1
LAST REFERENCE
PSALM 52 (TITLE)
KEY REFERENCES
1 SAMUEL 21:1, 6

2) A Hittite warrior who served King David.

ONLY REFERENCE
1 SAMUEL 26:6

AHIMOTH 1
Brother of death

A descendant of Levi through the family of Kohath.

ONLY REFERENCE
1 CHRONICLES 6:25

AHINADAB 1
Brother of liberality

One of King Solomon's twelve officials over provisions.

ONLY REFERENCE
1 KINGS 4:14

AHINOAM 7
Brother of pleasantness

1) The wife of Saul, Israel's first king.

ONLY REFERENCE
1 SAMUEL 14:50

2) A woman from Jezreel who became David's wife.

FIRST REFERENCE
1 SAMUEL 25:43
LAST REFERENCE
1 CHRONICLES 3:1

AHIO 6
Brotherly

1) A son of Abinadab, he went before the ark of the covenant then transported it into Jerusalem.

FIRST REFERENCE
2 SAMUEL 6:3
LAST REFERENCE
1 CHRONICLES 13:7

2) A descendant of Abraham through Jacob's son Benjamin. A son of Elpaal.

ONLY REFERENCE
I CHRONICLES 8:14

3) Another descendant of Abraham through Jacob's son Benjamin. His father was Jehiel.

FIRST REFERENCE
I CHRONICLES 8:31
LAST REFERENCE
I CHRONICLES 9:37

AHIRA 5

Brother of wrong

A prince of the tribe of Napthali, after the Exodus.

FIRST REFERENCE
NUMBERS 1:15
LAST REFERENCE
NUMBERS 10:27

AHIRAM 1

High

A descendant of Abraham through Jacob's son Benjamin.

ONLY REFERENCE
NUMBERS 26:38

AHISAMACH 3

Brother of support

A descendant of Dan and father of Aholiab, a workman on the temple.

FIRST REFERENCE
EXODUS 31:6
LAST REFERENCE
EXODUS 38:23

AHISHAHAR 1

Brother of the dawn

A descendant of Abraham through Jacob's son Benjamin.

ONLY REFERENCE
I CHRONICLES 7:10

AHISHAR 1

Brother of the singer

King Solomon's official over his household.

ONLY REFERENCE
I KINGS 4:6

AHITHOPHEL 20

Brother of folly

King David's counselor who conspired with David's son Absalom to overthrow the throne. Ahithophel advised Absalom to defile his father's concubines. "And the counsel of Ahithophel. . .was as if a man had enquired at the oracle of God" (2 Samuel 16:23). When Absalom did not follow his counselor's advice about attacking David and it became clear that Absalom was unlikely to win, Ahithophel hanged himself.

FIRST REFERENCE
2 SAMUEL 15:12
LAST REFERENCE
I CHRONICLES 27:34
KEY REFERENCE
2 SAMUEL 16:23

AHITUB 15

Brother of goodness

1) Son of Phineas and father of Ahiah and Ahimelech the priest of Nob.

FIRST REFERENCE
I SAMUEL 14:3
LAST REFERENCE
I SAMUEL 22:20

2) A descendant of Abraham through Jacob's son Levi and a priest

through the line of Aaron. Ahitub was the father of Zadok, the priest during King David's reign.

FIRST REFERENCE
2 SAMUEL 8:17
LAST REFERENCE
EZRA 7:2

3) Another descendant of Abraham through Jacob's son Levi and a priest through the line of Aaron.

FIRST REFERENCE
I CHRONICLES 6:11
LAST REFERENCE
I CHRONICLES 6:12

4) A priest described as "the ruler of the house of God" (Nehemiah 11:11).

FIRST REFERENCE
I CHRONICLES 9:11
LAST REFERENCE
NEHEMIAH 11:11

AHLAI 2
Wishful

1) A descendant of Abraham through Jacob's son Judah.

ONLY REFERENCE
I CHRONICLES 2:31

2) Father of one of King David's valiant warriors.

ONLY REFERENCE
I CHRONICLES 11:41

AHOAH 1
Brotherly

A descendant of Abraham through Jacob's son Benjamin.

ONLY REFERENCE
I CHRONICLES 8:4

AHOLIAB 5
Tent of his father

An engraver and embroiderer given special ability by God to work on the tabernacle, Israel's portable worship center begun in the time of Moses. Aholiab was "a cunning workman" and taught other craftsmen.

FIRST REFERENCE
EXODUS 31:6
LAST REFERENCE
EXODUS 38:23

AHOLIBAMAH 8
Tent of the height

1) A wife of Esau, "of the daughters of Canaan."

FIRST REFERENCE
GENESIS 36:2
LAST REFERENCE
GENESIS 36:25

2) A "duke of Edom" and a leader in the family line of Esau.

FIRST REFERENCE
GENESIS 36:41
LAST REFERENCE
I CHRONICLES 1:52

AHUMAI 1
Neighbor of water

A descendant of Abraham through Jacob's son Judah.

ONLY REFERENCE
I CHRONICLES 4:2

AHUZAM 1

Seizure

A descendant of Abraham through Jacob's son Judah.

ONLY REFERENCE
I CHRONICLES 4:6

AHUZZATH 1

Possession

A friend of Abimelech, king of Gerar.

ONLY REFERENCE
GENESIS 26:26

AIAH 5

Hawk

1) A descendant of Seir, who lived in Esau's "land of Edom."

ONLY REFERENCE
I CHRONICLES 1:40

2) Father of Rizpah, who was a concubine of King Saul.

FIRST REFERENCE
2 SAMUEL 3:7
LAST REFERENCE
2 SAMUEL 21:11

AJAH 1

Hawk

A descendant of Seir, who lived in Esau's "land of Edom."

ONLY REFERENCE
GENESIS 36:24

AKAN 1

Tortuous

A descendant of Seir, who lived in Esau's "land of Edom." Same as Jaakan and Jakan.

ONLY REFERENCE
GENESIS 36:27

AKKUB 8

Insidious

1) A descendant of Abraham through Jacob's son Judah, in the line of the nation of Judah's second-to-last king, Jeconiah (also known as Jehoiachin).

ONLY REFERENCE
I CHRONICLES 3:24

2) A Jewish exile from the tribe of Levi who resettled Jerusalem.

FIRST REFERENCE
I CHRONICLES 9:17
LAST REFERENCE
NEHEMIAH 12:25

3) Forefather of an exiled family that returned to Judah under Zerubbabel.

FIRST REFERENCE
EZRA 2:42
LAST REFERENCE
NEHEMIAH 7:45

4) Forefather of an exiled family that returned to Judah under Zerubbabel.

ONLY REFERENCE
EZRA 2:45

5) A Levite who helped Ezra to explain the law to exiles returned to Jerusalem.

ONLY REFERENCE
NEHEMIAH 8:7

ALAMETH 1

A covering

A descendant of Abraham through Jacob's son Benjamin.

ONLY REFERENCE
I CHRONICLES 7:8

ALEMETH 2

A covering

A descendant of Abraham through Jacob's son Benjamin, in the line of King Saul and his son Jonathan.

FIRST REFERENCE
1 CHRONICLES 8:36
LAST REFERENCE
1 CHRONICLES 9:42

ALEXANDER 6 4

Man-defender

1) One of two sons of Simon, a man from Cyrene forced by Roman soldiers to carry Jesus' cross to Golgotha, the crucifixion site.

ONLY REFERENCE
MARK 15:21

2) A relative of the high priest Annas, who was present when Jewish leaders questioned Peter and John about healing a lame beggar.

ONLY REFERENCE
ACTS 4:6

3) A Jewish participant in a riot in Ephesus, instigated by idol makers against the apostle Paul's teaching.

ONLY REFERENCE
ACTS 19:33

4) A blasphemous coppersmith who opposed the apostle Paul, doing him "much evil."

FIRST REFERENCE
1 TIMOTHY 1:20
LAST REFERENCE
2 TIMOTHY 4:14

ALIAH 1

Perverseness

A "duke of Edom" and a leader in the family line of Esau. Same as Alvah.

ONLY REFERENCE
1 CHRONICLES 1:51

ALIAN 1

Lofty

A descendant of Seir, who lived in Esau's "land of Edom." Same as Alvan.

ONLY REFERENCE
1 CHRONICLES 1:40

ALLON 1

Oak

A descendant of Abraham through Jacob's son Simeon.

ONLY REFERENCE
1 CHRONICLES 4:37

ALMODAD 2

A descendant of Noah through Noah's son Shem.

FIRST REFERENCE
GENESIS 10:26
LAST REFERENCE
1 CHRONICLES 1:20

ALPHAEUS 5 2

1) Father of one of two apostles named James. The phrase "James the son of Alphaeus" distinguishes this James from the brother of John and the "sons of Zebedee."

2) Father of the apostle Levi, also known as Matthew.

ONLY REFERENCE
MARK 2:14

ALVAH 1

Perverseness

A "duke of Edom" and a leader in the family line of Esau. Same as Aliah.

ONLY REFERENCE
GENESIS 36:40

ALVAN 1

Lofty

A descendant of Seir, who lived in Esau's "land of Edom." Same as Alian.

ONLY REFERENCE
GENESIS 36:23

AMAL 1

Worry

A descendant of Abraham through Jacob's son Asher.

ONLY REFERENCE
I CHRONICLES 7:35

AMALEK 3

A descendant of Abraham's grandson Esau, whose blessing as older brother was taken by the scheming Jacob. Amalek's descendants, the Amalekites, were longtime enemies of Israel, earning God's contempt: "The LORD hath sworn that the LORD will have war with Amalek from generation to generation" (Exodus 17:16).

FIRST REFERENCE
GENESIS 36:12
LAST REFERENCE
I CHRONICLES 1:36

AMARIAH 16 9

God has promised

1) A descendant of Abraham through Jacob's son Levi and a priest through the line of Aaron.

FIRST REFERENCE
I CHRONICLES 6:7
LAST REFERENCE
EZRA 7:3

2) Another descendant of Abraham through Jacob's son Levi and a priest through the line of Aaron.

ONLY REFERENCE
I CHRONICLES 6:11

3) A Levite who served at the time of King Solomon.

FIRST REFERENCE
I CHRONICLES 23:19
LAST REFERENCE
I CHRONICLES 24:23

4) The chief priest in the time of King Jehoshaphat of Judah.

ONLY REFERENCE
2 CHRONICLES 19:11

5) A priest in the time of King Hezekiah, he helped to distribute the people's freewill offerings to his fellow priests.

ONLY REFERENCE
2 CHRONICLES 31:15

6) An exiled Israelite who married a "strange" (foreign) woman.

ONLY REFERENCE
EZRA 10:42

7) A priest who renewed the covenant under Nehemiah.

FIRST REFERENCE
NEHEMIAH 10:3
LAST REFERENCE
NEHEMIAH 12:13

8) An ancestor of a man of the tribe of Judah who was chosen by lot to resettle Jerusalem after returning from the Babylonian Exile.

ONLY REFERENCE
NEHEMIAH 11:4

9) An ancestor of the prophet Zephaniah.

ONLY REFERENCE
ZEPHANIAH 1:1

AMASA 16
Burden

1) King David's nephew who became Absalom's commander during Absalom's rebellion against his father. When David regained the throne, he made Amasa commander of his army in Joab's place. When the king sent his new commander to gather the men of Judah, Joab followed Amasa, attacked him, and killed him.

FIRST REFERENCE
2 SAMUEL 17:25
LAST REFERENCE
1 CHRONICLES 2:17
KEY REFERENCE
2 SAMUEL 19:13

2) A man of the tribe of Ephraim who counseled Israel against enslaving fellow Jews from Judah who were captured in a civil war. Amasa helped to feed and clothe the prisoners before sending them home.

ONLY REFERENCE
2 CHRONICLES 28:12

AMASAI 5
Burdensome

1) A descendant of Abraham through Jacob's son Levi and the father of a Levite who cleansed the Jerusalem temple during the revival of King Hezekiah's day.

FIRST REFERENCE
1 CHRONICLES 6:25
LAST REFERENCE
2 CHRONICLES 29:12

2) A chief captain in David's army.

ONLY REFERENCE
1 CHRONICLES 12:18

3) A Levite who blew a trumpet before the ark of the covenant when David brought it to Jerusalem.

ONLY REFERENCE
1 CHRONICLES 15:24

AMASHAI 1
Burdensome

A Jewish exile from the tribe of Levi who resettled Jerusalem.

ONLY REFERENCE
NEHEMIAH 11:13

AMASIAH   1

God has loaded

A warrior who raised two hundred thousand brave men for King Jehoshaphat of Judah.

ONLY REFERENCE
2 CHRONICLES 17:16

AMAZIAH   40

Strength of God

1) Son and successor of King Joash of Judah. Though he did right, the new king did not remove the pagan altars from the land. He killed the servants who had murdered his father in his bed but did not kill their children. After raising an army in his country, he hired one hundred thousand men from Israel. But a man of God convinced the king to rely on God, not a hired army, so Amaziah sent the Israelites home. With his own men he went to war with Edom and won; meanwhile the scorned Israelite army attacked Judah, killed three thousand, and carried away spoils. Amaziah brought back idols from Edom and began to worship them. When God sent a prophet to correct him, he would not listen, and the prophet predicted Amaziah's downfall. Amaziah confronted Jehoash, king of Israel, who tried to make peace. Judah's king refused, but when he waged war on Israel, all his men fled. Jehoash broke down Jerusalem's wall and took the precious vessels from the temple and the treasures of the king's house. Later a conspiracy grew up against Amaziah, so he fled to Lachish, where he was killed.

FIRST REFERENCE
2 KINGS 12:21
LAST REFERENCE
2 CHRONICLES 26:4
KEY REFERENCES
2 CHRONICLES 25:1–2, 14–16

2) A descendant of Abraham through Jacob's son Simeon.

ONLY REFERENCE
1 CHRONICLES 4:34

3) A descendant of Abraham through Jacob's son Levi.

ONLY REFERENCE
1 CHRONICLES 6:45

4) A false priest of Bethel who accused the prophet Amos of conspiring against King Jeroboam of Israel.

FIRST REFERENCE
AMOS 7:10
LAST REFERENCE
AMOS 7:14

AMI   1

Skilled

Forefather of an exiled Israelite family.

ONLY REFERENCE
EZRA 2:57

AMINADAB   3

People of liberality

An ancestor of Jesus and the great-grandfather of David's great-grandfather Boaz.

FIRST REFERENCE
MATTHEW 1:4

LAST REFERENCE
LUKE 3:33

GENEALOGY OF JESUS
MATTHEW 1:4; LUKE 3:33

AMITTAI 2

Truthful

Father of the prophet Jonah, who preached in Nineveh.

FIRST REFERENCE
2 KINGS 14:25

LAST REFERENCE
JONAH 1:1

AMMIEL 6

People of God

1) One of the twelve spies sent by Moses to spy out the land of Canaan.

ONLY REFERENCE
NUMBERS 13:12

2) A man who housed Saul's crippled son, Mephibosheth, after the king's death. Ammiel's son Machir later brought food and supplies to King David and his soldiers as they fled from the army of David's son Absalom, who had staged a coup.

FIRST REFERENCE
2 SAMUEL 9:4

LAST REFERENCE
2 SAMUEL 17:27

3) Father of King David's wife Bath-sheba and grandfather of Solomon.

ONLY REFERENCE
1 CHRONICLES 3:5

4) A Levite "porter" (doorkeeper) in the house of the Lord.

ONLY REFERENCE
1 CHRONICLES 26:5

AMMIHUD 10

People of splendor

1) A descendant of Abraham through Joseph's son Ephraim and an ancestor of Joshua.

FIRST REFERENCE
NUMBERS 1:10

LAST REFERENCE
1 CHRONICLES 7:26

2) Forefather of Shemuel, prince of the tribe of Simeon when the Israelites entered the Promised Land.

ONLY REFERENCE
NUMBERS 34:20

3) Forefather of Pedahel, prince of the tribe of Naphtali when the Israelites entered the Promised Land.

ONLY REFERENCE
NUMBERS 34:28

4) Father of the king of Geshur, to whom Absalom fled after he killed Amnon.

ONLY REFERENCE
2 SAMUEL 13:37

5) A descendant of Judah and father of Uthai.

ONLY REFERENCE
1 CHRONICLES 9:4

AMMINADAB 13

People of liberality

1) Father-in-law of Aaron.

ONLY REFERENCE
EXODUS 6:23

2) A descendant of Judah. His son Nahshon became the prince of his tribe.

FIRST REFERENCE
NUMBERS 1:7
LAST REFERENCE
I CHRONICLES 2:10

3) A descendant of Abraham through Jacob's son Levi.

ONLY REFERENCE
I CHRONICLES 6:22

4) A descendant of Abraham through Jacob's son Levi. Amminadab was among a group of Levites appointed by King David to bring the ark of the covenant from the house of Obed-edom to Jerusalem.

FIRST REFERENCE
I CHRONICLES 15:10
LAST REFERENCE
I CHRONICLES 15:11

AMMISHADDAI 5

People of the Almighty

A descendant of Dan. His son Ahiezer became the prince of his tribe.

FIRST REFERENCE
NUMBERS 1:12
LAST REFERENCE
NUMBERS 10:25

AMMIZABAD 1

People of endowment

Son of Benaiah and an army officer of David.

ONLY REFERENCE
I CHRONICLES 27:6

AMNON 28

Faithful

1) David's firstborn son, born in Hebron to his wife Ahinoam. Amnon fell in love with his half sister Tamar. Pretending to be sick, he asked his father to send Tamar to him with food. When she came, he raped her. His love turned to hate, and he threw her out of his house. When Tamar's full brother, Absalom, heard of this, he hated Amnon and eventually had him killed.

FIRST REFERENCE
2 SAMUEL 3:2
LAST REFERENCE
I CHRONICLES 3:1
KEY REFERENCE
2 SAMUEL 13:1–2

2) A descendant of Abraham through Jacob's son Judah.

ONLY REFERENCE
I CHRONICLES 4:20

AMOK 2

Deep

An exiled priest who returned to Judah under Zerubbabel.

FIRST REFERENCE
NEHEMIAH 12:7
LAST REFERENCE
NEHEMIAH 12:20

AMON 19

Skilled

1) A governor of Samaria. When the prophet Micaiah did not please King Ahab, he sent the prophet to Amon.

FIRST REFERENCE
I KINGS 22:26
LAST REFERENCE
2 CHRONICLES 18:25

2) An evil king of Judah who reigned for two years. He wor-

shipped idols and "trespassed more and more" (2 Chronicles 33:23). His servants conspired against him and killed him in his own house.

FIRST REFERENCE
2 KINGS 21:18
LAST REFERENCE
MATTHEW 1:10
KEY REFERENCES
2 KINGS 21:19–20; 2 CHRONICLES 33:23
GENEALOGY OF JESUS
MATTHEW 1:10

3) Forefather of an exiled family—former servants of Solomon—that returned to Judah under Zerubbabel.

ONLY REFERENCE
NEHEMIAH 7:59

AMOS 8

Burdensome

1) A Judean prophet during the reigns of King Uzziah of Judah and King Jeroboam of Israel. He came from a rural setting in which he was a herdsman and fruit gatherer. When God called him as a prophet, he spoke to both Judah and Israel, condemning idolatry and disobedience.

FIRST REFERENCE
AMOS 1:1
LAST REFERENCE
AMOS 8:2

2) A descendant of Abraham through Isaac; forebear of Jesus' earthly father, Joseph.

ONLY REFERENCE
LUKE 3:25
GENEALOGY OF JESUS
LUKE 3:25

AMOZ 13

Strong

Father of the prophet Isaiah.

FIRST REFERENCE
2 KINGS 19:2
LAST REFERENCE
ISAIAH 38:1

AMPLIAS 1

Enlarged

A Roman Christian described as "my beloved in the Lord" by the apostle Paul.

ONLY REFERENCE
ROMANS 16:8

AMRAM 14 3

High people

1) Father of Moses, Aaron, and Miriam.

FIRST REFERENCE
EXODUS 6:18
LAST REFERENCE
1 CHRONICLES 24:20

2) An exiled Israelite who married a "strange" (foreign) woman.

ONLY REFERENCE
EZRA 10:34

3) A descendant of Seir the Horite, whose family married into Esau's family.

FIRST REFERENCE
1 CHRONICLES 1:41

AMRAPHEL 2

The king of Shinar in the days of Abram. Amraphel was part of a victorious battle alliance that kidnapped Abram's nephew Lot.

FIRST REFERENCE
GENESIS 14:1
LAST REFERENCE
GENESIS 14:9

AMZI 2
Strong

1) A descendant of Levi and fore-father of Hashabiah, who stood to the left of Heman the choir leader of the temple.

ONLY REFERENCE
I CHRONICLES 6:46

2) Forefather of a Jewish exile from the tribe of Levi who resettled Jerusalem.

ONLY REFERENCE
NEHEMIAH 11:12

ANAH 12
Answer

1) Mother of Aholibamah and mother-in-law of Esau.

FIRST REFERENCE
GENESIS 36:2
LAST REFERENCE
GENESIS 36:25

2) A descendant of Seir, who lived in Esau's "land of Edom."

FIRST REFERENCE
GENESIS 36:20
LAST REFERENCE
I CHRONICLES 1:38

3) Another descendant of Seir, who lived in Esau's "land of Edom." Anah discovered "mules in the wilderness" as he fed his father's donkeys.

FIRST REFERENCE
GENESIS 36:24
LAST REFERENCE
I CHRONICLES 1:41

ANAIAH 2
God has answered

1) A priest who assisted Ezra in reading the book of the law to the people of Jerusalem.

ONLY REFERENCE
NEHEMIAH 8:4

2) A Jewish leader who renewed the covenant under Nehemiah.

ONLY REFERENCE
NEHEMIAH 10:22

ANAK 9
Strangling

Founder of a tribe in Hebron. His gigantic sons lived there when Joshua's spies searched the land.

FIRST REFERENCE
NUMBERS 13:22
LAST REFERENCE
JUDGES 1:20

ANAN I
Cloud

A Jewish leader who renewed the covenant under Nehemiah.

ONLY REFERENCE
NEHEMIAH 10:26

ANANI I
Cloudy

A descendant of Abraham through Jacob's son Judah, in the line of the nation of Judah's second-to-last king, Jeconiah (also known as Jehoiachin).

ONLY REFERENCE
I CHRONICLES 3:24

ANANIAH 1

God has covered

Forefather of a man who repaired Jerusalem's walls under Nehemiah.

ONLY REFERENCE
NEHEMIAH 3:23

ANANIAS 11 3

God has favored

1) A Christian who lied to the apostle Peter, saying that he and his wife, Sapphira, had donated the full price of a land sale to the church. Peter confronted Ananias, asking why he had lied to God. Ananias died immediately.

FIRST REFERENCE
ACTS 5:1
LAST REFERENCE
ACTS 5:5

2) A Christian of Damascus whom God called to speak to Paul shortly after the apostle-to-be's conversion. When Ananias doubted the wisdom of meeting with Paul, God told him Paul would bear the gospel to the Gentiles.

FIRST REFERENCE
ACTS 9:10
LAST REFERENCE
ACTS 22:12

3) The high priest who accused and even hit Paul during interrogation, after the apostle was wrongly arrested for profaning the temple. Five days later Ananias appeared before Governor Felix, supporting charges of sedition against Paul.

FIRST REFERENCE
ACTS 23:2
LAST REFERENCE
ACTS 24:1

ANATH 2

Answer

Father of Israel's third judge, Shamgar.

FIRST REFERENCE
JUDGES 3:31
LAST REFERENCE
JUDGES 5:6

ANATHOTH 2 2

Answers

1) A descendant of Abraham through Jacob's son Benjamin.

ONLY REFERENCE
I CHRONICLES 7:8

2) A Jewish leader who renewed the covenant under Nehemiah.

ONLY REFERENCE
NEHEMIAH 10:19

ANDREW 13

Manly

Brother of Peter and one of Jesus' disciples and apostles. He met Jesus first and then told Peter he had found the Messiah. Jesus called both of these fishermen to leave their boat and become fishers of men. At the feeding of the five thousand, Andrew brought the boy with loaves and fish to Jesus' attention. With Philip, he brought some Greeks to meet Jesus. He was also one of the intimate group of disciples who questioned Jesus about the end times.

FIRST REFERENCE
MATTHEW 4:18
LAST REFERENCE
ACTS 1:13
KEY REFERENCES
MATTHEW 4:18–19; JOHN 6:8–9

ANDRONICUS 1
Man of victory

A Roman Christian who spent time in jail with the apostle Paul and who may have been related to Paul.

ONLY REFERENCE
ROMANS 16:7

ANER 2
Boy

An Amorite confederate of Abram who was part of a victorious battle alliance that kidnapped Abram's nephew Lot.

FIRST REFERENCE
GENESIS 14:13
LAST REFERENCE
GENESIS 14:24

ANIAM 1
Groaning of the people

A descendant of Abraham through Joseph's son Manasseh.

ONLY REFERENCE
I CHRONICLES 7:19

ANNA 1
Favored

A widowed prophetess who lived in the temple and recognized Jesus as the Messiah when He was first brought to the temple.

ONLY REFERENCE
LUKE 2:36

ANNAS 4
God has favored

High priest during Jesus' ministry. Though the Romans deposed him in favor of his son-in-law Caiaphas, many Jews still considered him the high priest. Jesus was first brought to him after Judas's betrayal. Annas was also one of the council that sought to keep Peter from preaching.

FIRST REFERENCE
LUKE 3:2
LAST REFERENCE
ACTS 4:6

ANTIPAS 1
Instead of father

A Christian martyr of Pergamos commended by Jesus.

ONLY REFERENCE
REVELATION 2:13

ANTOTHIJAH 1
Answers of God

A descendant of Abraham through Jacob's son Benjamin.

ONLY REFERENCE
I CHRONICLES 8:24

ANUB 1
Borne

A descendant of Abraham through Jacob's son Judah.

ONLY REFERENCE
I CHRONICLES 4:8

APELLES 1

A Christian acquaintance of the apostle Paul in Rome.

ONLY REFERENCE
ROMANS 16:10

APHIAH 1
Breeze

A descendant of Benjamin and forefather of King Saul.

ONLY REFERENCE
1 SAMUEL 9:1

APHSES 1
Sever

One of twenty-four priests in David's time who was chosen by lot to serve in the tabernacle.

ONLY REFERENCE
1 CHRONICLES 24:15

APOLLOS 10
The sun

A Jewish preacher from Alexandria who had been baptized into John's baptism and knew nothing of the Holy Spirit. Aquila and Priscilla "expounded unto him the way of God more perfectly" (Acts 18:26). He went to preach in Corinth. When a dispute arose in Corinth between church members who followed Paul and those who followed Apollos, Paul called them to recognize that they all followed Jesus.

FIRST REFERENCE
ACTS 18:24

LAST REFERENCE
TITUS 3:13
KEY REFERENCES
ACTS 18:24; 1 CORINTHIANS 3:5

APPAIM 2
Two nostrils

A descendant of Abraham through Jacob's son Judah.

FIRST REFERENCE
1 CHRONICLES 2:30
LAST REFERENCE
1 CHRONICLES 2:31

APPHIA 1

A Christian woman of Colosse called "beloved" by the apostle Paul.

ONLY REFERENCE
PHILEMON 1:2

AQUILA 6
Eagle

A tent-making Christian who lived in Corinth and met Paul there. Paul joined Aquila and his wife, Priscilla, in their craft. The couple became helpers in Paul's ministry and founded a house church in their home.

FIRST REFERENCE
ACTS 18:2
LAST REFERENCE
2 TIMOTHY 4:19

ARA 1
Lion

A descendant of Abraham through Jacob's son Asher.

ONLY REFERENCE
1 CHRONICLES 7:38

ARAD 3
Fugitive

1) A Canaanite king who fought the Israelites as they entered the Promised Land.

FIRST REFERENCE
NUMBERS 21:1
LAST REFERENCE
NUMBERS 33:40

2) A descendant of Abraham through Jacob's son Benjamin.

ONLY REFERENCE
I CHRONICLES 8:15

ARAH 4
Wayfaring

1) A descendant of Abraham through Jacob's son Asher.

ONLY REFERENCE
I CHRONICLES 7:39

2) Forefather of an exiled family that returned to Judah under Zerubbabel.

FIRST REFERENCE
EZRA 2:5
LAST REFERENCE
NEHEMIAH 7:10

3) Father of Tobiah, who opposed the rebuilding of Jerusalem's wall.

ONLY REFERENCE
NEHEMIAH 6:18

ARAM 8
The highland

1) A descendant of Noah through Noah's son Shem.

FIRST REFERENCE
GENESIS 10:22
LAST REFERENCE
I CHRONICLES 1:17

2) A descendant of Abraham's brother Nahor.

ONLY REFERENCE
GENESIS 22:21

3) A descendant of Abraham through Isaac; forebear of Jesus' earthly father, Joseph.

FIRST REFERENCE
I CHRONICLES 7:34
LAST REFERENCE
LUKE 3:33
GENEALOGY OF JESUS
LUKE 3:33

ARAN 2
Shrill

A descendant of Seir, who lived in Esau's "land of Edom."

FIRST REFERENCE
GENESIS 36:28
LAST REFERENCE
I CHRONICLES 1:42

ARAUNAH 9
Strong

A Jebusite who sold his threshing floor to King David so the king could build an altar and make a sacrifice there. Same as Ornan.

FIRST REFERENCE
2 SAMUEL 24:16
LAST REFERENCE
2 SAMUEL 24:24

ARBA 3
Four

Father of Anak. His city was given to the Levites when the land was divided among the tribes.

FIRST REFERENCE
JOSHUA 15:13
LAST REFERENCE
JOSHUA 21:11

ARCHELAUS 1

People-ruling

Son of Herod the Great who ruled over Judea when Joseph planned to return there with Mary and Jesus. Because Joseph feared Archelaus, he took his family to Galilee instead.

ONLY REFERENCE
MATTHEW 2:22

ARCHIPPUS 2

Horse-ruler

A Colossian Christian whom Paul encouraged in faithful ministry.

FIRST REFERENCE
COLOSSIANS 4:17
LAST REFERENCE
PHILEMON 1:2

ARD 3

Fugitive

1) A descendant of Abraham through Jacob's son Benjamin.

ONLY REFERENCE
GENESIS 46:21

2) Another descendant of Abraham through Jacob's son Benjamin. His father was Bela.

ONLY REFERENCE
NUMBERS 26:40

ARDON 1

Roaming

A descendant of Abraham through Jacob's son Judah.

ONLY REFERENCE
1 CHRONICLES 2:18

ARELI 2

Heroic

A descendant of Abraham through Jacob's son Gad.

FIRST REFERENCE
GENESIS 46:16
LAST REFERENCE
NUMBERS 26:17

ARETAS 1

An Arabian king who ruled over Syria.

ONLY REFERENCE
2 CORINTHIANS 11:32

ARGOB 1

Stony

An Israelite official assassinated along with King Pekahiah.

ONLY REFERENCE
2 KINGS 15:25

ARIDAI 1

One of ten sons of Haman, the villain of the story of Esther.

ONLY REFERENCE
ESTHER 9:9

ARIDATHA 1

One of ten sons of Haman, the villain of the story of Esther.

ONLY REFERENCE
ESTHER 9:8

ARIEH

Lion

An Israelite official assassinated along with King Pekahiah.

ONLY REFERENCE
2 KINGS 15:25

ARIEL

Lion of God

A Jewish exile charged with finding Levites and temple servants to travel to Jerusalem with Ezra.

ONLY REFERENCE
EZRA 8:16

ARIOCH

1) The king of Ellasar in the days of Abram. Arioch was part of a victorious battle alliance that kidnapped Abram's nephew Lot.

FIRST REFERENCE
GENESIS 14:1
LAST REFERENCE
GENESIS 14:9

2) Captain of King Nebuchadnezzar's guard. When none of Nebuchadnezzar's wise men could interpret the king's dream, Arioch was to kill all the wise men. Instead he brought Daniel to the king.

FIRST REFERENCE
DANIEL 2:14
LAST REFERENCE
DANIEL 2:25

ARISAI

One of ten sons of Haman, the villain of the story of Esther.

ONLY REFERENCE
ESTHER 9:9

ARISTARCHUS 5

Best ruling

One of Paul's companions at Ephesus who was captured by a crowd that objected to the Christians' teaching. He accompanied Paul on various travels, including his trip to Rome.

FIRST REFERENCE
ACTS 19:29
LAST REFERENCE
PHILEMON 1:24

ARISTOBULUS 1

Best counseling

A Christian acquaintance whom his the apostle Paul greeted in letter to the Romans.

ONLY REFERENCE
ROMANS 16:10

ARMONI

Palatial

A son of the late King Saul, delivered by King David to the Gibeonites. They hanged him in vengeance for Saul's mistreatment of their people.

ONLY REFERENCE
2 SAMUEL 21:8

ARNAN

Noisy

A descendant of Abraham through Jacob's son Judah, in the line of the nation of Judah's second-to-last king, Jeconiah (also known as Jehoiachin).

ONLY REFERENCE
1 CHRONICLES 3:21

AROD

Fugitive

A descendant of Abraham through Jacob's son Gad.

ONLY REFERENCE
NUMBERS 26:17

ARPHAXAD

A descendant of Noah through his son Shem.

FIRST REFERENCE
GENESIS 10:22
LAST REFERENCE
LUKE 3:36
KEY REFERENCE
GENESIS 11:11–13
GENEALOGY OF JESUS
LUKE 3:36

ARTAXERXES

1) Persian king who received letters objecting to the rebuilding of Jerusalem from those who opposed the Jews. Also called Longimanus.

FIRST REFERENCE
EZRA 4:7
LAST REFERENCE
EZRA 4:11

2) One of three Persian kings who commanded that the Jews rebuild Jerusalem. Also called Cambyses.

ONLY REFERENCE
EZRA 6:14

3) Another name for King Darius of Persia.

FIRST REFERENCE
EZRA 7:1
LAST REFERENCE
NEHEMIAH 13:6

ARTEMAS

Gift of Artemis

An acquaintance of the apostle Paul, whom Paul considered sending as a messenger to Titus.

ONLY REFERENCE
TITUS 3:12

ARZA

Earthiness

Palace steward of Israel's king Elah. A drunken Elah was assassinated in Arza's house.

ONLY REFERENCE
1 KINGS 16:9

ASA

1) King of Judah, son of King Abijam. Asa reigned forty-one years and removed many idols from Judah. While the country was peaceful, he built fortified cities and established his army. When an Ethiopian army attacked, he called on the Lord and was victorious. When Azariah prophetically encouraged the king to seek the Lord, Asa led

his people in making a covenant to seek God. He even removed his mother from her position as queen because she worshipped idols. But he did not remove the idols from the high places.

In the thirty-sixth year of his reign, Asa took the silver and gold from the temple and his own treasury and gave it to King Ben-hadad of Syria to convince him to end his alliance with Baasha, king of Israel, and support Judah instead. Through Hanani the prophet, God declared that Asa was not depending on Him and would end his reign in wars. The angry king imprisoned Hanani and oppressed people. Though he suffered an illness of his feet, Asa would not turn to the Lord.

FIRST REFERENCE
I KINGS 15:8
LAST REFERENCE
MATTHEW 1:8
KEY REFERENCES
2 CHRONICLES 14:2–4; 16:7–10
GENEALOGY OF JESUS
MATTHEW 1:8

2) A Jewish exile from the tribe of Levi who resettled Jerusalem.

ONLY REFERENCE
I CHRONICLES 9:16

ASAHEL   18

God has made

1) Brother of Joab, who was David's army commander. Asahel was also a commander in King David's army, overseeing twenty-four thousand men in the fourth month of each year. Abner, Saul's army commander, killed Asahel as he pursued the escaping Abner, following a battle at Gibeon.

FIRST REFERENCE
2 SAMUEL 2:18
LAST REFERENCE
I CHRONICLES 27:7

2) A Levite sent by King Jehoshaphat to teach the law of the Lord throughout the nation of Judah.

ONLY REFERENCE
2 CHRONICLES 17:8

3) A temple overseer during the reign of King Hezekiah of Judah.

ONLY REFERENCE
2 CHRONICLES 31:13

4) Forefather of Jonathan, who oversaw the dissolution of marriages to "strange" (foreign) women following the return from the Babylonian Exile.

ONLY REFERENCE
EZRA 10:15

ASAHIAH   2

God has made

A servant of King Josiah who was part of a delegation sent to the prophetess Huldah after the "book of the law" was discovered in the temple. Same as Asaiah (5).

FIRST REFERENCE
2 KINGS 22:12
LAST REFERENCE
2 KINGS 22:14

ASAIAH 6

God has made

1) A descendant of Abraham through Jacob's son Simeon.

ONLY REFERENCE
I CHRONICLES 4:36

2) A descendant of Abraham through Jacob's son Levi.

ONLY REFERENCE
I CHRONICLES 6:30

3) A Jewish exile from the tribe of Judah who resettled Jerusalem.

ONLY REFERENCE
I CHRONICLES 9:5

4) A descendant of Abraham through Jacob's son Levi. Asaiah was among a group of Levites appointed by King David to bring the ark of the covenant from the house of Obed-edom to Jerusalem.

FIRST REFERENCE
I CHRONICLES 15:6
LAST REFERENCE
I CHRONICLES 15:11

5) One of five men sent by King Josiah to ask God's prophetess Huldah what to do about the "book of the law" recently discovered in the temple. Same as Asahiah.

ONLY REFERENCE
2 CHRONICLES 34:20

ASAPH 45

Collector

1) Father of Joah, who represented King Hezekiah in a meeting with the Assyrian deputies of King Shalmaneser.

FIRST REFERENCE
2 KINGS 18:18
LAST REFERENCE
ISAIAH 36:22

2) A descendant of Abraham through Jacob's son Levi. Asaph was one of the key musicians serving in the Jerusalem temple. King David appointed Asaph's descendants to "prophesy with harps, with psalteries, and with cymbals" (1 Chronicles 25:1).

FIRST REFERENCE
I CHRONICLES 6:39
LAST REFERENCE
PSALM 83 (TITLE)

3) Forefather of a Jewish exile from the tribe of Levi who resettled Jerusalem.

ONLY REFERENCE
I CHRONICLES 9:15

4) Forefather of a Levite "porter" (doorkeeper) in the house of the Lord.

ONLY REFERENCE
I CHRONICLES 26:1

5) Keeper of the king's forest for King Artaxerxes of Persia.

ONLY REFERENCE
NEHEMIAH 2:8

ASAREEL 1

Right of God

A descendant of Abraham through Jacob's son Judah.

ONLY REFERENCE
I CHRONICLES 4:16

ASARELAH
Right toward God

A son of King David's musician Asaph, "which prophesied according to the order of the king" (1 Chronicles 25:2).

ONLY REFERENCE
I CHRONICLES 25:2

ASENATH

Daughter of an Egyptian priest and given as a wife to Joseph by the pharaoh. Asenath bore two sons to Joseph: Manasseh and Ephraim.

FIRST REFERENCE
GENESIS 41:45
LAST REFERENCE
GENESIS 46:20

ASER
Happy

Greek form of the Hebrew name *Asher*, one of twelve tribes of Israel.

FIRST REFERENCE
LUKE 2:36
LAST REFERENCE
REVELATION 7:6

ASHBEA
Adjurer

A descendant of Abraham through Jacob's son Judah. Ashbea's family was known for producing fine linen.

ONLY REFERENCE
I CHRONICLES 4:21

ASHBEL
Flowing

A descendant of Abraham through Jacob's son Benjamin. Ashbel was Benjamin's second son.

FIRST REFERENCE
GENESIS 46:21
LAST REFERENCE
I CHRONICLES 8:1

ASHCHENAZ

A descendant of Noah through his son Japheth. Same as Ashkenaz.

ONLY REFERENCE
I CHRONICLES 1:6

ASHER
Happy

A son of Jacob and Zilpah. He founded the tribe of Asher.

FIRST REFERENCE
GENESIS 30:13
LAST REFERENCE
I CHRONICLES 7:40

ASHKENAZ

A descendant of Noah through his son Japheth. Same as Ashchenaz.

ONLY REFERENCE
GENESIS 10:3

ASHPENAZ

Chief eunuch of the Babylonian king Nebuchadnezzar. Ashpenaz selected Daniel for the ruler's service.

ONLY REFERENCE
DANIEL 1:3

ASHRIEL

Right of God

A descendant of Abraham through Joseph's son Manasseh.

ONLY REFERENCE
I CHRONICLES 7:14

ASHUR 2

Successful

A descendant of Abraham through Jacob's son Judah.

FIRST REFERENCE
I CHRONICLES 2:24
LAST REFERENCE
I CHRONICLES 4:5

ASHVATH 1

Bright

A descendant of Abraham through Jacob's son Asher.

ONLY REFERENCE
I CHRONICLES 7:33

ASIEL 1

Made of God

A descendant of Abraham through Jacob's son Simeon.

ONLY REFERENCE
I CHRONICLES 4:35

ASNAH 1

Forefather of an exiled family that returned to Judah under Zerubbabel.

ONLY REFERENCE
EZRA 2:50

ASNAPPER 1

An Assyrian king who resettled Samaria with other people, after the Israelites were captured.

ONLY REFERENCE
EZRA 4:10

ASPATHA 1

One of ten sons of Haman, the villain of the story of Esther.

ONLY REFERENCE
ESTHER 9:7

ASRIEL 2

Right of God

A descendant of Joseph through his son Manasseh.

FIRST REFERENCE
NUMBERS 26:31
LAST REFERENCE
JOSHUA 17:2

ASSHUR 3

Successful

1) A descendant of Noah who built the cities of Nineveh, Rehoboth, and Calah.

ONLY REFERENCE
GENESIS 10:11

2) A descendant of Noah through Noah's son Shem.

FIRST REFERENCE
GENESIS 10:22
LAST REFERENCE
I CHRONICLES 1:17

ASSIR 5
Prisoner

1) A descendant of Abraham through Jacob's son Levi.

FIRST REFERENCE
EXODUS 6:24
LAST REFERENCE
I CHRONICLES 6:22

2) Another descendant of Abraham through Jacob's son Levi.

FIRST REFERENCE
I CHRONICLES 6:23
LAST REFERENCE
I CHRONICLES 6:37

3) A descendant of Abraham through Jacob's son Judah, in the line of the nation of Judah's second-to-last king, Jeconiah (also known as Jehoiachin).

ONLY REFERENCE
I CHRONICLES 3:17

ASYNCRITUS 1
Incomparable

A Christian acquaintance whom the apostle Paul greeted in his letter to the Romans.

ONLY REFERENCE
ROMANS 16:14

ATARAH 1
Crown

A wife of Jerahmeel, a descendant of Abraham through Jacob's son Judah.

ONLY REFERENCE
I CHRONICLES 2:26

ATER 5
Maimed

1) Forefather of a Jewish exile who returned to Judah under Zerubbabel.

FIRST REFERENCE
EZRA 2:16
LAST REFERENCE
NEHEMIAH 7:21

2) Forefather of an exiled family that returned to Judah under Zerubbabel.

FIRST REFERENCE
EZRA 2:42
LAST REFERENCE
NEHEMIAH 7:45

3) A Jewish leader who renewed the covenant under Nehemiah.

ONLY REFERENCE
NEHEMIAH 10:17

ATHAIAH 1
God has helped

A Jewish exile from the tribe of Judah who resettled Jerusalem.

ONLY REFERENCE
NEHEMIAH 11:4

ATHALIAH 17
God has constrained

1) Wife of Jehoram and mother of Ahaziah, two kings of Judah. When her son was killed by Jehu, she destroyed all possible heirs to the throne, missing only Joash, who was saved by his aunt Jehosheba. Wicked, idolatrous Athaliah ruled Judah for six years. In the seventh year of her reign, the priest

Jehoiada crowned Joash king while in the temple. When Athaliah saw this, she declared it treason. Jehoiada commanded his warriors to take her outside the temple and kill her. Judah did not mourn her death.

FIRST REFERENCE
2 KINGS 8:26
LAST REFERENCE
2 CHRONICLES 24:7
KEY REFERENCES
2 KINGS 11:1; 2 CHRONICLES 22:3

2) A descendant of Abraham through Jacob's son Benjamin.

ONLY REFERENCE
1 CHRONICLES 8:26

3) Forefather of a Jewish exile who returned to Judah under Ezra.

ONLY REFERENCE
EZRA 8:7

ATHLAI
Constricted

An exiled Israelite who married a "strange" (foreign) woman.

ONLY REFERENCE
EZRA 10:28

ATTAI
Timely

1) A descendant of Abraham through Jacob's son Judah. Attai descended from the line of an unnamed Israelite woman and her Egyptian husband, Jarha.

FIRST REFERENCE
1 CHRONICLES 2:35
LAST REFERENCE
1 CHRONICLES 2:36

2) One of several warriors from the tribe of Gad who left Saul to join David during his conflict with the king. Attai and his companions were "men of might. . .whose faces were like the faces of lions" (1 Chronicles 12:8).

ONLY REFERENCE
1 CHRONICLES 12:11

3) A son of Judah's king Rehoboam; grandson of Solomon.

ONLY REFERENCE
2 CHRONICLES 11:20

AUGUSTUS
August

The Roman emperor who called for the census that brought Mary and Joseph to Bethlehem. He was still ruling when Paul appealed to Caesar during his imprisonment in Jerusalem. Also called Caesar Augustus.

FIRST REFERENCE
LUKE 2:1
LAST REFERENCE
ACTS 27:1

AZALIAH
God has reserved

Father of a temple scribe who served in the time of King Joash of Judah.

FIRST REFERENCE
2 KINGS 22:3
LAST REFERENCE
2 CHRONICLES 34:8

AZANIAH

Heard by God

A Levite who renewed the covenant under Nehemiah.

ONLY REFERENCE
NEHEMIAH 10:9

AZARAEL

God has helped

A priest who helped to dedicate the rebuilt walls of Jerusalem by playing a musical instrument.

ONLY REFERENCE
NEHEMIAH 12:36

AZAREEL

God has helped

1) A "mighty man" who supported the future king David during his conflict with Saul.

ONLY REFERENCE
I CHRONICLES 12:6

2) One of twenty-four Levite musicians who was chosen by lot to serve in the house of the Lord.

ONLY REFERENCE
I CHRONICLES 25:18

3) Leader of the tribe of Dan in the days of King David.

ONLY REFERENCE
I CHRONICLES 27:22

4) An exiled Israelite who married a "strange" (foreign) woman.

ONLY REFERENCE
EZRA 10:41

5) Ancestor of a Jewish exile from the tribe of Levi who resettled Jerusalem.

ONLY REFERENCE
NEHEMIAH 11:13

AZARIAH

God has helped

1) An officer in Solomon's army. His father was Zadok the priest.

ONLY REFERENCE
I KINGS 4:2

2) Another prince under King Solomon. His father was Nathan.

ONLY REFERENCE
I KINGS 4:5

3) King of Judah who was obedient to God but did not remove the idolatrous altars from the high places. Though Azariah ruled for fifty-two years, God made him a leper, and his son judged the people in his place. Same as Uzziah (1).

FIRST REFERENCE
2 KINGS 14:21
LAST REFERENCE
I CHRONICLES 3:12

4) A descendant of Abraham through Jacob's son Judah.

ONLY REFERENCE
I CHRONICLES 2:8

5) Another descendant of Abraham through Jacob's son Judah. Azariah descended from the line of an unnamed Israelite woman and her Egyptian husband, Jarha.

FIRST REFERENCE
I CHRONICLES 2:38
LAST REFERENCE
I CHRONICLES 2:39

6) A descendant of Abraham through Jacob's son Levi and a priest through the line of Aaron.

ONLY REFERENCE
I CHRONICLES 6:9

7) Another descendant of Abraham through Jacob's son Levi and a priest through the line of Aaron. Azariah served in Solomon's temple in Jerusalem.

FIRST REFERENCE
I CHRONICLES 6:10
LAST REFERENCE
I CHRONICLES 6:11

8) Another descendant of Abraham through Jacob's son Levi and a priest through the line of Aaron.

FIRST REFERENCE
I CHRONICLES 6:13
LAST REFERENCE
EZRA 7:1

9) Ancestor of Heman, a singer who ministered in the tabernacle.

ONLY REFERENCE
I CHRONICLES 6:36

10) A prophet who encouraged King Asa of Judah to follow the Lord.

ONLY REFERENCE
2 CHRONICLES 15:1

11) A son of Judah's king Jehoshaphat who was given "great gifts of silver, and of gold, and of precious things" by his father (2 Chronicles 21:3).

ONLY REFERENCE
2 CHRONICLES 21:2

12) Another son of Judah's king Jehoshaphat who was given "great gifts of silver, and of gold, and of precious things" by his father (2 Chronicles 21:3).

ONLY REFERENCE
2 CHRONICLES 21:2

13) Son of Jehoram, king of Judah.

ONLY REFERENCE
2 CHRONICLES 22:6

14) A captain over hundreds for the priest Jehoiada, who crowned Joash king of Judah. His father was Jeroham.

ONLY REFERENCE
2 CHRONICLES 23:1

15) Another captain over hundreds for the priest Jehoiada, who crowned Joash king of Judah. His father was Obed.

ONLY REFERENCE
2 CHRONICLES 23:1

16) The chief priest who stood up to King Uzziah of Judah when he tried to burn incense on the temple altar.

FIRST REFERENCE
2 CHRONICLES 26:17
LAST REFERENCE
2 CHRONICLES 26:20

17) A man of the tribe of Ephraim who counseled Israel against enslaving fellow Jews from Judah who were captured in a civil war. Azariah helped to feed and clothe the prioners before sending them home.

ONLY REFERENCE
2 CHRONICLES 28:12

18) A descendant of Abraham through Jacob's son Levi and father of a Levite who cleansed the Jerusalem temple during the revival of King Hezekiah's day.

19) Another descendant of Abraham through Jacob's son Levi and father of a Levite who cleansed the Jerusalem temple during the revival of King Hezekiah's day.

20) "The ruler of the house of God" and chief priest during the reign of King Hezekiah of Judah (2 Chronicles 31:13).

21) Ancestor of Ezra, the scribe who led the Israelites into Jerusalem after the Babylonian Exile.

22) A man who repaired Jerusalem's walls under Nehemiah.

23) A Jewish exile who returned to Judah under Zerubbabel.

24) A Levite who helped Ezra to explain the law to exiles returned to Jerusalem.

25) A priest who renewed the covenant under Nehemiah.

26) A prince of Judah who joined in the dedication of Jerusalem's rebuilt walls.

27) A rebellious Israelite who refused to believe Jeremiah's warning to Israel's remnant, which was not to escape into Egypt.

28) The Hebrew name for Abednego, one of Daniel's companions in exile.

AZAZ

Strong

A descendant of Abraham through Jacob's son Reuben.

AZAZIAH

God has strengthened

1) A Levite musician who performed in celebration when King David brought the ark of the covenant to Jerusalem.

2) Father of Hoshea, a man of Ephraim who ruled over his tribe during King David's reign.

3) A temple overseer during the reign of King Hezekiah of Judah.

ONLY REFERENCE
2 CHRONICLES 31:13

AZBUK 1
Stern depopulator

Father of a man who repaired Jerusalem's walls under Nehemiah.

ONLY REFERENCE
NEHEMIAH 3:16

AZEL 6
Noble

A descendant of Abraham through Jacob's son Benjamin, through the line of King Saul and his son Jonathan.

FIRST REFERENCE
I CHRONICLES 8:37
LAST REFERENCE
I CHRONICLES 9:44

AZGAD 4
Stern troop

1) Forefather of an exiled family that returned to Judah under Zerubbabel.

FIRST REFERENCE
EZRA 2:12
LAST REFERENCE
NEHEMIAH 7:17

2) Forefather of a Jewish exile who returned from Babylon to Judah under Ezra.

ONLY REFERENCE
EZRA 8:12

3) A Jewish leader who renewed the covenant under Nehemiah.

ONLY REFERENCE
NEHEMIAH 10:15

AZIEL 1
Strengthened of God

A Levite musician who performed in celebration when King David brought the ark of the covenant to Jerusalem. Same as Jaaziel.

ONLY REFERENCE
I CHRONICLES 15:20

AZIZA 1
Strengthfulness

An exiled Israelite who married a "strange" (foreign) woman.

ONLY REFERENCE
EZRA 10:27

AZMAVETH 6
Strong one of death

1) One of King David's valiant warriors.

FIRST REFERENCE
2 SAMUEL 23:31
LAST REFERENCE
I CHRONICLES 11:33

2) A descendant of Abraham through Jacob's son Benjamin, in the line of King Saul and his son Jonathan.

FIRST REFERENCE
I CHRONICLES 8:36
LAST REFERENCE
I CHRONICLES 9:42

3) Father of David's "mighty men" Jeziel and Pelet, who supported the future king during his conflict with Saul.

4) A treasurer who served under King David.

ONLY REFERENCE
1 CHRONICLES 27:25

AZOR 2
Helpful

A descendant of Abraham through Isaac; forebear of Jesus' earthly father, Joseph.

FIRST REFERENCE
MATTHEW 1:13
LAST REFERENCE
MATTHEW 1:14
GENEALOGY OF JESUS
MATTHEW 1:13–14

AZRIEL 3
Help of God

1) One of the "mighty men of valour, famous men" who led the half tribe of Manasseh.

ONLY REFERENCE
1 CHRONICLES 5:24

2) Forefather of Ishmaiah, whom David made ruler over the Zebulunites.

ONLY REFERENCE
1 CHRONICLES 27:19

3) Father of Seraiah, whom Jehoiakim, king of Judah, commanded to seize the prophet Jeremiah and his scribe.

ONLY REFERENCE
JEREMIAH 36:26

AZRIKAM 6
Help of an enemy

1) A descendant of Abraham through Jacob's son Judah, in the line of the nation of Judah's second-to-last king, Jeconiah (also known as Jehoiachin).

ONLY REFERENCE
1 CHRONICLES 3:23

2) A descendant of Abraham through Jacob's son Benjamin, in the line of King Saul and his son Jonathan.

FIRST REFERENCE
1 CHRONICLES 8:38
LAST REFERENCE
1 CHRONICLES 9:44

3) Forefather of a Jewish exile from the tribe of Levi who resettled Jerusalem.

FIRST REFERENCE
1 CHRONICLES 9:14
LAST REFERENCE
NEHEMIAH 11:15

4) Official in charge of the palace of King Ahaz of Judah.

ONLY REFERENCE
2 CHRONICLES 28:7

AZUBAH 4
Desertion

1) Mother of King Jehoshaphat of Judah and daughter of Shilhi.

FIRST REFERENCE
1 KINGS 22:42
LAST REFERENCE
2 CHRONICLES 20:31

2) Wife of Caleb (2).

FIRST REFERENCE
1 CHRONICLES 2:18
LAST REFERENCE
1 CHRONICLES 2:19

AZUR 2

Helpful

1) A prophet whose son, Hanani, spoke prophetically to the prophet Jeremiah.

ONLY REFERENCE
JEREMIAH 28:1

2) A wicked counselor in Jerusalem following the Babylonian Exile.

ONLY REFERENCE
EZEKIEL 11:1

AZZAN 1

Strong one

Forefather of Paltiel, prince of the tribe of Issachar when the Israelites entered the Promised Land.

ONLY REFERENCE
NUMBERS 34:26

AZZUR 1

Helpful

A Jewish leader who renewed the covenant under Nehemiah.

ONLY REFERENCE
NEHEMIAH 10:17

BAAL 3

Master

1) A descendant of Abraham through Jacob's son Reuben.

ONLY REFERENCE
I CHRONICLES 5:5

2) Fourth son of the Benjaminite Jeiel, who founded the city of Gibeon.

FIRST REFERENCE
I CHRONICLES 8:30
LAST REFERENCE
I CHRONICLES 9:36

BAAL-HANAN 5

Possessor of grace

1) A king of Edom, "before there reigned any king over the children of Israel" (Genesis 36:31).

FIRST REFERENCE
GENESIS 36:38
LAST REFERENCE
I CHRONICLES 1:50

2) A Gederite who had charge of King David's olive and sycamore trees in the low plains.

ONLY REFERENCE
I CHRONICLES 27:28

BAALIS
In exultation

An Ammonite king who sent an assassin against Gedaliah, the Babylonian-appointed governor of Judah.

ONLY REFERENCE
JEREMIAH 40:14

BAANA
In affliction

1) One of King Solomon's twelve officials over provisions.

ONLY REFERENCE
I KINGS 4:12

2) Father of a man who repaired Jerusalem's walls under Nehemiah.

ONLY REFERENCE
NEHEMIAH 3:4

BAANAH
In affliction

1) A leader of one of the raiding bands of Saul's son Ish-bosheth. Baanah and his brother, Rechab, killed Ish-bosheth. In turn, David had the brothers killed.

FIRST REFERENCE
2 SAMUEL 4:2
LAST REFERENCE
2 SAMUEL 4:9

2) Father of one of King David's valiant warriors.

FIRST REFERENCE
2 SAMUEL 22:39
LAST REFERENCE
I CHRONICLES 11:30

3) One of King Solomon's twelve officials over provisions.

ONLY REFERENCE
I KINGS 4:16

4) A Jewish leader who renewed the covenant under Nehemiah.

FIRST REFERENCE
EZRA 2:2
LAST REFERENCE
NEHEMIAH 10:27

BAARA
Brutish

One of two wives of a Benjamite named Shaharaim. He divorced her in favor of other wives in Moab.

ONLY REFERENCE
I CHRONICLES 8:8

BAASEIAH
In the work of God

Forefather of Asaph, the Levite singer.

ONLY REFERENCE
I CHRONICLES 6:40

BAASHA
Offensiveness

The idolatrous king of Israel who fought with Asa, king of Judah. After conspiring against and killing King Nadab, he took Israel's throne. Baasha attempted to fortify Ramah, to limit access to Judah. But Asa bribed Ben-hadad, king of Syria, who had a covenant with both nations, to support him instead of Baasha. Asa's army tore down the unfinished fortifications at Ramah and carried the stones away. Baasha and Asa fought for the rest of their reigns. Jehu son of Hanani prophesied the destruction of Baasha's household. This occurred when Baasha's son Elah as killed by Zimri.

FIRST REFERENCE
I KINGS 15:16
LAST REFERENCE
JEREMIAH 41:9
KEY REFERENCES
I KINGS 15:16, 33; 16:1–4

BAKBAKKAR 1

Searcher

A Jewish exile from the tribe of Levi who resettled Jerusalem.

ONLY REFERENCE
I CHRONICLES 9:15

BAKBUK 2

Bottle

Forefather of an exiled family that returned to Judah under Zerubbabel.

FIRST REFERENCE
EZRA 2:51
LAST REFERENCE
NEHEMIAH 7:53

BAKBUKIAH 3

Emptying of God

An exiled Levite who resettled Jerusalem under Nehemiah.

FIRST REFERENCE
NEHEMIAH 11:17
LAST REFERENCE
NEHEMIAH 12:25

BALAAM 63

Foreigner

A Mesopotamian prophet, sent for by Balak, king of Moab, to curse the Israelites who were invading nearby nations and would soon come to his. Balak called for Balaam twice and offered the prophet great honor if he would come, so God allowed him to go to Moab. But the prophet had something perverse in mind. During his trip, his donkey first refused to follow the road then lay down upon it. Suffering a beating because of the prophet's anger, the beast spoke. Suddenly the angel of the Lord who had barred the donkey's way appeared before Balaam and reminded him that God had called for his obedience. Balaam continued on his way and would not curse Israel, no matter how the king pressed him; instead he prophesied blessings on Israel. But he gave the king an idea: distract Israel from its faith by leading its people into idolatry (Revelation 2:14–15).

FIRST REFERENCE
NUMBERS 22:5
LAST REFERENCE
REVELATION 2:14
KEY REFERENCES
NUMBERS 22:18; 23:12; REVELATION 2:14–15

BALAC 1

Waster

Greek form of the name *Balak;* a king of Moab.

ONLY REFERENCE
REVELATION 2:14

BALADAN 2
Bel is his lord

Father of the Babylonian king Berodach-baladan, who sent well wishes to Judah's ill king Hezekiah.

FIRST REFERENCE
2 KINGS 20:12
LAST REFERENCE
ISAIAH 39:1

BALAK 43
Waster

The king of Moab who saw the Israelites heading toward his country and sent for the Mesopotamian prophet Balaam to curse the intruders. At first, Balaam would not come to Moab. When he did come, Balak was angered by his unwillingness to curse Israel. Though Balak brought the prophet to numerous idolatrous high places and made many offerings, he could not sway the prophet's mind because God had told Balaam that Israel was blessed. But in the end Balaam did suggest that the king might influence Israel by leading the people into idolatry—and the idea was successful (Numbers 25:1–2).

FIRST REFERENCE
NUMBERS 22:2
LAST REFERENCE
MICAH 6:5
KEY REFERENCE
NUMBERS 22:5–6

BANI 15
Built

1) One of King David's warriors known as the "mighty men."

ONLY REFERENCE
2 SAMUEL 23:36

2) Ancestor of the sons of Merari, who ministered in the tabernacle.

ONLY REFERENCE
1 CHRONICLES 6:46

3) One of a group of Levites who led a revival among the Israelites in the time of Nehemiah.

ONLY REFERENCE
1 CHRONICLES 9:4

4) Forefather of exiled Israelites who returned to Judah under Zerubbabel.

FIRST REFERENCE
EZRA 2:10
LAST REFERENCE
EZRA 10:29

5) Father of an exiled Israelite who married a "strange" (foreign) woman.

ONLY REFERENCE
EZRA 10:34

6) An exiled Israelite who married a "strange" (foreign) woman.

ONLY REFERENCE
EZRA 10:38

7) A priest who helped Ezra to explain the law to exiles returned to Jerusalem; father of a rebuilder of the city walls.

FIRST REFERENCE
NEHEMIAH 3:17
LAST REFERENCE
NEHEMIAH 9:5

8) One of a group of Levites who led a revival among the Israelites in the time of Nehemiah.

FIRST REFERENCE
NEHEMIAH 9:4
LAST REFERENCE
NEHEMIAH 10:13

9) A Jewish leader who renewed the covenant under Nehemiah.

ONLY REFERENCE
NEHEMIAH 10:14

10) Forefather of a Jewish exile from the tribe of Levi who resettled Jerusalem.

ONLY REFERENCE
NEHEMIAH 11:22

BARABBAS   11
Son of Abba

A man variously described by the Gospel writers as a murderer, a robber, and one accused of sedition. Barabbas was in prison when Jesus came to trial, and Pilate offered the Jewish people a choice concerning which of the two men he should release for the Passover. At the instigation of the chief priests, the people chose Barabbas. He was released, and Jesus died on the cross instead.

FIRST REFERENCE
MATTHEW 27:16
LAST REFERENCE
JOHN 18:40
KEY REFERENCES
MATTHEW 27:17, 21–22

BARACHEL   2
God has blessed

Father of Job's young friend (and accuser) Elihu.

FIRST REFERENCE
JOB 32:2
LAST REFERENCE
JOB 32:6

BARACHIAS   1
Blessing of God

Father of Zacharias, who was killed between the temple and the altar.

ONLY REFERENCE
MATTHEW 23:35

BARAK   14
Lightning

The judge Deborah's battle captain, who refused to enter battle without her support. With Deborah, he went to Kadesh and joined battle against the Canaanite king Jabin's captain Sisera. Barak successfully routed the troops, but Sisera was killed by a woman—Jael, wife of Heber the Kenite.

FIRST REFERENCE
JUDGES 4:6
LAST REFERENCE
HEBREWS 11:32
KEY REFERENCES
JUDGES 4:8, 15–16

BARIAH
Fugitive

A descendant of Abraham through Jacob's son Judah, in the line of the nation of Judah's second-to-last king, Jeconiah (also known as Jehoiachin).

ONLY REFERENCE
I CHRONICLES 3:22

BAR-JESUS
Son of Jesus

A Jewish sorcerer, also called Elymas, who was miraculously blinded for opposing the apostle Paul's preaching of the gospel in Paphos. Same as Elymas.

ONLY REFERENCE
ACTS 13:6

BARJONA
Son of Jonas

Another name for the apostle Peter, used by Jesus Christ.

ONLY REFERENCE
MATTHEW 16:17

BARKOS 2

Forefather of an exiled family that returned to Judah under Zerubbabel.

FIRST REFERENCE
EZRA 2:53
LAST REFERENCE
NEHEMIAH 7:55

BARNABAS 29
Son of prophecy

A Cypriot Christian who sold some land and gave the profits to the church. After Saul's conversion, Barnabas introduced this previous persecutor of the church to the apostles and spoke up for him. When the Jerusalem church heard that Gentiles of Antioch had been converted, they sent Barnabas, who became one of the "prophets and teachers" at that church. Saul and Barnabas were sent on a missionary journey. In Lycaonia, the people wrongly proclaimed them gods. Together the two taught against the Judaizers, who wanted Gentiles to be circumcised. But these missionaries disagreed over the addition of John Mark to their ministry and separated. Barnabas and Mark went to Cyprus. Same as Joses (3).

FIRST REFERENCE
ACTS 4:36
LAST REFERENCE
COLOSSIANS 4:10
KEY REFERENCES
ACTS 9:26–27; 11:22–24

BARSABAS 2
Son of Sabas

1) Also called Joseph Justus, a potential apostolic replacement for Judas Iscariot. He lost by lot to the other candidate, Matthias. Same as Joseph (11) and Justus (1).

ONLY REFERENCE
ACTS 1:23

2) Surname of a Christian named Judas, who was sent by the Jerusalem Council to Antioch with Paul and Barnabas.

ONLY REFERENCE
ACTS 15:22

BARTHOLOMEW 4

Son of Tolmai

One of Jesus' disciples. Probably the same as Nathanael.

FIRST REFERENCE
MATTHEW 10:3
LAST REFERENCE
ACTS 1:13

BARTIMAEUS 1

Son of Timaeus

A blind beggar of Jericho who shouted for Jesus' attention, disturbing the crowds that had gathered to see the Lord. Jesus called for Bartimaeus and asked what he wanted. When the man said he wanted his sight, Jesus healed him, saying, "Thy faith hath made thee whole" (Mark 10:52).

ONLY REFERENCE
MARK 10:46

BARUCH 26 3

Blessed

1) A rebuilder of the walls of Jerusalem and a priest who renewed the covenant under Nehemiah.

FIRST REFERENCE
NEHEMIAH 3:20
LAST REFERENCE
NEHEMIAH 10:6

2) Forefather of a Jewish exile from the tribe of Judah who resettled Jerusalem.

ONLY REFERENCE
NEHEMIAH 11:5

3) A scribe who wrote down all the words the prophet Jeremiah received from God. He went to the temple and read these prophecies to the people. When he read them to the princes of the land, they warned him and Jeremiah to hide while they told Jehoiakim, king of Judah. After the king destroyed the first copy of the prophecies, Baruch rewrote it at Jeremiah's dictation. The proud men who opposed Jeremiah falsely accused Baruch of setting Jeremiah against Judah and trying to deliver the nation into the hands of the Chaldeans.

FIRST REFERENCE
JEREMIAH 32:12
LAST REFERENCE
JEREMIAH 45:2
KEY REFERENCE
JEREMIAH 36:4

BARZILLAI 12
Iron-hearted

1) An elderly man who brought food and supplies to King David and his soldiers as they fled from the army of David's son Absalom. When David returned to Jerusalem, Barzallai conducted him over the Jordan River. David invited him to Jerusalem, but he sent Chimham, who was probably his son, in his place.

FIRST REFERENCE
2 SAMUEL 17:27
LAST REFERENCE
NEHEMIAH 7:63

2) Father of Adriel, the husband of Merab, Saul's daughter.

ONLY REFERENCE
2 SAMUEL 21:8

BASHEMATH 6
Fragrance

1) The Hittite wife of Esau. Same as Adah (2).

ONLY REFERENCE
GENESIS 26:34

2) Ishmael's daughter and another wife of Esau. Mother of Reuel, Nahath, Zerah, Shammah, and Mizzah. Possibly the same as Bashemath (1).

FIRST REFERENCE
GENESIS 36:3
LAST REFERENCE
GENESIS 36:17

BASMATH 1
Fragrance

A daughter of King Solomon who married Ahimaaz, a royal official over the king's provisions.

ONLY REFERENCE
1 KINGS 4:15

BATH-SHEBA 11
Daughter of an oath

The beautiful wife of the warrior Uriah the Hittite. when her King David saw, bathing on her rooftop, he desired her and committed adultery with her, and she became pregnant. To solve his problem, he arranged for Uriah to die in battle and then married Bath-sheba. But God was displeased and the child died. After David repented, God gave them a son, Solomon, who became heir to David's throne. When David's son Adonijah tried to take the throne just before the king's death, Bath-sheba intervened, asking David to remember his promise. Later she intervened with Solomon when Adonijah sought to marry Abishag, David's concubine.

FIRST REFERENCE
2 SAMUEL 11:3
LAST REFERENCE
PSALM 51 (TITLE)
KEY REFERENCES
2 SAMUEL 11:3–4; 1 KINGS 1:11
GENEALOGY OF JESUS
MATTHEW 1:6

BATH-SHUA
Daughter of wealth

A form of the name *Bath-sheba;* a wife of King David.

ONLY REFERENCE
I CHRONICLES 3:5

BAVAI

A man who repaired Jerusalem's walls under Nehemiah.

ONLY REFERENCE
NEHEMIAH 3:18

BAZLITH
Peeling

Forefather of an exiled family that returned to Judah under Zerubbabel. Same as Bazluth.

ONLY REFERENCE
NEHEMIAH 7:54

BAZLUTH
Peeling

Forefather of an exiled family that returned to Judah under Zerubbabel. Same as Bazlith.

ONLY REFERENCE
EZRA 2:52

BEALIAH
God is master

A "mighty man" who supported the future king David during his conflict with Saul.

ONLY REFERENCE
I CHRONICLES 12:5

BEBAI 6

1) Forefather of an exiled family that returned to Judah under Zerubbabel.

FIRST REFERENCE
EZRA 2:11
LAST REFERENCE
NEHEMIAH 7:16

2) Forefather of an exiled family that returned to Judah under Ezra.

FIRST REFERENCE
EZRA 8:11
LAST REFERENCE
EZRA 10:28

3) A Jewish leader who renewed the covenant under Nehemiah.

ONLY REFERENCE
NEHEMIAH 10:15

BECHER 5
Young camel

1) A descendant of Abraham through Jacob's son Benjamin.

FIRST REFERENCE
GENESIS 46:21
LAST REFERENCE
I CHRONICLES 7:8

2) A descendant of Joseph through his son Ephraim.

ONLY REFERENCE
NUMBERS 26:35

BECHORATH
Firstborn

A man of the tribe of Benjamin, ancestor of Israel's king Saul.

ONLY REFERENCE
I SAMUEL 9:1

BEDAD 2
Solitary

Father of a king of Edom, "before there reigned any king over the children of Israel" (Genesis 36:31).

FIRST REFERENCE
GENESIS 36:35
LAST REFERENCE
I CHRONICLES 1:46

BEDAN 2
Servile

1) A judge of Israel who delivered the nation from its enemies.

ONLY REFERENCE
I SAMUEL 12:11

2) A descendant of Abraham through Joseph's son Manasseh.

ONLY REFERENCE
I CHRONICLES 7:17

BEDEIAH 1
Servant of Jehovah

An exiled Israelite who married a "strange" (foreign) woman.

ONLY REFERENCE
EZRA 10:35

BEELIADA 1
Baal has known

A son of King David, born in Jerusalem.

ONLY REFERENCE
I CHRONICLES 14:7

BEERA 1
A well

A descendant of Abraham through Jacob's son Asher.

ONLY REFERENCE
I CHRONICLES 7:37

BEERAH 1
A well

A descendant of Abraham through Jacob's son Reuben. Beerah, a leader of the tribe of Reuben, was taken captive by the Assyrian king Tiglath-pileser.

ONLY REFERENCE
I CHRONICLES 5:6

BEERI 2
Fountained

1) The Hittite father of Judith, a wife of Esau.

ONLY REFERENCE
GENESIS 26:34

2) Father of the prophet Hosea.

ONLY REFERENCE
HOSEA 1:1

BELA 11
A gulp

1) A king of Edom, "before there reigned any king over the children of Israel" (Genesis 36:31).

FIRST REFERENCE
GENESIS 36:32
LAST REFERENCE
I CHRONICLES 1:44

2) A descendant of Abraham through Jacob's son Benjamin. Bela was Benjamin's firstborn son.

FIRST REFERENCE
NUMBERS 26:38
LAST REFERENCE
I CHRONICLES 8:3

3) A descendant of Abraham through Jacob's son Reuben.

ONLY REFERENCE
I CHRONICLES 5:8

BELAH 1

A gulp

Another form of the name *Bela;* a son of Benjamin.

ONLY REFERENCE
GENESIS 46:21

BELSHAZZAR 8

A Babylonian king who saw handwriting on the wall and sought to have it interpreted. When his own soothsayers could not do so, the prophet Daniel read it to him. That night, Belshazzar was killed and Darius the Mede took his throne.

FIRST REFERENCE
DANIEL 5:1
LAST REFERENCE
DANIEL 8:1

BELTESHAZZAR 10

A Babylonian name given to the exiled Israelite Daniel upon entering King Nebuchadnezzar's service.

FIRST REFERENCE
DANIEL 1:7
LAST REFERENCE
DANIEL 10:1

BEN 1

Son

A Levite musician who performed in celebration when King David brought the ark of the covenant to Jerusalem.

ONLY REFERENCE
I CHRONICLES 15:18

BENAIAH 42 12

God has built

1) One of David's three mighty men and a commander in King David's army who oversaw the Cherethites and Pelethites. King Solomon commanded him to kill his brother Adonijah and his battle leader Joab. Solomon rewarded Benaiah by giving him Joab's command.

FIRST REFERENCE
2 SAMUEL 8:18
LAST REFERENCE
I CHRONICLES 27:6
KEY REFERENCES:
I KINGS 2:22–25, 29–34; I CHRONICLES 11:24

2) A commander in King David's army who oversaw twenty-four thousand men in the eleventh month of each year.

FIRST REFERENCE
2 SAMUEL 23:30
LAST REFERENCE
I CHRONICLES 27:14

3) A descendant of Abraham through Jacob's son Simeon.

ONLY REFERENCE
I CHRONICLES 4:36

4) A Levite musician who performed in celebration when King

David brought the ark of the covenant to Jerusalem.

FIRST REFERENCE
I CHRONICLES 15:18
LAST REFERENCE
I CHRONICLES 16:6

5) Son of the chief priest Jehoiada, he was military captain during the third month for King David.

ONLY REFERENCE
I CHRONICLES 27:34

6) Forefather of Jahaziel, a Levite worship leader who prophesied before King Jehoshaphat of Judah when Edom attacked.

ONLY REFERENCE
2 CHRONICLES 20:14

7) A temple overseer during the reign of Hezekiah, king of Judah.

ONLY REFERENCE
2 CHRONICLES 31:13

8) An exiled Israelite who married a "strange" (foreign) woman.

ONLY REFERENCE
EZRA 10:25

9) Another exiled Israelite who married a foreign woman.

ONLY REFERENCE
EZRA 10:30

10) Another exiled Israelite who married a foreign woman.

ONLY REFERENCE
EZRA 10:35

11) Another exiled Israelite who married a foreign woman.

ONLY REFERENCE
EZRA 10:43

12) Father of Pelatiah, a prince of Judah.

FIRST REFERENCE
EZEKIEL 11:1
LAST REFERENCE
EZEKIEL 11:13

BENAMMI 1
Son of my people

Forefather of the Ammonites and a son of Lot by an incestuous relationship with his younger daughter. After the destruction of Sodom and Gomorrah, Lot's two daughters devised a plan to continue their family line by making their father drunk and then lying with him.

ONLY REFERENCE
GENESIS 19:38

BEN-HADAD 26 3
Son of Hadad

1) King of Syria who supported Asa, king of Judah, against Israel.

FIRST REFERENCE
I KINGS 15:18
LAST REFERENCE
2 CHRONICLES 16:4

2) Another king of Syria who fought against King Ahab of Israel. When his army lost, Ben-hadad fled. Again Syria fought Israel and lost, and Ben-hadad fled to Aphek. He asked for mercy, and Ahab made a covenant with him. Elisha came to Damascus at a time when Ben-hadad was ill, and the king asked the prophet if he would live. Though Elisha told his messenger he would recover, he also prophesied his death. Ben-

hadad was murdered by Hazael, who took over his throne.

FIRST REFERENCE
I KINGS 20:1
LAST REFERENCE
2 KINGS 8:9

3) Another Syrian king, son of Hazael. Amos prophesied the burning of his palaces.

FIRST REFERENCE
2 KINGS 13:3
LAST REFERENCE
AMOS 1:4

BEN-HAIL
Son of might

A prince of Judah sent by King Jehoshaphat to teach the law of the Lord throughout the nation.

ONLY REFERENCE
2 CHRONICLES 17:7

BEN-HANAN
Son of Chanan

A descendant of Abraham through Jacob's son Judah.

ONLY REFERENCE
I CHRONICLES 4:20

BENINU
Our son

A Levite who renewed the covenant under Nehemiah.

ONLY REFERENCE
NEHEMIAH 10:13

Son of the right hand

1) Jacob's youngest son and the only full brother of Joseph. Their mother, Rachel, died when he was born. Benjamin became Jacob's favorite after Joseph was sold into slavery by his brothers. During a famine, Jacob sent his other sons to Egypt to get food but fearfully kept Benjamin home. Joseph, then prime minister of Egypt, imprisoned Simeon and insisted that his half brothers bring Benjamin to him. When they returned, Joseph gave his brothers more food but ordered that a silver cup be hidden in Benjamin's sack. When their half brothers came to Benjamin's defense, Joseph knew they had experienced a change of heart.

FIRST REFERENCE
GENESIS 35:18
LAST REFERENCE
I CHRONICLES 8:1

2) A descendant of Abraham through Jacob's son Benjamin.

ONLY REFERENCE
I CHRONICLES 7:10

3) An exiled Israelite who married a "strange" (foreign) woman.

ONLY REFERENCE
EZRA 10:32

4) A rebuilder of the walls of Jerusalem under Nehemiah.

ONLY REFERENCE
NEHEMIAH 3:23

5) A prince of Judah who joined in

the dedication of Jerusalem's rebuilt walls.

ONLY REFERENCE
NEHEMIAH 12:34

BENO 2
Son

A descendant of Abraham through Jacob's son Levi.

FIRST REFERENCE
I CHRONICLES 24:26
LAST REFERENCE
I CHRONICLES 24:27

BEN-ONI 1
Son of my sorrow

Name given by Rachel to her second son as she was dying in childbirth. The boy's father, Jacob, called him Benjamin.

ONLY REFERENCE
GENESIS 35:18

BEN-ZOHETH 1
Son of Zocheth

A descendant of Abraham through Jacob's son Judah.

ONLY REFERENCE
I CHRONICLES 4:20

BEOR 10 2
A lamp

1) Father of Bela, an Edomite king.

FIRST REFERENCE
GENESIS 36:32
LAST REFERENCE
I CHRONICLES 1:43

2) Father of the false prophet Balaam. Same as Bosor.

FIRST REFERENCE
NUMBERS 22:5
LAST REFERENCE
MICAH 6:5

BERA 1

The king of Sodom in the days of Abram. He was killed in battle near the slime pits of Siddim.

ONLY REFERENCE
GENESIS 14:2

BERACHAH 1
Benediction

A "mighty man" who supported the future king David during his conflict with Saul.

ONLY REFERENCE
I CHRONICLES 12:3

BERACHIAH 1
Blessing of God

Father of Asaph, musician for King David and King Solomon of Israel. Same as Berechiah.

ONLY REFERENCE
I CHRONICLES 6:39

BERAIAH 1
God has created

A descendant of Abraham through Jacob's son Benjamin.

ONLY REFERENCE
I CHRONICLES 8:21

BERECHIAH

Blessing of God

1) A descendant of Abraham through Jacob's son Judah, in the line of the nation of Judah's third-to-last king, Jeconiah (also known as Jehoiachin).

ONLY REFERENCE
I CHRONICLES 3:20

2) Father of Asaph, musician for King David and King Solomon of Israel. Same as Berachiah.

ONLY REFERENCE
I CHRONICLES 15:17

3) A Jewish exile from the tribe of Levi who resettled Jerusalem.

ONLY REFERENCE
I CHRONICLES 9:16

4) A doorkeeper for the ark of the covenant when David brought it to Jerusalem.

ONLY REFERENCE
I CHRONICLES 15:23

5) A man of the tribe of Ephraim who counseled his nation of Israel against enslaving fellow Jews from Judah who were captured in a civil war. Berechiah helped to feed and clothe the prisoners before sending them home.

ONLY REFERENCE
2 CHRONICLES 28:12

6) Father of a man who repaired Jerusalem's walls under Nehemiah.

FIRST REFERENCE
NEHEMIAH 3:4
LAST REFERENCE
NEHEMIAH 6:18

7) Father of the prophet Zechariah.

FIRST REFERENCE
ZECHARIAH 1:1
LAST REFERENCE
ZECHARIAH 1:7

BERED I

Hail

A descendant of Abraham through Joseph's son Ephraim.

ONLY REFERENCE
I CHRONICLES 7:20

BERI I

Fountained

A descendant of Abraham through Jacob's son Asher.

ONLY REFERENCE
I CHRONICLES 7:36

BERIAH II 4

In trouble

1) A descendant of Abraham through Jacob's son Asher.

FIRST REFERENCE
GENESIS 46:17
LAST REFERENCE
I CHRONICLES 7:31

2) A descendant of Abraham through Joseph's son Ephraim.

ONLY REFERENCE
I CHRONICLES 7:23

3) A descendant of Abraham through Jacob's son Benjamin. Beriah drove the original inhabitants out of the town of Gath.

FIRST REFERENCE
I CHRONICLES 8:13
LAST REFERENCE
I CHRONICLES 8:16

4) A Levite (worship leader) when Solomon was made king of Israel.

FIRST REFERENCE
I CHRONICLES 23:10
LAST REFERENCE
I CHRONICLES 23:11

BERNICE 3
Victorious

Daughter of Herod Agrippa and sister of Agrippa II. With her brother, she heard Paul's testimony before Festus.

FIRST REFERENCE
ACTS 25:13
LAST REFERENCE
ACTS 26:30

BERODACH-BALADAN 1

A Babylonian king who sent wishes for recovery to Judah's ill king Hezekiah.

ONLY REFERENCE
2 KINGS 20:12

BESAI 2
Domineering

Forefather of an exiled family that returned to Judah under Zerubbabel.

FIRST REFERENCE
EZRA 2:49
LAST REFERENCE
NEHEMIAH 7:52

BESODEIAH 1
In the counsel of Jehovah

Father of a man who repaired Jerusalem's walls under Nehemiah.

ONLY REFERENCE
NEHEMIAH 3:6

BETHLEHEM 3
Native of Bethlehem

A descendant of Abraham through Jacob's son Judah and a forefather of David.

FIRST REFERENCE
I CHRONICLES 2:51
LAST REFERENCE
I CHRONICLES 4:4

BETH-RAPHA 1
House of the giant

A descendant of Abraham through Jacob's son Judah.

ONLY REFERENCE
I CHRONICLES 4:12

BETHUEL 9
Destroyed of God

Son of Abraham's brother Nahor. Seeing God's hand in Jacob's request, Bethuel gave his daughter Rebekah in marriage to Isaac. He sent Rebekah off with a generous dowry.

FIRST REFERENCE
GENESIS 22:22
LAST REFERENCE
GENESIS 28:5

BETH-ZUR

House of the rock

A descendant of Abraham through Jacob's son Judah.

ONLY REFERENCE
I CHRONICLES 2:45

BEZAI 3

Domineering

1) Forefather of an exiled family that returned to Judah under Zerubbabel.

FIRST REFERENCE
EZRA 2:17
LAST REFERENCE
NEHEMIAH 7:23

2) A Jewish leader who renewed the covenant under Nehemiah.

ONLY REFERENCE
NEHEMIAH 10:18

BEZALEEL 9

In the shadow of God

1) A craftsman given special ability by God to work on the tabernacle, Israel's portable worship center begun in the time of Moses. Bezaleel was skilled in "cunning works" in gold, silver, brass, precious stones, and wood, along with teaching other craftsmen.

FIRST REFERENCE
EXODUS 31:2
LAST REFERENCE
2 CHRONICLES 1:5

2) An exiled Israelite who married a "strange" (foreign) woman.

ONLY REFERENCE
EZRA 10:30

BEZER 1

Inaccessible

A descendant of Abraham through Jacob's son Asher.

ONLY REFERENCE
I CHRONICLES 7:37

BICHRI 8

Youthful

Father of an Israelite who rebelled against King David.

FIRST REFERENCE
2 SAMUEL 20:1
LAST REFERENCE
2 SAMUEL 20:22

BIDKAR 1

Assassin

An army captain serving Israel's king Jehu. Bidkar was ordered to dispose of the body of the assassinated former king, Joram.

ONLY REFERENCE
2 KINGS 9:25

BIGTHA 1

A eunuch serving the Persian king Ahasuerus in Esther's time.

ONLY REFERENCE
ESTHER 1:10

BIGTHAN 1

One of two palace doorkeepers who conspired to kill their king, Ahasuerus of Persia. Their plot was uncovered by Mordecai, and both doorkeepers were hanged. Same as Bigthana.

ONLY REFERENCE
ESTHER 2:21

BIGTHANA 1

One of two palace doorkeepers who conspired to kill their king, Ahasuerus of Persia. Their plot was uncovered by Mordecai, and both doorkeepers were hanged. Same as Bigthan.

ONLY REFERENCE
ESTHER 6:2

BIGVAI 6

1) A Jewish exile who returned to Judah under Zerubbabel.

FIRST REFERENCE
EZRA 2:2
LAST REFERENCE
NEHEMIAH 7:7

2) Forefather of an exiled family that returned to Judah under Zerubbabel.

FIRST REFERENCE
EZRA 2:14
LAST REFERENCE
NEHEMIAH 7:19

3) Forefather of a Jewish exile who returned to Judah under Ezra.

ONLY REFERENCE
EZRA 8:14

4) A Jewish leader who renewed the covenant under Nehemiah.

ONLY REFERENCE
NEHEMIAH 10:16

BILDAD 5

One of three friends of Job who mourned his losses for a week then accused him of wrongdoing. God ultimately chastised the three for their criticism of Job, commanding them to sacrifice burnt offerings while Job prayed for them.

FIRST REFERENCE
JOB 2:11
LAST REFERENCE
JOB 42:9

BILGAH 3

Stopping

1) One of twenty-four priests in David's time who was chosen by lot to serve in the tabernacle.

ONLY REFERENCE
1 CHRONICLES 24:14

2) An exiled priest who returned to Judah under Zerubbabel.

FIRST REFERENCE
NEHEMIAH 12:5
LAST REFERENCE
NEHEMIAH 12:18

BILGAI 1

Stoppable

A priest who renewed the covenant under Nehemiah.

ONLY REFERENCE
NEHEMIAH 10:8

BILHAH 10

Timid

Rachel's handmaid, whom she gave to Jacob to bear children for her. As Jacob's concubine, Bilhah had two sons, Dan and Naphtali. Jacob's son Reuben also slept with her.

FIRST REFERENCE
GENESIS 29:29
LAST REFERENCE
1 CHRONICLES 7:13

BILHAN 4

Timid

1) A descendant of Seir, who lived in Esau's "land of Edom."

FIRST REFERENCE
GENESIS 36:27
LAST REFERENCE
I CHRONICLES 1:42

2) A descendant of Abraham through Jacob's son Benjamin.

ONLY REFERENCE
I CHRONICLES 7:10

BILSHAN 2

A Jewish exile who returned to Judah under Zerubbabel.

FIRST REFERENCE
EZRA 2:2
LAST REFERENCE
NEHEMIAH 7:7

BIMHAL 1

With pruning

A descendant of Abraham through Jacob's son Asher.

ONLY REFERENCE
I CHRONICLES 7:33

BINEA 2

A descendant of Abraham through Jacob's son Benjamin, in the line of King Saul and his son Jonathan.

FIRST REFERENCE
I CHRONICLES 8:37
LAST REFERENCE
I CHRONICLES 9:43

BINNUI 7

Built up

1) Father of a Levite who weighed the temple vessels after the Babylonian Exile.

ONLY REFERENCE
EZRA 8:33

2) An exiled Israelite who married a "strange" (foreign) woman.

ONLY REFERENCE
EZRA 10:30

3) Another exiled Israelite who married a foreign woman.

ONLY REFERENCE
EZRA 10:38

4) A Levite who repaired the walls of Jerusalem and renewed the covenant under Nehemiah.

FIRST REFERENCE
NEHEMIAH 3:24
LAST REFERENCE
NEHEMIAH 10:9

5) Forefather of an exiled family that returned to Judah under Zerubbabel.

ONLY REFERENCE
NEHEMIAH 7:15

6) An exiled Israelite who returned to Judah under Zerubbabel.

ONLY REFERENCE
NEHEMIAH 12:8

BIRSHA 1

With wickedness

The king of Sodom in the days of Abram. He was killed in battle near the slime pits of Siddim.

ONLY REFERENCE
GENESIS 14:2

BIRZAVITH
Holes

A descendant of Abraham through Jacob's son Asher.

ONLY REFERENCE
I CHRONICLES 7:31

BISHLAM

A man who tried to stop the rebuilding of Jerusalem's walls.

ONLY REFERENCE
EZRA 4:7

BITHIAH
Daughter of God

A daughter of an Egyptian pharaoh and the wife of Mered, a descendant of Judah.

ONLY REFERENCE
I CHRONICLES 4:18

BIZTHA

A eunuch serving the Persian king Ahasuerus in Esther's time.

ONLY REFERENCE
ESTHER 1:10

BLASTUS
To germinate

A eunuch serving Herod Agrippa I who helped the people of Tyre and Sidon gain an audience with the king.

ONLY REFERENCE
ACTS 12:20

BOANERGES
Sons of commotion

A nickname given to the disciples James and John, the sons of Zebedee, by Jesus.

ONLY REFERENCE
MARK 3:17

BOAZ 22

A relative of Naomi who acted as kinsman-redeemer for her and her daughter-in-law Ruth when they returned to Israel after their husbands' deaths. Ruth worked in Boaz's field, and he looked after her, having heard of her faithfulness to Naomi. At Naomi's urging, Ruth offered herself in marriage to Boaz. He accepted the responsibility of kinsman-redeemer. He bought back Naomi's husband's inherited land and promised that his first child would perpetuate Ruth's first husband's name. The couple married and had a son, Obed, who became the grandfather of King David. Same as Booz.

FIRST REFERENCE
RUTH 2:1
LAST REFERENCE
I CHRONICLES 2:12
KEY REFERENCES
RUTH 2:8–16; 4:9–11

BOCHERU 2

Firstborn

A descendant of Abraham through Jacob's son Benjamin, in the line of King Saul and his son Jonathan.

FIRST REFERENCE
1 CHRONICLES 8:38
LAST REFERENCE
1 CHRONICLES 9:44

BOOZ 3

Greek form of the name *Boaz;* the hero of the story of Ruth.

FIRST REFERENCE
MATTHEW 1:5
LAST REFERENCE
LUKE 3:32
GENEALOGY OF JESUS
MATTHEW 1:5; LUKE 3:32

BOSOR 1

A lamp

Father of the false prophet Balaam. Same as Beor.

ONLY REFERENCE
2 PETER 2:15

BUKKI 5

Wasteful

1) A descendant of Abraham through Jacob's son Levi and a priest through the line of Aaron.

FIRST REFERENCE
1 CHRONICLES 6:5
LAST REFERENCE
EZRA 7:4

2) Prince of the tribe of Dan when the Israelites entered the Promised Land

ONLY REFERENCE
NUMBERS 34:22

BUKKIAH 2

Wasting of God

A son of King David's musician Heman, who was "under the hands of [his] father for song in the house of the LORD" (1 Chronicles 25:6).

FIRST REFERENCE
1 CHRONICLES 25:4
LAST REFERENCE
1 CHRONICLES 25:13

BUNAH 1

Discretion

A descendant of Abraham through Jacob's son Judah.

ONLY REFERENCE
1 CHRONICLES 2:25

BUNNI 3

Built

1) One of a group of Levites (worship leaders) who led a revival among the Israelites in the time of Nehemiah.

ONLY REFERENCE
NEHEMIAH 9:4

2) Forefather of a Jewish exile from the tribe of Levi who resettled Jerusalem.

ONLY REFERENCE
NEHEMIAH 11:15

3) A Jewish leader who renewed the covenant under Nehemiah.

ONLY REFERENCE
NEHEMIAH 10:15

BUZ   2
Disrespect

1) A son of Nahor and a nephew of Abraham.

ONLY REFERENCE
GENESIS 22:21

2) A descendant of Abraham through Jacob's son Gad.

ONLY REFERENCE
I CHRONICLES 5:14

BUZI   1
Disrespect

Father of the prophet Ezekiel.

ONLY REFERENCE
EZEKIEL 1:3

CAIAPHAS   9
The dell

The Jewish high priest who judged Jesus at His trial. Caiaphas, who feared Roman authority, felt it was expedient to kill one man to protect his people and so accepted false testimony against Jesus. Since he could not kill anyone, he sent Jesus to Pilate for a death sentence. Following the resurrection of Jesus, Caiaphas tried to stop Peter from preaching.

FIRST REFERENCE
MATTHEW 26:3
LAST REFERENCE
ACTS 4:6

CAIN   19
Lance

Adam and Eve's first son who became jealous of his brother, Abel, when God refused Cain's unrighteous offering but accepted Abel's offering. Cain killed Abel and did not admit it when God asked where his brother was. For his sin, God made him "a fugitive and a vagabond" (Genesis 4:12). Cain moved to the land of Nod, had children, and built the city of Enoch.

FIRST REFERENCE
GENESIS 4:1
LAST REFERENCE
JUDE 1:11
KEY REFERENCES
GENESIS 4:9; HEBREWS 11:4

CAINAN   7 ♔ 👤

Fixed

Grandson of Seth and great-grandson of Adam and Eve. He lived for 910 years.

FIRST REFERENCE
GENESIS 5:9
LAST REFERENCE
LUKE 3:37
GENEALOGY OF JESUS
LUKE 3:37

CALCOL   1 👤

Sustenance

A descendant of Abraham through Jacob's son Judah.

ONLY REFERENCE
1 CHRONICLES 2:6

CALEB   36 👤

Forcible

1) Jephunneh's son, sent by Moses to spy out Canaan before the Israelites entered the Promised Land. When ten other spies warned that they could not win the land, Caleb believed Israel could do it. God blessed Caleb and Joshua, the only spies who believed the land could be taken. Of the twelve, only they entered the Promised Land. For his faithfulness, Caleb received Hebron as an inheritance. Caleb promised his daughter Achsah to the man who could conquer Kirjath-sepher. After his brother Othniel took it, Caleb kept his promise and the couple married.

FIRST REFERENCE
NUMBERS 13:6
LAST REFERENCE
1 CHRONICLES 6:56
KEY REFERENCES
NUMBERS 13:30; 32:11–12; JOSHUA 14:13

2) A descendant of Abraham through Jacob's son Judah. Brother of Jerahmeel. Same as Chelubai.

FIRST REFERENCE
1 CHRONICLES 2:18
LAST REFERENCE
1 CHRONICLES 2:42

3) A descendant of Abraham through Jacob's son Judah and Hur. Grandson of Caleb (2).

ONLY REFERENCE
1 CHRONICLES 2:50

CANAAN   9 👤

Humiliated

Son of Ham and grandson of Noah. Noah cursed Canaan because his father, Ham, did not cover Noah when he became drunk and fell asleep, naked, in his tent. Canaan became the ancestor of the Phoenicians and other peoples living between the Phoenician city of Sidon and Gaza.

FIRST REFERENCE
GENESIS 9:18
LAST REFERENCE
1 CHRONICLES 1:13

CANDACE

Queen of Ethiopia whose treasurer was converted to Christianity by Philip the evangelist.

ONLY REFERENCE
ACTS 8:27

CARCAS

A eunuch serving the Persian king Ahasuerus in Esther's time.

ONLY REFERENCE
ESTHER 1:10

CAREAH
Bald

Father of Johanan, a Jewish leader when the Chaldeans captured Jerusalem.

ONLY REFERENCE
2 KINGS 25:23

CARMI 8
Gardener

1) A descendant of Abraham through Jacob's son Judah.

FIRST REFERENCE
JOSHUA 7:1
LAST REFERENCE
1 CHRONICLES 4:1

2) A descendant of Abraham through Jacob's son Reuben.

FIRST REFERENCE
GENESIS 46:9
LAST REFERENCE
1 CHRONICLES 5:3

CARPUS 1
Fruit

A friend of Paul in Troas—one with whom the apostle once left a cloak.

ONLY REFERENCE
2 TIMOTHY 4:13

CARSHENA 1

One of seven Persian princes serving under King Ahasuerus.

ONLY REFERENCE
ESTHER 1:14

CEPHAS 6
The rock

A name Jesus gave the apostle Peter. It is used most often in the book of 1 Corinthians. Same as Peter.

FIRST REFERENCE
JOHN 1:42
LAST REFERENCE
GALATIANS 2:9

CHALCOL 1
Sustenance

A wise man, the son of Mahol, mentioned in comparison to Solomon's wisdom.

ONLY REFERENCE
1 KINGS 4:31

CHEDORLAOMER 5

The king of Elam in the days of Abram. Chedorlaomer was part of a victorious battle alliance that kidnapped Abram's nephew Lot.

CHELAL
Complete

An exiled Israelite who married a "strange" (foreign) woman.

ONLY REFERENCE
EZRA 10:30

CHELLUH
Completed

An exiled Israelite who married a "strange" (foreign) woman.

ONLY REFERENCE
EZRA 10:35

CHELUB
Basket

1) A descendant of Abraham through Jacob's son Judah.

ONLY REFERENCE
I CHRONICLES 4:11

2) Father of Ezri, the overseer of King David's servants who tilled the soil.

ONLY REFERENCE
I CHRONICLES 27:26

CHELUBAI
Forcible

A descendant of Abraham through Jacob's son Judah. Same as Caleb (2).

ONLY REFERENCE
I CHRONICLES 2:9

CHENAANAH 5
Humiliated

1) A false prophet who told King Ahab to fight against Ramoth-gilead.

FIRST REFERENCE
I KINGS 22:11
LAST REFERENCE
2 CHRONICLES 18:23

2) A descendant of Abraham through Jacob's son Benjamin.

ONLY REFERENCE
I CHRONICLES 7:10

CHENANI
Planted

One of a group of Levites who led a revival among the Israelites in the time of Nehemiah.

ONLY REFERENCE
NEHEMIAH 9:4

CHENANIAH 3
God has planted

1) A Levite musician, "the master of the song," who led singers in celebration when King David brought the ark of the covenant to Jerusalem.

FIRST REFERENCE
I CHRONICLES 15:22
LAST REFERENCE
I CHRONICLES 15:27

2) Head of a family appointed as officers and judges under King David.

ONLY REFERENCE
I CHRONICLES 26:29

CHERAN 2

A descendant of Seir, who lived in Esau's "land of Edom."

FIRST REFERENCE
GENESIS 36:26
LAST REFERENCE
I CHRONICLES 1:41

CHERUB 2

An exile of unclear ancestry who returned to Judah under Zerubbabel.

FIRST REFERENCE
EZRA 2:59
LAST REFERENCE
NEHEMIAH 7:61

CHESED 1

A son of Nahor and a nephew of Abraham.

ONLY REFERENCE
GENESIS 22:22

CHILEAB 1
Restraint of his father

A son of David, born to his wife Abigail in Hebron.

ONLY REFERENCE
2 SAMUEL 3:3

CHILION 3
Pining

One of Elimelech and Naomi's sons, he died in Moab.

FIRST REFERENCE
RUTH 1:2
LAST REFERENCE
RUTH 4:9

CHIMHAM 4
Pining

Possibly a son of Barzillai, who offered him to King David to serve in his place. David probably gave him a land grant near Bethlehem (Jeremiah 41:17).

FIRST REFERENCE
2 SAMUEL 19:37
LAST REFERENCE
JEREMIAH 41:17

CHISLON 1
Hopeful

Forefather of Elidad, prince of the tribe of Benjamin when the Israelites entered the Promised Land.

ONLY REFERENCE
NUMBERS 34:21

CHLOE 1
Green

A Corinthian Christian and acquaintance of Paul. Her family informed the apostle of divisions within the church.

ONLY REFERENCE
I CORINTHIANS 1:11

CHUSHAN-RISHATHAIM 4
Cushan of double wickedness

A Mesopotamian king into whose hands God gave the disobedient Israelites. When they repented, He raised up Othniel, Caleb's younger brother, to deliver the nation. Same as Cushan.

FIRST REFERENCE
JUDGES 3:8
LAST REFERENCE
JUDGES 3:10

CHUZA

King Herod's household manager whose wife, Joanna, financially supported the ministry of Jesus.

ONLY REFERENCE
LUKE 8:3

CIS

A bow

Father of Israel's first king, Saul. Same as Kish (1).

ONLY REFERENCE
ACTS 13:21

CLAUDIA

A Roman Christian who sent greetings to Timothy in Paul's second letter to his "dearly beloved son."

ONLY REFERENCE
2 TIMOTHY 4:21

CLAUDIUS 3

1) A Roman emperor who ruled when a famine affected the empire and the Antioch church took up a collection for the church in Judea. Claudius also commanded the Jews to leave Rome, causing Priscilla and Aquila to move to Corinth.

FIRST REFERENCE
ACTS 11:28
LAST REFERENCE
ACTS 18:2

2) A Roman military officer to whom Paul's nephew reported a plot against Paul's life. Also called Lysias.

ONLY REFERENCE
ACTS 23:26

CLEMENT

Merciful

A Philippian Christian and co-worker of the apostle Paul.

ONLY REFERENCE
PHILIPPIANS 4:3

CLEOPAS

Renowned father

A Christian who met Jesus on the road to Emmaus. Not recognizing Jesus, Cleopas described the events of the crucifixion and resurrection to Jesus. As they walked, Jesus interpreted the scriptures about Himself to Cleopas and his traveling companion. They shared dinner, Jesus blessed the bread, and they recognized Him.

ONLY REFERENCE
LUKE 24:18

CLEOPHAS

Husband of Mary, one of the women who stood at the cross when Jesus was crucified.

ONLY REFERENCE
JOHN 19:25

COL-HOZEH 2

Every seer

Forefather of a Jewish exile from the tribe of Judah who resettled Jerusalem.

FIRST REFERENCE
NEHEMIAH 3:15
LAST REFERENCE
NEHEMIAH 11:5

CONANIAH 1

God has sustained

A descendant of Abraham through Jacob's son Levi. Conaniah was among those who distributed sacrificial animals to fellow Levites preparing to celebrate the Passover under King Josiah.

ONLY REFERENCE
2 CHRONICLES 35:9

CONIAH 3

God will establish

An alternative name for Judah's king Jehoiachin. Same as Jeconiah.

FIRST REFERENCE
JEREMIAH 22:24
LAST REFERENCE
JEREMIAH 37:1

CONONIAH 2

God has sustained

A Levite (worship leader) in charge of tithes and offerings during King Hezekiah's reign.

FIRST REFERENCE
2 CHRONICLES 31:12
LAST REFERENCE
2 CHRONICLES 31:13

CORE 1

Ice

Greek form of the name *Korah;* a man who led a rebellion against Moses.

ONLY REFERENCE
JUDE 1:11

CORNELIUS 10

A God-fearing centurion of the Italian band. In a vision, an angel told him to call for Peter. Peter traveled to see Cornelius and preached to him and his companions. The Holy Spirit fell on them. They were the first Gentiles to be baptized by Peter.

FIRST REFERENCE
ACTS 10:1
LAST REFERENCE
ACTS 10:31

COSAM 1

Divination

A descendant of Abraham through Isaac; forebear of Jesus' earthly father, Joseph.

ONLY REFERENCE
LUKE 3:28
GENEALOGY OF JESUS
LUKE 3:28

COZ 1

Thorn

A descendant of Abraham through Jacob's son Judah.

ONLY REFERENCE
1 CHRONICLES 4:8

COZBI 2 👤
False

Daughter of a Midian prince, she was killed for consorting with an Israelite.

FIRST REFERENCE
NUMBERS 25:15
LAST REFERENCE
NUMBERS 25:18

CRESCENS 1 👤
Growing

A coworker of Paul who left the apostle in Rome before preaching in Galatia.

ONLY REFERENCE
2 TIMOTHY 4:10

CRISPUS 2 👤
Crisp

A head of the Corinthian synagogue who, along with his household, believed in Jesus. He was baptized by Paul.

FIRST REFERENCE
ACTS 18:8
LAST REFERENCE
I CORINTHIANS 1:14

CUSH 7 👤2

1) A grandson of Noah through his son Ham.

FIRST REFERENCE
GENESIS 10:6
LAST REFERENCE
I CHRONICLES 1:10

2) Author of Psalm 7, which David put to music.

ONLY REFERENCE
PSALM 7 (TITLE)

CUSHAN 1 👤

Mesopotamian king into whose hands God gave the disobedient Israelites. Same as Chushanrishathaim.

ONLY REFERENCE
HABAKKUK 3:7

CUSHI 10 👤3
A Cushite

1) The messenger who brought David the news that his son Absalom was dead.

FIRST REFERENCE
2 SAMUEL 18:21
LAST REFERENCE
2 SAMUEL 18:32

2) A messenger for the princes of Judah who called Jeremiah's scribe to read his prophecies to them.

ONLY REFERENCE
JEREMIAH 36:14

3) Father of the prophet Zephaniah.

ONLY REFERENCE
ZEPHANIAH 1:1

CYRENIUS 1 👤

Roman governor of Syria at the time when Jesus was born.

ONLY REFERENCE
LUKE 2:2

CYRUS 23 👤

The king of Persia who commanded that the temple in Jerusalem be rebuilt. He ordered all his people to give donations to help the Jews, and he returned the temple vessels that Nebuchadnezzar of Babylon had taken. When opposers objected to the work, the Jews reminded them of Cyrus's command, and the work went forward again. The prophet Daniel also lived and prospered during the early part of Cyrus's reign.

FIRST REFERENCE
2 CHRONICLES 36:22
LAST REFERENCE
DANIEL 10:1
KEY REFERENCES
2 CHRONICLES 36:23; EZRA 5:13–15

DALAIAH
God has delivered

A descendant of Abraham through Jacob's son Judah, in the line of the nation of Judah's second-to-last king, Jeconiah (also known as Jehoiachin).

ONLY REFERENCE
1 CHRONICLES 3:24

DALPHON
Dripping

One of ten sons of Haman, the villain of the story of Esther.

ONLY REFERENCE
ESTHER 9:7

DAMARIS
Gentle

A woman of Athens converted under the ministry of the apostle Paul.

ONLY REFERENCE
ACTS 17:34

DAN
Judge

Son of Jacob and Bilhah, Rachel's maid. Before his death, Jacob prophesied that Dan would judge his people and be as a "serpent by the way, an adder in the path" (Genesis 49:17).

DANIEL 83
Judge of God

1) A son of David, born to his wife Abigail in Hebron.

ONLY REFERENCE
1 CHRONICLES 3:1

2) A priest who renewed the covenant under Nehemiah.

FIRST REFERENCE
EZRA 8:2
LAST REFERENCE
NEHEMIAH 10:6

3) An Old Testament major prophet. As a child Daniel was taken into exile in Babylon. Because he refused to defile himself with meat and wine from the king's table, God blessed him with knowledge and wisdom. Daniel described and interpreted a dream about an image of various metals and clay for King Nebuchadnezzar, and the king made him ruler over the province of Babylon. Daniel revealed the meaning of a second dream to Nebuchadnezzar, predicting his downfall until he worshipped the Lord. During King Belshazzar's reign, Daniel interpreted the meaning of the mysterious handwriting on the wall. For this he was made third ruler in the kingdom, but Belshazzar died that night. Darius the Mede took over the kingdom of Babylonia and planned to make Daniel head of the whole kingdom. Other leaders plotted against Daniel. Knowing he would not worship anyone but the Lord, they convinced the king to punish any person who worshipped anyone but the king for thirty days. For disobeying this law, Daniel was thrown into the lions' den. But God closed the beasts' mouths. When his favored man came out safely, Darius honored the Lord. Daniel prospered in the reigns of Darius and Cyrus the Persian. Same as Belteshazzar.

FIRST REFERENCE
EZEKIEL 14:14
LAST REFERENCE
MARK 13:14
KEY REFERENCES
DANIEL 1:8, 17; 2:31–45; 6:22–23

DARA
Pearl of knowledge

A descendant of Abraham through Jacob's son Judah.

ONLY REFERENCE
1 CHRONICLES 2:6

DARDA
Pearl of knowledge

A wise man, the son of Mahol, whose wisdom is compared to Solomon's.

ONLY REFERENCE
1 KINGS 4:31

DARIUS   25

1) Son of Hystaspes and king of Persia. He followed in the footsteps of King Cyrus and supported the Jews in their efforts to rebuild Jerusalem. When those who opposed the rebuilding wrote to Darius, he looked into the question and then ordered the opposition to allow the building to continue.

FIRST REFERENCE
EZRA 4:5
LAST REFERENCE
ZECHARIAH 7:1

2) Darius the Persian. He was either Darius the II or Darius the III.

ONLY REFERENCE
NEHEMIAH 12:22

3) Darius the Mede, king of Persia during part of the prophet Daniel's life. Darius wanted to promote Daniel, but Daniel's enemies plotted against him. When Daniel refused to worship the king, Daniel was thrown into the lions' den despite Darius's efforts to save him. God protected his servant, and Darius glorified God.

FIRST REFERENCE
DANIEL 5:31
LAST REFERENCE
DANIEL 11:1

DARKON   2

Forefather of an exiled family—former servants of Solomon—that returned to Judah under Zerubbabel.

FIRST REFERENCE
EZRA 2:56
LAST REFERENCE
NEHEMIAH 7:58

DATHAN   10

With Korah and Abiram, Dathan conspired against Moses, declaring that all the people of Israel were holy. Dathan stayed in his tent when Moses called them before God, so Moses came to him. The ground broke open at Dathan's feet and swallowed him, his family, and his possessions.

FIRST REFERENCE
NUMBERS 16:1
LAST REFERENCE
PSALM 106:17

DAVID   1139

Loving

Popular king of Israel. As a young shepherd and musician, David was anointed king by the prophet Samuel in the place of disobedient King Saul. David vanquished the Philistine giant Goliath, and Saul brought young David to his court, where the king's son Jonathan befriended him. Because the new hero became popular with the people, Saul became jealous and first sent David to war then sought to kill him. With Jonathan's help, David fled. David escaped to Nob, where he received help from the priests, who were then killed by Saul. So began a period of war between the two men. Though David twice had opportunities to kill Saul, he would not touch the Lord's anointed. Fearing Saul, David eventually fled into Philistine territory but would not fight against his own people. He concealed from Achish, king of Gath, the fact that his troops never attacked Israel. When Achish prepared for battle against Israel, the king's troops refused to have David's men in their ranks. David never fought against Saul for the Philistines. Following the battle with the Philistines and the deaths of Saul and his sons, David was anointed king of Judah. Saul's remaining son, Ish-bosheth, was made king of Israel, but following Ish-bosheth's murder, these northern tribes made David their king. David defeated the Philistines and brought the ark of the covenant to Jerusalem. But God would not let him build a temple. The king continued to defeat his foreign enemies, until he fell into sin with Bathsheba and killed her husband, Uriah. Though David repented, this began a period of family troubles. David's son Amnon raped his half sister Tamar, and in retaliation her brother Absalom killed Amnon then attempted to take the throne. Though David's troops overcame Absalom's army, David grieved at the death of his rebellious son. Before David's death, when Adonijah tried to usurp his throne, David quickly had Solomon anointed king. David wrote many of the psalms and sang a song of praise about the victories God brought him (2 Samuel 22).

Despite his failings, scripture refers to David as a man after God's own heart (Acts 13:22).

FIRST REFERENCE
RUTH 4:17
LAST REFERENCE
REVELATION 22:16
KEY REFERENCES
I SAMUEL 16:13; 18:6–9; 24:6–7;
2 SAMUEL 12:13; 22
GENEALOGY OF JESUS
MATTHEW 1:1; LUKE 3:31

DEBIR   1
Shrine

A pagan king of Eglon during Joshua's conquest of the Promised Land, Debir allied with four other rulers to attack Gibeon, which had deceptively made a peace treaty with the Israelites. Joshua's soldiers defeated the five armies, and Joshua executed the allied kings.

ONLY REFERENCE
JOSHUA 10:3

DEBORAH   10
Bee

1) A nurse who accompanied Rebekah when she married Isaac (Genesis 24:59). This treasured servant's burial place, under an oak near Bethel, is recorded in Genesis 35:8.

ONLY REFERENCE
GENESIS 35:8

2) Israel's only female judge and prophetess, she held court under a palm tree. Deborah called Barak to lead warriors into battle against the Canaanite army commander,

Sisera. But Barak would fight only if Deborah went with him. For this, she prophesied that God would hand Sisera over to a woman. Deborah supported Barak as he gathered his troops on Mount Tabor, and she advised him to go into battle. With him she sang a song of victory that praised the Lord.

FIRST REFERENCE
JUDGES 4:4
LAST REFERENCE
JUDGES 5:15

DEDAN 5

1) A descendant of Noah through his son Ham.

FIRST REFERENCE
GENESIS 10:7
LAST REFERENCE
1 CHRONICLES 1:9

2) A descendant of Abraham by his second wife, Keturah.

FIRST REFERENCE
GENESIS 25:3
LAST REFERENCE
1 CHRONICLES 1:32

DEKAR 1
Stab

Father of one of King Solomon's royal officials over provisions.

ONLY REFERENCE
1 KINGS 4:9

DELAIAH 6
God has delivered

1) One of twenty-four priests in David's time who was chosen by lot to serve in the tabernacle.

ONLY REFERENCE
1 CHRONICLES 24:18

2) An exile of unclear ancestry who returned to Judah under Zerubbabel.

FIRST REFERENCE
EZRA 2:60
LAST REFERENCE
NEHEMIAH 7:62

3) A man who tried to terrify Nehemiah with threats on his life.

ONLY REFERENCE
NEHEMIAH 6:10

4) A prince of Judah who heard Jeremiah's prophecies.

FIRST REFERENCE
JEREMIAH 36:12
LAST REFERENCE
JEREMIAH 36:25

DELILAH 6
Languishing

A woman Samson fell in love with. Delilah was bribed by the Philistines to discover the source of her lover's strength. She nagged Samson until he told her that if his head was shaved, he would become weak. When this was done, Samson became weak and the Philistines overpowered him.

FIRST REFERENCE
JUDGES 16:4
LAST REFERENCE
JUDGES 16:18

DEMAS 3

A Christian worker who was with Paul at Corinth. He became attracted by worldly things and left Paul to go to Thessalonica.

FIRST REFERENCE
COLOSSIANS 4:14
LAST REFERENCE
PHILEMON 1:24

DEMETRIUS 3

1) A silversmith of Ephesus who opposed Paul and his teachings because they tended to destroy his business of making pagan shrines.

FIRST REFERENCE
ACTS 19:24
LAST REFERENCE
ACTS 19:38

2) A man to whose character the apostle John testified.

ONLY REFERENCE
3 JOHN 1:12

DEUEL 4
Known of God

Father of Eliasaph, who was a prince of the tribe of Gad.

FIRST REFERENCE
NUMBERS 1:14
LAST REFERENCE
NUMBERS 10:20

DIBLAIM 1
Two cakes

Father of Gomer, the wife of the prophet Hosea.

ONLY REFERENCE
HOSEA 1:3

DIBRI 1
Wordy

Father of Shelomith, whose son blasphemed the Lord.

ONLY REFERENCE
LEVITICUS 24:11

DIDYMUS 3
Twin

An alternate name for Thomas, one of the twelve disciples of Jesus.

FIRST REFERENCE
JOHN 11:16
LAST REFERENCE
JOHN 21:2

DIKLAH 2

A descendant of Noah through his son Shem.

FIRST REFERENCE
GENESIS 10:27
LAST REFERENCE
1 CHRONICLES 1:21

DINAH 8
Justice

Daughter of Jacob and Leah, who was sexually assaulted by the prince Shechem. Her brothers retaliated, killing the men of his city.

FIRST REFERENCE
GENESIS 30:21
LAST REFERENCE
GENESIS 46:15

DIONYSIUS

Reveler

A man of Athens converted under the ministry of the apostle Paul.

ONLY REFERENCE
ACTS 17:34

DIOTREPHES

Jove-nourished

An arrogant church member condemned by the apostle John. Diotrephes spoke out against the apostles and refused to welcome Christian visitors.

ONLY REFERENCE
3 JOHN 1:9

DISHAN

Antelope

A descendant of Seir, who lived in Esau's "land of Edom."

FIRST REFERENCE
GENESIS 36:21
LAST REFERENCE
1 CHRONICLES 1:42

DISHON

Antelope

1) A descendant of Seir, who lived in Esau's "land of Edom."

FIRST REFERENCE
GENESIS 36:21
LAST REFERENCE
1 CHRONICLES 1:38

2) Another descendant of Seir, who lived in Esau's "land of Edom."

FIRST REFERENCE
GENESIS 36:25
LAST REFERENCE
1 CHRONICLES 1:41

DODAI

Sick

A commander in King David's army overseeing twenty-four thousand men in the second month of each year.

ONLY REFERENCE
1 CHRONICLES 27:4

DODAVAH

Love of God

Father of the prophet Eliezer, who prophesied against Jehoshapat.

ONLY REFERENCE
2 CHRONICLES 20:37

DODO

Loving

1) Grandfather of Israel's seventh judge, Tola.

ONLY REFERENCE
JUDGES 10:1

2) Father of Eleazar, one of David's three mighty men.

FIRST REFERENCE
2 SAMUEL 23:9
LAST REFERENCE
1 CHRONICLES 11:12

3) Father of Elhanan, one of David's thirty mighty men.

FIRST REFERENCE
2 SAMUEL 23:24
LAST REFERENCE
1 CHRONICLES 11:26

DOEG 6
Anxious

King Saul's chief herdsman, who told the king that David had visited Nob. Doeg slaughtered the priests of Nob at Saul's command.

FIRST REFERENCE
I SAMUEL 21:7
LAST REFERENCE
PSALM 52 (TITLE)

DORCAS 2
Gazelle

A Christian of Joppa who did many good works. When she died, her friends called Peter, who raised her back to life. Same as Tabitha.

FIRST REFERENCE
ACTS 9:36
LAST REFERENCE
ACTS 9:39

DRUSILLA I

Wife of Felix, the Roman governor of Judea in Paul's time.

ONLY REFERENCE
ACTS 24:24

DUMAH 2

Silence

A descendant of Abraham through Ishmael, Abraham's son with his surrogate wife, Hagar.

FIRST REFERENCE
GENESIS 25:14
LAST REFERENCE
I CHRONICLES 1:30

EBAL 3
Bare

1) A descendant of Seir, who lived in Esau's "land of Edom."

FIRST REFERENCE
GENESIS 36:23
LAST REFERENCE
I CHRONICLES 1:40

2) A descendant of Noah through his son Shem.

ONLY REFERENCE
I CHRONICLES 1:22

EBED 6
Servant

1) Father of Gaal, who incited the men of Shechem against King Abimelech.

FIRST REFERENCE
JUDGES 9:26
LAST REFERENCE
JUDGES 9:35

2) A Jewish exile who returned from Babylon to Judah under Ezra.

ONLY REFERENCE
EZRA 8:6

EBED-MELECH 6
Servant of a king

An Ethiopian eunuch who rescued Jeremiah from a dungeon by reporting his situation to King Zedekiah. Jeremiah prophesied that God would deliver the faithful eunuch.

FIRST REFERENCE
JEREMIAH 38:7
LAST REFERENCE
JEREMIAH 39:16

ELISHAPHAT 12

Other side

1) Great-grandson of Shem and descendant of Noah.

FIRST REFERENCE
GENESIS 10:21
LAST REFERENCE
I CHRONICLES 1:25

2) A descendant of Abraham through Jacob's son Benjamin.

ONLY REFERENCE
I CHRONICLES 8:12

3) Forefather of a priest who returned to Jerusalem under Zerubbabel.

ONLY REFERENCE
NEHEMIAH 12:20

EBIASAPH 3

Gatherer

A descendant of Abraham through Jacob's son Levi.

FIRST REFERENCE
I CHRONICLES 6:23
LAST REFERENCE
I CHRONICLES 9:19

EDEN 2

Pleasure

1) A descendant of Abraham through Jacob's son Levi. Eden was among the Levites who cleansed the Jerusalem temple during the revival of King Hezekiah's day.

ONLY REFERENCE
2 CHRONICLES 29:12

2) A priest in the time of King Hezekiah who helped to distribute the people's freewill offerings to his fellow priests.

ONLY REFERENCE
2 CHRONICLES 31:15

EDER 2

Arrangement

A descendant of Abraham through Jacob's son Levi.

FIRST REFERENCE
I CHRONICLES 23:23
LAST REFERENCE
I CHRONICLES 24:30

EDOM 3

Red

A name given to Esau when he sold his birthright to his brother, Jacob, for a meal of red lentil stew. Because he was given this name, his descendants were called Edomites. Same as Esau.

FIRST REFERENCE
GENESIS 25:30
LAST REFERENCE
GENESIS 36:8

EGLAH 2

Calf

One of several wives of King David and mother of David's son Ithream.

FIRST REFERENCE
2 SAMUEL 3:5
LAST REFERENCE
I CHRONICLES 3:3

EGLON 5 👤
Calf-like

A king of Moab who attacked Israel. Eglon subjugated the Israelites for eighteen years but was killed by the Israelite judge Ehud.

FIRST REFERENCE
JUDGES 3:12
LAST REFERENCE
JUDGES 3:17

EHI 1 👤
Brotherly

A son of Benjamin who went to Egypt with Jacob.

ONLY REFERENCE
GENESIS 46:21

EHUD 10
United

1) The second judge of Israel who subdued the oppressing Moabites. A left-handed man, Ehud killed Eglon, the obese king of Moab, with a hidden dagger while pretending to be on a peace mission.

FIRST REFERENCE
JUDGES 3:15
LAST REFERENCE
JUDGES 4:1

2) A descendant of Abraham through Jacob's son Benjamin.

FIRST REFERENCE
I CHRONICLES 7:10
LAST REFERENCE
I CHRONICLES 8:6

EKER 1 👤
A transplanted person

A descendant of Abraham through Jacob's son Judah.

ONLY REFERENCE
I CHRONICLES 2:27

ELADAH 1 👤
God has decked

A descendant of Abraham through Joseph's son Ephraim.

ONLY REFERENCE
I CHRONICLES 7:20

ELAH 14
Oak

1) A "duke of Edom," a leader in the family line of Esau.

FIRST REFERENCE
GENESIS 36:41
LAST REFERENCE
I CHRONICLES 1:52

2) Father of Shimei, an officer under King Solomon.

ONLY REFERENCE
I KINGS 4:18

3) King of Israel, a contemporary of Asa, who was the king of Judah. Elah was killed by Zimri, who usurped his throne.

FIRST REFERENCE
I KINGS 16:6
LAST REFERENCE
I KINGS 16:14

4) Father of Hoshea, who killed King Pekah of Israel and usurped his throne.

FIRST REFERENCE
2 KINGS 15:30
LAST REFERENCE
2 KINGS 18:9

5) A descendant of Abraham through Jacob's son Judah.

ONLY REFERENCE
I CHRONICLES 4:15

6) A Jewish exile from the tribe of Benjamin who resettled Jerusalem.

ONLY REFERENCE
I CHRONICLES 9:8

ELAM 13

Distant

1) A descendant of Noah through his son Shem.

FIRST REFERENCE
GENESIS 10:22
LAST REFERENCE
I CHRONICLES 1:17

2) A descendant of Abraham through Jacob's son Benjamin.

ONLY REFERENCE
I CHRONICLES 8:24

3) A Levite "porter" (doorkeeper) in the house of the Lord.

ONLY REFERENCE
I CHRONICLES 26:3

4) Forefather of an exiled family that returned to Judah under Zerubbabel.

FIRST REFERENCE
EZRA 2:7
LAST REFERENCE
NEHEMIAH 7:12

5) Forefather of an exiled family that returned to Judah under Zerubbabel.

FIRST REFERENCE
EZRA 2:31
LAST REFERENCE
NEHEMIAH 7:34

6) Forefather of a Jewish exile who returned from Babylon to Judah under Ezra.

ONLY REFERENCE
EZRA 8:7

7) An Israelite whose descendants married "strange" (foreign) women.

FIRST REFERENCE
EZRA 10:2
LAST REFERENCE
EZRA 10:26

8) A Jewish leader who renewed the covenant under Nehemiah.

ONLY REFERENCE
NEHEMIAH 10:14

9) A priest who helped to dedicate the rebuilt walls of Jerusalem by giving thanks.

ONLY REFERENCE
NEHEMIAH 12:42

ELASAH 2

God has made

1) An exiled Israelite priest who married a "strange" (foreign) woman.

ONLY REFERENCE
EZRA 10:22

2) An ambassador of Judah's king Zedekiah sent to King Nebuchadnezzar of Babylon.

ONLY REFERENCE
JEREMIAH 29:3

ELDAAH 2
God of knowledge

A descendant of Abraham by his second wife, Keturah.

FIRST REFERENCE
GENESIS 25:4
LAST REFERENCE
I CHRONICLES 1:33

ELDAD 2
God has loved

A man who prophesied in the camp after God sent the Israelites quail to eat in the wilderness.

FIRST REFERENCE
NUMBERS 11:26
LAST REFERENCE
NUMBERS 11:27

ELEAD 1
God has testified

A descendant of Abraham through Joseph's son Ephraim. He was killed by men of Gath in a dispute over livestock.

ONLY REFERENCE
I CHRONICLES 7:21

ELEASAH 4
God has made

1) A descendant of Abraham through Jacob's son Judah. Eleasah descended from the line of an unnamed Israelite woman and her Egyptian husband, Jarha.

FIRST REFERENCE
I CHRONICLES 2:39
LAST REFERENCE
I CHRONICLES 2:40

2) A descendant of Abraham through Jacob's son Benjamin, in the line of King Saul and his son Jonathan.

FIRST REFERENCE
I CHRONICLES 8:37
LAST REFERENCE
I CHRONICLES 9:43

ELEAZAR 74
God is helper

1) Aaron's third son. His older brothers, Nadab and Abihu were killed by God for illicit worship practices, so Eleazar became the chief over the Levites. He oversaw the temple worship, including the use of the temple vessels, meat offerings, and anointing oil, and was in charge of the tabernacle. When Aaron died, Eleazar became high priest. With Moses, God commanded him to count the Israelites. After Israel came to the Promised Land, Eleazar and Joshua divided the territory among Israel's tribes. He died and was buried on a hill belonging to his son Phinehas.

FIRST REFERENCE
EXODUS 6:23
LAST REFERENCE
EZRA 7:5
KEY REFERENCES
NUMBERS 4:16; 26:1–2; DEUTERONOMY 10:6

2) Son of Abinadab (1), who was consecrated to guard the ark of the covenant.

ONLY REFERENCE
I SAMUEL 7:1

3) One of David's three mighty men.

FIRST REFERENCE
2 SAMUEL 23:9
LAST REFERENCE
I CHRONICLES 11:12

4) A descendant of Abraham through Jacob's son Levi.

FIRST REFERENCE
I CHRONICLES 23:21
LAST REFERENCE
I CHRONICLES 24:28

5) One of the men who weighed the temple vessels after the Babylonian Exile.

ONLY REFERENCE
EZRA 8:33

6) An exiled Israelite who married a "strange" (foreign) woman.

ONLY REFERENCE
EZRA 10:25

7) A priest who helped to dedicate the rebuilt wall of Jerusalem by giving thanks.

ONLY REFERENCE
NEHEMIAH 12:42

8) A descendant of Abraham through Isaac; forebear of Jesus' earthly father, Joseph.

ONLY REFERENCE
MATTHEW 1:15
GENEALOGY OF JESUS
MATTHEW 1:5

ELHANAN 4
God is gracious

1) A man from Bethlehem who killed Goliath's brother.

FIRST REFERENCE
2 SAMUEL 21:19
LAST REFERENCE
I CHRONICLES 20:5

2) One of King David's valiant warriors.

FIRST REFERENCE
2 SAMUEL 23:24
LAST REFERENCE
I CHRONICLES 11:26

ELI 33
Lofty

The high priest in Shiloh, where the ark of the covenant rested for a time. He rebuked Hannah for being drunk (though she wasn't) as she prayed for God to give her a child. When her son Samuel was born, she brought him to Eli and dedicated him to God. Eli acted as Samuel's foster father and trained him in the priesthood. Eli's own sons, Hophni and Phinehas, did not know the Lord and sinned greatly. Because Eli honored them above God, the priest had done little to restrain them. Yet God promised to raise up a faithful priest in their place. Samuel began to hear the Word of God, and Eli encouraged him to listen. Though his own sons were spiritual failures, Eli did much better with his foster son. Samuel went on to be a powerful prophet of the Lord. The Lord had told Eli that his sons would die on the same day, and they did—in a battle with the Philistines, who stole the ark. When Eli heard the news of his sons' deaths, he fell backward in his chair and broke his neck.

FIRST REFERENCE
1 SAMUEL 1:3
LAST REFERENCE
1 KINGS 2:27
KEY REFERENCES
1 SAMUEL 1:13–14; 2:29; 3:8–9

ELIAB 21

God of his father

1) A prince of Zebulun who assisted Moses in taking the census of his tribe.

FIRST REFERENCE
NUMBERS 1:9
LAST REFERENCE
NUMBERS 10:16

2) Father of Dathan and Abiram, who rebelled against Moses.

FIRST REFERENCE
NUMBERS 16:1
LAST REFERENCE
DEUTERONOMY 11:6

3) First son of Jesse and an older brother of King David. The prophet Samuel, sent by God to anoint the successor to King Saul, thought the tall and good-looking Eliab would be the Lord's choice—but God said, "The LORD seeth not as man seeth; for man looketh on the outward appearance, but the LORD looketh on the heart" (1 Samuel 16:7). A warrior in Saul's army, Eliab criticized his youngest brother when David questioned Israelite soldiers about their fear of Goliath.

FIRST REFERENCE
1 SAMUEL 16:6
LAST REFERENCE
2 CHRONICLES 11:18

4) A descendant of Abraham through Jacob's son Levi.

ONLY REFERENCE
1 CHRONICLES 6:27

5) One of several warriors from the tribe of Gad who left Saul to join David during his conflict with the king. Eliab and his companions were "men of might. . .whose faces were like the faces of lions" (1 Chronicles 12:8).

ONLY REFERENCE
1 CHRONICLES 12:9

6) A Levite musician who performed in celebration when King David brought the ark of the covenant to Jerusalem.

FIRST REFERENCE
1 CHRONICLES 15:18
LAST REFERENCE
1 CHRONICLES 16:5

ELIADA 3

God is knowing

1) A son of King David, born in Jerusalem.

FIRST REFERENCE
2 SAMUEL 5:16
LAST REFERENCE
1 CHRONICLES 3:8

2) A Benjaminite "mighty man of valour" who fought for King Jehoshaphat of Judah.

ONLY REFERENCE
2 CHRONICLES 17:17

ELIADAH   1
God is knowing

Father of Rezon, an opponent of Israel's king Solomon.

ONLY REFERENCE
1 KINGS 11:23

ELIAH   2
God of Jehovah

A descendant of Abraham through Jacob's son Benjamin. Eliah married a "strange" (foreign) woman in exile.

FIRST REFERENCE
1 CHRONICLES 8:27
LAST REFERENCE
EZRA 10:26

ELIAHBA   2
God will hide

One of King David's valiant warriors.

FIRST REFERENCE
2 SAMUEL 23:32
LAST REFERENCE
1 CHRONICLES 11:33

ELIAKIM   15   4
God of raising

1) Palace administrator for King Hezekiah of Judah. He confronted the king of Assyria's messengers who tried to convince Hezekiah and his people to submit to Assyria.

FIRST REFERENCE
2 KINGS 18:18
LAST REFERENCE
ISAIAH 37:2

2) Son of King Josiah of Judah. Pharaoh Necho of Egypt put him in power and changed his name to Jehoiakim. Same as Jehoiakim.

FIRST REFERENCE
2 KINGS 23:34
LAST REFERENCE
2 CHRONICLES 36:4

3) A priest who helped to dedicate the rebuilt walls of Jerusalem by giving thanks.

ONLY REFERENCE
NEHEMIAH 12:41

4) A descendant of Abraham through Isaac; forebear of Jesus' earthly father, Joseph.

FIRST REFERENCE
MATTHEW 1:13
LAST REFERENCE
LUKE 3:30
GENEALOGY OF JESUS
MATTHEW 1:13

ELIAM   2
God of the people

1) Father of Bath-sheba, the beautiful woman whom King David took as a wife.

ONLY REFERENCE
2 SAMUEL 11:3

2) One of King David's warriors known as the "mighty men."

ONLY REFERENCE
2 SAMUEL 23:34

ELIAS 30

God of Jehovah

Greek form of the name *Elijah*, used in six New Testament books.

FIRST REFERENCE
MATTHEW 11:14
LAST REFERENCE
JAMES 5:17

ELIASAPH 6

God is gatherer

1) A prince of Gad who helped Moses take a census of his tribe.

FIRST REFERENCE
NUMBERS 1:14
LAST REFERENCE
NUMBERS 10:20

2) The leader of the Gershonites under Moses.

ONLY REFERENCE
NUMBERS 3:24

ELIASHIB 17

God will restore

1) A descendant of Abraham through Jacob's son Judah, in the line of the nation of Judah's second-to-last king, Jeconiah (also known as Jehoiachin).

ONLY REFERENCE
I CHRONICLES 3:24

2) One of twenty-four priests in David's time who was chosen by lot to serve in the tabernacle.

ONLY REFERENCE
I CHRONICLES 24:12

3) A Levite worship leader, son of Jehoiakim and grandson of Jeshua, who returned from Babylon.

FIRST REFERENCE
EZRA 10:6
LAST REFERENCE
NEHEMIAH 12:23

4) An exiled Levite who married a "strange" (foreign) woman.

ONLY REFERENCE
EZRA 10:24

5) Another exiled Israelite who married a foreign woman.

ONLY REFERENCE
EZRA 10:27

6) Another exiled Israelite who married a foreign woman.

ONLY REFERENCE
EZRA 10:36

7) High priest during the rebuilding of Jerusalem's walls. He defiled the temple by assigning Tobiah the Ammonite a room there.

FIRST REFERENCE
NEHEMIAH 3:1
LAST REFERENCE
NEHEMIAH 13:28

ELIATHAH 2

God of his consent

A son of King David's musician Heman, who was "under the hands of [his] father for song in the house of the LORD" (1 Chronicles 25:6).

FIRST REFERENCE
I CHRONICLES 25:4
LAST REFERENCE
I CHRONICLES 25:27

ELIDAD

God of his love

Prince of the tribe of Benjamin when the Israelites entered the Promised Land.

ONLY REFERENCE
NUMBERS 34:21

ELIEL 10

God of his God

1) One of the "mighty men of valour, famous men" leading the half tribe of Manasseh.

ONLY REFERENCE
I CHRONICLES 5:24

2) An ancestor of the prophet Samuel. Same as Elihu (1).

ONLY REFERENCE
I CHRONICLES 6:34

3) A descendant of Abraham through Jacob's son Benjamin.

ONLY REFERENCE
I CHRONICLES 8:20

4) Another descendant of Abraham through Jacob's son Benjamin.

ONLY REFERENCE
I CHRONICLES 8:22

5) One of King David's valiant warriors.

ONLY REFERENCE
I CHRONICLES 11:46

6) Another of King David's valiant warriors.

ONLY REFERENCE
I CHRONICLES 11:47

7) One of several warriors from the tribe of Gad who left Saul to join David during his conflict with the king. Eliel and his companions were "men of might. . .whose faces were like the faces of lions" (1 Chronicles 12:8).

ONLY REFERENCE
I CHRONICLES 12:11

8) A descendant of Hebron who helped to bring the ark of the covenant to Jerusalem.

ONLY REFERENCE
I CHRONICLES 15:9

9) A descendant of Abraham through Jacob's son Levi. Eliel was among a group of Levites appointed by King David to bring the ark of the covenant from the house of Obed-edom to Jerusalem.

ONLY REFERENCE
I CHRONICLES 15:11

10) A supervisor of temple donations under King Hezekiah of Judah.

ONLY REFERENCE
2 CHRONICLES 31:13

ELIENAI 1

Toward Jehovah are my eyes

A descendant of Abraham through Jacob's son Benjamin.

ONLY REFERENCE
I CHRONICLES 8:20

ELIEZER 15

God of help

1) The steward of Abraham's house and Abraham's presumed heir before the miraculous birth of Isaac.

ONLY REFERENCE
GENESIS 15:2

2) A son of Moses by his wife, Zipporah.

FIRST REFERENCE
EXODUS 18:4
LAST REFERENCE
I CHRONICLES 26:25

3) A priest who blew a trumpet before the ark of the covenant when David brought it to Jerusalem.

ONLY REFERENCE
I CHRONICLES 15:24

4) Leader of the tribe of Reuben in the days of King David.

ONLY REFERENCE
I CHRONICLES 27:16

5) A prophet who predicted trouble for the ships of Judah's king Jehoshaphat, who had entered into a trading alliance with Ahaziah, king of Israel.

ONLY REFERENCE
2 CHRONICLES 20:37

6) A Jewish exile charged with finding Levites and temple servants to travel to Jerusalem with Ezra.

ONLY REFERENCE
EZRA 8:16

7) An exiled Israelite priest who married a "strange" (foreign) woman.

ONLY REFERENCE
EZRA 10:18

8) An exiled Levite who married a "strange" (foreign) woman.

ONLY REFERENCE
EZRA 10:23

9) An exiled Israelite who married a "strange" (foreign) woman.

ONLY REFERENCE
EZRA 10:31

10) An ancestor of Jesus Christ according to Luke's genealogy.

ONLY REFERENCE
LUKE 3:29
GENEALOGY OF JESUS
LUKE 3:29

ELIHOENAI

Toward Jehovah are my eyes

Forefather of a Jewish exile who returned from Babylon to Judah under Ezra.

ONLY REFERENCE
EZRA 8:4

ELIHOREPH

God of autumn

A scribe serving Israel's king Solomon.

ONLY REFERENCE
I KINGS 4:3

ELIHU

God of him

1) An ancestor of the prophet Samuel. Same as Eliel (2).

ONLY REFERENCE
I SAMUEL 1:1

2) A warrior who defected to David at Ziglag and became an army commander.

ONLY REFERENCE
I CHRONICLES 12:20

3) A Levite "porter" (doorkeeper) in the house of the Lord.

ONLY REFERENCE
I CHRONICLES 26:7

4) Leader of the tribe of Judah in the days of King David.

ONLY REFERENCE
I CHRONICLES 27:18

5) A young man who became a mediator in the discussion between Job and his comforters. Unlike the comforters, God did not accuse Elihu of any wrong.

FIRST REFERENCE
JOB 32:2
LAST REFERENCE
JOB 36:1

ELIJAH 69
God of Jehovah

1) One of the Old Testament's major prophets, Elijah came from Tishbe, in Gilead. His prophecy that no rain would fall in Israel except at his command angered wicked King Ahab, and Elijah had to flee across the Jordan River and on to Zarephath. God hid him for three years and sent him to Mount Carmel. At Carmel he had a showdown with the priests of Baal that proved the Lord was God. Baal could not ignite the offering made by the pagans, but God sent fire from heaven that lit a water-soaked offering made by Elijah. The people of Israel worshipped God, and rain fell. Angry that Elijah had all the priests of Baal killed, Queen Jezebel threatened his life, and the discouraged prophet fled to Horeb. God gave Elijah the prophet Elisha as a disciple. Elijah returned to Ahab to prophesy the ruling couple's end, and Ahab repented. Following Ahab's death, Elijah prophesied the death of King Ahaziah, who consulted the god of Ekron when he was ill. Knowing God would take Elijah to heaven, his disciple Elisha asked to receive a double portion of his spirit. Elijah said that if Elisha saw his ascension into heaven, he would have it. Suddenly a chariot with horses of fire appeared before the two men, and Elijah went up into heaven in a whirlwind. Same as Elias.

FIRST REFERENCE
I KINGS 17:1
LAST REFERENCE
MALACHI 4:5
KEY REFERENCES
I KINGS 17:1–6; 18:21–40; 2 KINGS 2:11

2) An exiled Israelite priest who married a "strange" (foreign) woman.

ONLY REFERENCE
EZRA 10:21

ELIKA 1
God of rejection

One of King David's mightiest warriors known as "the thirty."

ONLY REFERENCE
2 SAMUEL 23:25

ELIMELECH 6
God of the king

Naomi's husband. He died in Moab, where the family had moved from Bethlehem to escape a famine.

FIRST REFERENCE
RUTH 1:2
LAST REFERENCE
RUTH 4:9

ELIOENAI 8 7
Toward Jehovah are my eyes

1) A descendant of Abraham through Jacob's son Judah, in the line of the nation of Judah's second-to-last king, Jeconiah (also known as Jehoiachin).

FIRST REFERENCE
I CHRONICLES 3:23
LAST REFERENCE
I CHRONICLES 3:24

2) A descendant of Abraham through Jacob's son Simeon.

ONLY REFERENCE
I CHRONICLES 4:36

3) A descendant of Abraham through Jacob's son Benjamin.

ONLY REFERENCE
I CHRONICLES 7:8

4) A Levite "porter" (doorkeeper) in the house of the Lord.

ONLY REFERENCE
I CHRONICLES 26:3

5) An exiled Israelite priest who married a "strange" (foreign) woman.

ONLY REFERENCE
EZRA 10:22

6) An exiled Israelite who married a "strange" (foreign) woman.

ONLY REFERENCE
EZRA 10:27

7) A priest who helped to dedicate the rebuilt walls of Jerusalem by giving thanks.

ONLY REFERENCE
NEHEMIAH 12:41

ELIPHAL I
God of judgment

One of King David's valiant warriors.

ONLY REFERENCE
I CHRONICLES 11:35

ELIPHALET 2
God of deliverance

A son of King David, born to him in Jerusalem.

FIRST REFERENCE
2 SAMUEL 5:16
LAST REFERENCE
I CHRONICLES 14:7

ELIPHAZ 15 2
God of gold

1) A son of Esau. Esau's blessing as the older brother was taken by the scheming Jacob.

FIRST REFERENCE
GENESIS 36:4
LAST REFERENCE
I CHRONICLES 1:36

2) One of three friends of Job who mourned his losses for a week then accused him of wrongdoing. God ultimately chastised the three for their criticism of Job, commanding them to sacrifice burnt offerings while Job prayed for them.

FIRST REFERENCE
JOB 2:11
LAST REFERENCE
JOB 42:9

ELIPHELEH 2
God of his distinction

A Levite musician who performed in celebration when King David brought the ark of the covenant to Jerusalem.

FIRST REFERENCE
I CHRONICLES 15:18
LAST REFERENCE
I CHRONICLES 15:21

ELIPHELET 6
God of deliverance

1) One of King David's warriors known as the "mighty men."

ONLY REFERENCE
2 SAMUEL 23:34

2) A son of King David, born in Jerusalem.

ONLY REFERENCE
I CHRONICLES 3:6

3) Another son of King David, born in Jerusalem.

ONLY REFERENCE
I CHRONICLES 3:8

4) A descendant of Abraham through Jacob's son Benjamin, through the line of King Saul and his son Jonathan. Eliphelet was a courageous archer.

ONLY REFERENCE
I CHRONICLES 8:39

5) A Jewish exile who returned to Judah under Ezra.

ONLY REFERENCE
EZRA 8:13

6) An exiled Israelite who married a "strange" (foreign) woman.

ONLY REFERENCE
EZRA 10:33

ELISABETH 9
God of the oath

Wife of Zacharias and mother of John the Baptist. For many years Elisabeth had been barren, but her husband received a vision promising she would conceive. When Elisabeth heard, she rejoiced at God's favor. Her cousin Mary visited her for three months when Mary learned that she herself would bear the Messiah.

FIRST REFERENCE
LUKE 1:5
LAST REFERENCE
LUKE 1:57

ELISEUS 1
God of supplication

Greek form of the Old Testament name *Elisha*.

ONLY REFERENCE
LUKE 4:27

ELISHA 58
God of supplication

The prophet Elijah's successor and disciple, Elisha saw Elijah carried up to heaven in a whirlwind of fire and received a double portion of his spirit. Taking over the role of prophet, Elisha performed many miracles for individuals—he healed a polluted water source for the people of Jericho, provided oil for a widow, and caused a "great woman" of Shunem to have a child then brought him back to life after he died. He fed one hundred people from twenty loaves of bread, prefiguring Christ's feeding of the five thousand and the three thousand. At Elisha's command, Naaman, captain of the Syrian king, bathed in the Jordan and was healed of leprosy. At Elisha's request, God blinded a host of Syrian warriors. Elisha led them to Samaria then persuaded the king of Israel to send them home. This ended the incursion of Syria's raiding bands on Israel. The prophet prophesied the recovery and then the death of King Ben-hadad of Syria and told King Jeroboam of Israel that he would strike Syria three times but not fully defeat that nation. After Elisha died, some men put a body into his tomb for safekeeping. The man's body touched the prophet's bones and was revived. Same as Eliseus.

FIRST REFERENCE
1 KINGS 19:16
LAST REFERENCE
2 KINGS 13:21
KEY REFERENCES
2 KINGS 2:9; 4:8–37; 5:8–19

ELISHAH   3

A descendant of Noah, through his son Japheth.

FIRST REFERENCE
GENESIS 10:4
LAST REFERENCE
EZEKIEL 27:7

ELISHAMA   17

God of hearing

1) A descendant of Abraham through Joseph's son Ephraim and an ancestor of Joshua.

FIRST REFERENCE
NUMBERS 1:10
LAST REFERENCE
1 CHRONICLES 7:26

2) A son of King David, born in Jerusalem. Same as Elishua.

FIRST REFERENCE
2 SAMUEL 5:16
LAST REFERENCE
1 CHRONICLES 14:7

3) Forefather of Ishmael, who was the assassin of Gedaliah, governor of Israel.

ONLY REFERENCE
JEREMIAH 41:1

4) A descendant of Abraham through Jacob's son Judah. Elishama descended from the line of an unnamed Israelite woman and her Egyptian husband, Jarha.

ONLY REFERENCE
1 CHRONICLES 2:41

5) A priest sent by King Jehoshaphat to teach the law of the Lord throughout the nation of Judah.

ONLY REFERENCE
2 CHRONICLES 17:8

6) Forefather of Ishmael, who killed Gedaliah, governor of Jerusalem.

ONLY REFERENCE:
2 KINGS 25:25

7) Secretary to King Jehoiakim of Judah; he heard the prophecies of Jeremiah.

FIRST REFERENCE
JEREMIAH 36:12
LAST REFERENCE
JEREMIAH 36:21

ELISHAPHAT   1

God of judgment

A commander who entered into a covenant with the priest Jehoiada, young King Joash's protector.

ONLY REFERENCE
2 CHRONICLES 23:1

ELISHEBA   1

God of the oath

Aaron's wife, who bore him four sons.

ONLY REFERENCE
EXODUS 6:23

ELISHUA   2

God of supplication

A son of King David, born in Jerusalem. Same as Elishama (2).

FIRST REFERENCE
2 SAMUEL 5:15
LAST REFERENCE
1 CHRONICLES 14:5

ELIUD   2

God of majesty

The great-great-great-grandfather of Jesus' earthly father, Joseph, according to Matthew's genealogy of Jesus.

FIRST REFERENCE
MATTHEW 1:14
LAST REFERENCE
MATTHEW 1:15
GENEALOGY OF JESUS
MATTHEW 1:14–15

ELIZAPHAN   3

God of treasure

1) The leader of the Kohathite clans during the Exodus. Same as Elzaphan.

FIRST REFERENCE
NUMBERS 3:30
LAST REFERENCE
2 CHRONICLES 29:13

2) Prince of the tribe of Zebulun when the Israelites entered the Promised Land.

ONLY REFERENCE
NUMBERS 34:25

ELIZUR   5

God of the rock

A prince of Reuben who helped Moses take a census of his tribe and led the tribe out of Sinai.

FIRST REFERENCE
NUMBERS 1:5
LAST REFERENCE
NUMBERS 10:18

ELKANAH   20

God has obtained

1) A descendant of Abraham through Jacob's son Levi.

FIRST REFERENCE
EXODUS 6:24
LAST REFERENCE
1 CHRONICLES 6:23

2) Father of the prophet Samuel. Elkanah's wife Hannah was barren and prayed to have a child. When God gave her Samuel, Elkanah agreed with her that their son should become a priest under the high priest Eli.

3) Another descendant of Abraham through Jacob's son Levi.

FIRST REFERENCE
I CHRONICLES 6:25
LAST REFERENCE
I CHRONICLES 6:36

4) Another descendant of Abraham through Jacob's son Levi.

FIRST REFERENCE
I CHRONICLES 6:26
LAST REFERENCE
I CHRONICLES 6:35

5) A Jewish exile from the tribe of Levi who resettled Jerusalem.

ONLY REFERENCE
I CHRONICLES 9:16

6) A "mighty man" who supported the future king David during his conflict with Saul.

ONLY REFERENCE
I CHRONICLES 12:6

7) A doorkeeper for the ark of the covenant when David brought it to Jerusalem.

ONLY REFERENCE
I CHRONICLES 15:23

8) One of King Ahaz's officers, his second in command.

ONLY REFERENCE
2 CHRONICLES 28:7

ELMODAM

A descendant of Abraham through Isaac; forebear of Jesus' earthly father, Joseph.

ONLY REFERENCE
LUKE 3:28
GENEALOGY OF JESUS
LUKE 3:28

ELNAAM

God is his delight

Father of two of King David's valiant warriors.

ONLY REFERENCE
I CHRONICLES 11:46

ELNATHAN

God is the giver

1) Grandfather of King Jehoiachin of Judah.

FIRST REFERENCE
2 KINGS 24:8
LAST REFERENCE
JEREMIAH 36:25

2) A Jewish exile charged with finding Levites and temple servants to travel to Jerusalem with Ezra.

ONLY REFERENCE
EZRA 8:16

3) Another Jewish exile charged with finding Levites and temple servants to travel to Jerusalem with Ezra.

ONLY REFERENCE
EZRA 8:16

4) Yet another Jewish exile charged with finding Levites and temple servants to travel to Jerusalem with Ezra.

ONLY REFERENCE
EZRA 8:16

ELON 6
Oak grove

1) Father of Esau's wife Bashemath (or Adah).

FIRST REFERENCE
GENESIS 26:34
LAST REFERENCE
GENESIS 36:2

2) A son of Zebulun, founder of the tribe of the Elonites.

FIRST REFERENCE
GENESIS 46:14
LAST REFERENCE
NUMBERS 26:26

3) The eleventh judge of Israel, who led the nation for ten years.

FIRST REFERENCE
JUDGES 12:11
LAST REFERENCE
JUDGES 12:12

ELPAAL 3
God act

A descendant of Abraham through Jacob's son Benjamin.

FIRST REFERENCE
1 CHRONICLES 8:11
LAST REFERENCE
1 CHRONICLES 8:18

ELPALET 1
Meaning

A son of King David, born to him in Jerusalem.

ONLY REFERENCE
1 CHRONICLES 14:5

ELUZAI 1
God is defensive

A "mighty man" who supported the future king David during his conflict with Saul.

ONLY REFERENCE:
1 CHRONICLES 12:5

ELYMAS 1

A Jewish sorcerer, who was miraculously blinded for opposing the apostle Paul's preaching of the gospel in Paphos. Same as Bar-jesus.

ONLY REFERENCE
ACTS 13:8

ELZABAD 2
God has bestowed

1) One of several warriors from the tribe of Gad who left Saul to join David during his conflict with the king. Elzabad and his companions were "men of might. . .whose faces were like the faces of lions" (1 Chronicles 12:8).

ONLY REFERENCE
1 CHRONICLES 12:12

2) A Levite "porter" (doorkeeper) in the house of the Lord.

ONLY REFERENCE
1 CHRONICLES 26:7

ELZAPHAN 2 ♛ 🧍

God of treasure

A descendant of Levi and son of Uzziel who was part of the Exodus. Same as Elizaphan (1).

FIRST REFERENCE
EXODUS 6:22
LAST REFERENCE
LEVITICUS 10:4

EMMANUEL 1 🧍

God with us

A prophetic name for Jesus, given by the angel of the Lord to Joseph, husband of Mary.

ONLY REFERENCE
MATTHEW 1:23

EMMOR 1 🧍

Ass

A prince of Shechem whose sons sold Abraham a tomb.

ONLY REFERENCE
ACTS 7:16

ENAN 5 🧍

Having eyes

Forefather of a prince of Naphtali who helped Moses take a census of his tribe.

FIRST REFERENCE
NUMBERS 1:15
LAST REFERENCE
NUMBERS 10:27

ENOCH 11 ♛ 🧍

Initiated

1) Cain's eldest son, after whom he named a city.

FIRST REFERENCE
GENESIS 4:17
LAST REFERENCE
GENESIS 4:18

2) A descendant of Seth, son of Adam. "Enoch walked with God: and he was not; for God took him" (Genesis 5:24). He was immediately translated into eternity. Same as Henoch (1).

FIRST REFERENCE
GENESIS 5:18
LAST REFERENCE
JUDE 1:14
GENEALOGY OF JESUS
LUKE 3:37

ENOS 7 ♛ 🧍

Mortal

Son of Seth, Adam's son, and forebear of Jesus' earthly father, Joseph. Same as Enosh.

FIRST REFERENCE
GENESIS 4:26
LAST REFERENCE
LUKE 3:38
GENEALOGY OF JESUS:
LUKE 3:28

ENOSH 1 🧍

Mortal

Another form of the name *Enos;* son of Seth.

ONLY REFERENCE
1 CHRONICLES 1:1

EPAENETUS   1

Praised

A Christian acquaintance of the apostle Paul in Rome and the first Christian convert from Achaia.

ONLY REFERENCE
ROMANS 16:5

EPAPHRAS   3

Devoted

A fellow servant, with Paul, to the Colossian church. Epaphras was a native of Colossae.

FIRST REFERENCE
COLOSSIANS 1:7
LAST REFERENCE
PHILEMON 1:23

EPAPHRODITUS   2

Devoted

A fellow laborer with Paul whom the apostle sent to the church at Philippi. Epaphroditus also brought Paul some gifts from that church.

FIRST REFERENCE
PHILIPPIANS 2:25
LAST REFERENCE
PHILIPPIANS 4:18

EPHAH   5

Obscurity

1) A grandson of Abraham and Keturah through their son Midian.

FIRST REFERENCE
GENESIS 25:4
LAST REFERENCE
ISAIAH 60:6

2) Concubine of Caleb (2).

ONLY REFERENCE
I CHRONICLES 2:46

3) A descendant of Abraham through Jacob's son Judah.

ONLY REFERENCE
I CHRONICLES 2:47

EPHAI   1

Birdlike

Forefather of an Israelite family that stayed in Judah during the Babylonian captivity.

ONLY REFERENCE
JEREMIAH 40:8

EPHER   4

Gazelle

1) A descendant of Abraham by his second wife, Keturah.

FIRST REFERENCE
GENESIS 25:4
LAST REFERENCE
I CHRONICLES 1:33

2) A descendant of Abraham through Jacob's son Judah.

ONLY REFERENCE
I CHRONICLES 4:17

3) One of the "mighty men of valour, famous men" leading the half tribe of Manasseh.

ONLY REFERENCE
I CHRONICLES 5:24

EPHLAL   2

Judge

A descendant of Abraham through Jacob's son Judah. Ephlal descended from the line of an unnamed Israelite woman and her Egyptian husband, Jarha.

ONLY REFERENCE
I CHRONICLES 2:37

EPHOD
Girdle

Forefather of Hanniel, prince of the tribe of Manasseh when the Israelites entered the Promised Land.

ONLY REFERENCE
NUMBERS 34:23

EPHRAIM
Double fruit

Joseph and his wife Asenath's second son. Ephraim and his brother, Manasseh, were adopted and blessed by Jacob. But Ephraim received the greater blessing, for Jacob insisted he would be the greater brother. Eventually the brothers superseded Jacob's oldest sons, Reuben and Simeon.

FIRST REFERENCE
GENESIS 41:52
LAST REFERENCE
I CHRONICLES 7:22
KEY REFERENCES
GENESIS 48:5, 17–19

EPHRATAH
Fruitfulness

Wife of Hur; mother of Caleb, the son of Hur. Same as Ephrath.

FIRST REFERENCE
I CHRONICLES 2:50
LAST REFERENCE
I CHRONICLES 4:4

EPHRATH
Fruitfulness

An alternative form of the name *Ephratah.*

ONLY REFERENCE
I CHRONICLES 2:19

EPHRON
Fawn-like

The Hittite from whom Abraham bought the cave of Machpelah, where he buried Sarah. Though Ephron wanted to give Abraham the land, Abraham insisted on buying it.

FIRST REFERENCE
GENESIS 23:8
LAST REFERENCE
GENESIS 50:13
KEY REFERENCE
GENESIS 23:10–11

ER

Watchful

1) Judah's firstborn son, who was wicked. "The LORD. . .slew him" (Genesis 38:10). Both he and his brother Onan died in Canaan.

FIRST REFERENCE
GENESIS 38:3
LAST REFERENCE
I CHRONICLES 2:3

2) A son of Judah's son Shelah.

ONLY REFERENCE
I CHRONICLES 4:21

3) A descendant of Abraham through Isaac; forebear of Jesus' earthly father, Joseph.

ONLY REFERENCE
LUKE 3:28
GENEALOGY OF JESUS
LUKE 3:28

ERAN   1
Watchful

A descendant of Abraham through Jacob's son Ephraim.

ONLY REFERENCE
NUMBERS 26:36

ERASTUS   3   2
Beloved

1) A companion of Timothy on a mission to Macedonia. Erastus then went to Corinth.

FIRST REFERENCE
ACTS 19:22
LAST REFERENCE
2 TIMOTHY 4:20

2) The chamberlain (treasurer) of Corinth, who greeted the Roman Christians through Paul when the apostle wrote that church.

ONLY REFERENCE
ROMANS 16:23

ERI   2
Watchful

A descendant of Abraham through Jacob's son Gad.

FIRST REFERENCE
GENESIS 46:16
LAST REFERENCE
NUMBERS 26:16

ESAIAS   21
God has saved

Greek form of the name *Isaiah*, used in the New Testament.

FIRST REFERENCE
MATTHEW 3:3
LAST REFERENCE
ROMANS 15:12
KEY REFERENCE
LUKE 4:14–21

ESAR-HADDON   3

The son of Sennacherib who inherited the throne of Assyria. As king, following the Exile, Esar-haddon resettled people of other nations in Israel.

FIRST REFERENCE
2 KINGS 19:37
LAST REFERENCE
ISAIAH 37:38

ESAU   82
Rough

A son of Isaac and Rebekah and the twin brother of Jacob. Esau was a good hunter and the favorite of his father, but he sold his birthright to Jacob for some lentil stew. Then he disturbed his parents by marrying two Hittite women. Rebekah and Jacob plotted to trick Isaac into giving Jacob the elder son's blessing, and they succeeded, creating bad feelings between the brothers. Because the elder brother, Esau, received a lesser blessing, he plotted to kill Jacob, who had to flee. Years later, before Jacob returned to his homeland, he sent word to his brother. Fearing Esau's anger, he sent a peace offering of cattle before him. But Esau's rage had cooled, and he greeted him joyfully, refusing the gift Jacob offered. When the brothers' cattle became too many for them to live on the same land, Esau moved to Mount Seir. His descendants became the

Edomites, called after Esau's nickname, which came from the red stew for which he sold his birthright. Edom means "red." Same as Edom.

FIRST REFERENCE
GENESIS 25:25
LAST REFERENCE
HEBREWS 12:16
KEY REFERENCES
GENESIS 25:30–33; 27:41; 36:6–8

ESH-BAAL 2
Man of Baal

A son of Saul, who was Israel's first king.

FIRST REFERENCE
I CHRONICLES 8:33
LAST REFERENCE
I CHRONICLES 9:39

ESHBAN 2
Vigorous

A descendant of Seir, who lived in Esau's "land of Edom."

FIRST REFERENCE
GENESIS 36:26
LAST REFERENCE
I CHRONICLES 1:41

ESHCOL 2
Bunch of grapes

An Amorite confederate of Abram who went with him to recover Abram's nephew Lot from the king of Sodom.

FIRST REFERENCE
GENESIS 14:13
LAST REFERENCE
GENESIS 14:24

ESHEK 1
Oppression

A descendant of Abraham through Jacob's son Benjamin, the line of King Saul and his son Jonathan.

ONLY REFERENCE
I CHRONICLES 8:39

ESHTEMOA 2
Obedience

A descendant of Abraham through Jacob's son Judah.

FIRST REFERENCE
I CHRONICLES 4:17
LAST REFERENCE
I CHRONICLES 4:19

ESHTON 2
Restful

A descendant of Abraham through Jacob's son Judah.

FIRST REFERENCE
I CHRONICLES 4:11
LAST REFERENCE
I CHRONICLES 4:12

ESLI 1
Toward Jehovah are my eyes

A descendant of Abraham through Isaac; forebear of Jesus' earthly father, Joseph.

ONLY REFERENCE
LUKE 3:25
GENEALOGY OF JESUS
LUKE 3:25

ESROM 3
Courtyard

A descendant of Abraham through Isaac; forebear of Jesus' earthly father, Joseph.

FIRST REFERENCE
MATTHEW 1:3
LAST REFERENCE
LUKE 3:33
GENEALOGY OF JESUS
MATTHEW 1:3; LUKE 3:33

ESTHER 56
[star symbol]

The Jewish wife of the Persian king Ahasuerus. Angered by his first wife, Vashti, the king sought a new bride from among the most beautiful women of his kingdom. As a result of this search, he found Esther, fell in love with her, married her, and made her his queen. Ahasuerus's favorite counselor, Haman, lied to the king and plotted to kill the Jewish people. Esther's cousin Mordecai, who had raised her, convinced the new queen to confront her husband. When she expressed her doubts, he told her: "For if thou altogether holdest thy peace at this time, then shall there enlargement and deliverance arise to the Jews from another place; but thou and thy father's house shall be destroyed: and who knoweth whether thou art come to the kingdom for such a time as this?" (Esther 4:14). The queen boldly went to the king, though it could have meant her death to appear before him unrequested. She asked that he and Haman come to a banquet. On the second day of the banquet, Esther told the king of Haman's plan to kill her people. Angered, Ahasuerus had Haman killed, and Esther and her people were saved. Same as Hadassah.

FIRST REFERENCE
ESTHER 2:7
LAST REFERENCE
ESTHER 9:32
KEY REFERENCE
ESTHER 4:14–16

ETAM 1
Hawk-ground

A descendant of Abraham through Jacob's son Judah.

ONLY REFERENCE
I CHRONICLES 4:3

ETHAN 8
Permanent

1) The wise man who wrote Psalm 89. His wisdom was surpassed by Solomon's.

FIRST REFERENCE
I KINGS 4:31
LAST REFERENCE
PSALM 89 (TITLE)

2) A descendant of Abraham through Jacob's son Judah.

FIRST REFERENCE
I CHRONICLES 2:6
LAST REFERENCE
I CHRONICLES 2:8

3) A forefather of Asaph, a chief singer in the temple.

ONLY REFERENCE
I CHRONICLES 6:42

4) Another forefather of Asaph, a chief singer in the temple.

FIRST REFERENCE
I CHRONICLES 6:44
LAST REFERENCE
I CHRONICLES 15:19

ETHBAAL
With Baal

King of the Zidonians and father of Jezebel, the evil queen of Israel's king Ahab.

ONLY REFERENCE
I KINGS 16:31

ETHNAN
Gift

A descendant of Abraham through Jacob's son Judah.

ONLY REFERENCE
I CHRONICLES 4:7

ETHNI
Munificence

A forefather of Asaph, a chief singer in the temple.

ONLY REFERENCE
I CHRONICLES 6:41

EUBULUS
Good-willer

A Roman Christian who sent greetings to Timothy in Paul's second letter to his "dearly beloved son."

ONLY REFERENCE
2 TIMOTHY 4:21

EUNICE
Victorious

The Jewish mother of the apostle Paul's protégé Timothy. She was married to a Greek man (Acts 16:1), but Paul described Eunice as a person of "unfeigned faith" (2 Timothy 1:5).

ONLY REFERENCE
2 TIMOTHY 1:5

EUODIAS
Fine traveling

A Christian woman of Philippi who had "laboured with [Paul] in the gospel" (Philippians 4:3) but who had conflict with another church member, Syntyche. Paul begged them to "be of the same mind in the Lord" (Philippians 4:2).

ONLY REFERENCE
PHILIPPIANS 4:2

EUTYCHUS
Fortunate

A young man of Troas who drifted off to sleep during a late-night sermon of the apostle Paul. Eutychus fell from his window seat three floors to his death. Paul brought him back to life, and the Christians were "not a little comforted" (Acts 20:12).

ONLY REFERENCE
ACTS 20:9

EVE 4

Life-giver

Adam's wife, "the mother of all living." Tempted by the serpent, Eve ate the fruit of the tree of the knowledge of good and evil and offered it to her husband, who also ate. Suddenly fearful of God because of their sin, they hid from Him. God placed a curse on Adam and Eve. For her part, Eve would suffer greatly during childbirth, desire her husband, and be ruled over by him. God removed the couple from the Garden of Eden. Eve and Adam first had two children named in the Bible—Cain and Abel. After Cain murdered Abel, God gave them another child, Seth.

FIRST REFERENCE
GENESIS 3:20
LAST REFERENCE
I TIMOTHY 2:13

EVI 2

Desirous

A Midianite king killed by the Israelites at God's command.

FIRST REFERENCE
NUMBERS 31:8
LAST REFERENCE
JOSHUA 13:21

EVIL-MERODACH 2

Soldier of Merodak

Successor to the Babylonian king Nebuchadnezzar. Evil-merodach showed kindness to Judah's second-to-last king, Jehoiachin, who had been imprisoned in the first deportation of Jews to Babylon. Evil-merodach "spoke kindly" to Jehoiachin, "changed his prison garments," and allowed him to eat at the king's table for the rest of his life.

FIRST REFERENCE
2 KINGS 25:27
LAST REFERENCE
JEREMIAH 52:31

EZAR 1

Treasure

A descendant of Seir, who lived in Esau's "land of Edom."

ONLY REFERENCE
I CHRONICLES 1:38

EZBAI 1

Hyssop-like

Father of one of King David's valiant warriors.

ONLY REFERENCE
I CHRONICLES 11:37

EZBON 2

1) A son of Gad and a grandson of Jacob.

ONLY REFERENCE
GENESIS 46:16

2) A descendant of Abraham through Jacob's son Benjamin.

ONLY REFERENCE
I CHRONICLES 7:7

EZEKIAS 2 👑🧍
Strengthened of God

Greek form of the name *Hezekiah*, used in the New Testament.

FIRST REFERENCE
MATTHEW 1:9
LAST REFERENCE
MATTHEW 1:10
GENEALOGY OF JESUS
MATTHEW 1:9–10

EZEKIEL 2 🧍
God will strengthen

A priest, the son of Buzi, who was taken into exile at about age twenty-five when Nebuchadnezzar, king of Babylon, carried off most of Jerusalem. When Ezekiel was thirty and still in exile, God came to him in a vision and sent him to the rebellious Israelites as a prophet. The little we know about Ezekiel comes from his prophetic book. A contemporary of Daniel and Jeremiah, he was married, and his wife died before the Babylonians destroyed Jerusalem. His prophecies focus on judgment for both Israel and the other nations and God's grace and mercy for Israel. He is probably best known for his prophetic vision of the dry bones that came to life.

FIRST REFERENCE
EZEKIEL 1:3
LAST REFERENCE
EZEKIEL 24:24

EZER 9 🧍
Treasure, help

1) A descendant of Seir, who lived in Esau's "land of Edom."

FIRST REFERENCE
GENESIS 36:21
LAST REFERENCE
1 CHRONICLES 1:42

2) A descendant of Abraham through Jacob's son Judah.

ONLY REFERENCE
1 CHRONICLES 4:4

3) A descendant of Abraham through Joseph's son Ephraim. He was killed by men of Gath in a dispute over livestock.

ONLY REFERENCE
1 CHRONICLES 7:21

4) One of several warriors from the tribe of Gad who left Saul to join David during his conflict with the king. Ezer and his companions were "men of might. . .whose faces were like the faces of lions" (1 Chronicles 12:8).

ONLY REFERENCE
1 CHRONICLES 12:9

5) A man who repaired Jerusalem's walls under Nehemiah.

ONLY REFERENCE
NEHEMIAH 3:19

6) A priest who helped to dedicate the rebuilt walls of Jerusalem by giving thanks.

ONLY REFERENCE
NEHEMIAH 12:42

EZRA 26
Aid

1) A descendant of Abraham through Jacob's son Judah.

ONLY REFERENCE
I CHRONICLES 4:17

2) An Israelite scribe and teacher of the law who returned from the Babylonian Exile along with some priests, Levites, temple servants, and other Israelites. Ezra had received the backing of King Artaxerxes of Persia and returned with money and the temple vessels. Ezra also had the right to appoint magistrates and judges in Israel. When they reached Jerusalem, the officials told Ezra that many men of Israel had intermarried with the people around them and followed their ways. Ezra prayed for the people, read them the law, and called them to confess their sin. All Israel repented and put away their foreign spouses.

FIRST REFERENCE
EZRA 7:1
LAST REFERENCE
NEHEMIAH 12:36
KEY REFERENCE
EZRA 7:6

3) A priest who returned to Jerusalem under Zerubbabel.

ONLY REFERENCE
NEHEMIAH 12:1

EZRI 1
Helpful

A superintendent of agriculture who served under King David.

ONLY REFERENCE
I CHRONICLES 27:26

FELIX 9
Happy

Governor of Judea before whom Paul appeared after the Roman guard rescued him from his appearance at the Jewish council. Felix, hoping for a bribe and wanting to please the Jews, delayed in making a decision in Paul's case. When his successor, Porcius Festus, came, they heard his case together and sent Paul to Caesar in Rome.

FIRST REFERENCE
ACTS 23:24
LAST REFERENCE
ACTS 25:14
KEY REFERENCE
ACTS 24:24–26

FESTUS 13
Festal

The governor of Judea who replaced Felix. He heard Paul's case and determined to send Paul to Rome, since the apostle had appealed to Caesar. When Festus brought the case before King Agrippa, Agrippa agreed. Also called Porcius Festus.

FIRST REFERENCE
ACTS 24:27
LAST REFERENCE
ACTS 26:32
KEY REFERENCE
ACTS 25:24–25

FORTUNATUS
Fortunate

A Corinthian Christian who visited the apostle Paul in Ephesus and "refreshed [Paul's] spirit" (1 Corinthians 16:18).

ONLY REFERENCE
1 CORINTHIANS 16:17

-G-

GAAL   9
Loathing

A would-be ruler who got the men of Shechem drunk and convinced them to rise up against their king, Abimelech. Zebul, the ruler of the city, warned the king of their planned ambush. Abimelech stealthily returned to his city, fought, and won. Gaal and his relatives were banished from Shechem.

FIRST REFERENCE
JUDGES 9:26
LAST REFERENCE
JUDGES 9:41

GABBAI   1
Collective

A Jewish exile from the tribe of Benjamin who resettled Jerusalem.

ONLY REFERENCE
NEHEMIAH 11:8

GAD   19
Attack

1) A son of Jacob and Leah's handmaid Zilpah. At Gad's birth Leah said, "A troop cometh," so she gave him a name meaning "attack." Jacob prophesied that a troop would overcome Gad but that he would at last overcome.

FIRST REFERENCE
GENESIS 30:11
LAST REFERENCE
1 CHRONICLES 5:11

2) A prophet who warned David, when he ran from Saul, to leave Moab and return to Judea. When King David sinned by taking a census of the people, Gad came to him with God's choices for punishment and a way to end it.

FIRST REFERENCE
1 SAMUEL 22:5
LAST REFERENCE
2 CHRONICLES 29:25
KEY REFERENCES
1 SAMUEL 22:5; 1 CHRONICLES 21:9–14

GADDI 1

Fortunate

One of twelve spies sent by Moses to spy out the land of Canaan.

ONLY REFERENCE
NUMBERS 13:11

GADDIEL 1

Fortune of God

One of twelve spies sent by Moses to spy out the land of Canaan.

ONLY REFERENCE
NUMBERS 13:10

GADI 2

Fortunate

Father of Menahem, who killed King Shallum of Israel and reigned in his place.

FIRST REFERENCE
2 KINGS 15:14
LAST REFERENCE
2 KINGS 15:17

GAHAM 1

Flame

A nephew of Abraham, born to his brother Nahor's concubine, Reumah.

ONLY REFERENCE
GENESIS 22:24

GAHAR 2

Lurker

Forefather of an exiled family that returned to Judah under Zerubbabel.

FIRST REFERENCE
EZRA 2:47
LAST REFERENCE
NEHEMIAH 7:49

GAIUS 5

1) A man from Macedonia and a traveling companion of the apostle Paul. Gaius was caught in a riot started against Paul by Ephesian idol makers.

ONLY REFERENCE
ACTS 19:29

2) A man from Derbe and a traveling companion of the apostle Paul.

ONLY REFERENCE
ACTS 20:4

3) A Corinthian Christian who hosted the apostle Paul when he wrote the letter to the Romans. Gaius was one of a handful of believers whom Paul personally baptized.

FIRST REFERENCE
ROMANS 16:23
LAST REFERENCE
1 CORINTHIANS 1:14

4) The "wellbeloved" of John, addressee of John's third letter.

ONLY REFERENCE
3 JOHN·1:1

GALAL 3
Great

1) A Jewish exile from the tribe of Levi who resettled Jerusalem.

ONLY REFERENCE
1 CHRONICLES 9:15

2) Forefather of a Jewish exile who was chosen by lot to resettle Jerusalem.

FIRST REFERENCE
1 CHRONICLES 9:16
LAST REFERENCE
NEHEMIAH 11:17

GALLIO 3

Deputy (proconsul) of Achaia who refused to hear the case when the Jews accused Paul of breaking the law.

FIRST REFERENCE
ACTS 18:12
LAST REFERENCE
ACTS 18:17

GAMALIEL 7
Reward of God

1) Leader of the tribe of Manasseh under Moses during the Exodus.

FIRST REFERENCE
NUMBERS 1:10
LAST REFERENCE
NUMBERS 10:23

2) A Pharisee and doctor of the law who warned the Jews to leave the apostles alone. He was Paul's teacher.

FIRST REFERENCE
ACTS 5:34
LAST REFERENCE
ACTS 22:3

GAMUL 1
Rewarded

One of twenty-four priests in David's time who was chosen by lot to serve in the tabernacle.

ONLY REFERENCE
1 CHRONICLES 24:17

GAREB 2
Scabby

One of King David's valiant warriors.

FIRST REFERENCE
2 SAMUEL 23:38
LAST REFERENCE
1 CHRONICLES 11:40

GASHMU 1
A shower

A man who falsely reported to Sanballat that Nehemiah and his men meant to rebel.

ONLY REFERENCE
NEHEMIAH 6:6

GATAM 3

A descendant of Abraham's grandson Esau, whose blessing as older brother was taken by the scheming Jacob.

FIRST REFERENCE
GENESIS 36:11
LAST REFERENCE
1 CHRONICLES 1:36

GAZEZ 2

Shearer

1) A descendant of Abraham through Jacob's son Judah.

ONLY REFERENCE
I CHRONICLES 2:46

2) Another descendant of Abraham through Jacob's son Judah.

ONLY REFERENCE
I CHRONICLES 2:46

GAZZAM 2

Devourer

Forefather of an exiled family that returned to Judah under Zerubbabel.

FIRST REFERENCE
EZRA 2:48
LAST REFERENCE
NEHEMIAH 7:51

GEBER 2

Warrior

1) Father of one of King Solomon's twelve officials over provisions.

ONLY REFERENCE
I KINGS 4:13

2) One of King Solomon's twelve officials over provisions.

ONLY REFERENCE
I KINGS 4:19

GEDALIAH 32

God has become great

1) The ruler appointed by Nebuchadnezzar over the remnant of Jews left behind in Judah at the time of the Babylonian Exile. When the prophet Jeremiah was freed from prison, he chose to stay with Gedaliah and the people of Judah instead of heading for Babylon. Gedaliah persuaded the captains of Judah not to worry about serving the Chaldeans. Though one of his captains warned about a plot against him, Gedaliah refused to believe it. Ishmael, the son of Nethaniah, another captain, killed Gedaliah and all his men with him at Mizpah.

FIRST REFERENCE
2 KINGS 25:22
LAST REFERENCE
JEREMIAH 43:6
KEY REFERENCES
JEREMIAH 40:6–9, 16; 41:2

2) A son of King David's musician Jeduthun, "who prophesied with a harp, to give thanks and to praise the LORD" (1 Chronicles 25:3).

FIRST REFERENCE
I CHRONICLES 25:3
LAST REFERENCE
I CHRONICLES 25:9

3) An exiled Israelite priest who married a "strange" (foreign) woman.

ONLY REFERENCE
EZRA 10:18

4) Grandfather of the prophet Zephaniah.

ONLY REFERENCE
ZEPHANIAH 1:1

5) A prince of Judah who sought to have King Zedekiah kill Jeremiah because of his negative prophecy.

ONLY REFERENCE
JEREMIAH 38:1

GEDEON 1
Warrior

Greek form of the name *Gideon*, used in the New Testament.

ONLY REFERENCE
HEBREWS 11:32

GEDOR 4 2
Enclosure

1) A leader of the tribe of Benjamin who lived in Jerusalem.

FIRST REFERENCE
I CHRONICLES 8:31
LAST REFERENCE
I CHRONICLES 9:37

2) A descendant of Abraham through Jacob's son Judah.

FIRST REFERENCE
I CHRONICLES 4:4
LAST REFERENCE
I CHRONICLES 4:18

GEHAZI 12
Valley of a visionary

The prophet Elisha's servant, who pointed out to Elisha that the Shunnamite woman had no son. Elisha promised her one in a year. Gehazi later laid Elisha's staff on her son in an attempt to bring him back to life. After Elisha healed the Syrian captain Naaman of leprosy and refused gifts, Gehazi followed him to elicit money and clothing from him. For this, Gehazi was made leprous.

FIRST REFERENCE
2 KINGS 4:12
LAST REFERENCE
2 KINGS 8:5
KEY REFERENCES
2 KINGS 4:14; 5:25–27

GEMALLI 1
Camel driver

Father of one of the twelve spies sent by Moses to spy out the land of Canaan.

ONLY REFERENCE
NUMBERS 13:12

GEMARIAH 5 2
God has perfected

1) A scribe and prince of Judah in whose room Baruch read the prophecies of Jeremiah. Son of Shaphan.

FIRST REFERENCE
JEREMIAH 36:10
LAST REFERENCE
JEREMIAH 36:25

2) A messenger who took Jeremiah's letter to the exiles in Babylon. Son of Hilkiah.

ONLY REFERENCE
JEREMIAH 29:3

GENUBATH 2
Theft

Son of Hadad the Edomite, Solomon's adversary and leader of a marauding band.

ONLY REFERENCE
I KINGS 11:20

GERA 9
Grain

1) A son of Benjamin. He was a left-handed man.

ONLY REFERENCE
GENESIS 46:21

2) Father of Ehud, a left-handed man who became Israel's deliverer.

ONLY REFERENCE
JUDGES 3:15

3) Father of Shimei. Shimei cursed David but later recognized him as king.

FIRST REFERENCE
2 SAMUEL 16:5
LAST REFERENCE
I KINGS 2:8

4) A son of Bela, Benjamin's oldest son.

FIRST REFERENCE
I CHRONICLES 8:3
LAST REFERENCE
I CHRONICLES 8:7

GERSHOM 14
Refugee

1) Moses and Zipporah's firstborn son.

FIRST REFERENCE
EXODUS 2:22
LAST REFERENCE
I CHRONICLES 26:24

2) Firstborn son of Levi. Same as Gershon.

FIRST REFERENCE
I CHRONICLES 6:16
LAST REFERENCE
I CHRONICLES 15:7

3) A Jewish exile who returned to Judah from Babylon under Ezra.

ONLY REFERENCE
EZRA 8:2

4) Father of Jonathan. Jonathan was a priest to the tribe of Dan when they worshipped graven images.

ONLY REFERENCE
JUDGES 18:30

GERSHON 18
Refugee

Firstborn son of Levi. From his line came the Libnites and Shimites. His clan carried the curtains of the tabernacle, its cords, and the equipment. Same as Gershom (2).

FIRST REFERENCE
GENESIS 46:11
LAST REFERENCE
I CHRONICLES 23:6
KEY REFERENCE
GENESIS 46:11

GESHAM 1
Lumpish

A descendant of Abraham through Jacob's son Judah.

ONLY REFERENCE
I CHRONICLES 2:47

GESHEM 3
A shower

An Arabian who opposed Nehemiah's rebuilding of the walls of Jerusalem.

FIRST REFERENCE
NEHEMIAH 2:19
LAST REFERENCE
NEHEMIAH 6:2

GETHER 2

A descendant of Noah through his son Shem.

FIRST REFERENCE
GENESIS 10:23
LAST REFERENCE
I CHRONICLES 1:17

GEUEL 1
Majesty of God

A man from the tribe of Gad sent by Moses to spy out the land of Canaan.

ONLY REFERENCE
NUMBERS 13:15

GIBBAR 1
Warrior

Forefather of an exiled family that returned to Judah under Zerubbabel.

ONLY REFERENCE
EZRA 2:20

GIBEA 1
A hill

A descendant of Abraham through Jacob's son Judah.

ONLY REFERENCE
1 CHRONICLES 2:49

GIDDALTI 2
I have made great

A son of King David's musician Heman, who was "under the hands of [his] father for song in the house of the LORD" (1 Chronicles 25:6).

FIRST REFERENCE
1 CHRONICLES 25:4
LAST REFERENCE
1 CHRONICLES 25:29

GIDDEL 4
Stout

1) Forefather of an exiled family that returned to Judah under Zerubbabel.

FIRST REFERENCE
EZRA 2:47

LAST REFERENCE
NEHEMIAH 7:49

2) Forefather of an exiled family—former servants of Solomon—that returned to Judah under Zerubbabel.

FIRST REFERENCE
EZRA 2:56
LAST REFERENCE
NEHEMIAH 7:58

GIDEON 39
Warrior

The fifth judge of Israel, whom God raised up to lead his nation against the Midianites. The angel of the Lord appeared to Gideon when he was hiding his threshing from the enemy, told him God was with him, and called him a "mighty man of valour." Gideon's many doubts did not keep him from obeying God. He made an offering then tore down the altar to Baal and cut down its grove, for which the men of his town wanted to kill him. The Spirit of God came upon Gideon, and he sent to the tribes of Manasseh, Asher, Zebulun, and Naphtali, who came to him. Doubtful that God would save Israel, several times Gideon sought proof by placing a fleece on the floor and asking God to make either the fleece or the floor wet; every time God answered his request. When Israel gathered against Midian, God reduced Gideon's forces, cutting out the fearful and identifying the rest by the way they drank water. Gideon attacked

Midian with only three hundred men. Holding trumpets and pitchers filled with lamps, the men drew near the Midianite camp. They blew the trumpets and broke the pitchers, and their enemy fled. Gideon and his troops followed, capturing two princes and two kings and killing them. Same as Gedeon, Jerubbaal, and Jerubbesheth.

FIRST REFERENCE
JUDGES 6:11
LAST REFERENCE
JUDGES 8:35
KEY REFERENCES
JUDGES 6:11; 7:6–7, 20–22

GIDEONI 5
Warlike

Father of Abidan, a captain of the Benjaminites who helped Moses take a census and lead his people toward the Promised Land.

FIRST REFERENCE
NUMBERS 1:11
LAST REFERENCE
NUMBERS 10:24

GILALAI 1
Dungy

A priest who helped to dedicate the rebuilt walls of Jerusalem by playing a musical instrument.

ONLY REFERENCE
NEHEMIAH 12:36

GILEAD 13
Heap of testimony

1) A descendant of Abraham through Joseph's son Manasseh.

FIRST REFERENCE
NUMBERS 26:29
LAST REFERENCE
1 CHRONICLES 7:17

2) Father of Israel's ninth judge, Jephthah, by a relationship with a prostitute.

FIRST REFERENCE
JUDGES 11:1
LAST REFERENCE
JUDGES 11:2

3) A descendant of Abraham through Jacob's son Gad.

ONLY REFERENCE
1 CHRONICLES 5:14

GINATH 2

Father of Tibni. Half of Israel sought to make Tibni king after Zimri's death.

FIRST REFERENCE
1 KINGS 16:21
LAST REFERENCE
1 KINGS 16:22

GINNETHO 1
Gardener

An exiled priest who returned to Judah under Zerubbabel.

ONLY REFERENCE
NEHEMIAH 12:4

GINNETHON 2
Gardener

A priest who renewed the covenant under Nehemiah.

FIRST REFERENCE
NEHEMIAH 10:6
LAST REFERENCE
NEHEMIAH 12:16

GISPA 1
A Jewish exile of the Nethinims who resettled in Ophel.

ONLY REFERENCE
NEHEMIAH 11:21

GOG 11
1) A descendant of Abraham through Jacob's son Reuben.

ONLY REFERENCE
I CHRONICLES 5:4

2) A prince of Magog, a place perhaps in Scythia but certainly from the "north parts" (Ezekiel 39:2), against whom Ezekiel prophesied. God spoke of Gog's destruction and graves in Israel. In the book of Revelation, "Gog and Magog" refers to the Lord's last enemies.

FIRST REFERENCE
EZEKIEL 38:2
LAST REFERENCE
REVELATION 20:8

GOLIATH 6
Exile

A nine-foot-nine-inch-tall Philistine champion who was well armored and carried a spear that had a shaft like a weaver's beam. He challenged any Israelite to a fight; the losing nation would become the winner's servants. David fought Goliath with a slingshot and killed him and then cut off his head.

FIRST REFERENCE
I SAMUEL 17:4
LAST REFERENCE
I CHRONICLES 20:5

GOMER 5
Completion

1) Firstborn son of Japheth, Noah's son.

FIRST REFERENCE
GENESIS 10:2
LAST REFERENCE
I CHRONICLES 1:6

2) The unfaithful wife of the prophet Hosea. She represented the unfaithfulness of God's people. God told Hosea to redeem her from her lover and live with her again.

ONLY REFERENCE
HOSEA 1:3

GUNI 4
Protected

1) A descendant of Abraham through Jacob's son Naphtali.

FIRST REFERENCE
GENESIS 46:24
LAST REFERENCE
I CHRONICLES 7:13

2) A descendant of Abraham through Jacob's son Gad.

ONLY REFERENCE
I CHRONICLES 5:15

wicked. Habakkuk accepted God's judgment and glorified Him.

FIRST REFERENCE
HABAKKUK 1:1
LAST REFERENCE
HABAKKUK 3:1

HAAHASHTARI 1

Courier

A descendant of Abraham through Jacob's son Judah.

ONLY REFERENCE
1 CHRONICLES 4:6

HABAIAH 2

God has hidden

Forefather of an exile who returned to Jerusalem with Zerubbabel but lost his role as priest when his genealogical record could not be found.

FIRST REFERENCE
EZRA 2:6
LAST REFERENCE
NEHEMIAH 7:63

HABAKKUK 2

Embrace

An Old Testament minor prophet who served during the reign of King Josiah of Judah. He asked God why He was not delivering Israel and why the wicked seemed to win over the righteous. God replied that He would raise the Chaldeans against His sinful people and showed Habakkuk the profitlessness of the deeds of the

HABAZINIAH 1

Forefather of Jaazeniah, an obedient Rechabite whom God used as an example to Judah.

ONLY REFERENCE
JEREMIAH 35:3

HACHALIAH 2

Darkness of God

Father of the rebuilder of Jerusalem's walls, Nehemiah.

FIRST REFERENCE
NEHEMIAH 1:1
LAST REFERENCE
NEHEMIAH 10:1

HACHMONI 1

Skillful

Forefather of Jehiel, who was a tutor to King David's sons.

ONLY REFERENCE
1 CHRONICLES 27:32

HADAD 14

1) A king of Edom, "before there reigned any king over the children of Israel" (Genesis 36:31).

FIRST REFERENCE
GENESIS 36:35
LAST REFERENCE
1 CHRONICLES 1:47

2) Israel's Edomite adversary who arose after Solomon turned from the

Lord. Hadad formed a marauding band that attacked Israel for the rest of Solomon's reign.

FIRST REFERENCE
I KINGS 11:14
LAST REFERENCE
I KINGS 11:25

3) A descendant of Abraham through Ishmael, Abraham's son with his surrogate wife, Hagar.

ONLY REFERENCE
I CHRONICLES 1:30

4) Another king of Edom, "before there reigned any king over the children of Israel" (Genesis 36:31).

FIRST REFERENCE
I CHRONICLES 1:50
LAST REFERENCE
I CHRONICLES 1:51

HADADEZER 9

Hadad is his help

Syrian king of Zobah whose troops David defeated along with the Syrians of Damascus who supported Hadadezer. Same as Hadarezer.

FIRST REFERENCE
2 SAMUEL 8:3
LAST REFERENCE
I KINGS 11:23

HADAR 2

Magnificence

1) Eighth son of Ishmael.

ONLY REFERENCE
GENESIS 25:15

2) A king of Edom, "before there reigned any king over the children of Israel" (Genesis 36:31).

ONLY REFERENCE
GENESIS 36:39

HADAREZER 12

Hadad is his help

Syrian king of Zobar whom David defeated along with the Syrians of Damascus who supported him. Later, Hadarezer hired out his men to fight King David for the Ammonites. After they lost, Hadarezer made peace with Israel. Same as Hadadezer.

FIRST REFERENCE
2 SAMUEL 10:16
LAST REFERENCE
I CHRONICLES 19:19
KEY REFERENCES
I CHRONICLES 18:3–5; 19:6, 16

HADASSAH 1

Myrtle

An alternative name for Esther, the Jewish woman who became queen of Persia.

ONLY REFERENCE
ESTHER 2:7

HADLAI 1

Idle

A man of the tribe of Ephraim whose son Amasa counseled his nation of Israel against enslaving fellow Jews from Judah who were captured in a civil war.

ONLY REFERENCE
2 CHRONICLES 28:12

HADORAM 4

1) A descendant of Noah through Noah's son Shem.

FIRST REFERENCE
GENESIS 10:27
LAST REFERENCE
1 CHRONICLES 1:21

2) Son of Tou, king of Hamath, who sent Hadoram to congratulate King David on his victory over King Hadarezer.

ONLY REFERENCE
1 CHRONICLES 18:10

3) Taskmaster over forced labor for King Rehoboam of Israel. Hadoram was stoned to death by the Israelites.

ONLY REFERENCE
2 CHRONICLES 10:18

HAGAB 1

Locust

Forefather of an exiled family that returned to Judah under Zerubbabel. Same as Hagaba and Hagabah.

ONLY REFERENCE
EZRA 2:46

HAGABA 1

Locust

Forefather of an exiled family that returned to Judah under Zerubbabel. Same as Hagab and Hagabah.

ONLY REFERENCE
NEHEMIAH 7:48

HAGABAH 1

Locust

Forefather of an exiled family that returned to Judah under Zerubbabel. Same as Hagab and Hagaba.

ONLY REFERENCE
EZRA 2:45

HAGAR 12

Sarai's Egyptian maid who became a surrogate wife to Abram so he and Sarai could have a child. When Hagar conceived, she despised Sarai and fled from her. The angel of the Lord told Hagar to return and submit to Sarai. After Sarai's own child, Isaac, was born, she threw Hagar and her son, Ishmael, out of the camp. God provided Hagar with water in the wilderness and promised to make Ishmael into a great nation.

FIRST REFERENCE
GENESIS 16:1
LAST REFERENCE
GENESIS 25:12
KEY REFERENCES
GENESIS 16:1–2, 15; 21:10

HAGGAI 11

Festive

A prophet of Judah who wrote the book that bears his name. With the prophet Zechariah, he encouraged the disheartened Jews to continue in their efforts to rebuild the temple. During the era of Haggai's prophecies and the temple building project, the Jews prospered.

God promised this second temple would be greater than the original temple that Solomon had built.

FIRST REFERENCE
EZRA 5:1
LAST REFERENCE
HAGGAI 2:20
KEY REFERENCES
EZRA 6:14; HAGGAI 2:9–10

HAGGERI 1

Father of one of King David's valiant warriors.

ONLY REFERENCE
1 CHRONICLES 11:38

HAGGI 2
Festive

A descendant of Abraham through Jacob's son Gad.

FIRST REFERENCE
GENESIS 46:16
LAST REFERENCE
NUMBERS 26:15

HAGGIAH 1
Festival of God

A descendant of Abraham through Jacob's son Levi.

ONLY REFERENCE
1 CHRONICLES 6:30

HAGGITH 5
Festive

One of several wives of King David and mother of David's son Adonijah.

FIRST REFERENCE
2 SAMUEL 3:4
LAST REFERENCE
1 CHRONICLES 3:2

HAKKATAN 1
Small

Forefather of a Jewish exile who returned from Babylon to Judah under Ezra.

ONLY REFERENCE
EZRA 8:12

HAKKOZ 1
Thorn

One of twenty-four priests in David's time who was chosen by lot to serve in the tabernacle.

ONLY REFERENCE
1 CHRONICLES 24:10

HAKUPHA 2
Crooked

Forefather of an exiled family that returned to Judah under Zerubbabel.

FIRST REFERENCE
EZRA 2:51
LAST REFERENCE
NEHEMIAH 7:53

HALLOHESH 1
Enchanter

Father of a man who repaired Jerusalem's walls under Nehemiah. Same as Halohesh.

ONLY REFERENCE
NEHEMIAH 10:24

HALOHESH 1
Enchanter

Father of a man who repaired Jerusalem's walls under Nehemiah. Same as Hallohesh.

ONLY REFERENCE
NEHEMIAH 3:12

HAM 12
Hot

The youngest of Noah's three sons. After the flood, when Noah became drunk and lay naked in his tent, Ham looked on and reported it to his brothers. For this, Noah cursed Ham's youngest son and blessed the brothers who covered him without looking. Ham fathered four sons, from whom came many of Israel's worst enemies.

FIRST REFERENCE
GENESIS 5:32
LAST REFERENCE
I CHRONICLES 1:8
KEY REFERENCES
GENESIS 9:22–25; 10:6

HAMAN 53

King Ahasuerus's wicked counselor, who plotted to eradicate the Jews from the Persian kingdom. When Mordecai, the cousin of Ahasuerus's wife, Queen Esther, refused to bow before the king, Haman decided to destroy all the Jews. The counselor extracted permission from the king to create a law to that end. But Mordecai heard of his plan and reported it to the queen. When Haman came to the court one day, the king asked what should be done to honor a man in whom the king delighted. Thinking the king meant himself, Haman suggested that the man be dressed in the king's clothes, placed on a horse, and his good deeds proclaimed as he was led throughout the streets. To the counselor's horror, the king commanded him to do this for Haman's enemy, Mordecai. Queen Esther invited Haman and the king to a banquet. The proud counselor was honored until the second day of the feast, when the queen revealed the truth of his plans to the king. Ahasuerus, angry at the deceit of his counselor, had him hanged on the gallows that Haman had erected to destroy Mordecai.

FIRST REFERENCE
ESTHER 3:1
LAST REFERENCE
ESTHER 9:24
KEY REFERENCES
ESTHER 3:5–11

HAMMEDATHA 5

Father of Haman, the villain of the story of Esther.

FIRST REFERENCE
ESTHER 3:1
LAST REFERENCE
ESTHER 9:24

HAMMELECH 2 👤
King

Father of Jerameel and Malchiah. His sons imprisoned the prophet Jeremiah.

FIRST REFERENCE
JEREMIAH 36:26
LAST REFERENCE
JEREMIAH 38:6

HAMMOLEKETH 1 👩
Queen

Sister of Gilead and a descendant of Abraham through Joseph's son Manasseh.

ONLY REFERENCE
1 CHRONICLES 7:18

HAMOR 13 👤
Ass

A prince of Shechem whose son raped Dinah, Jacob's daughter. Hamor arranged a marriage, but Dinah's brothers, angered at the situation, killed all the men in the city.

FIRST REFERENCE
GENESIS 33:19
LAST REFERENCE
JUDGES 9:28
KEY REFERENCES
GENESIS 34:2, 8–10, 24–26

HAMUEL 1 👤
Anger of God

A descendant of Abraham through Jacob's son Simeon.

ONLY REFERENCE
1 CHRONICLES 4:26

HAMUL 3 👤
Pitied

A descendant of Abraham through Jacob's son Judah. Hamul founded the tribe of the Hamulites.

FIRST REFERENCE
GENESIS 46:12
LAST REFERENCE
1 CHRONICLES 2:5

HAMUTAL 3 👩
Father-in-law of dew

Mother of kings Jehoahaz and Zedekiah of Judah.

FIRST REFERENCE
2 KINGS 23:31
LAST REFERENCE
JEREMIAH 52:1

HANAMEEL 4 👤
God has favored

The prophet Jeremiah's cousin, from whom he bought land as a sign from God.

FIRST REFERENCE
JEREMIAH 32:7
LAST REFERENCE
JEREMIAH 32:12

HANAN 12 👤
Favor

1) A descendant of Abraham through Jacob's son Benjamin.

ONLY REFERENCE
1 CHRONICLES 8:23

2) A descendant of Abraham through Jacob's son Benjamin, in the line of King Saul and his son Jonathan.

3) One of King David's valiant warriors.

ONLY REFERENCE
I CHRONICLES 11:43

4) Forefather of an exiled family that returned to Judah under Zerubbabel.

FIRST REFERENCE
EZRA 2:46
LAST REFERENCE
NEHEMIAH 7:49

5) A Levite who helped Ezra to explain the law to exiles returned to Jerusalem.

ONLY REFERENCE
NEHEMIAH 8:7

6) A Levite who renewed the covenant under Nehemiah and became a temple treasurer.

FIRST REFERENCE
NEHEMIAH 10:10
LAST REFERENCE
NEHEMIAH 13:13

7) A Jewish leader who renewed the covenant under Nehemiah.

ONLY REFERENCE
NEHEMIAH 10:22

8) Another Jewish leader who renewed the covenant under Nehemiah.

ONLY REFERENCE
NEHEMIAH 10:26

9) A man of God in whose sons' chamber Jeremiah tested the obedience of the Rechabites.

ONLY REFERENCE
JEREMIAH 35:4

FIRST REFERENCE
I CHRONICLES 8:38
LAST REFERENCE
I CHRONICLES 9:44

HANANI 11 6
Gracious

1) A son of King David's musician Heman, who was "under the hands of [his] father for song in the house of the LORD" (1 Chronicles 25:6).

FIRST REFERENCE
I CHRONICLES 25:4
LAST REFERENCE
I CHRONICLES 25:25

2) A prophet who confronted Judah's king Asa for trusting his alliance with Syria more than trusting God. "The eyes of the LORD run to and fro throughout the whole earth, to shew himself strong in the behalf of them whose heart is perfect toward him," Hanani warned (2 Chronicles 16:9). Asa, furious, imprisoned Hanani.

ONLY REFERENCE
2 CHRONICLES 16:7

3) Father of King Jehu of Israel.

FIRST REFERENCE
I KINGS 16:1
LAST REFERENCE
2 CHRONICLES 20:34

4) An exiled Israelite priest who married a "strange" (foreign) woman.

ONLY REFERENCE
EZRA 10:20

5) A brother of the rebuilder of Jerusalem's walls, Nehemiah.

FIRST REFERENCE
NEHEMIAH 1:2
LAST REFERENCE
NEHEMIAH 7:2

6) A priest who helped to dedicate the rebuilt walls of Jerusalem by playing a musical instrument.

ONLY REFERENCE
NEHEMIAH 12:36

HANANIAH
God has favored

1) A son of King David's musician Heman, who was "under the hands of [his] father for song in the house of the LORD" (1 Chronicles 25:6).

FIRST REFERENCE
I CHRONICLES 25:4
LAST REFERENCE
I CHRONICLES 25:23

2) A commander under King Uzziah of Judah.

ONLY REFERENCE
2 CHRONICLES 26:11

3) Father of Zedekiah, one of the officials of King Jehoiakim of Judah.

ONLY REFERENCE
JEREMIAH 36:12

4) A false prophet who told King Zedekiah of Judah that the king of Babylon's yoke had been broken. He claimed that within two years, the temple vessels and King Jehoiakim's exiled son Jeconiah would be returned. Jeremiah was not convinced. God gave him a prophecy that denied Hananiah's and promised to take the false prophet's life within a year. Hananiah died in the seventh month.

FIRST REFERENCE
JEREMIAH 28:1
LAST REFERENCE
JEREMIAH 28:17

5) Forefather of a sentry who accused Jeremiah of deserting to the Chaldeans.

ONLY REFERENCE
JEREMIAH 37:13

6) A descendant of Abraham through Jacob's son Benjamin.

ONLY REFERENCE
I CHRONICLES 8:24

7) The Hebrew name of Daniel's friend better known as Shadrach.

FIRST REFERENCE
DANIEL 1:6
LAST REFERENCE
DANIEL 2:17

8) A descendant of Abraham through Jacob's son Judah, in the line of the nation of Judah's second-to-last king, Jeconiah (also known as Jehoiachin).

FIRST REFERENCE
I CHRONICLES 3:19
LAST REFERENCE
I CHRONICLES 3:21

9) An exiled Israelite who married a "strange" (foreign) woman.

ONLY REFERENCE
EZRA 10:28

10) Son of a perfume maker, Hananiah was a repairer of Jerusalem's walls under Nehemiah.

ONLY REFERENCE
NEHEMIAH 3:8

11) Another repairer of Jerusalem's walls under Nehemiah.

ONLY REFERENCE
NEHEMIAH 3:30

12) The overseer of Nehemiah's palace in Jerusalem, a "faithful man" given charge over the city's gates.

ONLY REFERENCE
NEHEMIAH 7:2

13) A Jewish leader who renewed the covenant under Nehemiah.

ONLY REFERENCE
NEHEMIAH 10:23

14) A priest who helped to dedicate the rebuilt wall of Jerusalem by giving thanks.

ONLY REFERENCE
NEHEMIAH 12:41

HANIEL
Favor of God

A descendant of Abraham through Jacob's son Asher.

ONLY REFERENCE
I CHRONICLES 7:39

HANNAH 13
Favored

Hannah could not bear a child, but her husband, Elkanah, loved her, though his second wife abused her. Distraught, Hannah went to the temple to pray and promised God that if He gave her a child, she would give the boy to Him for his whole life. As she fervently prayed in the temple, Eli the priest mistook her praying for drunkenness; then he discovered how wrong he had been. In time, Hannah conceived and bore Samuel. When he was weaned, the couple brought the boy to Eli to foster. Samuel became a powerful prophet of Israel who crowned Saul and David king.

FIRST REFERENCE
I SAMUEL 1:2
LAST REFERENCE
I SAMUEL 2:21
KEY REFERENCES
I SAMUEL 1:11; 15–16

HANNIEL 1
Favor of God

Prince of the tribe of Manasseh when the Israelites entered the Promised Land.

ONLY REFERENCE
NUMBERS 34:23

HANOCH 5
Initiated, favor of God

1) A descendant of Abraham by his second wife, Keturah. Same as Henoch (2).

ONLY REFERENCE
GENESIS 25:4

2) A descendant of Abraham through Jacob's son Reuben.

FIRST REFERENCE
GENESIS 46:9
LAST REFERENCE
I CHRONICLES 5:3

HANUN 11
Favored

1) An Ammonite king to whom David sent comforters after his father died. The princes of Ammon convinced Hanun these men were spies. So the new king shaved half their beards off, cut off half their clothing, and sent them home. Then Hanun hired Syrian warriors and unsuccessfully attacked Israel.

FIRST REFERENCE
2 SAMUEL 10:1
LAST REFERENCE
1 CHRONICLES 19:6

2) A man who repaired Jerusalem's walls under Nehemiah.

ONLY REFERENCE
NEHEMIAH 3:30

3) Another man who repaired Jerusalem's walls under Nehemiah. Hanun repaired the Valley Gate and "a thousand cubits" of the wall.

ONLY REFERENCE
NEHEMIAH 3:13

HARAN 9
Rest, mountaineer, parched

1) Brother of Abram. He died while they were still in Ur of the Chaldees. His son, Lot, traveled to Canaan with Abram and Sarai.

FIRST REFERENCE
GENESIS 11:26
LAST REFERENCE
GENESIS 11:31

2) A head Levite who was part of King David's religious-leadership reorganization.

ONLY REFERENCE
1 CHRONICLES 23:9

3) A descendant of Abraham through Jacob's son Judah.

ONLY REFERENCE
1 CHRONICLES 2:46

HARBONA 1

A eunuch serving the Persian king Ahasuerus in Esther's time. Same as Harbonah.

ONLY REFERENCE
ESTHER 1:10

HARBONAH 1

A eunuch serving the Persian king Ahasuerus in Esther's time. He informed the king of the gallows Haman had built for hanging Mordecai, gallows on which Haman himself was executed. Same as Harbona.

ONLY REFERENCE
ESTHER 7:9

HAREPH 1
Reproachful

A descendant of Abraham through Jacob's son Judah.

ONLY REFERENCE
1 CHRONICLES 2:51

HARHAIAH 1
Fearing God

Father of a man who repaired Jerusalem's walls under Nehemiah.

ONLY REFERENCE
NEHEMIAH 3:8

HARHAS 1
Shining

Grandfather of Shallum, husband of the prophetess Huldah in the days of King Josiah. Same as Hasrah.

ONLY REFERENCE
2 KINGS 22:14

HARHUR 2
Inflammation

Forefather of an exiled family that returned to Judah under Zerubbabel.

141

HARIM

Snub-nosed

1) One of twenty-four priests in David's time who was chosen by lot to serve in the tabernacle. Harim was also forefather of a man who repaired Jerusalem's walls under Nehemiah.

FIRST REFERENCE
I CHRONICLES 24:8
LAST REFERENCE
NEHEMIAH 12:15

2) Forefather of an exiled family that returned to Judah under Zerubbabel.

FIRST REFERENCE
EZRA 2:32
LAST REFERENCE
NEHEMIAH 7:35

3) Forefather of exiled Israelites who married "strange" (foreign) women.

ONLY REFERENCE
EZRA 10:31

4) A priest who renewed the covenant under Nehemiah.

ONLY REFERENCE
NEHEMIAH 10:5

5) A Jewish leader who renewed the covenant under Nehemiah.

ONLY REFERENCE
NEHEMIAH 10:27

HARIPH

Autumnal

1) Forefather of an exiled family that returned to Judah under Zerubbabel.

ONLY REFERENCE
NEHEMIAH 7:24

2) A Jewish leader who renewed the covenant under Nehemiah.

ONLY REFERENCE
NEHEMIAH 10:19

HARNEPHER

A descendant of Abraham through Jacob's son Asher.

ONLY REFERENCE
I CHRONICLES 7:36

HAROEH

Prophet

A descendant of Abraham through Jacob's son Judah.

ONLY REFERENCE
I CHRONICLES 2:52

HARSHA

Magician

Forefather of an exiled family that returned to Judah under Zerubbabel.

FIRST REFERENCE
EZRA 2:52
LAST REFERENCE
NEHEMIAH 7:54

HARUM

High

A descendant of Abraham through Jacob's son Judah.

ONLY REFERENCE
I CHRONICLES 4:8

HARUMAPH

Snub-nosed

Father of a man who repaired Jerusalem's walls under Nehemiah.

ONLY REFERENCE
NEHEMIAH 3:10

HARUZ

Earnest

Grandfather of King Amon of Judah.

ONLY REFERENCE
2 KINGS 21:19

HASADIAH

God has favored

A descendant of Abraham through Jacob's son Judah, in the line of the nation of Judah's second-to-last king, Jeconiah (also known as Jehoiachin).

ONLY REFERENCE
I CHRONICLES 3:20

HASENUAH

Pointed

Forefather of a Jewish exile from the tribe of Benjamin who resettled Jerusalem.

ONLY REFERENCE
I CHRONICLES 9:7

HASHABIAH   15

God has regarded

1) A descendant of Levi who stood next to Heman, the choir leader, in the temple.

ONLY REFERENCE
I CHRONICLES 6:45

2) Forefather of a Jewish exile from the tribe of Levi who resettled Jerusalem.

ONLY REFERENCE
I CHRONICLES 9:14

3) A son of King David's musician Jeduthun, "who prophesied with a harp, to give thanks and to praise the Lord" (1 Chronicles 25:3).

FIRST REFERENCE
I CHRONICLES 25:3
LAST REFERENCE
I CHRONICLES 25:19

4) A Hebronite who controlled Israel west of the Jordan River under King David's reorganization.

ONLY REFERENCE
I CHRONICLES 26:30

5) Leader of the tribe of Levi in the days of King David.

ONLY REFERENCE
I CHRONICLES 27:17

6) A descendant of Abraham through Jacob's son Levi. Hashabiah was among those who distributed sacrificial animals to fellow Levites preparing to celebrate the Passover under King Josiah.

ONLY REFERENCE
2 CHRONICLES 35:9

7) A Levite whom Ezra called to serve in the temple upon his return to Jerusalem.

ONLY REFERENCE
EZRA 8:19

8) A priest trusted by Ezra to carry money and temple vessels to Israel.

ONLY REFERENCE
EZRA 8:24

9) A rebuilder of the walls of Jerusalem under Nehemiah.

ONLY REFERENCE
NEHEMIAH 3:17

10) A Levite who renewed the covenant under Nehemiah.

ONLY REFERENCE
NEHEMIAH 10:11

11) Forefather of a Levite who returned to Jerusalem.

ONLY REFERENCE
NEHEMIAH 11:15

12) Forefather of a Levite overseer in Jerusalem after the Babylonian Exile.

ONLY REFERENCE
NEHEMIAH 11:22

13) Forefather of a priest who returned to Jerusalem under Zerubbabel.

ONLY REFERENCE
NEHEMIAH 12:21

14) A chief of the Levites in the time of Nehemiah.

ONLY REFERENCE
NEHEMIAH 12:24

HASHABNAH 1
Inventiveness

One of a group of Levites who led a revival among the Israelites in the time of Nehemiah.

ONLY REFERENCE
NEHEMIAH 10:25

HASHABNIAH 2
Thought of God

1) Father of a man who repaired Jerusalem's walls under Nehemiah.

ONLY REFERENCE
NEHEMIAH 3:10

2) A Levite worship leader when the Israelites confessed their sins following the Babylonian Exile.

ONLY REFERENCE
NEHEMIAH 9:5

HASHBADANA 1
Considerate judge

A priest who assisted Ezra in reading the book of the law to the people of Jerusalem.

ONLY REFERENCE
NEHEMIAH 8:4

HASHEM 1
Wealthy

Father of several of King David's valiant warriors.

ONLY REFERENCE
1 CHRONICLES 11:34

HASHUB 4
Intelligent

1) Forefather of a Levite who oversaw the outside work of the rebuilt temple.

ONLY REFERENCE
NEHEMIAH 11:15

2) A man who repaired Jerusalem's walls under Nehemiah. Hashub helped to rebuild "the tower of the furnaces."

ONLY REFERENCE
NEHEMIAH 3:11

3) Another man who repaired Jerusalem's walls under Nehemiah.

ONLY REFERENCE
NEHEMIAH 3:23

4) A Jewish leader who renewed the covenant under Nehemiah.

ONLY REFERENCE
NEHEMIAH 10:23

HASHUBAH 1
Estimation

A descendant of Abraham through Jacob's son Judah, in the line of the nation of Judah's second-to-last king, Jeconiah (also known as Jehoiachin).

ONLY REFERENCE
1 CHRONICLES 3:20

HASHUM 5
Enriched

1) Forefather of an exiled family that returned to Judah under Zerubbabel.

FIRST REFERENCE
EZRA 2:19
LAST REFERENCE
NEHEMIAH 7:22

2) A priest who assisted Ezra in reading the book of the law to the people of Jerusalem.

ONLY REFERENCE
NEHEMIAH 8:4

3) A Jewish leader who renewed the covenant under Nehemiah.

ONLY REFERENCE
NEHEMIAH 10:18

HASHUPHA 1
Nakedness

Forefather of an exiled family that returned to Judah under Zerubbabel.

ONLY REFERENCE
NEHEMIAH 7:46

HASRAH 1
Want

Grandfather of Shallum, husband of the prophetess Huldah in the days of King Josiah. Same as Harhas.

ONLY REFERENCE
2 CHRONICLES 34:22

HASSENAAH 1
Thorny

Father of several men who repaired Jerusalem's walls under Nehemiah.

ONLY REFERENCE
NEHEMIAH 3:3

HASSHUB
Intelligent

Forefather of a Levite exile to Babylon who resettled Jersualem.

ONLY REFERENCE
1 CHRONICLES 9:14

HASUPHA
Nakedness

Forefather of an exiled family that returned to Judah under Zerubbabel.

ONLY REFERENCE
EZRA 2:43

HATACH

One of King Ahasuerus's eunuchs, who attended Queen Esther. He acted as a messenger between her and Mordecai when Mordecai discovered Haman's plot.

FIRST REFERENCE
ESTHER 4:5
LAST REFERENCE
ESTHER 4:10

HATHATH
Dismay

A descendant of Abraham through Jacob's son Judah.

ONLY REFERENCE
1 CHRONICLES 4:13

HATIPHA
Robber

Forefather of an exiled family that returned to Judah under Zerubbabel.

FIRST REFERENCE
EZRA 2:54
LAST REFERENCE
NEHEMIAH 7:56

HATITA
Explorer

Forefather of an exiled family that returned to Judah under Zerubbabel.

FIRST REFERENCE
EZRA 2:42
LAST REFERENCE
NEHEMIAH 7:45

HATTIL
Fluctuating

Forefather of an exiled family—former servants of Solomon—that returned to Judah under Zerubbabel.

FIRST REFERENCE
EZRA 2:57
LAST REFERENCE
NEHEMIAH 7:59

HATTUSH

1) A descendant of Abraham through Jacob's son Judah, in the line of the nation of Judah's second-to-last king, Jeconiah (also known as Jehoiachin).

ONLY REFERENCE
1 CHRONICLES 3:22

2) An exiled priest who returned to Judah under Zerubbabel.

ONLY REFERENCE
EZRA 8:2

3) A priest who returned to Israel with Zerrubbabel.

ONLY REFERENCE
NEHEMIAH 12:12

4) A rebuilder of the walls of Jerusalem under Nehemiah.

ONLY REFERENCE
NEHEMIAH 3:10

5) A priest who renewed the covenant under Nehemiah.

ONLY REFERENCE
NEHEMIAH 10:4

HAVILAH 4
Circular

1) A descendant of Noah through his son Ham.

FIRST REFERENCE
GENESIS 10:7
LAST REFERENCE
I CHRONICLES 1:9

2) A descendant of Noah through his son Shem.

FIRST REFERENCE
GENESIS 10:29
LAST REFERENCE
I CHRONICLES 1:23

HAZAEL 23
God has seen

A king of Syria anointed to his position by Elijah. While Hazael served the Syrian king Ben-hadad, he was sent to Elisha to ask if the king would recover from an illness. Elisha replied that he would recover but told Hazael he would die. Hazael suffocated Ben-hadad and took his throne. Throughout his reign Hazael fought Israel and Judah. King Jehoash of Judah bribed him not to attack Jerusalem. Because Jehoash did not obey God, he continually fought Hazael and his son, Ben-hadad. Hazael oppressed Israel through King Jehoahaz's reign.

FIRST REFERENCE
I KINGS 19:15
LAST REFERENCE
AMOS 1:4
KEY REFERENCES
I KINGS 19:15; 2 KINGS 8:8–10; 12:18; 13:22

HAZAIAH I
God has seen

A Jewish exile from the tribe of Judah who resettled Jerusalem.

ONLY REFERENCE
NEHEMIAH 11:5

HAZARMAVETH 2
Village of death

A descendant of Noah through his son Shem.

FIRST REFERENCE
GENESIS 10:26
LAST REFERENCE
I CHRONICLES 1:20

HAZELELPONI I
Shade-facing

A descendant of Abraham through Jacob's son Judah.

ONLY REFERENCE
I CHRONICLES 4:3

HAZIEL I
Seen of God

A chief Levite who was part of King David's religious-leadership reorganization.

ONLY REFERENCE
I CHRONICLES 23:9

HAZO
Seer

A son of Nahor, Abraham's brother.

ONLY REFERENCE
GENESIS 22:22

HEBER
Community, across

1) A descendant of Abraham through Jacob's son Asher.

FIRST REFERENCE
GENESIS 46:17
LAST REFERENCE
LUKE 3:35
GENEALOGY OF JESUS
LUKE 3:35

2) Called Heber the Kenite, he was the husband of Jael, the woman who killed the Canaanite commander Sisera.

FIRST REFERENCE
JUDGES 4:11
LAST REFERENCE
JUDGES 5:24

3) A descendant of Abraham through Jacob's son Judah.

ONLY REFERENCE
I CHRONICLES 4:18

4) A descendant of Abraham through Jacob's son Benjamin.

ONLY REFERENCE
I CHRONICLES 8:17

5) A descendant of Abraham through Jacob's son Gad.

ONLY REFERENCE
I CHRONICLES 5:13

6) Another descendant of Abraham through Jacob's son Benjamin.

ONLY REFERENCE
I CHRONICLES 8:22

HEBRON
Association

1) A descendant of Abraham through Jacob's son Levi.

FIRST REFERENCE
EXODUS 6:18
LAST REFERENCE
I CHRONICLES 24:23

2) A descendant of Abraham through Jacob and Caleb the brother of Jerahmeel.

FIRST REFERENCE
I CHRONICLES 2:42
LAST REFERENCE
I CHRONICLES 15:9

HEGAI

The keeper of the harem for King Ahasuerus of Persia. He treated Esther preferentially, and she took his advice on what to take when she went to the king. Same as Hege.

FIRST REFERENCE
ESTHER 2:8
LAST REFERENCE
ESTHER 2:15

HEGE

An alternative name for Hegai, servant of the Persian king Ahasuerus.

ONLY REFERENCE
ESTHER 2:3

HELAH
Rust

Wife of Ashur, a descendant of Abraham through Jacob's son Judah.

FIRST REFERENCE
I CHRONICLES 4:5
LAST REFERENCE
I CHRONICLES 4:7

HELDAI 2
Worldliness

1) A commander in King David's army overseeing twenty-four thousand men in the twelfth month of each year.

ONLY REFERENCE
I CHRONICLES 27:15

2) Forefather of a family of Jewish exiles in Babylon who participated in a symbolic crowning of the future Messiah by the prophet Zechariah. Same as Helem (2).

ONLY REFERENCE
ZECHARIAH 6:10

HELEB 1
Fatness

One of King David's valiant warriors. Same as Heled.

ONLY REFERENCE
2 SAMUEL 23:29

HELED 1
To glide

One of King David's valiant warriors. Same as Heleb.

ONLY REFERENCE
I CHRONICLES 11:30

HELEK 2
Portion

A descendant of Abraham through Jacob's son Joseph.

FIRST REFERENCE
NUMBERS 26:30
LAST REFERENCE
JOSHUA 17:2

HELEM 2
Dream

1) A descendant of Abraham through Jacob's son Asher.

ONLY REFERENCE
I CHRONICLES 7:35

2) Forefather of a family of Jewish exiles who participated in a symbolic crowning of the future Messiah by the prophet Zechariah. Same as Heldai (2).

ONLY REFERENCE
ZECHARIAH 6:14

HELEZ 5
Strength

1) A commander in King David's army overseeing twenty-four thousand men in the seventh month of each year.

FIRST REFERENCE
2 SAMUEL 23:26
LAST REFERENCE
I CHRONICLES 27:10

2) A descendant of Abraham through Jacob's son Judah. Helez descended from the line of an unnamed Israelite woman and her Egyptian husband, Jarha.

ONLY REFERENCE
I CHRONICLES 2:39

HELI 1
Lofty

Father of Jesus' earthly father, Joseph.

ONLY REFERENCE
LUKE 3:23
GENEALOGY OF JESUS
LUKE 3:23

HELKAI 1

Apportioned

Forefather of a priest who returned to Jerusalem under Zerubbabel.

ONLY REFERENCE
NEHEMIAH 12:15

HELON 5

Strong

Father of a prince of Zebulun who helped Moses take a census of his tribe.

FIRST REFERENCE
NUMBERS 1:9
LAST REFERENCE
NUMBERS 10:16

HEMAM 1

Raging

A descendant of Seir, who lived in Esau's "land of Edom."

ONLY REFERENCE
GENESIS 36:22

HEMAN 16

Faithful

1) A wise man, the son of Mahol, mentioned in comparison to Solomon's wisdom.

FIRST REFERENCE
I KINGS 4:31
LAST REFERENCE
I CHRONICLES 2:6

2) A descendant of Abraham through Jacob's son Levi. Heman was one of the key musicians serving in the Jerusalem temple. King David appointed Heman's descendants to "prophesy with harps, with psalteries, and with cymbals" (1 Chronicles 25:1).

FIRST REFERENCE
I CHRONICLES 6:33
LAST REFERENCE
PSALM 88 (TITLE)

HEMATH 1

Walled

A descendant of Abraham through Jacob's son Judah.

ONLY REFERENCE
I CHRONICLES 2:55

HEMDAN 1

Pleasant

A descendant of Seir, who lived in Esau's "land of Edom."

ONLY REFERENCE
GENESIS 36:26

HEN 1

Grace

A son of Zephaniah who received a memorial crown in the temple.

ONLY REFERENCE
ZECHARIAH 6:14

HENADAD 4

Favor of Hadad

Father of a man who repaired Jerusalem's walls and led a revival under Nehemiah.

FIRST REFERENCE
EZRA 3:9
LAST REFERENCE
NEHEMIAH 10:9

HENOCH 2
Initiated

1) A descendant of Seth, son of Adam. "Enoch walked with God: and he was not; for God took him" (Genesis 5:24). He was immediately translated into eternity. Same as Enoch (2).

ONLY REFERENCE
1 CHRONICLES 1:3

2) A descendant of Abraham by his second wife, Keturah. Same as Hanoch (1).

ONLY REFERENCE
1 CHRONICLES 1:33

HEPHER 7
Shame

1) A descendant of Abraham through Jacob's son Joseph.

FIRST REFERENCE
NUMBERS 26:32
LAST REFERENCE
JOSHUA 17:3

2) A descendant of Abraham through Jacob's son Judah.

ONLY REFERENCE
1 CHRONICLES 4:6

3) One of King David's valiant warriors.

ONLY REFERENCE
1 CHRONICLES 11:36

HEPHZIBAH 1
My delight is in her

Wife of Judah's good king Hezekiah and mother of the evil king Manasseh.

ONLY REFERENCE
2 KINGS 21:1

HERESH 1
Magical craft

A Jewish exile from the tribe of Levi who resettled Jerusalem.

ONLY REFERENCE
1 CHRONICLES 9:15

HERMAS 1
To utter

A Christian acquaintance of the apostle Paul, greeted in Paul's letter to the Romans.

ONLY REFERENCE
ROMANS 16:14

HERMES 1
To utter

A Christian acquaintance of the apostle Paul, greeted in Paul's letter to the Romans.

ONLY REFERENCE
ROMANS 16:14

HERMOGENES 1
Born of Hermes

An Asian Christian who turned away from Paul.

ONLY REFERENCE
2 TIMOTHY 1:15

HEROD 44
Heroic

1) Known as Herod the Great, this evil king of Judea killed several of his own sons and completed many building projects, including improvements on the temple. He was much hated by those he ruled.

When the wise men from the East appeared, looking for the king of the Jews, Herod feared for his throne and killed all the male toddlers and infants in Bethlehem. But Joseph and his family had escaped into Egypt. Upon Herod's death, Joseph, Mary, and Jesus returned from Egypt but, fearing to live in the land ruled by his son, moved to Nazareth.

FIRST REFERENCE
MATTHEW 2:1
LAST REFERENCE
ACTS 23:35

2) Herod Antipas, son of Herod the Great, ruled as tetrarch of Galilee and Perea. John the Baptist opposed Antipas's marriage to Herodias, Antipas's brother's wife, saying that their union was unlawful. When the ruler's stepdaughter danced publicly and pleased him, Herod offered her whatever she wanted. He sorrowfully fulfilled her request—John the Baptist's head on a plate. Hearing of Jesus' miracles, he believed John had returned from the dead. When Pilate learned that Jesus was from Galilee, he passed him on to Herod to judge. Herod mocked Him and dressed Him in fine clothing. The two rulers became friends that day.

FIRST REFERENCE
MATTHEW 14:1
LAST REFERENCE
ACTS 12:21

3) Grandson of Herod the Great who ruled over the tetrarchy of Philip and Lysanias, Herod Agrippa I had the apostle James killed and arrested. Seeing that this pleased the Jewish leaders, he also imprisoned Peter. Herod Agrippa died suddenly and horribly when the people of Tyre and Sidon declared him a god and he did not correct them.

FIRST REFERENCE
ACTS 12:1
LAST REFERENCE
ACTS 13:1

4) Son of Herod Agrippa I, he ruled over the tetrarchy of Philip and Lysanias. This Herod (Herod Agrippa II) had an incestuous relationship with his sister Bernice, with whom he heard Paul's case with Porcius Festus. Paul almost convinced him to become a Christian. Same as Agrippa.

FIRST REFERENCE
ACTS 25:13
LAST REFERENCE
ACTS 26:28

HERODIAS 6
Heroic

Granddaughter of Herod the Great whose second marriage was opposed by John the Baptist. When Herodias's daughter asked what she should request from Herod Antipas, she pushed her to ask for John the Baptist's head on a plate.

HERODION   1

Heroic

A relative of the apostle Paul whom Paul greeted in his letter to the Romans.

ONLY REFERENCE
ROMANS 16:11

HESED   1

Favor

Father of one of King Solomon's twelve officials over provisions.

ONLY REFERENCE
1 KINGS 4:10

HETH   14

Terror

A descendant of Noah through his son Ham. Abraham bought a burial site for his wife, Sarah, from the descendants of Heth.

FIRST REFERENCE
GENESIS 10:15
LAST REFERENCE
1 CHRONICLES 1:13

HEZEKI   1

Strong

A descendant of Abraham through Jacob's son Benjamin.

ONLY REFERENCE
1 CHRONICLES 8:17

HEZEKIAH   128

Strengthened of God

1) King of Judah, son of Ahaz, who did right in God's eyes. Hezekiah removed pagan worship from the kingdom and kept God's commandments. Under his command, the Levites cleansed the temple and worship was restored. When the Assyrian king Sennacherib attacked his nation, Hezekiah gave him a large tribute. Sennacherib sent officials to confer with Hezekiah's aides and try to convince his people to side with Sennacherib against their king and God. As Assyria threatened, Isaiah brought the king a comforting prophecy. Sennacherib sent a message to Hezekiah that belittled God and threatened Judah. Hezekiah brought the letter before God and asked Him to save Judah. Again, Isaiah prophesied the Assyrians' fall. Hezekiah became ill to the point of death, and Isaiah told him he would not recover. After weeping and praying, the king received a message from the prophet that God had extended his life by fifteen years and would deliver and defend Jerusalem from its enemies. Isaiah confirmed this with the sign of a shadow moving back ten steps.

After Hezekiah showed the emissaries of the king of Babylon all that was in his house, Isaiah told him everything in his house would be carried away to that land. His sons would also be taken away and made eunuchs to the Babylonian king. Same as Ezekias.

FIRST REFERENCE
2 KINGS 16:20
LAST REFERENCE
MICAH 1:1
KEY REFERENCES
2 KINGS 18:1–7; 19:4–7; 20:9–11

2) A descendant of Abraham through Jacob's son Judah, in the line of the nation of Judah's third-to-last king, Jeconiah (also known as Jehoiachin).

ONLY REFERENCE
1 CHRONICLES 3:23

3) Forefather of an exiled family that returned to Judah under Zerubbabel.

FIRST REFERENCE
EZRA 2:16
LAST REFERENCE
NEHEMIAH 7:21

HEZION

Vision

Grandfather of Ben-hadad, the king of Syria in the days of Judah's king Asa.

ONLY REFERENCE
1 KINGS 15:18

HEZIR 2

Protected

1) One of twenty-four priests in David's time who was chosen by lot to serve in the tabernacle.

ONLY REFERENCE
1 CHRONICLES 24:15

2) A Jewish leader who renewed the covenant under Nehemiah.

ONLY REFERENCE
NEHEMIAH 10:20

HEZRAI 1

Enclosure

One of King David's valiant warriors. Same as Hezro.

ONLY REFERENCE
2 SAMUEL 23:35

HEZRO 1

Enclosure

One of King David's valiant warriors. Same as Hezrai.

ONLY REFERENCE
1 CHRONICLES 11:37

HEZRON 16

Courtyard

1) A descendant of Abraham through Jacob's son Judah.

FIRST REFERENCE
GENESIS 46:12
LAST REFERENCE
1 CHRONICLES 4:1

2) A descendant of Abraham through Jacob's son Reuben.

FIRST REFERENCE
GENESIS 46:9
LAST REFERENCE
1 CHRONICLES 5:3

HIDDAI 1

One of King David's warriors known as the "mighty men."

ONLY REFERENCE
2 SAMUEL 23:30

HIEL 1
Living of God

The rebuilder of Jericho. Joshua's prophecy was fulfilled (Joshua 6:26) as Hiel rebuilt the city at the cost of two of his sons' lives.

ONLY REFERENCE
1 KINGS 16:34

HILKIAH 34
Portion of God

1) A priest and father of Eliakim. His son met King Sennacherib's messengers for King Hezekiah of Judah.

FIRST REFERENCE
2 KINGS 18:18
LAST REFERENCE
ISAIAH 36:22

2) High priest during the reign of King Josiah of Judah. He oversaw the counting of the money collected for the work of restoring the temple, discovered the book of the law, and consulted the prophetess Huldah about the discovery.

FIRST REFERENCE
2 KINGS 22:4
LAST REFERENCE
JEREMIAH 29:3
KEY REFERENCE
2 KINGS 22:8

3) Forefather of Asaph, a chief singer in the temple.

ONLY REFERENCE
1 CHRONICLES 6:45

4) A Levite "porter" (doorkeeper) in the house of the Lord.

ONLY REFERENCE
1 CHRONICLES 26:11

5) A priest who assisted Ezra in reading the book of the law to the people of Jerusalem.

FIRST REFERENCE
NEHEMIAH 8:4
LAST REFERENCE
NEHEMIAH 12:7

6) Father of the prophet Jeremiah.

ONLY REFERENCE
JEREMIAH 1:1

HILLEL 2
Praising

Father of Israel's twelfth judge, Abdon.

FIRST REFERENCE
JUDGES 12:13
LAST REFERENCE
JUDGES 12:15

HIRAH 2
Splendor

A man from Adullam who became Judah's friend.

FIRST REFERENCE
GENESIS 38:1
LAST REFERENCE
GENESIS 38:12

HIRAM 23
Milk

1) A king of Tyre who provided cedar trees and workmen for building in Israel. "Hiram was ever a lover of David" (1 Kings 5:1) and offered David cedar trees and workmen to build a home. As he prepared to build the temple, Solomon ordered cedar and cypress from Hiram. The two men made a treaty, and Solomon gave Hiram twenty cities in Galilee. When Solomon built a

fleet of ships, Hiram provided experienced seamen to aid Solomon's sailors. Hiram's own fleet brought back almug wood, which was used to make supports for the temple.

FIRST REFERENCE
2 SAMUEL 5:11
LAST REFERENCE
1 CHRONICLES 14:1
KEY REFERENCES
1 KINGS 5:1, 8

2) A skilled craftsman who was especially gifted in working brass. He came from Tyre to help build Solomon's house and make utensils for the temple.

FIRST REFERENCE
1 KINGS 7:13
LAST REFERENCE
1 KINGS 7:45

HIZKIAH 1
Strengthened of God

An ancestor of the prophet Zephaniah.

ONLY REFERENCE
ZEPHANIAH 1:1

HIZKIJAH 1
Strengthened of God

A Jewish leader who renewed the covenant under Nehemiah.

ONLY REFERENCE
NEHEMIAH 10:17

HOBAB 2
Cherished

Father-in-law of Moses. Same as Jethro.

FIRST REFERENCE
NUMBERS 10:29
LAST REFERENCE
JUDGES 4:11

HOD 1
How?

A descendant of Abraham through Jacob's son Asher.

ONLY REFERENCE
1 CHRONICLES 7:37

HODAIAH 1
Majesty of God

A descendant of Abraham through Jacob's son Judah, in the line of the nation of Judah's second-to-last king, Jeconiah (also known as Jehoiachin).

ONLY REFERENCE
1 CHRONICLES 3:24

HODAVIAH 3
Majesty of God

1) One of the "mighty men of valour, famous men" leading the half tribe of Manasseh.

ONLY REFERENCE
1 CHRONICLES 5:24

2) A descendant of Abraham through Jacob's son Benjamin.

ONLY REFERENCE
1 CHRONICLES 9:7

3) Forefather of an exiled family that returned to Judah under Zerubbabel.

ONLY REFERENCE
EZRA 2:40

HODESH 1
A month

Third wife of Shaharaim, with whom she had children in Moab.

ONLY REFERENCE
1 CHRONICLES 8:9

HODEVAH
Majesty of God

Forefather of an exiled family that returned to Judah under Zerubbabel.

ONLY REFERENCE
NEHEMIAH 7:43

HODIAH
Celebrated

Wife of Mered, a descendant of Abraham through Jacob's son Judah.

ONLY REFERENCE
1 CHRONICLES 4:19

HODIJAH 5
Celebrated

1) A Levite who helped Ezra to explain the law to exiles returned to Jerusalem. Hodijah was among a group of Levites who led a revival among the Israelites in the time of Nehemiah.

FIRST REFERENCE
NEHEMIAH 8:7
LAST REFERENCE
NEHEMIAH 10:13

2) A Jewish leader who renewed the covenant under Nehemiah.

ONLY REFERENCE
NEHEMIAH 10:18

HOGLAH 4
Partridge

One of five daughters of Zelophehad, an Israelite who died during the wilderness wanderings. The women asked Moses if they could inherit their father's property in the Promised Land (a right normally reserved for sons), and God ruled that they should.

FIRST REFERENCE
NUMBERS 26:33
LAST REFERENCE
JOSHUA 17:3

HOHAM

A pagan king of Hebron during Joshua's conquest of the Promised Land, Hoham allied with four other rulers to attack Gibeon, which had deceptively made a peace treaty with the Israelites. Joshua's soldiers defeated the five armies, and Joshua executed the allied kings.

ONLY REFERENCE
JOSHUA 10:3

HOMAM
Raging

A descendant of Seir, who lived in Esau's "land of Edom."

ONLY REFERENCE
1 CHRONICLES 1:39

HOPHNI 5
Pugilist

Son of the high priest Eli, who had honored Hophni and his brother Phinehas more than the Lord. The brothers did not know the Lord, misused their priestly office, and disobeyed the law. A man of God prophesied that they would die on the same day. When the Philistines attacked and took the ark of the covenant, both Hophni and Phinehas were killed.

FIRST REFERENCE
I SAMUEL 1:3
LAST REFERENCE
I SAMUEL 4:17

HORAM 1
High

A king of Gezer who was killed, along with all of his people, by Joshua's army during the conquest of the Promised Land.

ONLY REFERENCE
JOSHUA 10:33

HORI 4 2
Cave dweller

1) A descendant of Seir, who lived in Esau's "land of Edom."

FIRST REFERENCE
GENESIS 36:22
LAST REFERENCE
I CHRONICLES 1:39

2) Father of one of the twelve spies sent by Moses to spy out the land of Canaan.

ONLY REFERENCE
NUMBERS 13:5

HOSAH 4
Hopeful

A Levite who was chosen by lot to guard the west side of the house of the Lord.

FIRST REFERENCE
I CHRONICLES 16:38
LAST REFERENCE
I CHRONICLES 26:16

HOSEA 3
Deliverer

A minor prophet told by God to marry a prostitute named Gomer. She took a lover and ran from him. God told Hosea to go to her and win her back. The prophet's tumultuous family life paralleled the unfaithfulness of the people of Israel, who had abandoned their covenant with God. The three children born during Hosea's marriage had symbolic names that pointed out Israel's sin. In the Old Testament book that bears his name, Hosea called God's people away from idolatry and back into an intimate relationship with Him.

FIRST REFERENCE
HOSEA 1:1
LAST REFERENCE
HOSEA 1:2

HOSHAIAH 3
God has saved

1) A prince of Judah who participated in the dedication of Jerusalem's rebuilt walls.

ONLY REFERENCE
NEHEMIAH 12:32

2) Captain of the Israelite forces and father of Azariah (27) who refused to believe Jeremiah's warning not to escape into Egypt.

FIRST REFERENCE
JEREMIAH 42:1
LAST REFERENCE
JEREMIAH 43:2

HOSHAMA I
Jehovah has heard

A descendant of Abraham through Jacob's son Judah, in the line of the nation of Judah's third-to-last king, Jeconiah (also known as Jehoiachin).

ONLY REFERENCE
1 CHRONICLES 3:18

HOSHEA II
Deliverer

1) Another name of Joshua, successor to Moses as leader of Israel.

ONLY REFERENCE
DEUTERONOMY 32:44

2) Leader of the tribe of Ephraim in the days of King David.

ONLY REFERENCE
1 CHRONICLES 27:20

3) The Israelite who conspired against King Pekah, killed him, and took his throne. He became a vassal to King Shalmaneser of Assyria but sent messengers to the king of Egypt. Shalmaneser imprisoned Hoshea, captured Samaria, and carried the Israelites off to Assyria.

FIRST REFERENCE
2 KINGS 15:30
LAST REFERENCE
2 KINGS 18:10

4) A Jewish leader who renewed the covenant under Nehemiah.

ONLY REFERENCE
NEHEMIAH 10:23

HOTHAM I
Seal

A descendant of Abraham through Jacob's son Asher.

ONLY REFERENCE
1 CHRONICLES 7:32

HOTHAN I
Seal

Father of one of King David's valiant warriors.

ONLY REFERENCE
1 CHRONICLES 11:44

HOTHIR 2
He has caused to remain

A son of King David's musician Heman, who was "under the hands of [his] father for song in the house of the LORD" (1 Chronicles 25:6).

FIRST REFERENCE
1 CHRONICLES 25:4
LAST REFERENCE
1 CHRONICLES 25:28

HUL 2
Circle

A descendant of Noah through his son Shem.

FIRST REFERENCE
GENESIS 10:23
LAST REFERENCE
1 CHRONICLES 1:17

HULDAH 2
Weasel

A prophetess who spoke to King Josiah's messengers about a coming judgment of God on Judah. Because King Josiah had heard the book of the law and responded to it, she told him God would defer judgment until after his death.

FIRST REFERENCE
2 KINGS 22:14
LAST REFERENCE
2 CHRONICLES 34:22

HUPHAM 1
Protection

A descendant of Abraham through Jacob's son Benjamin.

ONLY REFERENCE
NUMBERS 26:39

HUPPAH 1
Canopy

One of twenty-four priests in David's time who was chosen by lot to serve in the tabernacle.

ONLY REFERENCE
1 CHRONICLES 24:13

HUPPIM 3
Canopies

A descendant of Abraham through Jacob's son Benjamin.

FIRST REFERENCE
GENESIS 46:21
LAST REFERENCE
1 CHRONICLES 7:15

HUR 16
White

1) An Israelite who held up Moses' hand as the battle against the Amalekites raged so Israel could win. With Aaron, he ruled Israel while Moses was on Mount Sinai.

FIRST REFERENCE
EXODUS 17:10
LAST REFERENCE
EXODUS 24:14

2) Father of a craftsman who devised metal and stone designs for the tabernacle.

FIRST REFERENCE
EXODUS 31:2
LAST REFERENCE
2 CHRONICLES 1:5

3) A Midianite king killed by the Israelites at God's command to Moses.

FIRST REFERENCE
NUMBERS 31:8
LAST REFERENCE
JOSHUA 13:21

4) Father of one of King Solomon's twelve officials over provisions.

ONLY REFERENCE
1 KINGS 4:8

5) Father of Caleb (1), who spied out the land of Canaan.

FIRST REFERENCE
1 CHRONICLES 2:50
LAST REFERENCE
1 CHRONICLES 4:4

6) A descendant of Abraham through Jacob's son Judah.

ONLY REFERENCE
1 CHRONICLES 4:1

7) Father of a man who repaired Jerusalem's walls under Nehemiah.

ONLY REFERENCE
NEHEMIAH 3:9

HURAI 1

Linen worker

One of King David's valiant warriors.

ONLY REFERENCE
1 CHRONICLES 11:32

HURAM 12

Whiteness

1) A descendant of Abraham through Jacob's son Benjamin.

ONLY REFERENCE
1 CHRONICLES 8:5

2) Variation of the name Hiram. Same as Hiram (1).

FIRST REFERENCE
2 CHRONICLES 2:3
LAST REFERENCE
2 CHRONICLES 9:21

3) Variation of the name Hiram. Same as Hiram (2).

FIRST REFERENCE
2 CHRONICLES 4:11
LAST REFERENCE
2 CHRONICLES 4:16

HURI 1

Linen worker

A descendant of Abraham through Jacob's son Gad.

ONLY REFERENCE
1 CHRONICLES 5:14

HUSHAH 1

Haste

A descendant of Abraham through Jacob's son Judah.

ONLY REFERENCE
1 CHRONICLES 4:4

HUSHAI 14

Hasty

David's friend Hushai the Archite remained in Jerusalem when Absalom ousted the king from the city. At David's request, Hushai became Absalom's advisor, with the intent of protecting David. When Ahithophel wanted to attack his father quickly, Hushai advised against it; then he sent a warning to David to escape.

FIRST REFERENCE
2 SAMUEL 15:32
LAST REFERENCE
1 CHRONICLES 27:33
KEY REFERENCES
2 SAMUEL 15:32–34; 16:18

HUSHAM 4

Hastily

A king of Edom, "before there reigned any king over the children of Israel" (Genesis 36:31).

FIRST REFERENCE
GENESIS 36:34
LAST REFERENCE
1 CHRONICLES 1:46

HUSHIM 4

Hasters

1) A descendant of Abraham through Jacob's son Dan.

ONLY REFERENCE
GENESIS 46:23

2) A descendant of Abraham through Jacob's son Benjamin.

ONLY REFERENCE
1 CHRONICLES 7:12

3) One of two wives of a Benjamite named Shaharaim. He divorced her in favor of other wives in Moab.

FIRST REFERENCE
I CHRONICLES 8:8
LAST REFERENCE
I CHRONICLES 8:11

HUZ 1
Consultation

Firstborn son of Nahor, Abraham's brother.

ONLY REFERENCE
GENESIS 22:21

HYMENAEUS 2
Nuptial

A man who wrecked his faith and whom Paul accused of blasphemy. Second Timothy 2:18 indicates he had fallen into the Gnostic heresy.

FIRST REFERENCE
I TIMOTHY 1:20
LAST REFERENCE
2 TIMOTHY 2:17

IBHAR 3
Choice

A son of King David, born in Jerusalem.

FIRST REFERENCE
2 SAMUEL 5:15
LAST REFERENCE
I CHRONICLES 14:5

IBNEIAH 1
Built of God

A Jewish exile from the tribe of Benjamin who resettled Jerusalem.

ONLY REFERENCE
I CHRONICLES 9:8

IBNIJAH 1
Building of God

Forefather of a Jewish exile from the tribe of Benjamin who resettled Jerusalem.

ONLY REFERENCE
I CHRONICLES 9:8

IBRI 1
Eberite (Hebrew)

A Levite worship leader during David's reign. Lots were cast to determine his duties.

ONLY REFERENCE
I CHRONICLES 24:27

IBZAN 2
Splendid

The tenth judge of Israel, who led the nation for seven years. He was known for having thirty sons and thirty daughters. Ibzan sent his daughters abroad and brought in thirty foreign women as wives for his sons.

FIRST REFERENCE
JUDGES 12:8
LAST REFERENCE
JUDGES 12:10

I-CHABOD 2
There is no glory

Grandson of the high priest Eli, born just after Eli's death.

FIRST REFERENCE
I SAMUEL 4:21
LAST REFERENCE
I SAMUEL 14:3

IDBASH 1
Honeyed

A descendant of Abraham through Jacob's son Judah.

ONLY REFERENCE
I CHRONICLES 4:3

IDDO 14
Timely, appointed

1) Father of one of David's officers who provided food for King Solomon's household.

ONLY REFERENCE
I KINGS 4:14

2) A descendant of Abraham through Jacob's son Levi.

ONLY REFERENCE
I CHRONICLES 6:21

3) Leader of the half tribe of Manasseh in the days of King David.

ONLY REFERENCE
I CHRONICLES 27:21

4) A prophet who recorded the acts of kings Solomon, Rehoboam, and Abijah.

FIRST REFERENCE
2 CHRONICLES 9:29
LAST REFERENCE
2 CHRONICLES 13:22

5) Father of the prophet Zechariah.

FIRST REFERENCE
EZRA 5:1
LAST REFERENCE
ZECHARIAH 1:7

6) The leading man of Casiphia, whom Ezra asked for ministers for the temple.

ONLY REFERENCE
EZRA 8:17

7) An exiled priest who returned to Judah under Zerubbabel.

FIRST REFERENCE
NEHEMIAH 12:4
LAST REFERENCE
NEHEMIAH 12:16

IGAL 2
Avenger

1) One of twelve spies sent by Moses to spy out the land of Canaan.

ONLY REFERENCE
NUMBERS 13:7

2) One of King David's warriors known as the "mighty men."

ONLY REFERENCE
2 SAMUEL 23:36

IGDALIAH 1
Magnified of God

Father of Hanan, whose chambers Jeremiah borrowed when he tested the Rechabites' obedience.

ONLY REFERENCE
JEREMIAH 35:4

IGEAL 1
Avenger

A descendant of Abraham through Jacob's son Judah, in the line of the nation of Judah's second-to-last king, Jeconiah (also known as Jehoiachin).

ONLY REFERENCE
1 CHRONICLES 3:22

IKKESH 3
Perverse

Father of one of King David's valiant warriors.

FIRST REFERENCE
2 SAMUEL 23:36
LAST REFERENCE
1 CHRONICLES 27:9

ILAI 1
Elevated

One of King David's valiant warriors.

ONLY REFERENCE
1 CHRONICLES 11:29

IMLA 2
Full

Father of Micaiah, a prophet in the time of Israel's king Ahab. Same as Imlah.

FIRST REFERENCE
2 CHRONICLES 18:7
LAST REFERENCE
2 CHRONICLES 18:8

IMLAH 2
Full

Father of Micaiah, a prophet in the time of Israel's king Ahab. Same as Imla.

FIRST REFERENCE
1 KINGS 22:8
LAST REFERENCE
1 KINGS 22:9

IMMANUEL 2
With us is God

A prophetic name for a child promised to King Ahaz of Judah. Various Old Testament–era children have been identified as the fulfillment, but this most clearly prophesies the coming of Jesus.

FIRST REFERENCE
ISAIAH 7:14
LAST REFERENCE
ISAIAH 8:8

IMMER 10 5
Talkative

1) Forefather of a Levite who returned to Jerusalem following the Babylonian captivity.

FIRST REFERENCE
1 CHRONICLES 9:12
LAST REFERENCE
NEHEMIAH 11:13

2) One of twenty-four priests in David's time who was chosen by lot to serve in the tabernacle.

ONLY REFERENCE
1 CHRONICLES 24:14

3) An exile of unclear ancestry who returned to Judah under Zerubbabel.

FIRST REFERENCE
EZRA 2:59
LAST REFERENCE
NEHEMIAH 7:61

4) Father of a man who repaired Jerusalem's walls under Nehemiah.

ONLY REFERENCE
NEHEMIAH 3:29

5) Father of Pashur, a senior priest in the temple who put Jeremiah in the stocks.

ONLY REFERENCE
JEREMIAH 20:1

IMNA
He will restrain

A descendant of Abraham through Jacob's son Asher.

ONLY REFERENCE
1 CHRONICLES 7:35

IMNAH 2
Prosperity

1) A descendant of Abraham through Jacob's son Asher.

ONLY REFERENCE
1 CHRONICLES 7:30

2) A Levite worship leader whose son Kore had charge of freewill offerings under King Hezekiah.

ONLY REFERENCE
2 CHRONICLES 31:14

IMRAH
Interchange

A descendant of Abraham through Jacob's son Asher.

ONLY REFERENCE
1 CHRONICLES 7:36

IMRI 2
Force

1) Forefather of a Jewish exile who returned to Jerusalem.

ONLY REFERENCE
1 CHRONICLES 9:4

2) Father of a man who repaired Jerusalem's walls under Nehemiah.

ONLY REFERENCE
NEHEMIAH 3:2

IPHEDEIAH
God will liberate

A descendant of Abraham through Jacob's son Benjamin.

ONLY REFERENCE
1 CHRONICLES 8:25

IR
City

A descendant of Abraham through Jacob's son Benjamin.

ONLY REFERENCE
1 CHRONICLES 7:12

IRA 6
Wakefulness

1) A royal official serving under Israel's king David.

ONLY REFERENCE
2 SAMUEL 20:26

2) A commander in King David's army overseeing twenty-four thousand men in the sixth month of each year.

FIRST REFERENCE
2 SAMUEL 23:26
LAST REFERENCE
1 CHRONICLES 27:9

3) Another of King David's valiant warriors.

FIRST REFERENCE
2 SAMUEL 23:28
LAST REFERENCE
1 CHRONICLES 11:40

IRAD
Fugitive

A grandson of Cain and son of Enoch.

ONLY REFERENCE
GENESIS 4:18

IRAM
City-wise

A "duke of Edom," a leader in the family line of Esau.

FIRST REFERENCE
GENESIS 36:43
LAST REFERENCE
1 CHRONICLES 1:54

IRI
Urbane

A descendant of Abraham through Jacob's son Benjamin.

ONLY REFERENCE
1 CHRONICLES 7:7

IRIJAH
Fearful of God

A sentry who seized the prophet Jeremiah, accusing him of deserting to the Chaldeans.

FIRST REFERENCE
JEREMIAH 37:13
LAST REFERENCE
JEREMIAH 37:14

IRNAHASH
City of a serpent

A descendant of Abraham through Jacob's son Judah.

ONLY REFERENCE
1 CHRONICLES 4:12

IRU
City-wise

A descendant of Abraham through Jacob's son Judah.

ONLY REFERENCE
1 CHRONICLES 4:15

ISAAC
Laughter

The son of Abraham and Sarah whom God promised to the long-barren couple. After Sarah gave Abraham her servant Hagar to bear him a son, Ishmael, Sarah bore Isaac. God tested Abraham by asking him to sacrifice Isaac at Moriah. When Isaac commented on the lack of a lamb to sacrifice, Abraham replied that God would provide it. At the site of sacrifice, Abraham built an altar and placed his son atop it. But the angel of the Lord stopped the sacrifice, and God provided a ram instead. Abraham sent a servant to his brother Nahor's household to find a wife for Isaac. The man returned with Nahor's daughter Rebekah; Isaac married her and loved her. Rebekah had trouble conceiving, so Isaac prayed for a child. She bore two sons, Esau and Jacob. Esau was Isaac's favorite, but Jacob fooled his elderly, blind father into giving him the blessing of the firstborn child. Isaac had to give Esau a lesser blessing, which caused Esau to hate his brother and required Jacob to leave for a time. Isaac lived to be 180 years old, and his sons buried him.

FIRST REFERENCE
GENESIS 17:19
LAST REFERENCE
JAMES 2:21
KEY REFERENCES
GENESIS 22:7–9; 24:3–4; 25:19–34

ISAIAH 32

God has saved

A prophet of Jerusalem who served during the last year of the reign of King Uzziah and through the reigns of Jotham, Ahaz, and Hezekiah. This aristocratic prophet was married to a prophetess and had at least two children. Isaiah warned Ahaz of an attack by Syria. He supported Ahaz and Hezekiah as the Assyrians became aggressive and sought to expand their empire. But the prophet warned against making treaties with foreign nations. When Sennacherib, king of Assyria, attacked Judah and encouraged the people of Judah not to fight against him, Isaiah counseled Hezekiah to pray and prophesied that a spirit would enter the Assyrian king and he would return to his own land. Later he promised that God would not let Assyria enter Jerusalem. It happened as Isaiah had foretold. Hezekiah became sick, and Isaiah prophesied that he would die. Yet when the king prayed, God promised him fifteen more years of life. Isaiah proved it to the king by causing a shadow to go backward on the steps of Ahaz. But after Hezekiah showed his wealth to messengers from the king of Babylon, Isaiah foretold that everything in his house, including his sons, would be captured by Babylon. Same as Esaias.

FIRST REFERENCE
2 KINGS 19:2
LAST REFERENCE
ISAIAH 39:8
KEY REFERENCES
2 KINGS 19:20–24; 20; ISAIAH 1:1

ISCAH 1

Observant

Brother of Abram's sister-in-law Milcah.

ONLY REFERENCE
GENESIS 11:29

ISCARIOT 11
Inhabitant of Kerioth

A name identifying Judas, the disciple who betrayed Jesus. Same as Judas (1).

FIRST REFERENCE
MATTHEW 10:4
LAST REFERENCE
JOHN 14:22
KEY REFERENCES
MARK 14:10; JOHN 13:2, 26

ISHBAH 1
He will praise

A descendant of Abraham through Jacob's son Judah.

ONLY REFERENCE
1 CHRONICLES 4:17

ISHBAK 2
He will leave

A son of Abraham by his second wife, Keturah.

FIRST REFERENCE
GENESIS 25:2
LAST REFERENCE
1 CHRONICLES 1:32

ISHBI-BENOB 1
His dwelling is in Nob

A Philistine giant who planned to kill a weary King David in battle, but he was felled by David's soldier Abishai. Ishbi-benob carried a spear weighing more than seven pounds.

ONLY REFERENCE
2 SAMUEL 21:16

ISH-BOSHETH 12
Man of shame

King Saul's son who was made king over Israel by Abner, the captain of Saul's army. Ish-bosheth offended Abner by claiming that the captain had slept with Saul's concubine. So Abner turned to David, who sent word to Ish-bosheth and demanded that he return David's wife Michal. Ish-bosheth took her from her second husband and sent her to David. Baanah and Rechab killed Ish-bosheth. The murderers took his head to David, who had them killed and buried the dead king's head in Abner's tomb.

FIRST REFERENCE
2 SAMUEL 2:8
LAST REFERENCE
2 SAMUEL 4:12
KEY REFERENCES
2 SAMUEL 3:7; 4:5–8

ISHI 5 4
Saving

1) A descendant of Abraham through Jacob's son Judah.

ONLY REFERENCE
1 CHRONICLES 2:31

2) Another descendant of Abraham through Jacob's son Judah.

ONLY REFERENCE
1 CHRONICLES 4:20

3 Father of four sons who were captains over the sons of Simeon for King Hezekiah of Judah.

ONLY REFERENCE
1 CHRONICLES 4:42

4) One of the "mighty men of valour, famous men" leading the half tribe of Manasseh.

ONLY REFERENCE
1 CHRONICLES 5:24

ISHIAH   1

God will lend

A descendant of Abraham through Jacob's son Issachar.

ONLY REFERENCE
1 CHRONICLES 7:3

ISHIJAH   1

God will lend

An exiled Israelite who married a "strange" (foreign) woman.

ONLY REFERENCE
EZRA 10:31

ISHMA   1

Desolate

A descendant of Abraham through Jacob's son Judah.

ONLY REFERENCE
1 CHRONICLES 4:3

ISHMAEL   48

God will hear

1) Son of Hagar the Egyptian and Abram. He was born after Abram's barren wife, Sarai (later called Sarah), encouraged her husband to have a child with her maid. God rejected Ishmael, who was not the son of His covenant promise. But He promised to bless Ishmael and make him fruitful so he would found a great nation. Because Ishmael mocked Isaac, Sarah's son, Sarah insisted that Hagar and Ishmael be cast out of the camp. But God watched over them, and they made a home in the wilderness of Paran.

FIRST REFERENCE
GENESIS 16:11
LAST REFERENCE
1 CHRONICLES 1:31
KEY REFERENCES
GENESIS 17:18, 20; 21:9–12

2) An official who ruled over the household of Judah's King Jehoshaphat.

ONLY REFERENCE
2 CHRONICLES 19:11

3) A descendant of Abraham through Jacob's son Benjamin and the line of King Saul by his son Jonathan.

FIRST REFERENCE
1 CHRONICLES 8:38
LAST REFERENCE
1 CHRONICLES 9:44

4) A captain of hundreds under the priest Jehoiada, the regent for King Joash of Judah.

ONLY REFERENCE
2 CHRONICLES 23:1

5) An exiled Israelite priest who married a "strange" (foreign) woman.

ONLY REFERENCE
EZRA 10:22

6) An army captain of Judah under Gedaliah, the governor of Judah who was appointed by King Nebuchadnezzar of Babylon. Under the influence of the Ammonite king Baalis, Ishmael killed the governor and his men and fled with the

people of Judah toward Egypt. When the captain Johanan came to him, the people followed Johanan, and Ishmael escaped to the Ammonites.

FIRST REFERENCE
2 KINGS 25:23
LAST REFERENCE
JEREMIAH 41:18
KEY REFERENCES
JEREMIAH 40:13–16; 41:2–3, 15

ISHMAIAH
God will hear

Leader of the tribe of Zebulun in the days of King David.

ONLY REFERENCE
1 CHRONICLES 27:19

ISHMERAI
Preservative

A descendant of Abraham through Jacob's son Benjamin.

ONLY REFERENCE
1 CHRONICLES 8:18

ISHOD
Man of renown

A descendant of Abraham through Joseph's son Manasseh.

ONLY REFERENCE
1 CHRONICLES 7:18

ISHPAN
He will hide

A descendant of Abraham through Jacob's son Benjamin.

ONLY REFERENCE
1 CHRONICLES 8:22

ISHUAH
He will level

A descendant of Abraham through Jacob and his son Asher.

ONLY REFERENCE
GENESIS 46:17

ISHUAI
Level

A descendant of Abraham through Jacob's son Asher.

ONLY REFERENCE
1 CHRONICLES 7:30

ISHUI
Level

One of three sons of Israel's king Saul. Ishui and his brothers died with Saul in a battle against the Philistines on Mount Gilboa (1 Samuel 31:1–2). Same as Abinadab (3).

ONLY REFERENCE
1 SAMUEL 14:49

ISMACHIAH
God will sustain

A temple overseer of offerings during the reign of King Hezekiah of Judah.

ONLY REFERENCE
2 CHRONICLES 31:13

ISMAIAH

God will hear

One of King David's warriors known as the "mighty men." Ismaiah was part of an elite group called "the thirty."

ONLY REFERENCE
1 CHRONICLES 12:4

ISPAH

He will scratch

A descendant of Abraham through Jacob's son Benjamin.

ONLY REFERENCE
1 CHRONICLES 8:16

ISRAEL 55

He will rule as God

The name given to Jacob by God when he wrestled with Him at Peniel. After renaming him, God again appeared to Jacob, confirmed His covenant promises, and blessed him. Of his twelve sons, Israel loved Joseph more than the others, gave him a coat of many colors to show his preferred status, and put him in a position of authority. For this, Israel's other sons hated Joseph. They sold him into slavery and convinced their father that Joseph was dead. When famine came to the land, Israel sent all his sons except Benjamin to Egypt for food. Joseph had risen to second-in-command of the kingdom there, but his brothers did not recognize him.

Joseph demanded that they leave Simeon with him and bring Benjamin to Egypt. Israel reluctantly agreed to send Benjamin. When his sons returned again, telling him Egypt's second-in-command was Joseph, Israel could hardly believe it. At God's command he traveled to Egypt with all his family and flocks. Joseph met them in Goshen and was reunited with his father. With Pharaoh's approval, Joseph gave his family land in Goshen to settle on. Israel blessed Joseph's sons, Ephraim and Manasseh, taking them as his own sons. But he gave the younger, Ephraim, the greater blessing, saying he would be the greater one. Then he blessed all his sons and asked that he be buried in the field at Machpelah with his forefathers. When Israel died, Joseph had him embalmed and buried him as he requested. Same as Jacob (1).

FIRST REFERENCE
GENESIS 32:28
LAST REFERENCE
EZRA 8:18
KEY REFERENCES
GENESIS 35:10–12; 42:1–2; 48:1–5

ISSACHAR 8 2

He will bring a reward

1) Leah and Jacob's fifth son and Jacob's ninth son. His mother saw him as God's payment to her because she gave her servant, Zilpah, to Jacob. Issachar had four sons.

FIRST REFERENCE
GENESIS 30:18
LAST REFERENCE
I CHRONICLES 7:1

2) A Levite "porter" (doorkeeper) in the house of the Lord.

ONLY REFERENCE
I CHRONICLES 26:5

ISSHIAH 3

God will lend

1) A Levite worship leader during David's reign. Lots were cast to determine his duties.

ONLY REFERENCE
I CHRONICLES 24:21

2) Another Levite worship leader during David's reign. Lots were cast to determine his duties.

ONLY REFERENCE
I CHRONICLES 24:25

ISUAH 1

Level

A descendant of Abraham through Jacob's son Asher.

ONLY REFERENCE
I CHRONICLES 7:30

ISUI 1

Level

A descendant of Abraham through Jacob's son Asher.

ONLY REFERENCE
GENESIS 46:17

ITHAI 1

Near

Father of one of King David's valiant warriors.

ONLY REFERENCE
I CHRONICLES 11:31

ITHAMAR 21

Coast of the palm tree

A son of Aaron and his wife, Elisheba. With his father and brothers, Ithamar served as a priest. Moses became angry at Ithamar and his brother Eleazar because they would not eat the sin offering in the tabernacle. Ithamar oversaw the Gershonites and the duties of the sons of Merari in the tabernacle.

FIRST REFERENCE
EXODUS 6:23
LAST REFERENCE
EZRA 8:2
KEY REFERENCES
NUMBERS 3:4; 4:28, 33

ITHIEL 3

God has arrived

1) Ancestor of a Benjamite who was chosen by lot to resettle Jerusalem after returning from the Babylonian Exile.

ONLY REFERENCE
NEHEMIAH 11:7

2) A man to whom Agur spoke the words of Proverbs 30.

ONLY REFERENCE
PROVERBS 30:1

ITHMAH

Orphanage

One of King David's valiant warriors.

ONLY REFERENCE
1 CHRONICLES 11:46

ITHRA

Excellence

An Ishmaelite whose son, Amasa, replaced Joab as David's commander.

ONLY REFERENCE
2 SAMUEL 17:25

ITHRAN

Excellent

1) A descendant of Seir, who lived in Esau's "land of Edom."

FIRST REFERENCE
GENESIS 36:26
LAST REFERENCE
1 CHRONICLES 1:41

2) A descendant of Abraham through Jacob's son Asher.

ONLY REFERENCE
1 CHRONICLES 7:37

ITHREAM

Excellence of people

Sixth son of David, born to his wife Eglah in Hebron.

FIRST REFERENCE
2 SAMUEL 3:5
LAST REFERENCE
1 CHRONICLES 3:3

ITTAI

Near

1) A Gittite who remained faithful to David when Absalom tried to overthrow the king. David set Ittai over a third of the people who followed him out of Jerusalem.

FIRST REFERENCE
2 SAMUEL 15:19
LAST REFERENCE
2 SAMUEL 18:12

2) One of King David's warriors known as the "mighty men."

ONLY REFERENCE
2 SAMUEL 23:29

IZEHAR

Anointing

A descendant of Levi through his son Kohath.

ONLY REFERENCE
NUMBERS 3:19

IZHAR

Anointing

A descendant of Abraham through Jacob's son Levi.

FIRST REFERENCE
EXODUS 6:18
LAST REFERENCE
1 CHRONICLES 23:18

IZRAHIAH

God will shine

A descendant of Abraham through Jacob's son Issachar.

ONLY REFERENCE
1 CHRONICLES 7:3

IZRI
Trough

One of twenty-four Levite musicians who was chosen by lot to serve in the house of the Lord.

ONLY REFERENCE
1 CHRONICLES 25:11

JAAKAN
To twist

A descendant of Seir the Horite who lived in the land of Edom; founder of the Jaakanite tribe. Same as Akan and Jakan.

ONLY REFERENCE
DEUTERONOMY 10:6

JAAKOBAH
Heel catcher

A descendant of Abraham through Jacob's son Simeon.

ONLY REFERENCE
1 CHRONICLES 4:36

JAALA
Roe

Forefather of an exiled family—former servants of Solomon—that returned to Judah under Zerubbabel. Same as Jaalah.

ONLY REFERENCE
NEHEMIAH 7:58

JAALAH
Roe

Forefather of an exiled family—former servants of Solomon—that returned to Judah under Zerubbabel. Same as Jaala.

ONLY REFERENCE
EZRA 2:56

JAALAM 4
Occult

A son of Esau, whose blessing as older brother was taken by the scheming Jacob.

FIRST REFERENCE
GENESIS 36:5
LAST REFERENCE
I CHRONICLES 1:35

JAANAI 1
Responsive

A descendant of Abraham through Jacob's son Gad.

ONLY REFERENCE
I CHRONICLES 5:12

JAARE-OREGIM 1
Woods of weavers

Father of Elhanan. Same as Jair (4).

ONLY REFERENCE
2 SAMUEL 21:19

JAASAU 1
They will do

An exiled Israelite who married a "strange" (foreign) woman.

ONLY REFERENCE
EZRA 10:37

JAASIEL 1
Made of God

Leader of the tribe of Benjamin in the days of King David.

ONLY REFERENCE
I CHRONICLES 27:21

JAAZANIAH 4
Heard of God

1) A captain of the army of Judah under Nebuchadnezzar's governor, Gedaliah. Also called Jezaniah.

ONLY REFERENCE
2 KINGS 25:23

2) One of the Rechabites who refused to drink the wine Jeremiah offered them.

ONLY REFERENCE
JEREMIAH 35:3

3) A wicked counselor in Jerusalem after the Babylonian Exile.

ONLY REFERENCE
EZEKIEL 8:11

4) A prince of Judah whom God described as devising mischief and giving wicked counsel.

ONLY REFERENCE
EZEKIEL 11:1

JAAZIAH 2
Emboldened of God

A Levite worship leader during David's reign. Lots were cast to determine his duties.

FIRST REFERENCE
I CHRONICLES 24:26
LAST REFERENCE
I CHRONICLES 24:27

JAAZIEL 1
Emboldened of God

A Levite musician who performed in celebration when King David brought the ark of the covenant to Jerusalem. Same as Aziel.

ONLY REFERENCE
I CHRONICLES 15:18

JABAL

Stream

A descendant of Cain through Lamech and his wife Adah. Jabal was "the father of such as dwell in tents, and of such as have cattle."

ONLY REFERENCE
GENESIS 4:20

JABESH

Dry

Forefather of Shallum, who killed King Azariah of Judah and ruled in his place.

FIRST REFERENCE
2 KINGS 15:10
LAST REFERENCE
2 KINGS 15:14

JABEZ

To grieve

A pious man of the line of Judah who prayed for God's blessing, that He would enlarge his border and that God's hand would be with him and keep him from harm.

FIRST REFERENCE
1 CHRONICLES 4:9
LAST REFERENCE
1 CHRONICLES 4:10

JABIN

Intelligent

1) The king of Hazor who raised armies against Joshua and his invading troops.

ONLY REFERENCE
JOSHUA 11:1

2) The king of Canaan who had Sisera as the captain of his army. Since there was peace between Jabin and Heber the Kenite, Sisera fled to Heber's tents, where Heber's wife, Jael, killed him. God used this event to subdue Jabin.

FIRST REFERENCE
JUDGES 4:2
LAST REFERENCE
PSALM 83:9

JACHAN

Troublesome

A descendant of Abraham through Jacob's son Gad.

ONLY REFERENCE
1 CHRONICLES 5:13

JACHIN

He will establish

1) A descendant of Abraham through Jacob's son Simeon.

FIRST REFERENCE
GENESIS 46:10
LAST REFERENCE
NUMBERS 26:12

2) A Jewish exile and priest who resettled Jerusalem.

FIRST REFERENCE
1 CHRONICLES 9:10
LAST REFERENCE
NEHEMIAH 11:10

3) One of twenty-four priests in David's time who was chosen by lot to serve in the tabernacle.

ONLY REFERENCE
1 CHRONICLES 24:17

JACOB 280 ♔
Supplanter

1) Isaac and Rebekah's son who was born clinging to the heel of his twin brother, Esau. When the exhausted hunter, Esau, came home and asked Jacob for his lentil stew, Jacob offered to sell it to him for his birthright. Esau accepted. When Isaac was old and blind, he asked Esau to hunt game for him and promised his blessing. Rebekah overheard and warned Jacob. Together they plotted to gain the blessing for Jacob. Jacob covered himself with goatskins so he would seem as hairy as his brother, fed his father goat stew, and received the firstborn's greater blessing. Esau had to make do with a lesser one. To evade Esau's anger, Jacob fled to his uncle Laban's household. During his trip there, God promised to bring Jacob many descendants and bless the earth through them. Tricked by Laban, Jacob married both his daughters, Leah and Jacob's beloved Rachel. From them and their handmaids, Bilhah and Zilpah, Jacob had twelve sons, who became the founders of Israel's twelve tribes. After deceiving his father-in-law, Jacob fled toward home. He met God, wrestled with Him, was renamed Israel, and began to understand God's deliverance. When he met Esau, Jacob discovered that his fears were groundless. Esau was no longer angry. Same as Israel.

FIRST REFERENCE
GENESIS 25:26
LAST REFERENCE
HEBREWS 11:21
KEY REFERENCES
GENESIS 27:27–29, 39–40; 32:28–30
GENEALOGY OF JESUS
MATTHEW 1:2

2) A descendant of Abraham through Isaac; forebear of Jesus' earthly father, Joseph.

FIRST REFERENCE
MATTHEW 1:15
LAST REFERENCE
MATTHEW 1:16
GENEALOGY OF JESUS
MATTHEW 1:15–16

JADA 2 👤
Knowing

A descendant of Abraham through Jacob's son Judah.

FIRST REFERENCE
I CHRONICLES 2:28
LAST REFERENCE
I CHRONICLES 2:32

JADAU 1 👤
Praised

An exiled Israelite who married a "strange" (foreign) woman.

ONLY REFERENCE
EZRA 10:43

JADDUA 3
Knowing

1) A Jewish leader who renewed the covenant under Nehemiah.

ONLY REFERENCE
NEHEMIAH 10:21

177

2) A Levite worship leader who returned to Jerusalem with Zerubbabel.

FIRST REFERENCE
NEHEMIAH 12:11
LAST REFERENCE
NEHEMIAH 12:22

JADON 1 👤
Thankful

A man who repaired Jerusalem's walls under Nehemiah.

ONLY REFERENCE
NEHEMIAH 3:7

JAEL 6 👩
Ibex

The wife of Heber the Kenite who killed the Canaanite commander Sisera when he fled to her tent following his defeat by the Israelites. She invited him in and then took a tent peg and drove it through his temple. This death fulfilled the Israelite judge Deborah's prophecy.

FIRST REFERENCE
JUDGES 4:17
LAST REFERENCE
JUDGES 5:24

JAHATH 8 5️
Unity

1) A descendant of Abraham through Jacob's son Judah.

ONLY REFERENCE
I CHRONICLES 4:2

2) A descendant of Abraham through Jacob's son Levi.

FIRST REFERENCE
I CHRONICLES 6:20

LAST REFERENCE
I CHRONICLES 6:43

3) A Levite worship leader who was part of King David's reorganization of the Levites.

FIRST REFERENCE
I CHRONICLES 23:10
LAST REFERENCE
I CHRONICLES 23:11

4) A Levite worship leader during David's reign. Lots were cast to determine his duties.

ONLY REFERENCE
I CHRONICLES 24:22

5) A Levite worship leader who oversaw the repair of the temple under King Josiah.

ONLY REFERENCE
2 CHRONICLES 34:12

JAHAZIAH 1 👤
God will behold

A man who oversaw the Israelites who needed to put away "strange" (foreign) wives under Ezra.

ONLY REFERENCE
EZRA 10:15

JAHAZIEL 6 5️
Beheld of God

1) A "mighty man" who supported the future king David during his conflict with Saul.

ONLY REFERENCE
I CHRONICLES 12:4

2) A priest who blew a trumpet when David brought the ark of the Lord to Jerusalem.

ONLY REFERENCE
I CHRONICLES 16:6

3) A Levite worship leader who was part of David's reorganization of the Levites.

FIRST REFERENCE
I CHRONICLES 23:19
LAST REFERENCE
I CHRONICLES 24:23

4) A Levite worship leader who prophesied before King Jehoshaphat of Judah when Edom attacked.

ONLY REFERENCE
2 CHRONICLES 20:14

5) Forefather of a Jewish exile who returned from Babylon to Judah under Ezra.

ONLY REFERENCE
EZRA 8:5

JAHDAI   1

Jehovah fired

A descendant of Abraham through Jacob's son Judah.

ONLY REFERENCE
I CHRONICLES 2:47

JAHDIEL   1

Unity of God

One of the "mighty men of valour, famous men" leading the half tribe of Manasseh.

ONLY REFERENCE
I CHRONICLES 5:24

JAHDO   1

His unity, together

A descendant of Abraham through Jacob's son Gad.

ONLY REFERENCE
I CHRONICLES 5:14

JAHLEEL   2

Wait for God

A descendant of Abraham through Jacob's son Zebulun.

FIRST REFERENCE
GENESIS 46:14
LAST REFERENCE
NUMBERS 26:26

JAHMAI   1

Hot

A descendant of Abraham through Jacob's son Issachar.

ONLY REFERENCE:
I CHRONICLES 7:2

JAHZEEL   2

God will allot

A descendant of Abraham through Jacob's son Naphtali. Same as Jahziel.

FIRST REFERENCE
GENESIS 46:24
LAST REFERENCE
NUMBERS 26:48

JAHZERAH   1

Protection

Forefather of a Levite who returned to Jerusalem after the Babylonian captivity.

ONLY REFERENCE
I CHRONICLES 9:12

JAHZIEL   1

Allotted of God

A descendant of Abraham through Jacob's son Naphtali. Same as Jahzeel.

ONLY REFERENCE
I CHRONICLES 7:13

JAIR 9

Enlightener

1) A descendant of Manasseh who captured twenty-three cities of Bashan and named them Havvoth-jair.

FIRST REFERENCE
NUMBERS 32:41
LAST REFERENCE
I CHRONICLES 2:22

2) The eighth judge of Israel, who led the nation for twenty-two years. He was known for having thirty sons who rode thirty donkeys.

FIRST REFERENCE
JUDGES 10:3
LAST REFERENCE
JUDGES 10:5

3) Father of Mordecai, Queen Esther's cousin.

ONLY REFERENCE
ESTHER 2:5

4) Father of Elhanan, who killed Goliath's brother. Same as Jaare-oregim.

ONLY REFERENCE
I CHRONICLES 20:5

JAIRUS 2

Enlightener

A synagogue ruler who asked Jesus to come and heal his daughter. She died before they could reach her, but Jesus brought her back to life.

FIRST REFERENCE
MARK 5:22
LAST REFERENCE
LUKE 8:41

JAKAN 1

Tortuous

A descendant of Seir the Horite who lived in the land of Edom. Same as Akan or Jaakan.

ONLY REFERENCE
I CHRONICLES 1:42

JAKEH 1

Obedient

Father of the little-known biblical writer who wrote the thirtieth chapter of Proverbs.

ONLY REFERENCE
PROVERBS 30:1

JAKIM 2

He will raise

1) A descendant of Abraham through Jacob's son Benjamin.

ONLY REFERENCE
I CHRONICLES 8:19

2) One of twenty-four priests in David's time who was chosen by lot to serve in the tabernacle.

ONLY REFERENCE
I CHRONICLES 24:12

JALON 1

Lodging

A descendant of Abraham through Jacob's son Judah.

ONLY REFERENCE
I CHRONICLES 4:17

JAMBRES 1

An opponent of Moses mentioned by the apostle Paul as an example of apostasy.

ONLY REFERENCE
2 TIMOTHY 3:8

JAMES 42

1) Zebedee's son and John's brother. With John, this fisherman was called by Jesus to become a fisher of men as one of His disciples. He was part of the intimate group of disciples who witnessed the healing of Simon's mother-in-law, the raising of Jairus's daughter, and the transfiguration of Jesus. With his brother, he boldly sought to call down fire on an unbelieving village and asked to sit at Jesus' right or left hand in glory. He was among the disciples who asked when the temple would fall and who spent the night in Gethsemane with Jesus. Following Jesus' death, James remained with the disciples in the upper room in prayer. He was executed by Herod Agrippa I.

FIRST REFERENCE
MATTHEW 4:21
LAST REFERENCE
ACTS 12:2
KEY REFERENCES
MARK 1:17–20; 5:37; 9:2–3; ACTS 12:1–2

2) Son of Alphaeus and disciple of Jesus. Scripture only mentions him in lists of the disciples. He was one of those in the upper room, praying, following Jesus' death.

FIRST REFERENCE
MATTHEW 10:3
LAST REFERENCE
ACTS 1:13

3) Jesus' brother, called James the less (younger). When the people of the synagogue were astonished at Jesus' teachings, they asked if this was not the brother of James. James became a leader in the Jerusalem church. Paul visited him after returning from Arabia. When he saw that Paul had received God's grace, James and some other disciples accepted him for ministry. Freed from prison, Peter requested that James be informed, and James spoke for the disciples during the Jerusalem Council, which had convened to address the subject of Gentile circumcision. Paul again consulted James on this subject when he returned to Jerusalem. This James is believed by many to be the writer of the book of James in the New Testament.

FIRST REFERENCE
MATTHEW 13:55
LAST REFERENCE
JUDE 1:1
KEY REFERENCES
MARK 6:3; 15:40; 1 CORINTHIANS 15:7; GALATIANS 2:9

JAMIN 6
Right hand

1) A descendant of Abraham through Jacob's son Simeon.

FIRST REFERENCE
GENESIS 46:10
LAST REFERENCE
1 CHRONICLES 4:24

2) A descendant of Abraham through Jacob's son Judah.

ONLY REFERENCE
I CHRONICLES 2:27

3) A Levite who helped Ezra to explain the law to exiles who returned to Jerusalem.

ONLY REFERENCE:
NEHEMIAH 8:7

JAMLECH
He will make king

A descendant of Abraham through Jacob's son Simeon.

ONLY REFERENCE
I CHRONICLES 4:34

JANNA
Oppressor

A descendant of Abraham through Isaac; forebear of Jesus' earthly father, Joseph.

ONLY REFERENCE
LUKE 3:24
GENEALOGY OF JESUS
LUKE 3:24

JANNES
To cure

An opponent of Moses mentioned by the apostle Paul as an example of apostasy.

ONLY REFERENCE
2 TIMOTHY 3:8

JAPHETH
Expansion

Noah's third son, who joined his family in the ark. After leaving the ark, when Noah became drunk and lay unclothed in his tent, Japheth and his brother Shem covered their father without looking at him. For this, Noah asked that God would bless him. Japheth had seven sons and became forefather of the coastland peoples.

FIRST REFERENCE
GENESIS 5:32
LAST REFERENCE
I CHRONICLES 1:5

JAPHIA
Bright

1) The king of Lachish during Joshua's conquest of the Promised Land. Japhia allied with four other rulers to attack Gibeon, which had deceptively made a peace treaty with the Israelites. Joshua's soldiers defeated the five armies, and Joshua executed the allied kings.

ONLY REFERENCE
JOSHUA 10:3

2) A son of King David, born in Jerusalem.

FIRST REFERENCE
2 SAMUEL 5:15
LAST REFERENCE
I CHRONICLES 14:6

JAPHLET
He will deliver

A descendant of Abraham through Jacob's son Asher.

FIRST REFERENCE
I CHRONICLES 7:32
LAST REFERENCE
I CHRONICLES 7:33

JARAH 2
Honey in the comb

A descendant of Abraham through Jacob's son Benjamin. Same as Jehoadah.

ONLY REFERENCE
I CHRONICLES 9:42

JAREB 2
He will contend

An Assyrian king mentioned in the prophecies of Hosea.

FIRST REFERENCE
HOSEA 5:13
LAST REFERENCE
HOSEA 10:6

JARED 6
A descent

A descendant of Adam through Adam's son Seth. Jared was the second-longest-lived indiviual in the Bible at 962 years. Same as Jered.

FIRST REFERENCE
GENESIS 5:15
LAST REFERENCE
LUKE 3:37

JARESIAH 1
Uncertain

A descendant of Abraham through Jacob's son Benjamin.

ONLY REFERENCE
I CHRONICLES 8:27

JARHA 2

The Egyptian servant of Sheshan, a descendant of Abraham through Jacob's son Judah. Jarha married a daughter of Sheshan.

FIRST REFERENCE
I CHRONICLES 2:34
LAST REFERENCE
I CHRONICLES 2:35

JARIB 3
He will contend

1) A descendant of Abraham through Jacob's son Simeon.

ONLY REFERENCE
I CHRONICLES 4:24

2) A Jewish exile in Babylon charged with finding Levites and temple servants to travel to Jerusalem with Ezra.

ONLY REFERENCE
EZRA 8:16

3) An exiled Israelite priest who married a "strange" (foreign) woman.

ONLY REFERENCE
EZRA 10:18

JAROAH 1
Born at the new moon

A descendant of Abraham through Jacob's son Gad.

ONLY REFERENCE
I CHRONICLES 5:14

JASHEN 1
Sleepy

Father of several of King David's warriors known as the "mighty men."

ONLY REFERENCE
2 SAMUEL 23:32

JASHOBEAM 3

People will return

1) A commander in King David's army, overseeing twenty-four thousand men in the first month of each year. Jashobeam was one of David's "mighty men," who once single-handedly killed three hundred enemy soldiers.

FIRST REFERENCE
I CHRONICLES 11:11
LAST REFERENCE
I CHRONICLES 27:2

2) A "mighty man" who supported the future king David during his conflict with Saul.

ONLY REFERENCE
I CHRONICLES 12:6

JASHUB 3

He will return

1) A descendant of Abraham through Jacob's son Issachar. Same as Job (1).

FIRST REFERENCE
NUMBERS 26:24
LAST REFERENCE
I CHRONICLES 7:1

2) An exiled Israelite who married a "strange" (foreign) woman.

ONLY REFERENCE
EZRA 10:29

JASHUBI-LEHEM 1

Returner of bread

A descendant of Abraham through Jacob and his son Judah.

ONLY REFERENCE
I CHRONICLES 4:22

JASIEL 1

Made of God

One of King David's valiant warriors.

ONLY REFERENCE
I CHRONICLES 11:47

JASON 5

About to cure

1) A Christian from Thessalonica whose house was attacked by jealous Jews who dragged him and other Christians before the city officials. The Jews claimed the Christians had said there was another King, Jesus. After taking money from the Christians as security the Roman officials released them.

FIRST REFERENCE
ACTS 17:5
LAST REFERENCE
ACTS 17:9

2) A relative of Paul, living in Rome, who was greeted in the apostle's letter to the Romans.

ONLY REFERENCE
ROMANS 16:21

JATHNIEL 1

Continued of God

A Levite "porter" (doorkeeper) in the house of the Lord.

ONLY REFERENCE
I CHRONICLES 26:2

JAVAN 4
Effervescing

A grandson of Noah through his son Japheth. Javan had four sons.

FIRST REFERENCE
GENESIS 10:2
LAST REFERENCE
I CHRONICLES 1:7

JAZIZ 1
He will make prominent

Called Jaziz the Hagarite, he was in charge of King David's flocks.

ONLY REFERENCE
I CHRONICLES 27:31

JEATERAI 1
Stepping

A descendant of Abraham through Jacob's son Levi.

ONLY REFERENCE
I CHRONICLES 6:21

JEBERECHIAH 1
Blessed of God

Forefather of Zechariah (27).

ONLY REFERENCE
ISAIAH 8:2

JECAMIAH 1
God will rise

A descendant of Abraham through Jacob's son Judah, in the line of the nation of Judah's second-to-last king, Jeconiah (also known as Jehoiachin). Same as Jekamiah.

ONLY REFERENCE
I CHRONICLES 3:18

JECHOLIAH 1
Jehovah will enable

Mother of Judah's good king Azariah, also known as Uzziah. Same as Jecoliah.

ONLY REFERENCE
2 KINGS 15:2

JECHONIAS 2
Jehovah will establish

Greek form of the name *Jeconiah*, used in the New Testament.

FIRST REFERENCE
MATTHEW 1:11
LAST REFERENCE
MATTHEW 1:12
GENEALOGY OF JESUS
MATTHEW 1:11–12

JECOLIAH 1
God will enable

Mother of Judah's good king Uzziah, also known as Azariah. Same as Jecholiah.

ONLY REFERENCE
2 CHRONICLES 26:3

JECONIAH 7
God will establish

King of Judah and son of King Jehoiakim. King Nebuchandnezzar carried him and his nobles to Babylon. Hananiah prophesied that he would return to Jerusalem, but, through Jeremiah, God revealed that he would not. Same as Coniah, Jechonias, and Jehoiachin.

FIRST REFERENCE
I CHRONICLES 3:16
LAST REFERENCE
JEREMIAH 29:2

JEDAIAH 13
Praised of God

1) A descendant of Abraham through Jacob's son Simeon.

ONLY REFERENCE
I CHRONICLES 4:37

2) A rebuilder of the walls of Jerusalem under Nehemiah.

ONLY REFERENCE
NEHEMIAH 3:10

3) One of twenty-four priests in David's time who was chosen by lot to serve in the tabernacle.

FIRST REFERENCE
I CHRONICLES 9:10
LAST REFERENCE
NEHEMIAH 7:39

4) A priest who returned from exile with Zerubbabel and lived in Jerusalem. The prophet Zechariah prophesied that there would be a memorial to him in the temple.

FIRST REFERENCE
NEHEMIAH 11:10
LAST REFERENCE
ZECHARIAH 6:14

5) An exiled priest who returned to Judah under Zerubbabel.

FIRST REFERENCE
NEHEMIAH 12:7
LAST REFERENCE
NEHEMIAH 12:21

JEDIAEL 6
Knowing God

1) A descendant of Abraham through Jacob's son Benjamin.

FIRST REFERENCE
I CHRONICLES 7:6
LAST REFERENCE
I CHRONICLES 7:11

2) One of King David's valiant warriors.

ONLY REFERENCE
I CHRONICLES 11:45

3) A captain of thousands for the tribe of Manasseh, which supported David against Saul.

ONLY REFERENCE
I CHRONICLES 12:20

4) A Levite "porter" (doorkeeper) in the house of the Lord.

ONLY REFERENCE
I CHRONICLES 26:2

JEDIDAH I
Beloved

Mother of Judah's good king Josiah.

ONLY REFERENCE
2 KINGS 22:1

JEDIDIAH I
Beloved of God

God's special name for Solomon, as delivered by the prophet Nathan.

ONLY REFERENCE
2 SAMUEL 12:25

JEDUTHUN 17
Laudatory

A descendant of Abraham through Jacob's son Levi. Jeduthun was one of the key musicians serving in the Jerusalem temple. King David appointed Jeduthun's descendants to "prophesy with harps, with psalteries, and with cymbals" (1 Chronicles 25:1).

FIRST REFERENCE
I CHRONICLES 9:16
LAST REFERENCE
PSALM 77 (TITLE)

JEEZER 1
Helpless

A descendant of Joseph's son Manasseh and a son of Gilead.

ONLY REFERENCE
NUMBERS 26:30

JEHALELEEL 1
Praising God

A descendant of Abraham through Jacob's son Judah.

ONLY REFERENCE
I CHRONICLES 4:16

JEHALELEL 1
Praising God

Father of a Levite who cleansed the temple under King Hezekiah of Judah.

ONLY REFERENCE
2 CHRONICLES 29:12

JEHDEIAH 2
Unity of God

1) A descendant of Abraham through Jacob's son Levi.

ONLY REFERENCE
I CHRONICLES 24:20

2) An official responsible for King David's herds of donkeys.

ONLY REFERENCE
I CHRONICLES 27:30

JEHEZEKEL 1
God will strengthen

One of twenty-four priests in David's time who was chosen by lot to serve in the tabernacle.

ONLY REFERENCE
I CHRONICLES 24:16

JEHIAH 1
God will live

A doorkeeper of the ark of the covenant under King David.

ONLY REFERENCE
I CHRONICLES 15:24

JEHIEL 16 13
God will live

1) A Levite musician who performed in celebration when King David brought the ark of the covenant to Jerusalem.

FIRST REFERENCE
I CHRONICLES 15:18
LAST REFERENCE
I CHRONICLES 16:5

2) A leader of the Gershonites who cared for the precious stones donated for Solomon's temple.

FIRST REFERENCE
I CHRONICLES 23:8
LAST REFERENCE
I CHRONICLES 29:8

3) Tutor to King David's sons.

ONLY REFERENCE
I CHRONICLES 27:32

4) A son of Judah's king Jehoshaphat, given "great gifts of silver, and of gold, and of precious things" by his father (2 Chronicles 21:3).

ONLY REFERENCE
2 CHRONICLES 21:2

5) A descendant of Abraham through Jacob's son Levi. Jehiel was among the Levites who cleansed the Jerusalem temple during the revival of King Hezekiah's day.

ONLY REFERENCE
2 CHRONICLES 29:14

6) A temple overseer during the reign of King Hezekiah of Judah.

ONLY REFERENCE
2 CHRONICLES 31:13

7) A chief temple officer under King Josiah of Judah.

ONLY REFERENCE
2 CHRONICLES 35:8

8) Forefather of a Jewish exile who returned to Judah under Ezra.

ONLY REFERENCE
EZRA 8:9

9) Father of Shechaniah, an exiled Israelite who married a "strange" (foreign) woman but suggested to Ezra that he and his fellow offenders "make a covenant with our God to put away all the wives, and such as are born of them" (Ezra 10:3).

ONLY REFERENCE
EZRA 10:2

10) An exiled Israelite priest who married a "strange" (foreign) woman.

ONLY REFERENCE
EZRA 10:21

11) Another exiled Israelite who married a foreign woman.

ONLY REFERENCE
EZRA 10:26

12) Forefather of King Saul.

ONLY REFERENCE
1 CHRONICLES 9:35

13) One of King David's valiant warriors.

ONLY REFERENCE
1 CHRONICLES 11:44

JEHIELI 2
God will live

A Levite whose sons were in charge of the temple treasury.

FIRST REFERENCE
1 CHRONICLES 26:21
LAST REFERENCE
1 CHRONICLES 26:22

JEHIZKIAH 1
Strengthened of God

A man of the tribe of Ephraim who counseled his nation of Israel against enslaving fellow Jews from Judah who were captured in a civil war. Jehizkiah helped to feed and clothe the prisoners before sending them home.

ONLY REFERENCE
2 CHRONICLES 28:12

JEHOADAH 2 👤
Jehovah adorned

A descendant of Abraham through Jacob's son Benjamin, through the line of King Saul and his son Jonathan. Same as Jarah.

ONLY REFERENCE
I CHRONICLES 8:36

JEHOADDAN 2 👤
Jehovah pleased

Mother of Amaziah, king of Judah.

FIRST REFERENCE
2 KINGS 14:2
LAST REFERENCE
2 CHRONICLES 25:1

JEHOAHAZ 23 👤
Jehovah seized

1) King of Israel and son of King Jehu, Jehoahaz did what was evil in God's sight. He fought and lost battles with Hazael, king of Syria. When he sought the Lord concerning the oppression that the nation inflicted upon Israel, God provided a savior.

FIRST REFERENCE
2 KINGS 10:35
LAST REFERENCE
2 CHRONICLES 25:25
KEY REFERENCE
2 KINGS 13:4–5

2) King of Judah, son of King Josiah. This evil king reigned only three months before Pharaohnecho of Egypt captured Jehoahaz and sent him to Egypt, where he died. Same as Shallum (1).

FIRST REFERENCE
2 KINGS 23:30
LAST REFERENCE
2 CHRONICLES 36:4

3) Son of King Jehoram of Judah. When the Philistines and Arabians attacked Judah, they carried away all of Jehoram's sons but Jehoahaz.

FIRST REFERENCE
2 CHRONICLES 21:17
LAST REFERENCE
2 CHRONICLES 25:23

JEHOASH 17 👤
Jehovah fired

1) Another name for Joash (5).

FIRST REFERENCE
2 KINGS 11:21
LAST REFERENCE
2 KINGS 14:13

2) An evil king of Israel, son of King Jehoahaz. Jehoash regained from Hazael, king of Syria, the cities Hazael had won from Israel in battle. Jehoash fought King Amaziah of Judah, broke down Jerusalem's wall, and took gold and silver from the temple and the king. With hostages, he returned to Samaria. Same as Joash (6).

FIRST REFERENCE
2 KINGS 13:10
LAST REFERENCE
2 KINGS 14:17

JEHOHANAN 6 👤
Jehovah favored

1) A Levite "porter" (doorkeeper) in the house of the Lord.

ONLY REFERENCE
I CHRONICLES 26:3

2) A military captain of Judah who stood next to Adnah, the commander.

ONLY REFERENCE
2 CHRONICLES 17:15

3) Father of a captain of hundreds under the priest Jehoiada of Judah.

ONLY REFERENCE
2 CHRONICLES 23:1

4) An exiled Israelite who married a "strange" (foreign) woman.

ONLY REFERENCE
EZRA 10:28

5) Forefather of a priest who returned to Jerusalem under Zerubbabel.

ONLY REFERENCE
NEHEMIAH 12:13

6) A priest who helped to dedicate the rebuilt wall of Jerusalem by giving thanks.

ONLY REFERENCE
NEHEMIAH 12:42

JEHOIACHIN 10

Jehovah will establish

King of Judah and son of King Jehoiakim, this evil king reigned only three months before King Nebuchadnezzar of Babylon carried him and the best of his people to Babylon. In the thirty-seventh year of Jehoiachin's captivity, King Evil-merodach brought him out of prison and gave him preferential treatment. Same as Coniah, Jeconiah, and Jeconias.

FIRST REFERENCE
2 KINGS 24:6
LAST REFERENCE
JEREMIAH 52:31

JEHOIADA 52

Jehovah known

1) Father of Benaiah, a commander in King David's army, who also served Solomon.

FIRST REFERENCE
2 SAMUEL 8:18
LAST REFERENCE
1 CHRONICLES 27:5

2) The high priest who made a covenant with the army's leaders to protect young King Joash. For six years Jehoiada protected Joash from his grandmother Athaliah, who had usurped Judah's throne. In the seventh year, the priest anointed and crowned Joash. When Athaliah objected, he had her killed then made a covenant between Joash and his people. At the king's command, Jehoiada took up a collection for refurbishing the temple, which Athaliah had caused to be damaged. Because Jehoiada had done much good for the people, he was buried with the kings of Judah.

FIRST REFERENCE
2 KINGS 11:4
LAST REFERENCE
2 CHRONICLES 24:25
KEY REFERENCES
2 CHRONICLES 23:1; 24:6–7, 15–16

3) A leader descended from Aaron who joined David at Hebron to make him king over Israel.

ONLY REFERENCE
1 CHRONICLES 12:27

4) Son of Benaiah, who succeeded Ahithophel as David's counselor.

ONLY REFERENCE
I CHRONICLES 27:34

5) A man who repaired Jerusalem's walls under Nehemiah.

ONLY REFERENCE
NEHEMIAH 3:6

6) A priest mentioned by Jeremiah in his prophecy against the false prophet Shemaiah.

ONLY REFERENCE
JEREMIAH 29:26

JEHOIAKIM 37

Jehovah will raise

Originally named Eliakim, he was a son of King Josiah of Judah. After the Egyptian pharaoh Necho killed Josiah and later deposed his son Jehoahaz, the pharaoh made Eliakim king of Judah and changed his name to Jehoiakim. Following Necho's defeat by King Nebuchadnezzar, Jehoiakim served the Babylonian king. But three years later, Jehoiakim rebelled. When Jeremiah's prophetic, warning words were read to this wicked king, piece by piece he burned the scroll they were written on—so God declared that Babylon would destroy Judah. Nebuchadnezzar attacked and defeated Jerusalem, bound Jehoiakim in chains, and carried him to Babylon, along with most of the people of Judah. Following Jehoiakim's capture, a prophet told how he murdered another prophet who spoke out against him then had his body dumped in a common burial ground. Same as Eliakim (27).

FIRST REFERENCE
2 KINGS 23:34
LAST REFERENCE
DANIEL 1:2
KEY REFERENCES
2 KINGS 23:34; 24:1; JEREMIAH 26:20–23;
36:22–24

JEHOIARIB 2

Jehovah will contend

1) A priest who returned to Jerusalem after the Babylonian captivity.

ONLY REFERENCE
I CHRONICLES 9:10

2) One of twenty-four priests of David's time who was chosen by lot to serve in the tabernacle.

ONLY REFERENCE
I CHRONICLES 24:7

JEHONADAB 3

Jehovah largessed

One of the Rechabites, who were known for their spiritual austerity. He met King Jehu in Samaria and saw his destruction of the temple of Baal, with all the worshippers in it.

FIRST REFERENCE
2 KINGS 10:15
LAST REFERENCE
2 KINGS 10:23

JEHONATHAN 3
Jehovah given

1) An official in charge of King David's storehouses.

ONLY REFERENCE
I CHRONICLES 27:25

2) A Levite sent by King Jehoshaphat to teach the law of the Lord throughout the nation of Judah.

ONLY REFERENCE
2 CHRONICLES 17:8

3) Forefather of a priest who returned to Jerusalem under Zerubbabel.

ONLY REFERENCE
NEHEMIAH 12:18

JEHORAM 23
Jehovah raised

1) Firstborn son of King Jehoshaphat of Judah. After Jehoram became king, he killed all his brothers. He married the daughter of King Ahab of Israel and led his nation into idolatry. Philistines and Arabians invaded Judah and captured Jehoram's family. As God had warned, Jehoram died, unmourned, of an incurable bowel disease. He was not buried in the kings' tombs. Same as Joram (2).

FIRST REFERENCE
I KINGS 22:50
LAST REFERENCE
2 CHRONICLES 22:11
KEY REFERENCES
2 CHRONICLES 21:4–6, 11, 20

2) King of Israel, son of Ahab, and brother of Ahaziah, from whom he inherited the throne. Though he did not worship Baal, neither did he stop his nation from worshipping Jeroboam's golden calves. With Jehoshaphat, king of Judah, he went to war against Moab. Discouraged, they consulted the prophet Elijah, who told them how to win their battle. Jehoram was killed by Jehu (2), who took his throne. Same as Joram (2).

FIRST REFERENCE
2 KINGS 1:17
LAST REFERENCE
2 CHRONICLES 22:7

3) A priest sent by King Jehoshaphat to teach the law of the Lord throughout the nation of Judah.

ONLY REFERENCE
2 CHRONICLES 17:8

JEHOSHABEATH 2
Jehovah sworn

Daughter of Judah's king Jehoram and sister of Judah's king Ahaziah. When Ahaziah was killed, Jehoshabeath saved her infant nephew Joash from a family massacre engineered by Ahaziah's mother, Athaliah, who wanted to make herself queen. Same as Hehosheba.

ONLY REFERENCE
2 CHRONICLES 22:11

JEHOSHAPHAT 83
Jehovah judged

1) An official in King David's court who was his recorder.

FIRST REFERENCE
2 SAMUEL 8:16
LAST REFERENCE
1 CHRONICLES 18:15

2) One of King Solomon's twelve officials over provisions.

ONLY REFERENCE
1 KINGS 4:17

3) King of Judah, who inherited the throne from his father, Asa. Though he had blessings and "riches and honour in abundance" (2 Chronicles 17:5; 18:1), he repeatedly allied himself with Israel. Though he followed God, Jehoshaphat became inconsistent in his obedience and did not completely end idolatry in Judah. Despite the warning of the prophet Micaiah, he joined King Ahab of Israel in a disastrous attack on Ramoth-gilead. Later, as a great army came against his own nation, Jehoshaphat sought the Lord. When King Jehoram of Israel asked Jehoshaphat to join him in attacking Moab, Judah's king suggested they consult a prophet. Elijah gave them the winning battle plan.

FIRST REFERENCE
1 KINGS 15:24
LAST REFERENCE
2 CHRONICLES 22:9
KEY REFERENCES
1 KINGS 22:4–5, 43; 2 KINGS 3:11–20;
2 CHRONICLES 18:1, 31; 20:5–12

4) Father of Jehu, king of Israel.

FIRST REFERENCE
2 KINGS 9:2
LAST REFERENCE
2 KINGS 9:14

5) A priest who blew a trumpet as David moved the ark of the covenant.

ONLY REFERENCE
1 CHRONICLES 15:24

JEHOSHEBA 2
Jehovah sworn

King Joash's aunt, who protected him from his wicked grandmother Athaliah. Same as Jehoshabeath.

ONLY REFERENCE
2 KINGS 11:2

JEHOSHUA 1
Jehovah saved

A variant name for Joshua, son of Nun, successor to Moses.

ONLY REFERENCE
NUMBERS 13:16

JEHOSHUAH 1
Jehovah saved

A variant name for Joshua, son of Nun, successor to Moses.

ONLY REFERENCE
1 CHRONICLES 7:27

JEHOZABAD 4
Jehovah endowed

1) One of two royal officials who conspired to kill Judah's king Joash.

FIRST REFERENCE
2 KINGS 12:21
LAST REFERENCE
2 CHRONICLES 24:26

2) A Levite "porter" (doorkeeper) in the house of the Lord.

ONLY REFERENCE
I CHRONICLES 26:4

3) A commander in the army of King Jehoshaphat of Israel.

ONLY REFERENCE
2 CHRONICLES 17:18

JEHOZADAK 2

Jehovah righted

A descendant of Abraham through Jacob's son Levi and a priest through the line of Aaron. Jehozadak served when the Babylonians overran Judah, and he was carried into captivity.

FIRST REFERENCE
I CHRONICLES 6:14
LAST REFERENCE
I CHRONICLES 6:15

JEHU 59

Jehovah (is) He

1) A prophet who prophesied the destruction of Baasha, king of Israel, and Baasha's heirs. He also confronted King Jehoshaphat of Judah with his inconsistent faith.

FIRST REFERENCE
I KINGS 16:1
LAST REFERENCE
2 CHRONICLES 20:34

2) A king of Israel. God commanded Elijah to anoint Jehu king to destroy King Ahab and his dynasty. Stunned, Jehu received Elijah's servant and the anointing. Jehu killed kings Joram of Israel and Ahaziah of Judah. Then he killed Jezebel by commanding servants to throw her from a window, made the Samaritans slaughter Ahab's sons, and killed forty-two of King Ahaziah's relatives. After calling the priests of Baal and the idol's worshippers together, Jehu had his men put them all to the sword. But Jehu did not walk carefully in God's ways and lost part of Israel to Syria.

FIRST REFERENCE
I KINGS 19:16
LAST REFERENCE
HOSEA 1:4
KEY REFERENCES
2 KINGS 9:6–10, 23–24, 27, 33; 10:18–27

3) A descendant of Abraham through Jacob's son Judah. Jehu descended from the line of an unnamed Israelite woman and her Egyptian husband, Jarha.

ONLY REFERENCE
I CHRONICLES 2:38

4) A descendant of Abraham through Jacob's son Simeon.

ONLY REFERENCE
I CHRONICLES 4:35

5) A "mighty man" who supported the future king David during his conflict with Saul.

ONLY REFERENCE
I CHRONICLES 12:3

JEHUBBAH 1

Hidden

A descendant of Abraham through Jacob's son Asher.

ONLY REFERENCE
I CHRONICLES 7:34

JEHUCAL
Potent

A man sent by King Zedekiah to ask Jeremiah to pray for Judah as Egypt attacked.

ONLY REFERENCE
JEREMIAH 37:3

JEHUDI
Descendant of Jehudah

Nethaniah's son who carried a message from King Josiah's court to Jeremiah's scribe, commanding him to read Judah's princes the word God sent through the prophet.

FIRST REFERENCE
JEREMIAH 36:14
LAST REFERENCE
JEREMIAH 36:23

JEHUDIJAH
Female descendant of Jehudah

A wife of Ezra (1).

ONLY REFERENCE
1 CHRONICLES 4:18

JEHUSH
Hasty

A descendant of Abraham through Jacob's son Benjamin, in the line of King Saul and his son Jonathan. Jehush was a courageous archer.

ONLY REFERENCE
1 CHRONICLES 8:39

JEIEL
Carried away of God

1) A descendant of Abraham through Jacob's son Reuben.

ONLY REFERENCE
1 CHRONICLES 5:7

2) A Levite worship leader who played a harp as the ark of the covenant was brought into Jerusalem.

FIRST REFERENCE
1 CHRONICLES 15:18
LAST REFERENCE
1 CHRONICLES 16:5

3) Forefather of Jahaziel, who prophesied to King Jehoshaphat that he would not be overcome by his enemies.

ONLY REFERENCE
2 CHRONICLES 20:14

4) A scribe who counted the men who went to battle with King Uzziah of Judah.

ONLY REFERENCE
2 CHRONICLES 26:11

5) A descendant of Abraham through Jacob's son Levi. Jeiel was among the Levites who cleansed the Jerusalem temple during the revival in King Hezekiah's reign.

ONLY REFERENCE
2 CHRONICLES 29:13

6) A descendant of Abraham through Jacob's son Levi. Jeiel was among those who distributed sacrificial animals to fellow Levites preparing to celebrate the Passover under King Josiah.

ONLY REFERENCE
2 CHRONICLES 35:9

7) A Jewish exile who returned from Babylon to Judah under Ezra.

ONLY REFERENCE
EZRA 8:13

8) An exiled Israelite who married a "strange" (foreign) woman.

ONLY REFERENCE
EZRA 10:43

JEKAMEAM 2
The people will rise

A descendant of Abraham through Jacob's son Levi.

FIRST REFERENCE
I CHRONICLES 23:19
LAST REFERENCE
I CHRONICLES 24:23

JEKAMIAH 2
God will rise

A descendant of Abraham through Jacob's son Judah. Jekamiah descended from the line of an unnamed Israelite woman and her Egyptian husband, Jarha. Same as Jecamiah.

ONLY REFERENCE
I CHRONICLES 2:41

JEKUTHIEL 1
Obedience of God

A descendant of Abraham through Jacob's son Judah.

ONLY REFERENCE
I CHRONICLES 4:18

JEMIMA 1
Dove

A daughter of Job. Jemima was the oldest of three daughters born to Job after God restored his fortunes. Jemima and her two sisters, Kezia and Keren-happuch, were said to be more beautiful than any other woman "in all the land" (Job 42:15).

ONLY REFERENCE
JOB 42:14

JEMUEL 2
Day of God

A descendant of Abraham through Jacob's son Simeon. Same as Nemuel (2).

FIRST REFERENCE
GENESIS 46:10
LAST REFERENCE
EXODUS 6:15

JEPHTHAE 1
He will open

Greek form of the name *Jephthah*, used in the New Testament.

ONLY REFERENCE
HEBREWS 11:32

JEPHTHAH 29
He will open

The eighth judge of Israel, Jephthah the Gileadite was Gilead's son by a prostitute. His half brothers drove him out, and he went to the land of Tob. When the Ammonites fought Israel, he became Gilead's leader. He unsuccessfully tried to make peace with these enemies. Then Jephthah promised God that he would give Him whatever greeted him when he came home, should he be victorious. After winning the battle, his daughter, his only child, came to greet him on his return. After giving his daughter a two-month reprieve, Jephthah kept his vow. For passing over Ephraim's land, he battled the Ephraimites. Jephthah judged Israel for six years. Same as Jephthae.

FIRST REFERENCE
JUDGES 11:1
LAST REFERENCE
I SAMUEL 12:11
KEY REFERENCES
JUDGES 11:5–10, 29–30

JEPHUNNEH 16

He will be prepared

1) Father of Caleb, one of two spies (along with Joshua) who argued in favor of entering the Promised Land.

FIRST REFERENCE
NUMBERS 13:6
LAST REFERENCE
I CHRONICLES 6:56

2) A descendant of Abraham through Jacob's son Asher.

ONLY REFERENCE
I CHRONICLES 7:38

JERAH 2

Month

A descendant of Noah through his son Shem.

FIRST REFERENCE
GENESIS 10:26
LAST REFERENCE
I CHRONICLES 1:20

JERAHMEEL 8

God will be compassionate

1) A descendant of Abraham through Jacob's son Pharez.

FIRST REFERENCE
I CHRONICLES 2:9
LAST REFERENCE
I CHRONICLES 2:42

2) A descendant of Abraham through Jacob's son Levi.

ONLY REFERENCE
I CHRONICLES 24:29

3) A man ordered by King Jehoiakim to imprison the prophet Jeremiah and his scribe.

ONLY REFERENCE
JEREMIAH 36:26

JERED 2

A descent

1) A descendant of Adam through his son Seth. Jered was the second-longest-lived individual in the Bible at 962 years. Same as Jared.

ONLY REFERENCE
I CHRONICLES 1:2

2) A descendant of Abraham through Jacob's son Judah.

ONLY REFERENCE
I CHRONICLES 4:18

JEREMAI 1

Elevated

An exiled Israelite who married a "strange" (foreign) woman.

ONLY REFERENCE
EZRA 10:33

God will rise

1) Grandfather of kings Jehoahaz and Zedekiah of Judah.

FIRST REFERENCE
2 KINGS 23:31
LAST REFERENCE
JEREMIAH 52:1

2) One of the "mighty men of valour, famous men" leading the half tribe of Manasseh.

ONLY REFERENCE
1 CHRONICLES 5:24

3) One of King David's mightiest warriors known as "the thirty."

ONLY REFERENCE
1 CHRONICLES 12:4

4) One of several warriors from the tribe of Gad who left Saul to join David during his conflict with the king. Jeremiah and his companions were "men of might...whose faces were like the faces of lions" (1 Chronicles 12:8).

ONLY REFERENCE
1 CHRONICLES 12:10

5) Another of several warriors from the tribe of Gad who left Saul to join David during his conflict with the king. Jeremiah and his companions were "men of might. . .whose faces were like the faces of lions" (1 Chronicles 12:8).

ONLY REFERENCE
1 CHRONICLES 12:13

6) A prophet of Judah during the reigns of kings Josiah, Jehoahaz, Jehoiakim, Jehoiachin, and Zedekiah. Following Assyria's destruction of Israel, Babylon threatened Judah. The turmoil of his age was clearly reflected in the gloomy prophecies of Jeremiah. He condemned Judah for idolatry and called the nation to repentance. God warned of Judah's destruction and mourned over it, yet Jerusalem refused to repent, and Jeremiah warned of the people's judgment. When Pashur (3), chief officer of the temple, heard Jeremiah's prophecies, he put him in the stocks. Released, the prophet spoke against this false prophet, predicting the fall of Judah to Babylon. Pashur was only one of many men who became angry with the prophet, because Jeremiah contended with kings and false prophets as he spoke God's Word. Before the fall of Jerusalem, Jeremiah was imprisoned and accused of deserting to the enemy. For a while he was cast into a muddy cistern. When Jerusalem fell, Nebuchadnezzar treated him well. Jeremiah warned the remnant of people who remained in Judah not to go to Egypt. But the commanders of Judah took the people, including Jeremiah, there anyway. Jeremiah may have died in Egypt. Same as Jeremias and Jeremy.

FIRST REFERENCE
2 CHRONICLES 35:25
LAST REFERENCE
DANIEL 9:2
KEY REFERENCES
JEREMIAH 1:1, 5; 20:1–6; 21:3–6; 35:8–17; 37:12–15; 38:6

7) A priest who renewed the covenant under Nehemiah.

FIRST REFERENCE
NEHEMIAH 10:2
LAST REFERENCE
NEHEMIAH 12:34

JEREMIAS

God will rise

Greek form of the name *Jeremiah*, used in the New Testament. Same as Jeremiah (6).

ONLY REFERENCE
MATTHEW 16:14

JEREMOTH

Elevations

1) A descendant of Abraham through Jacob's son Benjamin.

ONLY REFERENCE
I CHRONICLES 8:14

2) An exiled Israelite who married a "strange" (foreign) woman.

ONLY REFERENCE
EZRA 10:26

3) Another exiled Israelite who married a "strange" (foreign) woman.

ONLY REFERENCE
EZRA 10:27

4) A descendant of Abraham through Jacob's son Levi. Same as Jerimoth (4).

ONLY REFERENCE
I CHRONICLES 23:23

5) One of twenty-four Levite musicians who was chosen by lot to serve in the house of the Lord.

ONLY REFERENCE
I CHRONICLES 25:22

JEREMY

God will rise

Latin form of the name *Jeremiah*, used in the New Testament. Same as Jeremiah (6).

FIRST REFERENCE
MATTHEW 2:17
LAST REFERENCE
MATTHEW 27:9

JERIAH

God will throw

A descendant of Abraham through Jacob's son Levi.

FIRST REFERENCE
I CHRONICLES 23:19
LAST REFERENCE
I CHRONICLES 24:23

JERIBAI

Contentious

One of King David's valiant warriors.

ONLY REFERENCE
I CHRONICLES 11:46

JERIEL

Thrown of God

A descendant of Abraham through Jacob's son Issachar.

ONLY REFERENCE
I CHRONICLES 7:2

JERIJAH

Chief of the Hebronites whom King David gave authority over the Reubenites, Gadites, and half tribe of Manasseh.

ONLY REFERENCE
I CHRONICLES 26:31

199

JERIMOTH 8
Elevations

1) A descendant of Abraham through Jacob's son Benjamin.

ONLY REFERENCE
I CHRONICLES 7:7

2) Another descendant of Abraham through Jacob's son Benjamin.

ONLY REFERENCE
I CHRONICLES 7:8

3) A "mighty man" who supported the future king David during his conflict with Saul.

ONLY REFERENCE
I CHRONICLES 12:5

4) A descendant of Abraham through Jacob's son Levi. Same as Jeremoth (4).

ONLY REFERENCE
I CHRONICLES 24:30

5) A son of King David's musician Heman, who was "under the hands of [his] father for song in the house of the LORD" (1 Chronicles 25:6).

ONLY REFERENCE
I CHRONICLES 25:4

6) Leader of the tribe of Naphtali in the days of King David.

ONLY REFERENCE
I CHRONICLES 27:19

7) Father-in-law of King Rehoboam of Judah.

ONLY REFERENCE
2 CHRONICLES 11:18

8) A temple overseer during the reign of King Hezekiah of Judah.

ONLY REFERENCE
2 CHRONICLES 31:13

JERIOTH 1
Curtains

A descendant of Abraham through Jacob's son Judah.

ONLY REFERENCE
I CHRONICLES 2:18

JEROBOAM 104
The people will contend

1) A servant of King Solomon who had authority over the forced labor for the tribes of Ephraim and Manasseh. The prophet Ahijah the Shilonite prophesied that Jeroboam would be king over ten tribes of Israel when Solomon died. Solomon heard this and sought to kill Jeroboam, who fled to Egypt. Israel rebelled against Solomon's son, King Rehoboam, and made Jeroboam king. Fearing that his people would return to Rehoboam if they worshipped in Jerusalem, Jeroboam established idolatrous worship in Israel. Because Jeroboam did not obey God, the prophet Abijah warned the king's wife that God would cut off all the men of Jeroboam's household and burn his house. Jeroboam's son became ill and died. When Jeroboam went to war with King Abijah of Judah, God routed Jeroboam. Israel never regained its power during Jeroboam's lifetime.

FIRST REFERENCE
I KINGS 11:26
LAST REFERENCE
2 CHRONICLES 13:20
KEY REFERENCES
I KINGS 12:20, 28;
2 CHRONICLES 13:14–16, 20

2) King of Israel, son of King Joash, Jeroboam continued the idolatrous worship established by Jeroboam (1). God used Jeroboam to regain Israel's lost territory, and he even took the Syrian capital, Damascus. The prophet Amos predicted Jeroboam's death by the sword.

FIRST REFERENCE
2 KINGS 13:13
LAST REFERENCE
AMOS 7:11
KEY REFERENCES
2 KINGS 14:25–27; AMOS 7:11

JEROHAM   10

Compassionate

1) A descendant of Abraham through Jacob's son Levi. Jeroham was the grandfather of the prophet Samuel.

FIRST REFERENCE
I SAMUEL 1:1
LAST REFERENCE
I CHRONICLES 6:34

2) A descendant of Abraham through Jacob's son Benjamin.

ONLY REFERENCE
I CHRONICLES 8:27

3) Forefather of a Levite who returned to Jerusalem following the Babylonian captivity.

ONLY REFERENCE
I CHRONICLES 9:8

4) Forefather of a priest who lived in Jerusalem following the return from exile.

FIRST REFERENCE
I CHRONICLES 9:12
LAST REFERENCE
NEHEMIAH 11:12

5) Father of David's "mighty men" Joelah and Zebadiah, who supported the future king during his conflict with Saul.

ONLY REFERENCE
I CHRONICLES 12:7

6) A prince of the tribe of Dan, assigned to rule by King David.

ONLY REFERENCE
I CHRONICLES 27:22

7) Father of one of the captains of Jehoiada the priest.

ONLY REFERENCE
2 CHRONICLES 23:1

JERUBBAAL   14

Baal will contend

A name given to Gideon by his father after he destroyed the altars to Baal.

FIRST REFERENCE
JUDGES 6:32
LAST REFERENCE
I SAMUEL 12:11
KEY REFERENCE
JUDGES 6:32

JERUBBESHETH I

Shame will contend

An alternative name for the judge Gideon.

ONLY REFERENCE
2 SAMUEL 11:21

JERUSHA

Possessed (married)

Mother of Jotham, king of Judah.

ONLY REFERENCE
2 KINGS 15:33

JERUSHAH

Possessed (married)

A variant spelling of *Jerusha*; mother of King Jotham of Judah.

ONLY REFERENCE
2 CHRONICLES 27:1

JESAIAH

God has saved

1) A descendant of Abraham through Jacob's son Judah, in the line of the nation of Judah's third-to-last king, Jeconiah (also known as Jehoiachin).

ONLY REFERENCE
1 CHRONICLES 3:21

2) Forefather of a descendant of Benjamin who was chosen by lot to resettle Jerusalem after returning from the Babylonian Exile.

ONLY REFERENCE
NEHEMIAH 11:7

JESHAIAH

God has saved

1) A son of King David's musician Jeduthun, "who prophesied with a harp, to give thanks and to praise the LORD" (1 Chronicles 25:3).

FIRST REFERENCE
1 CHRONICLES 25:3
LAST REFERENCE
1 CHRONICLES 25:15

2) A Levite worship leader under King David.

ONLY REFERENCE
1 CHRONICLES 26:25

3) A Jewish exile who returned from Babylon to Judah under Ezra.

ONLY REFERENCE
EZRA 8:7

4) A temple minister sent to Ezra by Iddo, the chief at Casiphia.

ONLY REFERENCE
EZRA 8:19

JESHARELAH

Right toward God

One of twenty-four Levite musicians in David's time who was chosen by lot to serve in the house of the Lord.

ONLY REFERENCE
1 CHRONICLES 25:14

JESHEBEAB

People will return

One of twenty-four priests in David's time who was chosen by lot to serve in the tabernacle.

ONLY REFERENCE
1 CHRONICLES 24:13

JESHER

The right

A descendant of Abraham through Jacob's son Judah.

ONLY REFERENCE
1 CHRONICLES 2:18

JESHISHAI 1

Aged

A descendant of Abraham through Jacob's son Gad.

ONLY REFERENCE
1 CHRONICLES 5:14

JESHOHAIAH 1

God will empty

A descendant of Abraham through Jacob's son Simeon.

ONLY REFERENCE
1 CHRONICLES 4:36

JESHUA 29

He will save

1) Forefather of a priestly family who returned from captivity with Zerubbabel.

FIRST REFERENCE
EZRA 2:36
LAST REFERENCE
NEHEMIAH 7:39

2) A priest in the time of King Hezekiah who helped to distribute the people's freewill offerings to his fellow priests.

FIRST REFERENCE
1 CHRONICLES 24:11
LAST REFERENCE
2 CHRONICLES 31:15

3) High priest who returned from exile with Zerubbabel and built the temple altar with him. With the priests and Levites, Jeshua took part in a praise service when the temple foundation was laid. When Judah's adversaries wanted to help build the temple, Jeshua and other leaders refused to allow it.

FIRST REFERENCE
EZRA 2:2
LAST REFERENCE
NEHEMIAH 12:26
KEY REFERENCE
EZRA 3:2

4) Father of a Levite worship leader who weighed the temple vessels after the Babylonian Exile.

ONLY REFERENCE
EZRA 8:33

5) Forefather of an exiled family that returned to Judah under Zerubbabel.

FIRST REFERENCE
EZRA 2:6
LAST REFERENCE
NEHEMIAH 7:11

6) Father of a man who repaired Jerusalem's walls under Nehemiah.

ONLY REFERENCE
NEHEMIAH 3:19

7) A Levite who helped Ezra to explain the law to exiles returned to Jerusalem. Jeshua was among a group of Levites who led a revival among the Israelites in the time of Nehemiah.

FIRST REFERENCE
NEHEMIAH 8:7
LAST REFERENCE
NEHEMIAH 12:24

8) Another form of the name *Joshua*. Same as Joshua (1).

ONLY REFERENCE
NEHEMIAH 8:17

9) A Jewish leader who renewed the covenant under Nehemiah.

ONLY REFERENCE
NEHEMIAH 10:9

JESIAH 2 [2]
God will lend

1) A "mighty man" who supported the future king David during his conflict with Saul.

ONLY REFERENCE
I CHRONICLES 12:6

2) A descendant of Abraham through Jacob's son Levi.

ONLY REFERENCE
I CHRONICLES 23:20

JESIMIEL 1 [image]
God will place

A descendant of Abraham through Jacob's son Simeon.

ONLY REFERENCE
I CHRONICLES 4:36

JESSE 47 [image]
Extant

Father of David. Jesse had seven of his sons pass before the prophet Samuel, but none was the king Samuel was seeking. Only when the youngest, David, was brought before Samuel did the prophet anoint him king. Jesse allowed his youngest son to become King Saul's harpist and then his armor bearer. After David returned home, his father sent him to bring food to his brothers, who were with Saul's army, and there David fought Goliath. The prophet Isaiah foresaw the coming of the Messiah with the words "There shall come forth a rod out the stem of Jesse, and a Branch shall grow out of his roots" (Isaiah 11:1). Jesus' earthly lineage stems from Jesse, through David.

FIRST REFERENCE
RUTH 4:17
LAST REFERENCE
ROMANS 15:12
KEY REFERENCES
I SAMUEL 16:8–11; ISAIAH 11:1
GENEALOGY OF JESUS
MATTHEW 1:5–6

JESUI 1 [image]
Level

A descendant of Abraham through Jacob's son Asher.

ONLY REFERENCE
NUMBERS 26:44

JESUS 983 [3]
Jehovah saved

1) God's Son and humanity's Savior, Jesus existed from the beginning. Through the Holy Spirit, He became incarnated within the womb of Mary and was born in a humble Bethlehem stable. He grew up in Nazareth, learning the carpentry trade of His earthly father, Joseph. At twelve he amazed the religious leaders of Jerusalem with his understanding of spiritual things. Jesus began His ministry when he was about thirty. Baptized by his cousin John, Jesus went into the wilderness, where He was tempted by Satan but did not fail. After announcing His new ministry in the synagogue, He called twelve disciples to leave their

work and follow Him. With them, He traveled through Israel, teaching and calling people to repentance and new relationship with God. During His ministry Jesus preached about the kingdom of God and corrected the false beliefs of the Pharisees and Sadducees. Jesus taught the spiritual ruler Nicodemus that he needed to be born again. In the Sermon on the Mount, He gave the multitudes a short course in what it meant to truly love God and serve Him. With signs and miracles, He proved His own divine status and drew curious crowds to whom He preached. Jesus healed many people of illnesses and broke through their spiritual darknesses. But when He raised Lazarus from the dead, the chief priests and Pharisees began to plot to kill Him because they feared the Romans' reaction to this news. As His enemies sought to kill Him, Jesus entered Jerusalem on a donkey. The people spread garments before him and greeted Him as the Messiah, calling out, "Hosanna." A week later, after Judas betrayed Him, the crowd agreed with the chief priests and cried, "Crucify Him!" Following an illegal trial, Jesus, who had done no wrong, died for humanity's sin on the cross. After His resurrection, three days later, He showed Himself to Mary Magdalene and then the disciples and others. He appeared to the faithful for forty days then commissioned the apostles to spread the Good News, afterward ascending to heaven. The book of Revelation pictures Jesus as the Lamb who is Lord of lords and King of kings. He will return to judge the world. Finally He will establish a New Jerusalem, where He will live with those who trust in Him.

FIRST REFERENCE
MATTHEW 1:1
LAST REFERENCE
REVELATION 22:21
KEY REFERENCES
MATTHEW 5–7; MARK 11:7–9; LUKE 4:18;
24:28–32; JOHN 1:1, 14; 3:3–21; 20:10–22;
REVELATION 17:14; 19:11–16; 21:1–3

2) Another form of the name *Joshua*. Same as Joshua (1).

ONLY REFERENCE
HEBREWS 4:8

3) A believing Jew and fellow worker with the apostle Paul in Rome. Paul called Jesus, also known as Justus, "a comfort unto me."

ONLY REFERENCE
COLOSSIANS 4:11

JETHER 8

Superiority

1) Gideon's son who fearfully disobeyed when his father told him to kill Zebah and Zalmunna.

ONLY REFERENCE
JUDGES 8:20

2) Father of Amasa, one of David's army commanders.

FIRST REFERENCE
I KINGS 2:5
LAST REFERENCE
I CHRONICLES 2:17

3) A descendant of Abraham through Jacob's son Judah.

ONLY REFERENCE
I CHRONICLES 2:32

4) Another descendant of Abraham through Jacob's son Judah.

ONLY REFERENCE
I CHRONICLES 4:17

5) A descendant of Abraham through Jacob's son Asher.

ONLY REFERENCE
I CHRONICLES 7:38

JETHETH 2

A "duke of Edom," a leader in the family line of Esau.

FIRST REFERENCE
GENESIS 36:40
LAST REFERENCE
I CHRONICLES 1:51

JETHRO 10
His excellence

Moses' father-in-law, for whom Moses kept flocks until God called him to Egypt. For a time, Moses' wife, Zipporah, along with her two sons, lived with Jethro. The four of them joined up at Mt. Sinai. There Jethro advised Moses to appoint others who could help him rule over the people. Same as Hobab.

FIRST REFERENCE
EXODUS 3:1
LAST REFERENCE
EXODUS 18:12

JETUR 2
Encircled, enclosed

A descendant of Abraham through Ishmael, Abraham's son by his surrogate wife, Hagar.

FIRST REFERENCE
GENESIS 25:15
LAST REFERENCE
I CHRONICLES 1:31

JEUEL 1
Carried away of God

A Jewish exile from the tribe of Judah who resettled Jerusalem.

ONLY REFERENCE
I CHRONICLES 9:6

JEUSH 8
Hasty

1) A son of Esau.

FIRST REFERENCE
GENESIS 36:5
LAST REFERENCE
I CHRONICLES 1:35

2) A descendant of Abraham through Jacob's son Benjamin.

ONLY REFERENCE
I CHRONICLES 7:10

3) A descendant of Gershon who was numbered when David counted the Levites.

FIRST REFERENCE
I CHRONICLES 23:10
LAST REFERENCE
I CHRONICLES 23:11

4) A son of Judah's king Rehoboam and a grandson of Solomon.

ONLY REFERENCE
2 CHRONICLES 11:19

JEUZ 1
Counselor

A descendant of Abraham through Jacob's son Benjamin.

ONLY REFERENCE
I CHRONICLES 8:10

JEZANIAH 2
Heard of God

A captain of Israel's forces under Nebuchadnezzar's governor, Gedaliah. Same as Jaazaniah (1).

FIRST REFERENCE
JEREMIAH 40:8
LAST REFERENCE
JEREMIAH 42:1

JEZEBEL 22
Chaste

A Sidonian princess who married King Ahab of Israel, Jezebel killed or persecuted Israel's prophets, including Elijah, who fled from her wrath after he killed the priests of her god Baal. When Ahab coveted Naboth's vineyard, Jezebel arranged for charges of blasphemy to be brought against Naboth. After he was stoned, she commanded Ahab to take the vineyard. God ordered Jehu to strike Jezebel down. After assassinating her son, King Joram, Jehu went to Jezreel. There he commanded Jezebel's slaves to throw her from a window. When he ordered her burial, only her skull, her feet, and the palms of her hands were left, fulfilling Elijah's prophecy that dogs would eat her.

FIRST REFERENCE
I KINGS 16:31
LAST REFERENCE
REVELATION 2:20
KEY REFERENCES
I KINGS 18:13; 19:1–3; 21:8–16; 2 KINGS 9:7–10

JEZER 3
Form

A descendant of Abraham through Jacob's son Naphtali.

FIRST REFERENCE
GENESIS 46:24
LAST REFERENCE
I CHRONICLES 7:13

JEZIAH 1
Sprinkled of God

An exiled Israelite who married a "strange" (foreign) woman.

ONLY REFERENCE
EZRA 10:25

JEZIEL 1
Sprinkled of God

A "mighty man" who supported the future king David during his conflict with Saul.

ONLY REFERENCE
I CHRONICLES 12:3

207

JEZLIAH   1 👤
He will draw out

A descendant of Abraham through Jacob's son Benjamin.

ONLY REFERENCE
1 CHRONICLES 8:18

JEZOAR   1 👤
He will shine

A descendant of Abraham through Jacob's son Judah.

ONLY REFERENCE
1 CHRONICLES 4:7

JEZRAHIAH   1 👤
God will shine

A priest who helped to dedicate the rebuilt wall of Jerusalem by leading the singing.

ONLY REFERENCE
NEHEMIAH 12:42

JEZREEL   4 👤2
God will sow

1) A descendant of Abraham through Jacob's son Judah.

ONLY REFERENCE
1 CHRONICLES 4:3

2) Firstborn son of the prophet Hosea whose name signified the judgment God planned for the rebellious people of Judah.

FIRST REFERENCE
HOSEA 1:4
LAST REFERENCE
HOSEA 1:11

JIBSAM   1 👤
Fragrant

A descendant of Abraham through Jacob's son Issachar.

ONLY REFERENCE
1 CHRONICLES 7:2

JIDLAPH   1 👤
Tearful

A son of Nahor, Abraham's brother.

ONLY REFERENCE
GENESIS 22:22

JIMNA   1 👤
Prosperity

A descendant of Abraham through Jacob's son Asher. Same as Jimnah.

ONLY REFERENCE
NUMBERS 26:44

JIMNAH   1 👤
Prosperity

A variant spelling of *Jimna;* a descendant of Abraham.

ONLY REFERENCE
GENESIS 46:17

JOAB   146 👤5
Jehovah fathered

1) Though he displeased David when he killed Saul's army commander, Abner, for many years Joab was commander of David's army. He fought the Ammonites for David and obeyed David's command to put Uriah the Hittite on the front lines so he would be killed.

Joab sought to bring David and his estranged son Absalom together by sending a wise woman to him with a story similar to David's own. David immediately guessed that Joab was behind her story and allowed the exiled Absalom to come home. Two years later, Joab intervened again to bring Absalom into his father's favor. David set Amasa as commander over Joab, but he sent Joab and a third of the army into battle against Absalom, who was trying to dethrone his father. Though David asked Joab to deal gently with his son, when the commander heard that Absalom was caught in a tree, Joab killed him. Joab killed Amasa, too, and again commanded the whole army. He obeyed David—but not God—when he took a census of Israel. At the end of David's life, Joab supported David's son Adonijah as king instead of Solomon. On his deathbed, David warned Solomon not to let Joab die peacefully. Solomon had Joab killed in the tabernacle, where he had fled.

FIRST REFERENCE
I SAMUEL 26:6
LAST REFERENCE
PSALM 60 (TITLE)
KEY REFERENCES
2 SAMUEL 3:26–30; 11:14–17; 14:2–3; 18:14; I KINGS 2:33–34

2) A descendant of Abraham through Jacob's son Judah.

ONLY REFERENCE
I CHRONICLES 2:54

3) Another descendant of Abraham through Jacob's son Judah.

ONLY REFERENCE
I CHRONICLES 4:14

4) Forefather of an exiled family that returned to Judah under Zerubbabel.

FIRST REFERENCE
EZRA 2:6
LAST REFERENCE
NEHEMIAH 7:11

5) Forefather of a Jewish exile who returned from Babylon to Judah under Ezra.

ONLY REFERENCE
EZRA 8:9

JOAH

Jehovah brothered

1) An officer of King Hezekiah of Judah. With Eliakim and Shebna, he confronted the king of Assyria's messengers, who tried to convince Hezekiah and his people to submit to Assyria.

FIRST REFERENCE
2 KINGS 18:18
LAST REFERENCE
ISAIAH 36:22

2) A descendant of Abraham through Jacob's son Levi. Joah was among the Levites who cleansed the Jerusalem temple during the revival of King Hezekiah's day.

FIRST REFERENCE
I CHRONICLES 6:21
LAST REFERENCE
2 CHRONICLES 29:12

3) A Levite "porter" (doorkeeper) in the house of the Lord.

ONLY REFERENCE
I CHRONICLES 26:4

4) An official under King Josiah of Judah, whom the king sent to repair the temple.

ONLY REFERENCE
2 CHRONICLES 34:8

JOAHAZ 1

Jehovah seized

Father of Joah, an official whom King Josiah of Judah sent to repair the temple.

ONLY REFERENCE
2 CHRONICLES 34:8

JOANNA 3

1) A woman who followed Jesus and provided for his financial needs. Joanna was the wife of one of King Herod's officials and was later one of the first to learn of and tell others about Jesus' resurrection.

FIRST REFERENCE
LUKE 8:3
LAST REFERENCE
LUKE 24:10

2) A descendant of Abraham through Isaac; forebear of Jesus' earthly father, Joseph.

ONLY REFERENCE
LUKE 3:27
GENEALOGY OF JESUS
LUKE 3:27

JOASH 49

Jehovah hastened

1) A descendant of Abraham through Jacob's son Benjamin.

ONLY REFERENCE
1 CHRONICLES 7:8

2) The official over stores of oil under King David.

ONLY REFERENCE
1 CHRONICLES 27:28

3) Father of Gideon, Joash stood up for his son when their neighbors wanted to kill Gideon for destroying the altar of Baal.

FIRST REFERENCE
JUDGES 6:11
LAST REFERENCE
JUDGES 8:32

4) A son of King Ahab of Israel.

FIRST REFERENCE
1 KINGS 22:26
LAST REFERENCE
2 CHRONICLES 18:25

5) King of Judah, son of King Ahaziah. He was hidden from his wicked grandmother Athaliah and protected by the priest Jehoiada, who instructed him. Though he followed the Lord, Joash did not remove idolatry from the nation. He ordered that money be collected to refurbish the temple. But when Hazael, king of Syria, was about to attack, Joash took the gold from the temple and his own house and sent it as tribute to Hazael. Joash was killed by his servants, who formed a conspiracy against him. Same as Jehoash (1).

FIRST REFERENCE
2 KINGS 11:2
LAST REFERENCE
2 CHRONICLES 25:25
KEY REFERENCES
2 CHRONICLES 22:11; 24:2, 25

6) Another name for Jehoash (2), a king of Israel.

FIRST REFERENCE
2 KINGS 13:9
LAST REFERENCE
AMOS 1:1

7) A descendant of Abraham through Jacob's son Judah. Joash was a potter.

ONLY REFERENCE
1 CHRONICLES 4:22

8) A "mighty man" who supported the future king David during his conflict with Saul.

ONLY REFERENCE
1 CHRONICLES 12:3

JOATHAM 2 👑 🧍

A descendant of Abraham through Isaac; forebear of Jesus' earthly father, Joseph.

ONLY REFERENCE
MATTHEW 1:9
GENEALOGY OF JESUS
MATTHEW 1:9

JOB 60 🧍

Hated, persecuted

1) A descendant of Abraham through Jacob's son Issachar. Same as Jashub (1).

ONLY REFERENCE
GENESIS 46:13

2) A righteous man from the land of Uz whom God tested to prove to Satan that Job was not faithful to Him because he had many physical blessings. For a time, God gave Job into Satan's power. First Job lost his cattle and servants. Then a messenger came with news that all his children had been killed. Yet Job continued to worship God. Satan then covered Job with sores, and his wife told him, "Curse God, and die" (Job 2:9). Yet he still remained faithful. Three comfortless comforters, his friends, came to share his misery. For a week they were silent. But when Job began to speak, they answered with accusations that he had done something wrong. Eliphaz, Bildad, and Zophar took turns attempting to convince him that he needed to repent. Job made his case against them. Aware that no one is completely righteous before God, Job remained at a loss to understand what he had done wrong and voiced many moving expressions of faith. A young man, Elihu, confronted them with God's justice and power, until God intervened and made Job aware of his own lack of understanding. Job repented. God rebuked his three friends and restored all of Job's original blessings.

FIRST REFERENCE
JOB 1:1
LAST REFERENCE
JAMES 5:11
KEY REFERENCES
JOB 1:21; 9:1–3; 13:12, 15; 19:25–27; 38:1–3;
40:4–5; 42:1–17

JOBAB 9 [5]
Howler

1) A descendant of Noah through his son Shem.

FIRST REFERENCE
GENESIS 10:29
LAST REFERENCE
I CHRONICLES 1:23

2) A king of Edom, "before there reigned any king over the children of Israel" (Genesis 36:31).

FIRST REFERENCE
GENESIS 36:33
LAST REFERENCE
I CHRONICLES 1:45

3) The king of Madon who joined an alliance to attack the Israelites under Joshua.

ONLY REFERENCE
JOSHUA 11:1

4) A descendant of Abraham through Jacob's son Benjamin.

ONLY REFERENCE
I CHRONICLES 8:9

5) Another descendant of Abraham through Jacob's son Benjamin.

ONLY REFERENCE
I CHRONICLES 8:18

JOCHEBED 2
Jehovah gloried

Wife of Amram and mother of Moses, Aaron, and Miriam. She was a daughter of Levi.

FIRST REFERENCE
EXODUS 6:20
LAST REFERENCE
NUMBERS 26:59

JOED 1
Appointer

Ancestor of a Benjamite who was chosen by lot to resettle Jerusalem after returning from the Babylonian Exile.

ONLY REFERENCE
NEHEMIAH 11:7

JOEL 20 [14]
Jehovah is his God

1) Firstborn son of the prophet Samuel. Joel and his brother, Abiah, served as judges in Beersheba, but their poor character caused Israel's leaders to ask Samuel for a king to rule over them. Joel's son Heman was a well-known singer. Same as Vashni.

FIRST REFERENCE
I SAMUEL 8:2
LAST REFERENCE
I CHRONICLES 15:17

2) A descendant of Abraham through Jacob's son Simeon.

ONLY REFERENCE
I CHRONICLES 4:35

3) A descendant of Abraham through Jacob's son Reuben.

FIRST REFERENCE
I CHRONICLES 5:4
LAST REFERENCE
I CHRONICLES 5:8

4) A descendant of Abraham through Jacob's son Gad.

ONLY REFERENCE
I CHRONICLES 5:12

5) Ancestor of Heman, a singer who ministered in the tabernacle.

6) A descendant of Abraham through Jacob's son Issachar.

7) One of King David's valiant warriors.

8) A descendant of Abraham through Jacob's son Levi. Joel was among a group of Levites appointed by King David to bring the ark of the covenant from the house of Obed-edom to Jerusalem.

9) A Levite worship leader in charge of the temple treasures during David's reign.

10) Leader of the half tribe of Manasseh in the days of King David.

11) A descendant of Abraham through Jacob's son Levi. Joel was among the Levites who cleansed the Jerusalem temple during the revival of King Hezekiah's day.

12) An exiled Israelite who married a "strange" (foreign) woman.

13) A descendant of Benjamin who was chosen by lot to resettle Jerusalem after returning from the Babylonian Exile.

14) An Old Testament minor prophet who spoke of the coming day of the Lord and prophesied that God would pour out His Spirit on all flesh in the last days.

JOELAH

To ascend

A "mighty man" who supported the future king David during his conflict with Saul.

JOEZER

Jehovah is his help

A "mighty man" who supported the future king David during his conflict with Saul.

JOGLI

Exiled

Forefather of Bukki, prince of the tribe of Dan when the Israelites entered the Promised Land.

JOHA 2

Jehovah revived

1) A descendant of Abraham through Jacob's son Benjamin.

ONLY REFERENCE
I CHRONICLES 8:16

2) One of King David's valiant warriors.

ONLY REFERENCE
I CHRONICLES 11:45

JOHANAN 27

Jehovah favored

1) A rebellious Jewish leader. Johanan supported the new Chaldean governor, Gedaliah, after the fall of Jerusalem. Following the governor's murder, he disobeyed God and took the remaining Israelites to Egypt.

FIRST REFERENCE
2 KINGS 25:23
LAST REFERENCE
JEREMIAH 43:5
KEY REFERENCE
JEREMIAH 43:2

2) A descendant of King Solomon through his son Rehoboam.

ONLY REFERENCE
I CHRONICLES 3:15

3) A descendant of Abraham through Jacob's son Judah, in the line of the nation of Judah's second-to-last king, Jeconiah (also known as Jehoiachin).

ONLY REFERENCE
I CHRONICLES 3:24

4) A descendant of Abraham through Jacob's son Levi and a priest through the line of Aaron.

FIRST REFERENCE
I CHRONICLES 6:9
LAST REFERENCE
I CHRONICLES 6:10

5) A "mighty man" who supported the future king David during his conflict with Saul.

ONLY REFERENCE
I CHRONICLES 12:4

6) One of several warriors from the tribe of Gad who left Saul to join David during his conflict with the king. Johanan and his companions were "men of might. . .whose faces were like the faces of lions" (1 Chronicles 12:8).

ONLY REFERENCE
I CHRONICLES 12:12

7) A man of the tribe of Ephraim whose son Azariah counseled his nation of Israel against enslaving fellow Jews from Judah who were captured in a civil war.

ONLY REFERENCE
2 CHRONICLES 28:12

8) A Jewish exile who returned from Babylon to Judah under Ezra.

ONLY REFERENCE
EZRA 8:12

9) A Levite worship leader in whose room Ezra fasted over Judah's sins.

ONLY REFERENCE
EZRA 10:6

10) Son of Tobiah, an enemy of

Israel during the rebuilding of Jerusalem's walls under Nehemiah.

ONLY REFERENCE
NEHEMIAH 6:18

11) A high priest and descendant of the high priest Jeshua (3), who went to Jerusalem with Zerubbabel. Same as Jonathan (10).

FIRST REFERENCE
NEHEMIAH 12:22
LAST REFERENCE
NEHEMIAH 12:23

JOHN 133

1) Called "the Baptist," John was Jesus' cousin. He was born to the elderly couple Zacharias and Elisabeth after an angel told the doubtful Zacharias of the expected birth then temporarily struck him dumb for unbelief. Before Jesus began His ministry, John preached a message of repentance in the desert and, in the Jordan River, baptized those who confessed their sins. He also confronted the Pharisees and Sadducees with their lack of repentance. John foretold that another worthier than he would baptize with the Holy Spirit. He hesitantly baptized Jesus and saw the Spirit of God descend on Him. Because John had objected to Herod the tetrarch's marriage to Herod's brother's wife, Herodias, the ruler threw John into prison. Yet Herod was afraid to kill John, because the people believed he was a prophet. From prison, John sent word to ask Jesus if He was the expected Messiah. Jesus replied by telling the messengers to report on the healings they had seen and the preaching they had heard. When Herod's stepdaughter danced before his birthday guests, Herod offered to give her whatever she wanted. Her mother, Herodias, pressed her to ask for John the Baptist's head. Herod reluctantly gave her what she asked for. John's disciples took his body and buried it.

FIRST REFERENCE
MATTHEW 3:1
LAST REFERENCE
ACTS 19:4
KEY REFERENCES
MATTHEW 3:7–10; 11:2–4; 14:1–12;
MARK 1:6–8; LUKE 1:5–20

2) A son of Zebedee and brother of James, John became Jesus' disciple when the Master called the brothers to leave their fishing boat and follow Him. Describing himself in his Gospel as the disciple whom Jesus loved, John indicated their intimate relationship. As Jesus' closest disciples, he, James, and Peter experienced events such as the healings of Peter's mother-in-law and Jairus's daughter and the transfiguration of Jesus. Jesus called Zebedee's sons the Sons of Thunder, perhaps for their quick-tempered personalities. When a town refused to house the Master and his men, the brothers wanted to call down fire on them. These two overly confident men asked Jesus if they could sit at his left and right hands in glory. John and

James fell asleep in the Garden of Gethsemane as Jesus prayed before His arrest. John may also have been the "another disciple" who was known to the high priest and brought Peter into the courtyard during Jesus' trial (John 18:15). At the crucifixion, Jesus placed his mother, Mary, in John's care. After Jesus' death and resurrection, John was often with Peter. Together they investigated the empty tomb and went fishing while they awaited their new ministry. John was with Peter when he healed the beggar at the temple gate. John wrote the Gospel and letters that bear his name and the book of Revelation.

FIRST REFERENCE
MATTHEW 4:21
LAST REFERENCE
REVELATION 22:8
KEY REFERENCES
MATTHEW 4:21–22; 17:1–3; MARK 10:35–37; JOHN 13:23; 19:26; 20:1–2

3) A member of the family of the high priest Caiaphas, or Annas.

ONLY REFERENCE
ACTS 4:6

4) Also called Mark, he joined his cousin Barnabas and the apostle Paul on Paul's first missionary journey but left them at Perga. This caused Paul to lose confidence in John Mark for a time.

FIRST REFERENCE
ACTS 12:12
LAST REFERENCE
ACTS 15:37

JOIADA 4
Jehovah knows

A high priest and descendant of the priest Jeshua.

FIRST REFERENCE
NEHEMIAH 12:10
LAST REFERENCE
NEHEMIAH 13:28

JOIAKIM 4
Jehovah will raise

A high priest and descendant of the high priest Jeshua (3). Joiakim returned to Jerusalem with Zerubbabel.

FIRST REFERENCE
NEHEMIAH 12:10
LAST REFERENCE
NEHEMIAH 12:26

JOIARIB 5 3
Jehovah will contend

1) A Jewish exile charged with finding Levites and temple servants to travel to Jerusalem with Ezra.

ONLY REFERENCE
EZRA 8:16

2) A Jewish exile from the tribe of Judah who resettled Jerusalem.

ONLY REFERENCE
NEHEMIAH 11:5

3) An exiled priest who returned to Judah under Zerubbabel.

FIRST REFERENCE
NEHEMIAH 11:10
LAST REFERENCE
NEHEMIAH 12:19

JOKIM 1

Jehovah will establish

A descendant of Abraham through Jacob's son Judah. Jokim was a potter.

ONLY REFERENCE
1 CHRONICLES 4:22

JOKSHAN 4

Insidious

A son of Abraham by his second wife, Keturah.

FIRST REFERENCE
GENESIS 25:2
LAST REFERENCE
1 CHRONICLES 1:32

JOKTAN 6

He will be made little

A descendant of Noah through his son Shem. Joktan had thirteen sons.

FIRST REFERENCE
GENESIS 10:25
LAST REFERENCE
1 CHRONICLES 1:23

JONA 1

A dove

Greek form of the name *Jonah*, used in the New Testament.

ONLY REFERENCE
JOHN 1:42

JONADAB 12

Jehovah largessed

1) A friend and cousin of David's son Amnon, "a very subtil man" (2 Samuel 13:3) who advised him to pretend to be ill so his half sister Tamar would come to him. He reported Amnon's death to King David, telling him that Absalom had killed his brother.

FIRST REFERENCE
2 SAMUEL 13:3
LAST REFERENCE
2 SAMUEL 13:35

2) The Rechabite who commanded his descendants not to drink any wine.

FIRST REFERENCE
JEREMIAH 35:6
LAST REFERENCE
JEREMIAH 35:19

JONAH 19

A dove

An Old Testament minor prophet whom God commanded to preach in Nineveh, home of Israel's Assyrian enemies. Fearing God would give mercy to his enemies, Jonah fled on a ship headed for Tarshish. When a tempest struck the ship, the sailors threw Jonah overboard. Jonah was swallowed by a fish. When he praised God, the fish vomited him onto land. Jonah went to Nineveh, and the people repented. The angry prophet, wanting to die, fled the city. God pointed out that Jonah had more compassion for a plant that died than for the people of the city. Same as Jona and Jonas (1).

FIRST REFERENCE
2 KINGS 14:25
LAST REFERENCE
JONAH 4:9
KEY REFERENCES
JONAH 1:10–15; 4:10–11

JONAN   1   👑 🧍

A descendant of Abraham through Isaac; forebear of Jesus' earthly father, Joseph.

ONLY REFERENCE
LUKE 3:30
GENEALOGY OF JESUS
LUKE 3:30

JONAS   12   2

1) Greek form of the name *Jonah*, used in the New Testament.

FIRST REFERENCE
MATTHEW 12:39
LAST REFERENCE
LUKE 11:32

2) Father of Simon Peter.

FIRST REFERENCE
JOHN 21:15
LAST REFERENCE
JOHN 21:17

JONATHAN   121   14

Jehovah given

1) A priest to the idolatrous tribe of Dan in the time of the judges.

ONLY REFERENCE
JUDGES 18:30

2) Eldest son of King Saul. He and his armor bearer attacked the Philistines at Michmash and brought them into confusion so Saul and his men could attack them. Jonathan and David became great friends, and Jonathan made a covenant with him. When Saul jealously tried to kill David, Jonathan warned his friend. He spoke well of David to his father and earned him a reprieve, but again Saul's anger raged against David, who fled. David later consulted Jonathan, who spoke to his father then warned David away for good. When Saul again fought the Philistines, Jonathan was killed in battle.

FIRST REFERENCE
I SAMUEL 13:2
LAST REFERENCE
JEREMIAH 38:26
KEY REFERENCES
I SAMUEL 14:6–15; 18:1–4; 20:1–23; 31:2

3) Son of Abiathar, the high priest during King David's reign. He acted as messenger to David for the counselor Hushai. When David made Solomon king, Jonathan brought the news to David's son Adonijah.

FIRST REFERENCE
2 SAMUEL 15:27
LAST REFERENCE
I KINGS 1:43

4) David's nephew, who killed a Philistine giant from Gath.

FIRST REFERENCE
2 SAMUEL 21:21
LAST REFERENCE
I CHRONICLES 20:7

5) One of King David's valiant warriors.

FIRST REFERENCE
2 SAMUEL 23:32
LAST REFERENCE
I CHRONICLES 11:34

6) A descendant of Abraham through Jacob's son Judah.

FIRST REFERENCE
I CHRONICLES 2:32
LAST REFERENCE
I CHRONICLES 2:33

7) David's uncle and counselor, who took care of the king's sons.

8) Forefather of a Jewish exile who returned from Babylon to Judah under Ezra.

ONLY REFERENCE
EZRA 8:6

9) A man who joined Ezra in urging the Israelites to give up their "strange" (foreign) wives.

ONLY REFERENCE
EZRA 10:15

10) A high priest and descendant of the priest Jeshua who went to Jerusalem with Zerubbabel. Same as Johanan (11).

ONLY REFERENCE
NEHEMIAH 12:11

11) Forefather of a priest who returned to Jerusalem under Zerubbabel.

ONLY REFERENCE
NEHEMIAH 12:14

12) Father of a priest who helped to dedicate the rebuilt walls of Jerusalem by playing a musical instrument.

ONLY REFERENCE
NEHEMIAH 12:35

13) The scribe in whose home Jeremiah was imprisoned.

FIRST REFERENCE
JEREMIAH 37:15
LAST REFERENCE
JEREMIAH 37:20

14) A captain of Israel's forces under Nebuchadnezzar's governor Gedaliah.

ONLY REFERENCE
JEREMIAH 40:8

JORAH 1
Rainy

Forefather of an exiled family that returned to Judah under Zerubbabel.

ONLY REFERENCE
EZRA 2:18

JORAI 1
Rainy

A descendant of Abraham through Jacob's son Gad.

ONLY REFERENCE
1 CHRONICLES 5:13

JORAM 29
Jehovah raised

1) The son of the king of Hamath who brought gifts to David.

ONLY REFERENCE
2 SAMUEL 8:10

2) King of Judah and son of King Jehoshaphat. Edom revolted during his reign. When Joram fought them, his troops fled. Same as Jehoram (1).

FIRST REFERENCE
2 KINGS 8:21
LAST REFERENCE
MATTHEW 1:8
GENEALOGY OF JESUS
MATTHEW 1:8

3) Son of King Ahab and king of Israel. When he went to war with King Ahaziah of Judah against the Syrians, Joram was wounded. While he was recovering in Jezreel, he was killed by Jehu, who took his throne. Same as Jehoram (2).

FIRST REFERENCE
2 KINGS 8:16
LAST REFERENCE
2 CHRONICLES 22:7

219

4) A Levite worship leader who worked in the temple treasury during King David's reign.

ONLY REFERENCE
1 CHRONICLES 26:25

JORIM

A descendant of Abraham through Isaac; forebear of Jesus' earthly father, Joseph.

ONLY REFERENCE
LUKE 3:29
GENEALOGY OF JESUS
LUKE 3:29

JORKOAM

People will be poured forth

A descendant of Abraham through Jacob's son Judah.

ONLY REFERENCE
1 CHRONICLES 2:44

JOSABAD

Jehovah endowed

A "mighty man" who supported the future king David during his conflict with Saul.

ONLY REFERENCE
1 CHRONICLES 12:4

JOSAPHAT 2

A descendant of Abraham through Isaac; forebear of Jesus' earthly father, Joseph.

ONLY REFERENCE
MATTHEW 1:8
GENEALOGY OF JESUS
MATTHEW 1:8

JOSE 1

A descendant of Abraham through Isaac; forebear of Jesus' earthly father, Joseph.

ONLY REFERENCE
LUKE 3:29
GENEALOGY OF JESUS
LUKE 3:29

JOSEDECH 6

Jehovah righted

Father of the high priest Joshua, who took part in rebuilding the temple.

FIRST REFERENCE
HAGGAI 1:1
LAST REFERENCE
ZECHARIAH 6:11

JOSEPH 250

Let him add

1) Son of Jacob and Rachel. Joseph was Jacob's favorite son, which made his other sons jealous. Joseph angered his brothers when he told them of his dream that he would rule over them. While watching their flocks, the brothers plotted to kill Joseph. They threw him into an empty pit then sold him to some passing traders. Killing a goat, they dipped Joseph's robe in it and told Jacob he had been killed by a wild animal. Carried to Egypt, Joseph became a slave to the captain of Pharaoh's guard. After the captain's wife accused him of trying to seduce her, Joseph landed in prison, where he interpreted the dreams of two of Pharaoh's servants.

Given an opportunity to interpret Pharaoh's dream, he became second-in-command in Egypt. During the famine he had predicted, Joseph's ten half brothers came to buy food from him and did not recognize him. Joseph tested them to be certain they would not treat his full brother, Benjamin, as they had treated him. The brothers passed the test, and Joseph revealed himself. The family was reunited in Egypt, where they settled in Goshen.

FIRST REFERENCE
GENESIS 30:24
LAST REFERENCE
HEBREWS 11:22
KEY REFERENCES
GENESIS 37:3–8, 24–28; 41:14–40; 42:6–28; 44:16–34; 45:3–10

2) Father of one of the twelve spies sent by Moses to spy out the land of Canaan.

ONLY REFERENCE
NUMBERS 13:7

3) A son of King David's musician Asaph, "which prophesied according to the order of the king" (1 Chronicles 25:2).

FIRST REFERENCE
1 CHRONICLES 25:2
LAST REFERENCE
1 CHRONICLES 25:9

4) An exiled Israelite who married a "strange" (foreign) woman.

ONLY REFERENCE
EZRA 10:42

5) Forefather of a priest who returned to Jerusalem under Zerubbabel.

ONLY REFERENCE
NEHEMIAH 12:14

6) Husband of Mary and earthly father of Jesus. The carpenter Joseph was betrothed to Mary when she conceived Jesus. He planned to divorce her quietly, but an angel told him not to fear marrying her, for she would bear the Messiah. With Mary, he traveled to Bethlehem, where the child was born. He was with Mary when Jesus was dedicated at the temple and when they visited the temple when Jesus was twelve years old.

FIRST REFERENCE
MATTHEW 1:16
LAST REFERENCE
JOHN 6:42
KEY REFERENCES
MATTHEW 1:18–25; LUKE 2:4–7
GENEALOGY OF JESUS
MATTHEW 1:16

7) A wealthy man of Arimathea and member of the Sanhedrin who became Jesus' disciple. After Jesus' death, Joseph went to Pilate and asked for His body, which Joseph laid in his own tomb.

FIRST REFERENCE
MATTHEW 27:57
LAST REFERENCE
JOHN 19:38

8) A descendant of Abraham through Isaac; forebear of Jesus' earthly father, Joseph.

ONLY REFERENCE
LUKE 3:24
GENEALOGY OF JESUS
LUKE 3:24

9) Another descendant of Abraham through Isaac; another forebear of Jesus' earthly father, Joseph.

ONLY REFERENCE
LUKE 3:26
GENEALOGY OF JESUS
LUKE 3:26

10) Another descendant of Abraham through Isaac; another forebear of Jesus' earthly father, Joseph.

ONLY REFERENCE
LUKE 3:30
GENEALOGY OF JESUS
LUKE 3:30

11) A potential apostolic replacement for Judas Iscariot who lost by lot to the other candidate, Matthias. Same as Barsabas and Justus (1).

ONLY REFERENCE
ACTS 1:23

JOSES 6

1) One of four brothers of Jesus, as recorded in the Gospels of Matthew and Mark.

FIRST REFERENCE
MATTHEW 13:55
LAST REFERENCE
MARK 6:3

2) Son of one of the Marys who witnessed Jesus' crucifixion.

FIRST REFERENCE
MATTHEW 27:56
LAST REFERENCE
MARK 15:47

3) Another name for Barnabas.

ONLY REFERENCE
ACTS 4:36

JOSHAH 1
Jehovah set

A descendant of Abraham through Jacob's son Simeon.

ONLY REFERENCE
I CHRONICLES 4:34

JOSHAPHAT 1
Jehovah judged

One of King David's valiant warriors.

ONLY REFERENCE
I CHRONICLES 11:43

JOSHAVIAH 1
Jehovah set

One of King David's valiant warriors.

ONLY REFERENCE
I CHRONICLES 11:46

JOSHBEKASHAH 2
Hard seat

A son of King David's musician Heman, who was "under the hands of [his] father for song in the house of the LORD" (1 Chronicles 25:6).

FIRST REFERENCE
I CHRONICLES 25:4
LAST REFERENCE
I CHRONICLES 25:24

JOSHUA 216
Jehovah saved

1) Moses' right-hand man, Joshua son of Nun led Israel to victory against the Amalekites. He spied

out Canaan before the Israelites entered it and came back with a positive report. For his faith, he was one of only two men of his generation who entered the Promised Land. God chose Joshua to succeed Moses as Israel's leader. After Moses' death, Joshua led the Israelites into the Promised Land. After they crossed the Jordan River, Joshua led his warriors to attack Jericho using trumpets, the ark of the covenant, and their own voices. The walls fell flat from God's power. Through their own disobedience, the Israelites lost at Ai; then they won when they obeyed God. Joshua renewed their covenant with God and wrote a copy of Moses' law then continued to conquer the new land. As they fought the king of Jerusalem and his allies, Joshua needed a longer day and asked God to make the sun stand still. It remained in place until Israel won. When Joshua was old and the land had not all been conquered, God promised to win the land for His people, so Joshua allotted all the lands to the tribes of Israel and charged the people to obey God. Same as Hoshea (1) and Jesus (2).

FIRST REFERENCE
EXODUS 17:9
LAST REFERENCE
I KINGS 16:34
KEY REFERENCES
NUMBERS 14:6–7, 30; 27:18–23; JOSHUA 6:2–21; 10:12–13; 13:1, 6; 24:15

2) Owner of the land where an ox cart bearing the ark of the covenant stopped when the Philistines sent it to Israel.

FIRST REFERENCE
I SAMUEL 6:14
LAST REFERENCE
I SAMUEL 6:18

3) Governor of the city of Jerusalem under King Josiah.

ONLY REFERENCE
2 KINGS 23:8

4) The high priest who served under Governor Zerubbabel. Through their leadership, Israel rebuilt the temple. The prophet Zechariah saw a vision of Joshua. Satan accused him as he stood in filthy garments, but an angel reclothed him in clean clothes symbolizing righteousness.

FIRST REFERENCE
HAGGAI 1:1
LAST REFERENCE
ZECHARIAH 6:11
KEY REFERENCES
HAGGAI 1:14; ZECHARIAH 3:1–10

JOSIAH 53
Founded of God

1) Son of King Amon of Judah, Josiah became king when he was eight years old and followed the Lord closely through his life. Josiah collected money and repaired the temple. When the book of the law was discovered by Hilkiah the priest, Josiah had it read to him and consulted the prophetess Huldah. Then Josiah read the book to the elders of his nation, made a covenant

to follow the Lord, and caused his people to follow his example. He put down idolatry in the land and celebrated the Passover. Josiah died in battle against Necho, king of Egypt, who fought at Carchemish.

FIRST REFERENCE
I KINGS 13:2
LAST REFERENCE
ZEPHANIAH 1:1
KEY REFERENCES
2 KINGS 22:1–2, 10–13; 23:1–3, 5, 21, 29;
2 CHRONICLES 34:1–3, 31–33; 35:20–24

2) A man in whose house the high priest Joshua received a prophecy from Zechariah.

ONLY REFERENCE
ZECHARIAH 6:10

JOSIAS 2

Founded of God

A descendant of Abraham through Isaac; forebear of Jesus' earthly father, Joseph.

FIRST REFERENCE
MATTHEW 1:10
LAST REFERENCE
MATTHEW 1:11
GENEALOGY OF JESUS
MATTHEW 1:10–11

JOSIBIAH I

Jehovah will cause to dwell

A descendant of Abraham through Jacob's son Simeon.

ONLY REFERENCE
I CHRONICLES 4:35

JOSIPHIAH I

God is adding

Forefather of a Jewish exile who returned from Babylon to Judah under Ezra.

ONLY REFERENCE
EZRA 8:10

JOTHAM 24

Jehovah is perfect

1) The youngest son of Jerubbaal (also known as Gideon). Jotham hid from his brother Abimelech, who tried to kill all his brothers.

FIRST REFERENCE
JUDGES 9:5
LAST REFERENCE
JUDGES 9:57

2) Son of Azariah, king of Judah, Jotham governed for his father, who had become a leper. After he inherited the throne, he built the upper gate of the temple and obeyed God, but he did not destroy idolatry in the land. He defeated the Ammonites and received tribute from them.

FIRST REFERENCE
2 KINGS 15:5
LAST REFERENCE
MICAH 1:1
KEY REFERENCES
2 KINGS 15:32–35; 2 CHRONICLES 27:1–5

3) A descendant of Abraham through Jacob's son Judah.

ONLY REFERENCE
I CHRONICLES 2:47

JOZABAD 9

Jehovah has conferred

1) A mighty man of valor who joined David at Ziklag.

ONLY REFERENCE
1 CHRONICLES 12:20

2) An overseer of the temple treasury during King Hezekiah's reign.

ONLY REFERENCE
2 CHRONICLES 31:13

3) A descendant of Abraham through Jacob's son Levi. Jozabad was among those who distributed sacrificial animals to fellow Levites preparing to celebrate the Passover under King Josiah.

ONLY REFERENCE
2 CHRONICLES 35:9

4) A Levite who weighed the temple vessels after the Babylonian Exile.

ONLY REFERENCE
EZRA 8:33

5) An exiled Israelite priest who married a "strange" (foreign) woman.

ONLY REFERENCE
EZRA 10:22

6) An exiled Levite who married a "strange" (foreign) woman.

ONLY REFERENCE
EZRA 10:23

7) A Levite who helped Ezra to explain the law to exiles after they returned to Jerusalem.

ONLY REFERENCE
NEHEMIAH 8:7

8) A Levite who oversaw the outside of the Jerusalem temple in the time of Nehemiah.

ONLY REFERENCE
NEHEMIAH 11:16

JOZACHAR 1

Jehovah remembered

A servant of King Joash of Judah who conspired against him and murdered him.

ONLY REFERENCE
2 KINGS 12:21

JOZADAK 5

Jehovah righted

Father of Jeshua, the high priest who returned to Israel with Zerubbabel.

FIRST REFERENCE
EZRA 3:2
LAST REFERENCE
NEHEMIAH 12:26

JUBAL 1

Stream

A descendant of Cain through Lamech and his wife Adah. Jubal was "the father of all such as handle the harp and organ."

ONLY REFERENCE
GENESIS 4:21

JUCAL 1

Potent

A prince of Judah who urged King Zedekiah to kill Jeremiah because of his negative prophecy.

ONLY REFERENCE
JEREMIAH 38:1

JUDA 4 ♛ 🧍4
Judah

1) One of four brothers of Jesus, as recorded in Mark's Gospel. Same as Judas (2).

ONLY REFERENCE
MARK 6:3

2) Son of Jacob and ancestor of Jesus.

ONLY REFERENCE
LUKE 3:26
GENEALOGY OF JESUS:
LUKE 3:26

3) A descendant of David and another ancestor of Jesus.

ONLY REFERENCE:
LUKE 3:30
GENEALOGY OF JESUS
LUKE 3:30

4) A descendant of Abraham through Isaac; forebear of Jesus' earthly father, Joseph.

ONLY REFERENCE:
LUKE 3:33
GENEALOGY OF JESUS
LUKE 3:33

JUDAH 49 🧍7
Celebrated

1) Fourth son of Jacob and Leah. Judah convinced his brothers not to kill Joseph but to sell him to some Midianite traders instead. Because Judah would not give his widowed daughter-in-law his third son as a husband, she sat by the roadside and pretended she was a harlot. Judah went to her and she had twins. In Egypt, Judah spoke up for Benjamin when he was accused of stealing Joseph's cup and offered himself in Benjamin's place. His father's final blessing described Judah as one whom his brothers would praise.

FIRST REFERENCE
GENESIS 29:35
LAST REFERENCE
JEREMIAH 38:22
KEY REFERENCES
GENESIS 37:26–27; 44:18–34; 49:8–9

2) Father of several men who oversaw the workmen rebuilding the temple after the Babylonian Exile.

ONLY REFERENCE
EZRA 3:9

3) An exiled Levite who married a "strange" (foreign) woman.

ONLY REFERENCE
EZRA 10:23

4) A descendant of Benjamin who was chosen by lot to resettle Jerusalem after returning from the Babylonian Exile.

ONLY REFERENCE
NEHEMIAH 11:9

5) A Levite who returned to Judah with Zerubbabel.

ONLY REFERENCE
NEHEMIAH 12:8

6) A leader of Judah who took part in the dedication of Jerusalem's rebuilt wall.

ONLY REFERENCE
NEHEMIAH 12:34

7) A priest who helped to dedicate the rebuilt walls of Jerusalem by playing a musical instrument.

ONLY REFERENCE
NEHEMIAH 12:36

JUDAS 33
Celebrated

1) The disciple who betrayed Jesus, usually identified as Judas Iscariot. He was given his position by Jesus and was put in charge of the money, but he was not honest with it (John 12:6). Judas went to the chief priests and promised to betray Jesus for forty pieces of silver. At the Last Supper, Jesus predicted Judas's betrayal and even handed him a morsel of food to indicate his identity as the betrayer. Sorrowful at his own betrayal, following Jesus' death, Judas returned the money to the priests and hanged himself. Same as Iscariot.

FIRST REFERENCE
MATTHEW 10:4
LAST REFERENCE
ACTS 1:25
KEY REFERENCES
MATTHEW 27:3–5; MARK 14:10; JOHN 13:2, 26

2) One of four brothers of Jesus, as recorded by Matthew's Gospel. Same as Juda (1).

ONLY REFERENCE
MATTHEW 13:55

3) Identified as "the brother of James," another of Jesus' disciples, not to be confused with Judas Iscariot. He was with the disciples in the upper room after Jesus' resurrection. Same as Jude, Lebbaeus, and Thaddaeus.

FIRST REFERENCE
LUKE 6:16
LAST REFERENCE
ACTS 1:13

4) A man of Galilee whom Gamaliel used as an example of fleetingly popular religious figures.

ONLY REFERENCE
ACTS 5:37

5) A man of Damascus with whom Saul stayed while he was blinded.

ONLY REFERENCE
ACTS 9:11

6) Judas surnamed Barsabbas. The Jerusalem Council sent Judas to Antioch with Paul and Barnabas to address the issue of Gentile circumcision.

FIRST REFERENCE
ACTS 15:22
LAST REFERENCE
ACTS 15:32

7) Greek form of the name *Judah*. Same as Judah (1).

FIRST REFERENCE
MATTHEW 1:2
LAST REFERENCE
MATTHEW 1:3

JUDE 1

A disciple of Jesus, author of the epistle of Jude, and the brother of James. Same as Judas (3), Lebbaeus, and Thaddaeus.

ONLY REFERENCE
JUDE 1:1

JUDITH 1
Jew, descendant of Judah

One of Esau's Hittite wives, the daughter of Beeri.

ONLY REFERENCE
GENESIS 26:34

JULIA 1

A Christian acquaintance of the apostle Paul, greeted in his letter to the Romans.

ONLY REFERENCE
ROMANS 16:15

JULIUS 2

A Roman centurion who guarded Paul when he sailed to Rome.

FIRST REFERENCE
ACTS 27:1
LAST REFERENCE
ACTS 27:3

JUNIA 1

A Roman Christian who spent time in jail with the apostle Paul and who also may have been related to Paul.

ONLY REFERENCE
ROMANS 16:7

JUSHABHESED 1

Jehovah is perfect

A descendant of Abraham through Jacob's son Judah, in the line of the nation of Judah's second-to-last king, Jeconiah (also known as Jehoiachin).

ONLY REFERENCE
I CHRONICLES 3:20

JUSTUS 3
Just

1) Surname of Joseph (11), a potential apostolic replacement for Judas Iscariot who lost by lot to the other candidate, Matthias. Same as Barsabas (1).

ONLY REFERENCE
ACTS 1:23

2) A Corinthian Christian in whose home Paul stayed.

ONLY REFERENCE
ACTS 18:7

3) A Christian Jew and fellow worker with the apostle Paul in Rome. Paul called Justus, also known as Jesus, "a comfort unto me."

ONLY REFERENCE
COLOSSIANS 4:11

-K-

KADMIEL 8

Presence of God

1) Head of a Levite family whose descendants returned from captivity with Zerubbabel.

FIRST REFERENCE
EZRA 2:40
LAST REFERENCE
NEHEMIAH 7:43

2) A man who supervised the workmen in the temple when it was rebuilt under Zerubbabel.

ONLY REFERENCE
EZRA 3:9

3) One of a group of Levites who led a revival among the Israelites in the time of Nehemiah.

FIRST REFERENCE
NEHEMIAH 9:4
LAST REFERENCE
NEHEMIAH 12:24

KALLAI 1

Frivolous

Forefather of a priest who returned to Jerusalem under Zerubbabel.

ONLY REFERENCE
NEHEMIAH 12:20

KAREAH 13

Bald

Father of Johanan and Jonathan, captains of the Israelite forces under Governor Gedaliah, who was placed in authority by King Nebuchadnezzar of Babylon.

FIRST REFERENCE
JEREMIAH 40:8
LAST REFERENCE
JEREMIAH 43:5

KEDAR 2

Dusky

A descendant of Abraham through Ishmael, Abraham's son with his surrogate wife, Hagar.

FIRST REFERENCE
GENESIS 25:13
LAST REFERENCE
I CHRONICLES 1:29

KEDEMAH 2

Precedence

A descendant of Abraham through Ishmael, Abraham's son with his surrogate wife, Hagar.

FIRST REFERENCE
GENESIS 25:15
LAST REFERENCE
I CHRONICLES 1:31

KEILAH 1

Enclosing, citadel

Called a Garmite, Keilah was a descendant of Abraham through Jacob's son Judah.

ONLY REFERENCE
I CHRONICLES 4:19

KELAIAH
Insignificance

An exiled Levite who married a "strange" (foreign) woman. Same as Kelita (1).

ONLY REFERENCE
EZRA 10:23

KELITA
Maiming

1) An exiled Levite who married a "strange" (foreign) woman. Same as Kelaiah.

ONLY REFERENCE
EZRA 10:23

2) A Levite who helped Ezra to explain the law to exiles returned to Jerusalem.

FIRST REFERENCE
NEHEMIAH 8:7
LAST REFERENCE
NEHEMIAH 10:10

KEMUEL
Raised of God

1) A son of Abraham's brother Nahor.

ONLY REFERENCE
GENESIS 22:21

2) Prince of the tribe of Ephraim when the Israelites entered the Promised Land.

ONLY REFERENCE
NUMBERS 34:24

3) Father of Hashabiah, a ruler over the Levites during King David's reign.

ONLY REFERENCE
I CHRONICLES 27:17

KENAN
A nest

A descendant of Adam through his son Seth. Kenan was the sixth-longest-lived person in the Bible at 910 years.

ONLY REFERENCE
I CHRONICLES 1:2

KENAZ
Hunter

1) A descendant of Abraham's grandson Esau.

FIRST REFERENCE
GENESIS 36:11
LAST REFERENCE
I CHRONICLES 1:36

2) A "duke of Edom," a leader in the family line of Esau.

FIRST REFERENCE
GENESIS 36:42
LAST REFERENCE
I CHRONICLES 1:53

3) Younger brother of Caleb and father of Othniel, the first judge of Israel after Caleb's death.

FIRST REFERENCE
JOSHUA 15:17
LAST REFERENCE
I CHRONICLES 4:13

4) A descendant of Abraham through Jacob's son Judah and through Caleb.

ONLY REFERENCE
I CHRONICLES 4:15

KEREN-HAPPUCH   1

Horn of cosmetic

A daughter of Job. Keren-happuch was the youngest of three daughters born to Job when God restored his fortunes. Keren-happuch and her two sisters, Jemima and Kezia, were said to be more beautiful than any other women "in all the land" (Job 42:15).

ONLY REFERENCE
JOB 42:14

KEROS   2

Ankled

Forefather of an exiled family that returned to Judah under Zerubbabel.

FIRST REFERENCE
EZRA 2:44
LAST REFERENCE
NEHEMIAH 7:47

KETURAH   4

Perfumed

Abraham's concubine (1 Chronicles 1:32) and wife (Genesis 25:1). He may have married her following Sarah's death, but her children were not part of God's promised line.

FIRST REFERENCE
GENESIS 25:1
LAST REFERENCE
I CHRONICLES 1:33

KEZIA   1

Cassia

A daughter of Job. Kezia was the second of three daughters born to Job when God restored his fortunes.

Kezia and her two sisters, Jemima and Keren-happuch, were said to be more beautiful than any other women "in all the land" (Job 42:15).

ONLY REFERENCE
JOB 42:14

KIRJATH-JEARIM   3

City of forests

A descendant of Abraham through Jacob's son Judah.

FIRST REFERENCE
I CHRONICLES 2:50
LAST REFERENCE
I CHRONICLES 2:53

KISH   21   5

A bow

1) A Benjaminite, the father of King Saul. Seeking his father's donkeys, Saul came to Samuel, who anointed him king. Kish's brother was Abner, Saul's battle commander. Saul and his son Jonathan were buried in Kish's tomb. Same as Cis.

FIRST REFERENCE
I SAMUEL 9:1
LAST REFERENCE
I CHRONICLES 26:28
KEY REFERENCES
I SAMUEL 14:50–51; 2 SAMUEL 21:14

2) A descendant of Abraham through Jacob's son Benjamin.

FIRST REFERENCE
I CHRONICLES 8:30
LAST REFERENCE
I CHRONICLES 9:36

3) A descendant of Abraham through Jacob's son Levi.

FIRST REFERENCE
I CHRONICLES 23:21
LAST REFERENCE
I CHRONICLES 24:29

4) Another descendant of Abraham through Jacob's son Levi. Kish was among the Levites who cleansed the temple during the revival of King Hezekiah's day.

ONLY REFERENCE
2 CHRONICLES 29:12

5) Forefather of Mordecai, Esther's cousin.

ONLY REFERENCE
ESTHER 2:5

KISHI   1
War, battle

A descendant of Abraham through Jacob's son Levi.

ONLY REFERENCE
I CHRONICLES 6:44

KITTIM   2
Islander

A descendant of Noah through his son Japheth.

FIRST REFERENCE
GENESIS 10:4
LAST REFERENCE
I CHRONICLES 1:7

KOHATH   32
Allied

A son of Levi. Kohath's family was designated by God to care for the most holy things of the tabernacle.

FIRST REFERENCE
GENESIS 46:11
LAST REFERENCE
I CHRONICLES 23:12
KEY REFERENCES
NUMBERS 4:15; 7:9

KOLAIAH   2
Voice of God

1) Ancestor of a Benjaminite who was chosen by lot to resettle Jerusalem after returning from the Babylonian Exile.

ONLY REFERENCE
NEHEMIAH 11:7

2) Father of Ahab, a false prophet at the time of the Babylonian Exile.

ONLY REFERENCE
JEREMIAH 29:21

KORAH   37
To make bald

1) A son of Esau.

FIRST REFERENCE
GENESIS 36:5
LAST REFERENCE
I CHRONICLES 1:35

2) A descendant of Esau and a "duke" of Edom.

ONLY REFERENCE
GENESIS 36:16

3) A descendant of Levi and Kohath who opposed Moses when the prophet said all the Israelites were not holy. Moses commanded Korah and his company to come before the Lord, with their censers filled with incense, and stand in the door of the tabernacle. God warned Moses and Aaron to stand back while He consumed these rebels. Though the prophet and priest prayed for them, God made the earth swallow all 250 men, along with their tents.

FIRST REFERENCE
EXODUS 6:21
LAST REFERENCE
I CHRONICLES 9:19
KEY REFERENCES
NUMBERS 16:1–11, 16–19, 32–35; 26:9–11

4) A descendant of Judah through his son Perez.

ONLY REFERENCE
I CHRONICLES 2:43

5) A descendant of Abraham through Jacob's son Levi. Korah's sons are named in the titles of eleven psalms: 42, 44–49, 84–85, and 87–88.

FIRST REFERENCE
I CHRONICLES 6:22
LAST REFERENCE
PSALM 88 (TITLE)

KORE 4

1) Father of Shallum, a tabernacle gatekeeper.

FIRST REFERENCE
I CHRONICLES 9:19
LAST REFERENCE
I CHRONICLES 26:19

2) A Levite worship leader who kept the temple's east gate under King Hezekiah and had charge of the freewill and most holy offerings.

ONLY REFERENCE
2 CHRONICLES 31:14

KOZ 4

1) Forefather of an exile who returned to Jerusalem with Zerubbabel. Koz lost his role as a priest when his genealogical record could not be found.

FIRST REFERENCE
EZRA 2:61
LAST REFERENCE
NEHEMIAH 7:63

2) Forefather of a man who repaired Jerusalem's walls under Nehemiah.

FIRST REFERENCE
NEHEMIAH 3:4
LAST REFERENCE
NEHEMIAH 3:21

KUSHAIAH 1

Entrapped of God

Father of a Levite musician appointed during King David's reign.

ONLY REFERENCE
I CHRONICLES 15:17

LAADAH

A descendant of Abraham through Jacob's son Judah.

ONLY REFERENCE
I CHRONICLES 4:21

LAADAN 7

1) A descendant of Abraham through Joseph's son Ephraim.

ONLY REFERENCE
I CHRONICLES 7:26

2) A Levite worship leader who was part of David's reorganization of the Levites.

FIRST REFERENCE
I CHRONICLES 23:7
LAST REFERENCE
I CHRONICLES 26:21

LABAN 55

To be white or to make bricks

Called Laban the Syrian (Genesis 25:20), this brother of Rebekah approved of her marriage to Isaac. When Rebekah's son Esau became angry at his brother, Jacob, for stealing their father's blessing from him, Isaac sent Jacob to Laban. Jacob loved Rachel, Laban's second daughter, and offered to work for him for seven years in order to win her. At the end of that time, Laban tricked Jacob into marrying his first daughter, Leah. Then he offered Rachel to Jacob for another seven years of service. When Jacob wanted to go home, Laban asked him to stay, recognizing that God had blessed him because Jacob was in his camp. Jacob, in turn, tricked Laban into giving him the best of his flocks. Jacob saw the anger of Laban and his sons, and God called him to return home, so he left. Laban pursued Jacob and confronted him for slipping away without warning and taking his household gods. Laban did not find the gods because Rachel, who had taken them, was sitting on them. He made a covenant with Jacob. Then, blessing them, Laban departed.

FIRST REFERENCE
GENESIS 24:29
LAST REFERENCE
GENESIS 46:25
KEY REFERENCES
GENESIS 28:2; 29:18–28; 30:31–43

LAEL

Belonging to God

Chief of the Gershonites when Moses led Israel.

ONLY REFERENCE
NUMBERS 3:24

LAHAD

To glow, to be earnest

A descendant of Abraham through Jacob's son Judah.

ONLY REFERENCE
I CHRONICLES 4:2

LAHMI

Foodful

Brother of the Philistine giant Goliath. Lahmi was killed in battle by King David's warrior Elhanan. Lahmi's spear handle "was like a weaver's beam."

ONLY REFERENCE
I CHRONICLES 20:5

LAISH 2

Crushing

Father of Phalti, Michal's second husband, whom she was forced to leave to return to her first husband, King David.

FIRST REFERENCE
I SAMUEL 25:44
LAST REFERENCE
2 SAMUEL 3:15

LAMECH 12

A descendant of Cain through his son Enoch. Lamech's father was Methuselah, and Lamech was the father of Noah. Lamech is the first man whom the Bible records as having more than one wife.

FIRST REFERENCE
GENESIS 4:18
LAST REFERENCE
LUKE 3:36
KEY REFERENCES
GENESIS 4:19; 5:28–29
GENEALOGY OF JESUS
LUKE 3:36

LAPIDOTH 1

To shine, or a lamp or flame

Husband of Israel's only female judge, Deborah.

ONLY REFERENCE
JUDGES 4:4

LAZARUS 11

The brother of Mary and Martha, Lazarus was loved by Jesus, who often came to visit the family. When Lazarus became ill, his sisters sent for Jesus, who waited several days before arriving. By the time He appeared in Bethany, Lazarus had died. Jesus promised Martha, "Thy brother shall rise again" (John 11:23), and told her He was the resurrection and the life. After weeping at Lazarus's tomb, Jesus had the stone removed from the mouth of this cave then called Lazarus forth. Lazarus walked out, still bound by the grave clothes. This Lazarus is not to be confused with the beggar named Lazarus in Jesus' parable in Luke 16.

FIRST REFERENCE
JOHN 11:1
LAST REFERENCE
JOHN 12:17

LEAH 34

Weary

Laban's tender-eyed daughter who was less beautiful than her sister, Rachel. Though Jacob loved Rachel and arranged to marry her, Laban insisted that Jacob marry Leah first. He tricked Jacob into marriage with Leah but then allowed him to marry Rachel, too. Leah had four children, while Rachel was barren. When Rachel gave Jacob her maid, Bilhah, to have children with him and Leah had had no more children, Leah gave her maid, Zilpah, to Jacob, too. But Leah later had two more sons and a daughter. When Jacob returned to his home after serving Laban for many years, he placed Leah in more danger than her sister as they neared Jacob's wronged brother, Esau. Leah's daughter, Dinah, was raped by the prince of Shechem, and Leah's sons Simeon and Levi killed the men of Shechem. Leah was buried at Machpelah with Abraham, Sarah, Isaac, and Rebekah.

FIRST REFERENCE
GENESIS 29:16
LAST REFERENCE
RUTH 4:11
KEY REFERENCES
GENESIS 29:20–28, 31–35; 30:9, 17–21; 33:1–2; 34:1–2; 49:31

LEBANA

The white, the moon

Forefather of a family that returned to Jerusalem with Zerubbabel. Same as Lebanah.

ONLY REFERENCE
NEHEMIAH 7:48

LEBANAH

The white, the moon

Forefather of a family that returned to Jerusalem with Zerubbabel. Same as Lebana.

ONLY REFERENCE
EZRA 2:45

LEBBAEUS

Uncertain

Also called Thaddaeus, he was one of Jesus' twelve disciples, as listed by Matthew. Also called "Judas, the brother of James" in Luke's Gospel and the book of Acts. Same as Judas (3) and Jude.

ONLY REFERENCE
MATTHEW 10:3

LECAH

A journey

A descendant of Abraham through Jacob's son Judah.

ONLY REFERENCE
1 CHRONICLES 4:21

LEHABIM

Flames

A descendant of Noah through his son Ham.

FIRST REFERENCE
GENESIS 10:13
LAST REFERENCE
1 CHRONICLES 1:11

LEMUEL 2

Belonging to God

An otherwise unknown king credited with writing Proverbs 31. Lemuel credited the words to "the prophecy that his mother taught him" (Proverbs 31:1).

FIRST REFERENCE
PROVERBS 31:1
LAST REFERENCE
PROVERBS 31:4

LETUSHIM 1

Oppressed

A descendant of Abraham by his second wife, Keturah.

ONLY REFERENCE
GENESIS 25:3

LEUMMIM 1

Night specter

A descendant of Abraham by his second wife, Keturah.

ONLY REFERENCE
GENESIS 25:3

LEVI 21

Attached

1) Leah and Jacob's third child. After Dinah was raped by the prince of Shechem, Levi and his brother Simeon attacked the men of the city and killed them. Through his line, God established the priests and Levites, beginning with Aaron and his sons.

FIRST REFERENCE
GENESIS 29:34
LAST REFERENCE
EZRA 8:18
KEY REFERENCE
GENESIS 34:25

2) Son of Alphaeus, a tax collector who became Jesus' disciple. He left his work when Jesus called him to follow Him. Same as Matthew.

FIRST REFERENCE
MARK 2:14
LAST REFERENCE
LUKE 5:29

3) A descendant of Abraham through Isaac; forebear of Jesus' earthly father, Joseph.

ONLY REFERENCE
LUKE 3:24
GENEALOGY OF JESUS
LUKE 3:24

4) Another descendant of Abraham through Isaac; another forebear of Jesus' earthly father, Joseph.

ONLY REFERENCE
LUKE 3:29
GENEALOGY OF JESUS
LUKE 3:29

LIBNI 5

White

1) A descendant of Abraham through Jacob's son Levi.

FIRST REFERENCE
EXODUS 6:17
LAST REFERENCE
I CHRONICLES 6:20

2) Another descendant of Abraham through Jacob's son Levi.

ONLY REFERENCE
I CHRONICLES 6:29

LIKHI

Learned

A descendant of Abraham through Joseph's son Manasseh.

ONLY REFERENCE
1 CHRONICLES 7:19

LINUS

A Christian whose greetings Paul passed on to Timothy when Paul wrote his second letter to the young pastor.

ONLY REFERENCE
2 TIMOTHY 4:21

LO-AMMI

Not my people

Third child of the prophet Hosea's adulterous wife, Gomer. God gave the boy the prophetic name Lo-ammi to indicate that the Jewish people "are not my people, and I will not be your God."

ONLY REFERENCE
HOSEA 1:9

LOIS

Grandmother of the apostle Paul's protégé Timothy. Paul described Lois as a person of "unfeigned faith."

ONLY REFERENCE
2 TIMOTHY 1:5

LO-RUHAMAH 2

Not pitied

Second child of the prophet Hosea's adulterous wife, Gomer. God gave the girl the prophetic name Lo-ruhamah to indicate that "I will no more have mercy upon the house of Israel" (Hosea 1:6).

FIRST REFERENCE
HOSEA 1:6
LAST REFERENCE
HOSEA 1:8

LOT 37

Abram's nephew, who traveled with him to the Promised Land. Once their grazing area was unable to support all their flocks, Lot chose to move to the plain of the Jordan River and live near Sodom. An alliance of Canaanite kings attacked Sodom and Gomorrah and captured Lot, his people, and his goods. When Abram heard about this, he went to Lot's rescue and regained everything. Lot returned to Sodom, where two angels visited him. Lot offered them his hospitality, but the men of Sodom demanded that he bring the two angels out so they could know them. Instead, Lot offered the men his two virgin daughters, whom they refused. The angels blinded the men and told Lot they were about to destroy the city. Lot tried to gather his extended family, but his sons-in-law would not listen. So Lot took his wife and daughters and left the city. They were warned not to look back, but his wife did and was turned into a pillar of salt. After the destruction of the cities of the plain, Lot's daughters lay with their father. The children of these unions became the founders of the Moabites and Ammonites.

FIRST REFERENCE
GENESIS 11:27
LAST REFERENCE
2 PETER 2:7
KEY REFERENCES
GENESIS 13:5–11; 14:14–16; 19:1–38

LOTAN 7
Covering

A descendant of Seir, who lived in Esau's "land of Edom."

FIRST REFERENCE
GENESIS 36:20
LAST REFERENCE
I CHRONICLES 1:39

LUCAS 2

A variation on the name *Luke*; a biblical writer and traveling companion of the apostle Paul.

ONLY REFERENCE
PHILEMON 1:24

LUCIUS 2
Illuminative

1) Called Lucius of Cyrene, he was a prophet or teacher who ministered in Antioch when Paul and Barnabas were chosen for missionary work.

ONLY REFERENCE
ACTS 13:1

2) A relative of Paul who lived in Rome and was greeted in the apostle's letter to the Romans.

ONLY REFERENCE
ROMANS 16:21

LUD 2

A descendant of Noah through his son Shem.

FIRST REFERENCE
GENESIS 10:22
LAST REFERENCE
I CHRONICLES 1:17

LUDIM 2
A Ludite

A descendant of Noah through his son Ham.

FIRST REFERENCE
GENESIS 10:13
LAST REFERENCE
I CHRONICLES 1:11

LUKE 2

Known as the "beloved physician," Luke was probably a Gentile believer who became a companion of Paul. Writer of a Gospel and the book of Acts, he was also an excellent historian, as is shown by the exactness with which he describes the details of the gospel events and the places where they happened. The use of "we" in Acts 16:10 indicates that Luke joined Paul and Silas on their missionary journey. He was with Paul during his imprisonment in Rome. Same as Lucas.

FIRST REFERENCE
COLOSSIANS 4:14
LAST REFERENCE
2 TIMOTHY 4:11

LYDIA 2 👤

A woman of Thyatira who sold goods dyed with an expensive purple color. After hearing Paul's preaching, she became a Christian believer.

FIRST REFERENCE
ACTS 16:14
LAST REFERENCE
ACTS 16:40

LYSANIAS 1 👤
Grief dispelling

Tetrarch of Abilene when John the Baptist began preaching.

ONLY REFERENCE
LUKE 3:1

LYSIAS 3 👤

The Roman soldier who heard information from Paul's nephew about a plot to kill Paul. Lysias sent Paul to the governor, Felix, in Caesarea. Also called Claudius Lysias. See Claudius (2).

FIRST REFERENCE
ACTS 23:26
LAST REFERENCE
ACTS 24:22

MAACAH 2 👥
Depression

1) One of David's wives who was daughter of Talmai, king of Geshur, and mother of Absalom. Same as Maachah (6).

ONLY REFERENCE
2 SAMUEL 3:3

2) A king who provided hired soldiers to the Ammonites when they attacked King David.

ONLY REFERENCE
2 SAMUEL 10:6

MAACHAH 18 👥
Depression

1) A son of Nahor (2), Abraham's brother, by his concubine Reumah.

ONLY REFERENCE
GENESIS 22:24

2) Father of Achish, a king of Gath with whom David once sought refuge.

ONLY REFERENCE
1 KINGS 2:39

3) A daughter of David's son Absalom and the favorite among King Rehoboam's eighteen wives and sixty concubines.

4) Mother of King Asa of Judah.

FIRST REFERENCE
I KINGS 15:13
LAST REFERENCE
2 CHRONICLES 15:16

5) A concubine of Caleb, the brother of Jerahmeel.

ONLY REFERENCE
I CHRONICLES 2:48

6) One of David's wives who was daughter of Talmai, the king of Geshur, and mother of Absalom. Same as Maacah (1).

ONLY REFERENCE
I CHRONICLES 3:2

7) Wife of a descendant of Manasseh named Machir.

FIRST REFERENCE
I CHRONICLES 7:15
LAST REFERENCE
I CHRONICLES 7:16

8) Wife of Jehiel, the leader of Gibeon.

FIRST REFERENCE
I CHRONICLES 8:29
LAST REFERENCE
I CHRONICLES 9:35

9) Father of one of King David's valiant warriors.

ONLY REFERENCE
I CHRONICLES 11:43

10) Father of a leader of the Simeonites who served under David.

ONLY REFERENCE
I CHRONICLES 27:16

MAADAI

Ornamental

An exiled Israelite who married a "strange" (foreign) woman.

ONLY REFERENCE
EZRA 10:34

MAADIAH

Ornament of God

A chief priest who went up to Jerusalem with Zerubbabel.

ONLY REFERENCE
NEHEMIAH 12:5

MAAI

Sympathetic

A priest who helped to dedicate the rebuilt wall of Jerusalem by playing a musical instrument.

ONLY REFERENCE
NEHEMIAH 12:36

MAASEIAH   25

Work of God

1) A Levite musician who performed in celebration when King David brought the ark of the covenant to Jerusalem.

FIRST REFERENCE
I CHRONICLES 15:18
LAST REFERENCE
I CHRONICLES 15:20

2) A captain of hundreds under Jehoiada the priest, who crowned King Joash.

ONLY REFERENCE
2 CHRONICLES 23:1

3) An official under King Uzziah who prepared his army.

ONLY REFERENCE
2 CHRONICLES 26:11

4) A son of King Ahaz who was killed in a battle with Syria.

ONLY REFERENCE
2 CHRONICLES 28:7

5) Jerusalem's governor who repaired the temple at King Josiah's command.

ONLY REFERENCE
2 CHRONICLES 34:8

6) An exiled Israelite priest who married a "strange" (foreign) woman.

ONLY REFERENCE
EZRA 10:18

7) Another exiled Israelite priest who married a foreign woman.

ONLY REFERENCE
EZRA 10:21

8) Another exiled Israelite priest who married a foreign woman.

ONLY REFERENCE
EZRA 10:22

9) Another exiled Israelite who married a foreign woman.

ONLY REFERENCE
EZRA 10:30

10) A rebuilder of the walls of Jerusalem under Nehemiah.

ONLY REFERENCE
NEHEMIAH 3:23

11) A priest who assisted Ezra in reading the book of the law to the people of Jerusalem.

ONLY REFERENCE
NEHEMIAH 8:4

12) A Levite who helped Ezra to explain the law to exiles returned to Jerusalem.

ONLY REFERENCE
NEHEMIAH 8:7

13) A Jewish leader who renewed the covenant under Nehemiah.

ONLY REFERENCE
NEHEMIAH 10:25

14) A Jewish exile from the tribe of Judah who resettled Jerusalem in the time of Nehemiah.

ONLY REFERENCE
NEHEMIAH 11:5

15) Ancestor of a Benjaminite who was chosen by lot to resettle Jerusalem after returning from the Babylonian Exile.

ONLY REFERENCE
NEHEMIAH 11:7

16) A priest who helped to dedicate the rebuilt wall of Jerusalem by giving thanks.

ONLY REFERENCE
NEHEMIAH 12:41

17) A priest who gave thanks with a trumpet at the dedication of Jerusalem's rebuilt walls.

ONLY REFERENCE
NEHEMIAH 12:42

18) Father of the priest Zephaniah, who served during the reign of King Zedekiah of Judah.

FIRST REFERENCE
JEREMIAH 21:1
LAST REFERENCE
JEREMIAH 37:3

19) A false prophet aganist whom Jeremiah prophesied.

ONLY REFERENCE
JEREMIAH 29:21

20) Father of a temple "porter" (doorkeeper) during the reign of King Jehoiakim of Judah.

ONLY REFERENCE
JEREMIAH 35:4

21) Forefather of Baruch, scribe of the prophet Jeremiah.

FIRST REFERENCE
JEREMIAH 32:12
LAST REFERENCE
JEREMIAH 51:59

MAASIAI 1

Operative

Forefather of a Levite who returned to Jerusalem following the Babylonian captivity.

ONLY REFERENCE
1 CHRONICLES 9:12

MAATH 1

A descendant of Abraham through Isaac; forebear of Jesus' earthly father, Joseph.

ONLY REFERENCE
LUKE 3:26
GENEALOGY OF JESUS
LUKE 3:26

MAAZ 1

Closure

A descendant of Abraham through Jacob's son Judah and Judah's son Pharez.

ONLY REFERENCE
1 CHRONICLES 2:27

MAAZIAH 2

Rescue of God

1) One of twenty-four priests in David's time who was chosen by lot to serve in the tabernacle.

ONLY REFERENCE
1 CHRONICLES 24:18

2) A priest who renewed the covenant under Nehemiah.

ONLY REFERENCE
NEHEMIAH 10:8

MACHBANAI 1

Native of Macbena

One of several warriors from the tribe of Gad who left Saul to join David during his conflict with the king. Machbanai and his companions were "men of might. . .whose faces were like the faces of lions" (1 Chronicles 12:8).

ONLY REFERENCE
1 CHRONICLES 12:13

MACHBENAH 1

Knoll

A descendant of Abraham through Jacob's son Judah.

ONLY REFERENCE
1 CHRONICLES 2:49

MACHI 1

Pining

Father of one of the twelve spies sent by Moses to spy out the land of Canaan.

ONLY REFERENCE
NUMBERS 13:15

MACHIR 22
Salesman

1) Grandson of Joseph through his son Manasseh and his Syrian concubine. Machir's family took Gilead from the Amorites. Moses gave him the land, and he lived there.

FIRST REFERENCE
GENESIS 50:23
LAST REFERENCE
I CHRONICLES 7:17
KEY REFERENCES
NUMBERS 32:39–40; I CHRONICLES 7:14

2) A man who brought food and supplies to King David and his soldiers as they fled from the army of David's son Absalom.

FIRST REFERENCE
2 SAMUEL 9:4
LAST REFERENCE
2 SAMUEL 17:27

MACHNADEBAI I
What is like a liberal man?

An exiled Israelite who married a "strange" (foreign) woman.

ONLY REFERENCE
EZRA 10:40

MADAI 2
Mede

A grandson of Noah through his son Japheth.

FIRST REFERENCE
GENESIS 10:2
LAST REFERENCE
I CHRONICLES 1:5

MADMANNAH I

A descendant of Abraham through Jacob's son Judah.

ONLY REFERENCE
I CHRONICLES 2:49

MAGBISH I
Stiffening

Forefather of an exiled family that returned to Judah under Zerubbabel.

ONLY REFERENCE
EZRA 2:30

MAGDALENE 12
Woman of Magdala

Surname of Mary (2).

FIRST REFERENCE
MATTHEW 27:56
LAST REFERENCE
JOHN 20:18

MAGDIEL 2
Preciousness of God

A "duke of Edom," a leader in the family line of Esau.

FIRST REFERENCE
GENESIS 36:43
LAST REFERENCE
I CHRONICLES 1:54

MAGOG 2

A son of Japheth and a grandson of Noah.

FIRST REFERENCE
GENESIS 10:2
LAST REFERENCE
I CHRONICLES 1:5

MAGOR-MISSABIB

Afright from around

A name God gave Pashur (3), the "chief governor" of the temple, when he put the prophet Jeremiah in the stocks.

ONLY REFERENCE
JEREMIAH 20:3

MAGPIASH

Exterminator of the moth

A Jewish leader who renewed the covenant under Nehemiah.

ONLY REFERENCE
NEHEMIAH 2:10

MAHALAH

Sickness

A descendant of Abraham through Joseph's son Manasseh.

ONLY REFERENCE
I CHRONICLES 7:18

MAHALALEEL 7

Praise of God

1) A descendant of Adam through his son Seth.

FIRST REFERENCE
GENESIS 5:12
LAST REFERENCE
I CHRONICLES 1:2

2) A Jewish exile from the tribe of Judah who resettled Jerusalem.

ONLY REFERENCE
NEHEMIAH 11:4

MAHALATH 2

Sickness

1) A daughter of Ishmael who married Esau.

ONLY REFERENCE
GENESIS 28:9

2) Granddaughter of David and wife of Rehoboam, king of Judah.

ONLY REFERENCE
2 CHRONICLES 11:18

MAHALI

Sick

A grandson of Levi and a great-grandson of Jacob.

ONLY REFERENCE
EXODUS 6:19

MAHARAI 3

Hasty

A commander in King David's army overseeing twenty-four thousand men in the tenth month of each year.

FIRST REFERENCE
2 SAMUEL 23:28
LAST REFERENCE
I CHRONICLES 27:13

MAHATH 3

Erasure

1) A descendant of Abraham through Jacob's son Levi.

FIRST REFERENCE
I CHRONICLES 6:35
LAST REFERENCE
2 CHRONICLES 29:12

2) An overseer of temple offerings under King Hezekiah.

ONLY REFERENCE
2 CHRONICLES 31:13

MAHAZIOTH 2
Visions

A son of King David's musician Heman, "under the hands of [his] father for song in the house of the LORD" (1 Chronicles 25:6).

FIRST REFERENCE
1 CHRONICLES 25:4
LAST REFERENCE
1 CHRONICLES 25:30

MAHER-SHALAL-HASH-BAZ 2
Hasting is he to the booty

A son of the prophet Isaiah, named at God's command to describe the Assyrian attack on Damascus and Samaria.

FIRST REFERENCE
ISAIAH 8:1
LAST REFERENCE
ISAIAH 8:3

MAHLAH 4
Sickness

One of Zelophehad's five daughters who received his inheritance because he had no sons. Each had to marry within their tribe, Manasseh.

FIRST REFERENCE
NUMBERS 26:33
LAST REFERENCE
JOSHUA 17:3

MAHLI 11
Sick

1) A descendant of Abraham through Jacob's son Levi. His father was Merari.

FIRST REFERENCE
NUMBERS 3:20
LAST REFERENCE
EZRA 8:18

2) Forefather of the sons of Merari, who ministered in the tabernacle, and a descendant of Levi.

FIRST REFERENCE
1 CHRONICLES 6:47
LAST REFERENCE
1 CHRONICLES 24:30

MAHLON 4
Sick

A son of Naomi and her husband, Elimelech. Mahlon, his father, and his brother died in Moab, forcing Naomi and Mahlon's wife, Ruth, to return to Bethlehem.

FIRST REFERENCE
RUTH 1:2
LAST REFERENCE
RUTH 4:10

MAHOL 1
Dancing

The father of two wise men who were not as wise as Solomon.

ONLY REFERENCE
1 KINGS 4:31

MALACHI 1

Ministrative

Writer of the last book of the Old Testament. Malachi lived in the time of Nehemiah and Ezra.

ONLY REFERENCE
MALACHI 1:1

MALCHAM 1

A descendant of Abraham through Jacob's son Benjamin.

ONLY REFERENCE:
I CHRONICLES 8:9

MALCHIAH 9 7

King of [appointed by] God

1) Forefather of the temple musician Asaph.

ONLY REFERENCE
I CHRONICLES 6:40

2) An exiled Israelite who married a "strange" (foreign) woman.

FIRST REFERENCE
EZRA 10:25
LAST REFERENCE
NEHEMIAH 11:12

3) Another exiled Israelite who married a foreign woman.

ONLY REFERENCE
EZRA 10:31

4) A man who repaired Jerusalem's walls under Nehemiah.

ONLY REFERENCE
NEHEMIAH 3:14

5) A goldsmith's son who repaired Jerusalem's walls under Nehemiah.

ONLY REFERENCE
NEHEMIAH 3:31

6) A priest who assisted Ezra in reading the book of the law to the people of Jerusalem.

ONLY REFERENCE
NEHEMIAH 8:4

7) Owner of the dungeon in which the prophet Jeremiah was imprisoned.

FIRST REFERENCE
JEREMIAH 38:1
LAST REFERENCE
JEREMIAH 38:6

MALCHIEL 3

King of [appointed by] God

A descendant of Abraham through Jacob's son Asher. His father was Beriah.

FIRST REFERENCE
GENESIS 46:17
LAST REFERENCE
I CHRONICLES 7:31

MALCHIJAH 6 5

King of [appointed by] God

1) Forefather of a priest who returned to Jerusalem after the Babylonian captivity.

ONLY REFERENCE
I CHRONICLES 9:12

2) One of twenty-four priests in David's time who was chosen by lot to serve in the tabernacle.

ONLY REFERENCE
I CHRONICLES 24:9

3) An exiled Israelite who married a "strange" (foreign) woman.

ONLY REFERENCE
EZRA 10:25

4) A rebuilder of the walls of Jerusalem under Nehemiah.

ONLY REFERENCE
NEHEMIAH 3:11

5) A priest who helped to dedicate the rebuilt walls of Jerusalem by giving thanks.

FIRST REFERENCE
NEHEMIAH 10:3
LAST REFERENCE
NEHEMIAH 12:42

MALCHIRAM   1

King of a high one [or exaltation]

A descendant of Abraham through Jacob's son Judah, in the line of the nation of Judah's third-to-last king, Jeconiah (also known as Jehoiachin).

ONLY REFERENCE
1 CHRONICLES 3:18

MALCHI-SHUA 3

A son of King Saul. Same as Melchi-shua.

FIRST REFERENCE
1 CHRONICLES 8:33
LAST REFERENCE
1 CHRONICLES 10:2

MALCHUS   1

The high priest's servant whose ear Simon Peter cut off when Jesus was arrested.

ONLY REFERENCE
JOHN 18:10

MALELEEL   1

A descendant of Abraham through Isaac; forebear of Jesus' earthly father, Joseph.

ONLY REFERENCE
LUKE 3:37
GENEALOGY OF JESUS
LUKE 3:27

MALLOTHI   2

I have talked, loquacious

A son of King David's musician Heman, who was "under the hands of [his] father for song in the house of the LORD" (1 Chronicles 25:6).

FIRST REFERENCE
1 CHRONICLES 25:4
LAST REFERENCE
1 CHRONICLES 25:26

MALLUCH   6   5

Regnant

1) A descendant of Levi and forefather of the sons of Merari who ministered in the tabernacle.

ONLY REFERENCE
1 CHRONICLES 6:44

2) An exiled Israelite who married a "strange" (foreign) woman.

ONLY REFERENCE
EZRA 10:29

3) Another exiled Israelite who married a foreign woman.

ONLY REFERENCE
EZRA 10:32

4) A priest who renewed the covenant under Nehemiah.

FIRST REFERENCE
NEHEMIAH 10:4
LAST REFERENCE
NEHEMIAH 12:2

5) A Jewish leader who renewed the covenant under Nehemiah.

ONLY REFERENCE
NEHEMIAH 10:27

MAMRE 2

Lusty (meaning "vigorous")

An Amorite ally of Abram who went with him to recover Abram's nephew Lot from the king of Sodom.

FIRST REFERENCE
GENESIS 14:13
LAST REFERENCE
GENESIS 14:24

MANAEN 1

Uncertain

A prophet or teacher at Antioch when Barnabas and Saul were commissioned as missionaries.

ONLY REFERENCE
ACTS 13:1

MANAHATH 2

Rest

A descendant of Seir, who lived in Esau's "land of Edom."

FIRST REFERENCE
GENESIS 36:23
LAST REFERENCE
I CHRONICLES 1:40

MANASSEH 55 5

Causing to forget

1) The elder child of Joseph and Asenath who was adopted, with his brother, Ephraim, by Joseph's father, Jacob. When Jacob blessed the two boys, he gave Ephraim the greater blessing. But he prophesied that both nations that came from the boys would be great.

FIRST REFERENCE
GENESIS 41:51
LAST REFERENCE
I CHRONICLES 7:17
KEY REFERENCE
GENESIS 48:17–19

2) A priest of the tribe of Dan, which worshipped idols, in the period of the judges.

ONLY REFERENCE
JUDGES 18:30

3) King of Judah and son of King Hezekiah, Manasseh was an evil ruler who erected pagan altars in the temple and led his nation into idolatry. He burned his own sons as offerings to the idols and became involved in witchcraft. The Lord caused the Assyrian army to capture Manasseh and bring him to Babylon. Manasseh repented, and God brought him back to Jerusalem. Manasseh removed the idols from Jerusalem, repaired God's altar, and commanded his nation to follow God.

FIRST REFERENCE
2 KINGS 20:21
LAST REFERENCE
JEREMIAH 15:4
KEY REFERENCE
2 CHRONICLES 33:1–20

4) An exiled Israelite who married a "strange" (foreign) woman.

ONLY REFERENCE
EZRA 10:30

5) Another exiled Israelite who married a foreign woman.

ONLY REFERENCE
EZRA 10:33

MANASSES 2

Causing to forget

A descendant of Abraham through Isaac; forebear of Jesus' earthly father, Joseph. Greek form of *Manasseh*.

ONLY REFERENCE
MATTHEW 1:10
GENEALOGY OF JESUS
MATTHEW 1:10

MANOAH 18

Rest

Father of Samson, whose wife was barren. The woman received a visit from the angel of the Lord, who told her not to have strong drink or anything unclean, because the child she would bear would be a Nazarite. When Manoah heard this, he prayed that God would send the angel again, so he could know what to do when the child was born. Again the angel appeared to the woman, and she brought her husband to Him. When Manoah received the instructions

he recognized that he had seen God and made an offering to Him.

FIRST REFERENCE
JUDGES 13:2
LAST REFERENCE
JUDGES 16:31
KEY REFERENCE
JUDGES 13

MAOCH 1

Oppressed

Father of Achish, the Philistine king of Gath with whom David sought refuge.

ONLY REFERENCE
I SAMUEL 27:2

MAON 2

A residence

A descendant of Abraham through Jacob's son Judah.

ONLY REFERENCE
I CHRONICLES 2:45

MARA 1

Bitter

A name Naomi gave herself after the men of her family died and she felt that God had dealt bitterly with her.

ONLY REFERENCE
RUTH 1:20

MARCUS 3

Latin form of Mark. Same as Mark.

FIRST REFERENCE
COLOSSIANS 4:10
LAST REFERENCE
I PETER 5:13

MARESHAH 2

Summit

1) A descendant of Abraham through Jacob's son Judah.

ONLY REFERENCE
1 CHRONICLES 2:42

2) Another descendant of Abraham through Jacob's son Judah.

ONLY REFERENCE
1 CHRONICLES 4:21

MARK 5

Nephew of Barnabas and fellow missionary with Barnabas and Saul. At Pamphylia, Mark left the mission. When his uncle wanted to bring him on a second journey, Paul objected. So Barnabas took Mark back with him to Cyprus. Mark was the writer of the Gospel that bears his name. Same as Marcus.

FIRST REFERENCE
ACTS 12:12
LAST REFERENCE
2 TIMOTHY 4:11

MARSENA 1

One of seven Persian princes serving under King Ahasuerus.

ONLY REFERENCE
ESTHER 1:14

MARTHA 13

Mistress

Sister of Lazarus and Mary (5). Jesus became friendly with the family when Martha invited Him to her home in Bethany. Martha, encumbered with serving, asked Jesus to tell Mary to help her, but Jesus pointed out that Mary had chosen the better part—listening to His teaching. When their brother became ill, Martha and Mary called for Jesus. While He delayed, Lazarus died. When Jesus reached Bethany, Martha commented, "If thou hadst been here, my brother had not died" (John 11:21). Jesus pointed out that He was the resurrection and brought her brother back to life.

FIRST REFERENCE
LUKE 10:38
LAST REFERENCE
JOHN 12:2
KEY REFERENCES
LUKE 10:38–42; JOHN 11:1–44

MARY 54

1) Jesus' mother, who as a virgin received the news from an angel that she would bear the Messiah. Mary traveled to Bethlehem with her betrothed, Joseph. Jesus was born there, and there Mary saw the shepherds and kings worship Him. When she and Joseph brought Jesus to the temple, Mary heard Simeon's and Anna's prophecies about her son. When Jesus was twelve years old, the couple brought Him to the temple, did not realize He had not left with their group, and had to return for Him. Mary stood by the cross and saw her son crucified. She was also in the upper

room, praying with the disciples after His ascension.

FIRST REFERENCE
MATTHEW 1:16
LAST REFERENCE
ACTS 1:14
KEY REFERENCES
MATTHEW 1:18–25; LUKE 1:26–35; 2;
JOHN 19:25
GENEALOGY OF JESUS:
MATTHEW 1:16

2) Called Mary Magdelene, she had seven devils cast out of her by Jesus. Mary was present throughout the crucifixion of Jesus. Following His resurrection, she came to the tomb with the other women to anoint His body and saw the angels who reported that Jesus had risen from the dead. She and the other women told the disciples. As Mary wept at the tomb, Jesus appeared to her. She did not recognize Him until He spoke her name.

FIRST REFERENCE
MATTHEW 27:56
LAST REFERENCE
JOHN 20:18
KEY REFERENCES
MARK 15:40–41, 16:9; LUKE 24:10–11;
JOHN 20:1–18

3) Mary, the mother of James and Joses, was with Mary Magdalene and other women at the crucifixion of Jesus and at the tomb following His resurrection.

FIRST REFERENCE
MATTHEW 27:56
LAST REFERENCE
LUKE 24:10

4) Wife of Cleophas. Possibly the same as Mary (3).

ONLY REFERENCE
JOHN 19:25

5) The sister of Lazarus and Martha, Mary of Bethany listened at Jesus' feet while her sister became encumbered in household matters. When their brother became ill, Martha and Mary called for Jesus. While He delayed, Lazarus died. Mary saw her brother, Lazarus, resurrected by Jesus and anointed Jesus with spikenard before His death.

FIRST REFERENCE
LUKE 10:39
LAST REFERENCE
JOHN 12:3
KEY REFERENCES
LUKE 10:39–42; JOHN 11:28–32; 12:3

6) Mother of John (4).

ONLY REFERENCE
ACTS 12:12

7) A Christian whom Paul greeted in his letter to the church at Rome.

ONLY REFERENCE
ROMANS 16:6

MASH

A descendant of Noah through his son Shem.

ONLY REFERENCE
GENESIS 10:23

MASSA

Burden

A son of Ishmael.

FIRST REFERENCE
GENESIS 25:14
LAST REFERENCE
1 CHRONICLES 1:30

MATHUSALA

A descendant of Abraham through Isaac; forebear of Jesus' earthly father, Joseph.

ONLY REFERENCE
LUKE 3:37
GENEALOGY OF JESUS
LUKE 3:37

MATRED

Propulsive

Mother-in-law of a king of Edom, "before there reigned any king over the children of Israel" (Genesis 36:31).

FIRST REFERENCE
GENESIS 36:39
LAST REFERENCE
I CHRONICLES 1:50

MATRI

Forefather of King Saul.

ONLY REFERENCE
I SAMUEL 10:21

MATTAN

1) A priest of Baal killed by the people of Judah after Jehoiada made a covenant between them, King Joash, and God.

FIRST REFERENCE
2 KINGS 11:18
LAST REFERENCE
2 CHRONICLES 23:17

2) Father of Shephatiah, who threw Jeremiah into a dungeon.

ONLY REFERENCE
JEREMIAH 38:1

MATTANIAH

Gift of God

1) When Nebuchadnezzar, king of Babylon, conquered Judah, Mattaniah was made king in his uncle Jehoiachin's place and renamed Zedekiah.

ONLY REFERENCE
2 KINGS 24:17

2) A Jewish exile from the tribe of Levi who resettled Jerusalem.

FIRST REFERENCE
I CHRONICLES 9:15
LAST REFERENCE
NEHEMIAH 12:35

3) A son of King David's musician Heman, who was "under the hands of [his] father for song in the house of the LORD" (1 Chronicles 25:6).

FIRST REFERENCE
I CHRONICLES 25:4
LAST REFERENCE
I CHRONICLES 25:16

4) A descendant of Abraham through Jacob's son Levi. Mattaniah was among the Levites who cleansed the Jerusalem temple during the revival of King Hezekiah's day.

ONLY REFERENCE
2 CHRONICLES 29:13

5) An exiled Israelite who married a "strange" (foreign) woman.

ONLY REFERENCE
EZRA 10:26

6) Another exiled Israelite who married a foreign woman.

ONLY REFERENCE
EZRA 10:27

7) Another exiled Israelite who married a foreign woman.

ONLY REFERENCE
EZRA 10:30

8) Another exiled Israelite who married a foreign woman.

ONLY REFERENCE
EZRA 10:37

9) Forefather of one of the temple treasurers appointed by Nehemiah.

ONLY REFERENCE
NEHEMIAH 13:13

MATTATHA 1
Gift of God

A descendant of Abraham through Isaac; forebear of Jesus' earthly father, Joseph.

ONLY REFERENCE
LUKE 3:31
GENEALOGY OF JESUS
LUKE 3:31

MATTATHAH 1
Gift of God

An exiled Israelite who married a "strange" (foreign) woman.

ONLY REFERENCE
EZRA 10:33

MATTATHIAS 2
Gift of God

1) A descendant of Abraham through Isaac; forebear of Jesus' earthly father, Joseph.

ONLY REFERENCE
LUKE 3:25
GENEALOGY OF JESUS
LUKE 3:25

2) Another descendant of Abraham through Isaac; another forebear of Jesus' earthly father, Joseph.

ONLY REFERENCE
LUKE 3:26
GENEALOGY OF JESUS
LUKE 3:26

MATTENAI 3
Liberal

1) An exiled Israelite who married a "strange" (foreign) woman.

ONLY REFERENCE
EZRA 10:33

2) Another exiled Israelite who married a foreign woman.

ONLY REFERENCE
EZRA 10:37

3) Forefather of a priest who returned to Jerusalem under Zerubbabel.

ONLY REFERENCE
NEHEMIAH 12:19

MATTHAN 2

A descendant of Abraham through Isaac; forebear of Jesus' earthly father, Joseph.

ONLY REFERENCE
MATTHEW 1:15
GENEALOGY OF JESUS
MATTHEW 1:15

MATTHAT 2
Gift of God

1) A descendant of Abraham through Isaac; forebear of Jesus' earthly father, Joseph.

ONLY REFERENCE
LUKE 3:24
GENEALOGY OF JESUS
LUKE 3:24

2) Another descendant of Abraham through Isaac; forebear of Jesus' earthly father, Joseph.

ONLY REFERENCE
LUKE 3:29
GENEALOGY OF JESUS
LUKE 3:29

MATTHEW 5

A tax collector (or publican), also called Levi, who left his tax booth to follow Jesus. Disciple Matthew was in the upper room, following Jesus' resurrection, praying. Although Matthew does not list himself as the writer of the Gospel named after him, the early church ascribed it to him. Same as Levi (2).

FIRST REFERENCE
MATTHEW 9:9
LAST REFERENCE
ACTS 1:13

MATTHIAS 2

One of two potential apostolic replacements for Judas Iscariot. Matthias won the position but is not mentioned afterward in scripture.

FIRST REFERENCE
ACTS 1:23
LAST REFERENCE
ACTS 1:26

MATTITHIAH 8 5
Gift of God

1) A Levite official in charge of the goods baked in the temple sanctuary.

ONLY REFERENCE
I CHRONICLES 9:31

2) A Levite musician who performed in celebration when King David brought the ark of the covenant to Jerusalem.

FIRST REFERENCE
I CHRONICLES 15:18
LAST REFERENCE
I CHRONICLES 16:5

3) A son of King David's musician Jeduthun, "who prophesied with a harp, to give thanks and to praise the LORD" (1 Chronicles 25:3).

FIRST REFERENCE
I CHRONICLES 25:3
LAST REFERENCE
I CHRONICLES 25:21

4) An exiled Israelite who married a "strange" (foreign) woman.

ONLY REFERENCE
EZRA 10:43

5) A priest who assisted Ezra in reading the book of the law to the people of Jerusalem.

ONLY REFERENCE
NEHEMIAH 8:4

MEBUNNAI 1
Built up

One of King David's warriors known as the "mighty men."

ONLY REFERENCE
2 SAMUEL 23:27

MEDAD 2
Loving, affectionate

A man who prophesied after God sent the Israelites quail to eat in the wilderness.

FIRST REFERENCE
NUMBERS 11:26
LAST REFERENCE
NUMBERS 11:27

MEDAN 2
Discord, strife

A son of Abraham by his second wife, Keturah.

FIRST REFERENCE
GENESIS 25:2
LAST REFERENCE
1 CHRONICLES 1:32

MEHETABEEL 1
Bettered of God

Forefather of Shemaiah, who falsely told Nehemiah that he would be killed.

ONLY REFERENCE
NEHEMIAH 6:10

MEHETABEL 2
Bettered of God

Wife of a king of Edom, "before there reigned any king over the children of Israel" (Genesis 36:31).

FIRST REFERENCE
GENESIS 36:39
LAST REFERENCE
1 CHRONICLES 1:50

MEHIDA 2
Junction

Forefather of an exiled family that returned to Judah under Zerubbabel.

FIRST REFERENCE
EZRA 2:52
LAST REFERENCE
NEHEMIAH 7:54

MEHIR 1
Price

A descendant of Abraham through Jacob's son Judah.

ONLY REFERENCE
1 CHRONICLES 4:11

MEHUJAEL 2
Smitten of God

A descendant of Cain through his son Enoch.

ONLY REFERENCE
GENESIS 4:18

MEHUMAN 1

A eunuch serving the Persian king Ahasuerus in Esther's time.

ONLY REFERENCE
ESTHER 1:10

MEHUNIM 1
A Muenite or inhabitant of Maon

Forefather of an exiled family that returned to Judah under Zerubbabel.

ONLY REFERENCE
EZRA 2:50

MELATIAH 1
God has delivered

A man who repaired Jerusalem's walls under Nehemiah.

ONLY REFERENCE
NEHEMIAH 3:7

MELCHI 2
My king

1) A descendant of Abraham through Isaac; forebear of Jesus' earthly father, Joseph.

ONLY REFERENCE
LUKE 3:24
GENEALOGY OF JESUS
LUKE 3:24

2) Another descendant of Abraham through Isaac; forebear of Jesus' earthly father, Joseph.

ONLY REFERENCE
LUKE 3:28
GENEALOGY OF JESUS
LUKE 3:28

MELCHIAH 1
King of [appointed by] God

Forefather of Pashur, who served King Zedekiah of Judah.

ONLY REFERENCE
JEREMIAH 21:1

MELCHISEDEC 9
King of right

King and high priest of Salem who blessed Abram after he recovered his nephew Lot (Genesis 14:18; Hebrews 7:1). The writer of Hebrews refers to Jesus as high priest "after the order of Melchisedec," since He was not a priest from the line of Levi. Same as Melchizedek.

FIRST REFERENCE
HEBREWS 5:6
LAST REFERENCE
HEBREWS 7:21

MELCHI-SHUA 2
King of wealth

A son of King Saul. He was killed by the Philistines along with his father and two brothers. Same as Malchi-shua.

FIRST REFERENCE
I SAMUEL 14:49
LAST REFERENCE
I SAMUEL 31:2

MELCHIZEDEK 2
King of right

Hebrew form of the name *Melchisedec*.

FIRST REFERENCE
GENESIS 14:18
LAST REFERENCE
PSALM 110:4

MELEA 1

A descendant of Abraham through Isaac; forebear of Jesus' earthly father, Joseph.

ONLY REFERENCE
LUKE 3:31
GENEALOGY OF JESUS
LUKE 3:31

MELECH 2

King

A descendant of Abraham through Jacob's son Benjamin, in the line of King Saul and his son Jonathan.

FIRST REFERENCE
I CHRONICLES 8:35
LAST REFERENCE
I CHRONICLES 9:41

MELICU 1

Regnant

Forefather of a household of priests who returned to Jerusalem under Zerubbabel.

ONLY REFERENCE
NEHEMIAH 12:14

MELZAR 2

A Babylonian official in charge of Daniel and his three friends.

FIRST REFERENCE
DANIEL 1:11
LAST REFERENCE
DANIEL 1:16

MEMUCAN 3

One of seven Persian princes serving under King Ahasuerus.

FIRST REFERENCE
ESTHER 1:14
LAST REFERENCE
ESTHER 1:21

MENAHEM 8

Comforter

A king of Israel who usurped the throne from King Shallum. During his ten-year reign, the idolatrous Menahem did evil. To keep his throne, he raised money from the wealthy men of Israel and gave it to Pul, the king of Assyria, as tribute.

FIRST REFERENCE
2 KINGS 15:14
LAST REFERENCE
2 KINGS 15:23

MENAN 1

A descendant of Abraham through Isaac; forebear of Jesus' earthly father, Joseph.

ONLY REFERENCE
LUKE 3:31
GENEALOGY OF JESUS
LUKE 3:31

MEONOTHAI 1

Habitative

A descendant of Abraham through Jacob's son Judah.

ONLY REFERENCE
I CHRONICLES 4:14

MEPHIBOSHETH 15

Dispeller of shame

1) Grandson of King Saul and son of Jonathan. As a child, Mephibosheth was dropped by his nurse and became lame. When David took the throne of Israel, he treated Mephibosheth kindly because of his friendship with Jonathan. When Absalom ousted David from Jerusalem, Mephibosheth's servant Ziba reported that Mephibosheth

remained in Jerusalem, confident he would be made king. David gave Mephibosheth's land to Ziba. When David returned to Jerusalem, Mephibosheth claimed that Ziba had deceived him and lied to David. The king ordered the two men to split the land, but Mephibosheth agreed that Ziba should have all, as long as David had returned in peace. Same as Merib-baal.

FIRST REFERENCE
2 SAMUEL 4:4
LAST REFERENCE
2 SAMUEL 21:7
KEY REFERENCES
2 SAMUEL 9:6–10; 16:3–4; 19:24–30

2) One of King Saul's sons whom David handed over to the Gibeonites, who sought vengeance on Saul's house.

ONLY REFERENCE
2 SAMUEL 21:8

MERAB   3

Increase

King Saul's firstborn daughter who was promised to David but married another man.

FIRST REFERENCE
I SAMUEL 14:49
LAST REFERENCE
I SAMUEL 18:19

MERAIAH   I

Rebellion

A priest in the days of the high priest Joiakim.

ONLY REFERENCE
NEHEMIAH 12:12

MERAIOTH   7   3

Rebellious

1) Forefather of Ezra (2) and a descendant of Abraham through Jacob's son Levi.

FIRST REFERENCE
I CHRONICLES 6:6
LAST REFERENCE
EZRA 7:3

2) Forefather of a priest who returned to Jerusalem following the Babylonian captivity.

FIRST REFERENCE
I CHRONICLES 9:11
LAST REFERENCE
NEHEMIAH 11:11

3) A descendant of Abraham through Jacob's son Levi, and a priest through the line of Aaron.

ONLY REFERENCE
NEHEMIAH 12:15

MERARI   39

Bitter

Levi's third son. His family was in charge of the boards, bars, pillars, sockets, and vessels of the tabernacle, along with the pillars of the court and their sockets, pins, and cords.

FIRST REFERENCE
GENESIS 46:11
LAST REFERENCE
EZRA 8:19
KEY REFERENCES
EXODUS 6:19; NUMBERS 3:33–37

MERED 2
Rebellion

A descendant of Abraham through Jacob's son Judah.

FIRST REFERENCE
I CHRONICLES 4:17
LAST REFERENCE
I CHRONICLES 4:18

MEREMOTH 6
Heights

1) A priest's son who weighed the valuable utensils that King Artaxerxes of Persia and his officials had given Ezra to take back to Jerusalem's temple.

FIRST REFERENCE
EZRA 8:33
LAST REFERENCE
NEHEMIAH 3:21

2) An exiled Israelite who married a "strange" (foreign) woman.

ONLY REFERENCE
EZRA 10:36

3) A priest who renewed the covenant under Nehemiah.

FIRST REFERENCE
NEHEMIAH 10:5
LAST REFERENCE
NEHEMIAH 12:3

MERES I

One of seven Persian princes serving under King Ahasuerus.

ONLY REFERENCE
ESTHER 1:14

MERIB-BAAL 4
Quarreler of Baal

A descendant of Abraham through Jacob's son Benjamin, in the line of King Saul and his son Jonathan. Same as Mephibosheth (1).

FIRST REFERENCE
I CHRONICLES 8:34
LAST REFERENCE
I CHRONICLES 9:40

MERODACH-BALADAN I

King of Babylon during the reign of King Hezekiah of Judah.

ONLY REFERENCE
ISAIAH 39:1

MESHA 3
Safety

1) A king of Moab at the time of King Jehoram of Israel.

ONLY REFERENCE
2 KINGS 3:4

2) A descendant of Abraham through Jacob's son Judah.

ONLY REFERENCE
I CHRONICLES 2:42

3) A descendant of Benjamin and son of Shaharaim.

ONLY REFERENCE
I CHRONICLES 8:9

MESHACH 15

The Babylonian name for Mishael, one of Daniel's companions in exile. Daniel had King Nebuchadnezzar make Meshach a ruler in Babylon. When some Chaldeans accused Meshach and his friends, fellow Jews and corulers Shadrach and Abed-nego, of not worshipping the king's golden idol, the three faithful Jews were thrown into a furnace. God protected His men, who were not even singed. The king recognized the power of their God and promoted them in his service. Same as Mishael.

FIRST REFERENCE
DANIEL 1:7
LAST REFERENCE
DANIEL 3:30
KEY REFERENCE
DANIEL 3:16–18

MESHECH 3

1) One of Noah's grandsons through his son Japheth.

FIRST REFERENCE
GENESIS 10:2
LAST REFERENCE
I CHRONICLES 1:5

2) A descendant of Noah through his son Shem.

ONLY REFERENCE
I CHRONICLES 1:17

MESHELEMIAH 4

A Levite "porter" (doorkeeper) in the house of the Lord.

FIRST REFERENCE
I CHRONICLES 9:21
LAST REFERENCE
I CHRONICLES 26:9

MESHEZABEEL 3

Delivered of God

1) Forefather of a man who repaired Jerusalem's walls under Nehemiah.

ONLY REFERENCE
NEHEMIAH 3:4

2) A Levite who renewed the covenant under Nehemiah.

FIRST REFERENCE
NEHEMIAH 10:21
LAST REFERENCE
NEHEMIAH 11:24

MESHILLEMITH 1

Reconciliation

Forefather of a priest who returned to Jerusalem after the Babylonian captivity.

ONLY REFERENCE
I CHRONICLES 9:12

MESHILLEMOTH 2

Reconciliations

1) A man of the tribe of Ephraim whose son Berechiah counseled his nation of Israel against enslaving fellow Jews from Judah who were captured in a civil war.

ONLY REFERENCE
2 CHRONICLES 28:12

2) A forefather of Amashai, who worked in the temple following Judah's return from exile.

ONLY REFERENCE
NEHEMIAH 11:13

MESHOBAB 1

Returned

A descendant of Abraham through Jacob's son Simeon.

ONLY REFERENCE
I CHRONICLES 4:34

MESHULLAM 25

Allied

1) Forefather of a scribe who worked for King Josiah.

ONLY REFERENCE
2 KINGS 22:3

2) A descendant of Abraham through Jacob's son Judah, in the line of the nation of Judah's second-to-last king, Jeconiah (also known as Jehoiachin).

ONLY REFERENCE
I CHRONICLES 3:19

3) A descendant of Abraham through Jacob's son Gad.

ONLY REFERENCE
I CHRONICLES 5:13

4) A descendant of Benjamin and a chief of that tribe who lived in Jerusalem.

ONLY REFERENCE
I CHRONICLES 8:17

5) Father of a Benjaminite who was chosen by lot to resettle Jerusalem after returning from the Babylonian Exile.

ONLY REFERENCE
I CHRONICLES 9:7

6) A descendant of Abraham through Jacob's son Benjamin.

ONLY REFERENCE
I CHRONICLES 9:8

7) Forefather of a priest who returned to Jerusalem under Zerubbabel.

FIRST REFERENCE
I CHRONICLES 9:11
LAST REFERENCE
NEHEMIAH 11:11

8) Another forefather of a priest who returned to Jerusalem under Zerubbabel.

ONLY REFERENCE
I CHRONICLES 9:12

9) Forefather of several Kohathites who rebuilt the temple under King Josiah.

ONLY REFERENCE
2 CHRONICLES 34:12

10) A Jewish leader whom Ezra requested to send Levites to join the exiles returning to Jerusalem.

ONLY REFERENCE
EZRA 8:16

11) A Levite who urged the Israelites to give up their "strange" (foreign) wives.

ONLY REFERENCE
EZRA 10:15

12) An exiled Israelite who married a "strange" (foreign) woman.

ONLY REFERENCE
EZRA 10:29

13) A man who repaired Jerusalem's walls under Nehemiah. His daughter married Tobiah, one of Judah's enemies who tried to stop the walls from being rebuilt.

FIRST REFERENCE
NEHEMIAH 3:4
LAST REFERENCE
NEHEMIAH 6:18

14) Another man who repaired Jerusalem's walls under Nehemiah.

ONLY REFERENCE
NEHEMIAH 3:6

15) A priest who assisted Ezra in reading the book of the law to the people of Jerusalem.

ONLY REFERENCE
NEHEMIAH 8:4

16) A Jewish leader who renewed the covenant under Nehemiah.

ONLY REFERENCE
NEHEMIAH 10:7

17) A Levite who renewed the covenant under Nehemiah.

ONLY REFERENCE
NEHEMIAH 10:20

18) Forefather of a Jewish exile from the tribe of Benjamin who resettled Jerusalem.

ONLY REFERENCE
NEHEMIAH 11:7

19) A priest who helped to dedicate Jerusalem's rebuilt walls.

FIRST REFERENCE
NEHEMIAH 12:13
LAST REFERENCE
NEHEMIAH 12:33

20) A priest who returned to Jerusalem with Zerubbabel after the exile.

ONLY REFERENCE
NEHEMIAH 12:16

21) A Levite "porter" (doorkeeper) at the temple gates in Nehemiah's day.

ONLY REFERENCE
NEHEMIAH 12:25

MESHULLEMETH 1

A mission or a favorable release

Mother of King Amon of Judah.

ONLY REFERENCE
2 KINGS 21:19

METHUSAEL 2

Man who is of God

A descendant of Adam through his son Cain.

ONLY REFERENCE
GENESIS 4:18

METHUSELAH 6

Man of a dart

A descendant of Seth who lived for 969 years, the longest-recorded life span in the Bible.

FIRST REFERENCE
GENESIS 5:21
LAST REFERENCE
1 CHRONICLES 1:3

MEUNIM 1

A Meunite

Forefather of an exiled family that returned to Judah under Zerubbabel.

ONLY REFERENCE
NEHEMIAH 7:52

MEZAHAB 2
Water of gold

Grandmother of a wife of a king of Edom, "before there reigned any king over the children of Israel" (Genesis 36:31).

FIRST REFERENCE
GENESIS 36:39
LAST REFERENCE
I CHRONICLES 1:50

MIAMIN 2
From the right hand

1) An exiled Israelite who married a "strange" (foreign) woman.

ONLY REFERENCE
EZRA 10:25

2) A chief priest who went up to Jerusalem with Zerubbabel.

ONLY REFERENCE
NEHEMIAH 12:5

MIBHAR 1
Select, the best

One of King David's warriors known as the "mighty men."

ONLY REFERENCE
I CHRONICLES 11:38

MIBSAM 3
Fragrant

1) Fourth son of Ishmael.

FIRST REFERENCE
GENESIS 25:13
LAST REFERENCE
I CHRONICLES 1:29

2) A descendant of Abraham through Jacob's son Simeon.

ONLY REFERENCE
I CHRONICLES 4:25

MIBZAR 2
Fortification, castle, or fortified city

A "duke of Edom," a leader in the family line of Esau.

FIRST REFERENCE
GENESIS 36:42
LAST REFERENCE
I CHRONICLES 1:53

MICAH 31
Who is like God?

1) A man of Mt. Ephraim who took eleven hundred shekels from his mother. When he returned them, she had two idols made for him. Micah consecrated one of his sons to be his priest. When a Levite came to his area, Micah hired him as a priest and consecrated him. Some men from Dan stole his idols and took the priest, who went with them willingly. Though Micah and his neighbors tried to recover the items, the Danites were too strong. The thieves set up the idol in Laish, a city they had conquered.

FIRST REFERENCE
JUDGES 17:1
LAST REFERENCE
JUDGES 18:27
KEY REFERENCES
JUDGES 17:1–6, 10–12; 18:17–27

2) A descendant of Abraham through Jacob's son Reuben.

ONLY REFERENCE
I CHRONICLES 5:5

3) A descendant of Abraham through Jacob's son Benjamin, in the line of King Saul and his son Jonathan.

FIRST REFERENCE
I CHRONICLES 8:34
LAST REFERENCE
I CHRONICLES 9:41

4) A Jewish exile from the tribe of Levi who resettled Jerusalem.

ONLY REFERENCE
I CHRONICLES 9:15

5) A descendant of Levi's son Kohath. Micah was the head of his father's household.

ONLY REFERENCE
I CHRONICLES 23:20

6) Father of Abdon, whom King Josiah sent to Huldah the prophetess to ask about the book of the law he had discovered.

ONLY REFERENCE
2 CHRONICLES 34:20

7) Called Micah the Morasthite, this Old Testament minor prophet ministered during the reign of Hezekiah, king of Judah.

FIRST REFERENCE
JEREMIAH 26:18
LAST REFERENCE
MICAH 1:1

MICAIAH 18

A prophet whom King Ahab of Israel hated because he never prophesied anything good to him. When King Jehoshaphat of Israel asked Ahab for a prophet who would tell the truth, Ahab had Micaiah called. Though Ahab's messenger warned him to give a good message, the prophet would only say what God told him. Micaiah mocked the false prophets' message then told Ahab that if he attacked Ramoth-gilead, his soldiers would be scattered. Micaiah condemned the lying prophets and was struck by one of their number. Micaiah prophesied against him.

FIRST REFERENCE
I KINGS 22:8
LAST REFERENCE
2 CHRONICLES 18:27
KEY REFERENCES
I KINGS 22:13–17; 2 CHRONICLES 18:1–16

MICHA 4 3

1) Son of Mephibosheth and grandson of King Saul's son Jonathan.

ONLY REFERENCE
2 SAMUEL 9:12

2) A Jewish leader who renewed the covenant under Nehemiah.

ONLY REFERENCE
NEHEMIAH 10:11

3) A Jewish exile of the tribe of Levi who resettled Jerusalem.

FIRST REFERENCE
NEHEMIAH 11:17
LAST REFERENCE
NEHEMIAH 11:22

MICHAEL 10

Who is like God?

1) Father of one of the twelve spies sent by Moses to spy out the land of Canaan.

ONLY REFERENCE
NUMBERS 13:13

2) A descendant of Abraham through Jacob's son Gad.

ONLY REFERENCE
I CHRONICLES 5:13

3) Another descendant of Abraham through Jacob's son Gad.

ONLY REFERENCE
I CHRONICLES 5:14

4) Father of a temple musician appointed by King David.

ONLY REFERENCE
I CHRONICLES 6:40

5) A descendant of Abraham through Jacob's son Issachar.

ONLY REFERENCE
I CHRONICLES 7:3

6) A descendant of Abraham through Jacob's son Benjamin.

ONLY REFERENCE
I CHRONICLES 8:16

7) A mighty man of valor who defected to David at Ziklag.

ONLY REFERENCE
I CHRONICLES 12:20

8) Father or a ruler of the tribe of Issachar in David's time.

ONLY REFERENCE
I CHRONICLES 27:18

9) A son of Judah's king Jehoshaphat, Michael was given "great gifts of silver, and of gold, and of precious things" by his father (2 Chronicles 21:3).

ONLY REFERENCE
2 CHRONICLES 21:2

10) Forefather of a Jewish exile who returned from Babylon to Judah under Ezra.

ONLY REFERENCE
EZRA 8:8

MICHAH 3

Who is like God?

A Levite worship leader during David's reign. Lots were cast to determine Michah's duties.

FIRST REFERENCE
I CHRONICLES 24:24
LAST REFERENCE
I CHRONICLES 24:25

MICHAIAH 7

Who is like God?

1) Father of Achbor. Same as Micah (6).

ONLY REFERENCE
2 KINGS 22:12

2) Mother of King Abijah of Judah.

ONLY REFERENCE
2 CHRONICLES 13:12

3) A prince of Judah sent by King Jehoshaphat to teach the law of the Lord throughout the nation.

ONLY REFERENCE
2 CHRONICLES 17:7

4) A priest who helped to dedicate the rebuilt walls of Jerusalem by giving thanks.

FIRST REFERENCE
NEHEMIAH 12:35
LAST REFERENCE
NEHEMIAH 12:41

5) A man who heard the prophet Jeremiah's words, read by his scribe, and related them to Judah's princes.

FIRST REFERENCE
JEREMIAH 36:11
LAST REFERENCE
JEREMIAH 36:13

MICHAL 18
Rivulet

Daughter of King Saul and wife of David. To win her, David had to give Saul a hundred Philistine foreskins; he killed two hundred of the enemy, fulfilling the king's request twice over. When Saul sought to kill David, Michal warned her husband and let him out a window. She told Saul's men that David was sick. Discovered, she claimed David threatened to kill her.

Saul married Michal to Phalti. When David sent for her, after he became king, she was returned to him. But when David danced before the ark, Michal despised and berated him. She had no children.

FIRST REFERENCE
I SAMUEL 14:49
LAST REFERENCE
I CHRONICLES 15:29
KEY REFERENCES
I SAMUEL 18:20–27; 19:11–12; 25:44

MICHRI 1
Salesman

Forefather of one of Benjamin's descendants who returned to Jerusalem after the Babylonian Exile.

ONLY REFERENCE
I CHRONICLES 9:8

MIDIAN 4
Brawling, contentious

A son of Abraham by his second wife, Keturah.

FIRST REFERENCE
GENESIS 25:2
LAST REFERENCE
I CHRONICLES 1:33

MIJAMIN 2

1) One of twenty-four priests in David's time who was chosen by lot to serve in the tabernacle.

ONLY REFERENCE
I CHRONICLES 24:9

2) A priest who renewed the covenant under Nehemiah.

ONLY REFERENCE
NEHEMIAH 10:7

MIKLOTH 4
Rods

1) A descendant of Abraham through Jacob's son Benjamin.

FIRST REFERENCE
I CHRONICLES 8:32
LAST REFERENCE
I CHRONICLES 9:38

2) One of David's officers who served him during the second month.

ONLY REFERENCE
I CHRONICLES 27:4

MIKNEIAH 2
Possession of God

A Levite musician who performed in celebration when King David brought the ark of the covenant to Jerusalem.

FIRST REFERENCE
I CHRONICLES 15:18
LAST REFERENCE
I CHRONICLES 15:21

MILALAI 1
Talkative

A priest who helped to dedicate the rebuilt walls of Jerusalem by playing a musical instrument.

ONLY REFERENCE
NEHEMIAH 12:36

MILCAH 11
Queen

1) Wife of Nahor (2), Abraham's brother. The couple had eight children together. Milcah was Rebekah's grandmother.

FIRST REFERENCE
GENESIS 11:29
LAST REFERENCE
GENESIS 24:47

2) One of Zelophehad's five daughters who received his inheritance because he had no sons. Each had to marry within their tribe, Manasseh.

FIRST REFERENCE
NUMBERS 26:33
LAST REFERENCE
JOSHUA 17:3

MINIAMIN 3
From the right hand

1) A priest in the time of King Hezekiah who helped to distribute the people's freewill offerings to his fellow priests.

ONLY REFERENCE
2 CHRONICLES 31:15

2) A priest who helped to dedicate the rebuilt wall of Jerusalem by giving thanks.

FIRST REFERENCE
NEHEMIAH 12:17
LAST REFERENCE
NEHEMIAH 12:41

MIRIAM 15
Rebelliously

1) Sister of Moses and Aaron and a prophetess of Israel. Miriam led the praises after Israel crossed the Red Sea. She and Aaron objected to Moses' marrying an Ethiopian woman. "Hath the LORD indeed spoken only by Moses?" they asked, seeking acknowledgment of their own prophetic gifts (Numbers 12:2). The Lord became angry, confronted them publicly, and made Miriam leprous. Moses prayed for her. God had her stay outside the camp for a week until she was healed. She died in the Desert of Zin.

FIRST REFERENCE
EXODUS 15:20
LAST REFERENCE
MICAH 6:4
KEY REFERENCES
EXODUS 15:20–21; NUMBERS 12:1–15; 20:1

2) A descendant of Jacob through his son Judah.

ONLY REFERENCE
1 CHRONICLES 4:17

MIRMA 1
Deceiving, fraud

A descendant of Abraham through Jacob's son Benjamin.

ONLY REFERENCE
1 CHRONICLES 8:10

MISHAEL 8 3
Who is what God is?

1) A cousin of Moses. When God killed Aaron's two oldest sons, Mishael and his brother carried them from the sanctuary.

FIRST REFERENCE
EXODUS 6:22
LAST REFERENCE
LEVITICUS 10:4

2) A friend of the prophet Daniel who would not defile himself by eating the king's meat. Along with two others, he would not worship an idol and was cast into the fiery furnace by King Nebuchadnezzar. Also called Meshach.

FIRST REFERENCE
DANIEL 1:6
LAST REFERENCE
DANIEL 2:17

3) A priest who assisted Ezra in reading the book of the law to the people of Jerusalem.

ONLY REFERENCE
NEHEMIAH 8:4

MISHAM 1
Inspection

A descendant of Abraham through Jacob's son Benjamin.

ONLY REFERENCE
1 CHRONICLES 8:12

MISHMA 4
A report, hearing

A descendant of Abraham through Jacob's son Simeon.

FIRST REFERENCE
GENESIS 25:14
LAST REFERENCE
1 CHRONICLES 4:26

MISHMANNAH 1
Fatness

One of several warriors from the tribe of Gad who left Saul to join David during his conflict with the king. Mishmannah and his companions were "men of might... whose faces were like the faces of lions" (1 Chronicles 12:8).

ONLY REFERENCE
1 CHRONICLES 12:10

MISPERETH 1
Enumeration

Forefather of an exiled family that returned to Judah under Zerubbabel.

ONLY REFERENCE
NEHEMIAH 7:7

MITHREDATH 2

Treasurer for Cyrus, king of Persia. He joined in writing a letter of complaint to King Artaxerxes about the rebuilding of Jerusalem.

FIRST REFERENCE
EZRA 1:8
LAST REFERENCE
EZRA 4:7

MIZPAR

Number

Forefather of an exiled family that returned to Judah under Zerubbabel.

ONLY REFERENCE
EZRA 2:2

MIZRAIM 4

Upper and Lower Egypt

A descendant of Noah through his son Ham.

FIRST REFERENCE
GENESIS 10:6
LAST REFERENCE
I CHRONICLES 1:11

MIZZAH 3

To faint with fear

A descendant of Abraham's grandson Esau, whose blessing as older brother was taken by the scheming Jacob.

FIRST REFERENCE
GENESIS 36:13
LAST REFERENCE
I CHRONICLES 1:37

MNASON

An elderly Christian from Cyprus who accompanied Paul to Jerusalem.

ONLY REFERENCE
ACTS 21:16

MOAB

From her (the mother's) father

Son of one of Lot's daughters who lay with her father and became pregnant. Moab became the forefather of the Moabites.

ONLY REFERENCE
GENESIS 19:37

MOADIAH

Assembly of God

A priest under the leadership of Joiakim following the return from exile.

ONLY REFERENCE
NEHEMIAH 12:17

MOLID

Genitor

A descendant of Abraham through Jacob's son Judah.

ONLY REFERENCE
I CHRONICLES 2:29

MORDECAI 60

1) An exiled Israelite who returned to Judah under Zerubbabel.

FIRST REFERENCE
EZRA 2:2
LAST REFERENCE
NEHEMIAH 7:7

2) Cousin of Queen Esther, who was wife of the Persian king Ahasuerus. Though he was an exiled Jew, Mordecai was faithful to his king and warned him of a plot against him by some officers of the king's household. Then Mordecai discovered a plot against the Jews, set up by the king's scheming counselor, Haman. Mordecai warned Esther and encouraged her to confront the king for the good of her people. Before the king and Haman came to the banquet at which she intended to reveal Haman's plans, the king discovered that Mordecai had never been honored

for his role in foiling the plot against him. The king commanded Haman to honor Mordecai by publicly proclaiming his deeds. When Esther revealed Haman's plan against the Jews to her husband, he became angry and commanded that Haman be hanged on the gallows his counselor had prepared for Mordecai. Then he commanded Mordecai to write a law that would defend the Jews against attack and made him first counselor in Haman's place. Mordecai received all of Haman's household as a reward.

FIRST REFERENCE
ESTHER 2:5
LAST REFERENCE
ESTHER 10:3
KEY REFERENCE
ESTHER 4:13–14

MOSES   848

Drawing out (of the water), rescued

The Old Testament prophet through whom God gave Israel the law. Because Pharaoh commanded that all male newborn Israelites should be killed, Moses' mother placed him in a basket in the Nile River. There he was found by an Egyptian princess, who raised him. Once grown, Moses killed a man for abusing an Israelite slave and fled to Midian, where he met God in a burning bush. The Lord sent Moses back to Egypt, where his brother, Aaron, became his spokesman. As God's prophet in Egypt, Moses confronted Pharaoh. God visited ten plagues on Egypt because Egypt's ruler would not let Israel go. After all Egypt's firstborn died, Pharaoh finally sent Israel away. But Egyptian troops followed, planning to recapture them. God parted the Red Sea's waters for His people, but the Egyptians were caught in the returning waves. On the way to the Promised Land, God gave His people the Ten Commandments and other laws. At their goal, ten spies sent into Canaan discouraged Israel from entering their Promised Land. So Moses and his people wandered in the desert for forty years. Moses died on Mt. Nebo, just before Israel finally entered the Promised Land.

FIRST REFERENCE
EXODUS 2:10
LAST REFERENCE
REVELATION 15:3
KEY REFERENCES
EXODUS 3:2–18; 11:4–10; 12:29–30; 14:21–27;
20:1–17; DEUTERONOMY 34:5

MOZA   5

1) A descendant of Abraham through Jacob's son Judah.

ONLY REFERENCE
I CHRONICLES 2:46

2) A descendant of Abraham through Jacob's son Benjamin, in the line of King Saul and his son Jonathan.

FIRST REFERENCE
I CHRONICLES 8:36
LAST REFERENCE
I CHRONICLES 9:43

MUPPIM
Wavings

A son of Benjamin and descendant of Abraham.

ONLY REFERENCE
GENESIS 46:21

MUSHI 8
Sensitive

A descendant of Abraham through Jacob's son Levi.

FIRST REFERENCE
EXODUS 6:19
LAST REFERENCE
I CHRONICLES 24:30

NAAM 1
Pleasure

A descendant of Abraham through Jacob's son Judah. Naam was Caleb's son.

ONLY REFERENCE
I CHRONICLES 4:15

NAAMAH 4
Pleasantness

1) A descendant of Cain and sister of Tubal-cain.

ONLY REFERENCE
GENESIS 4:22

2) Mother of King Rehoboam, she was an Ammonite.

FIRST REFERENCE
I KINGS 14:21
LAST REFERENCE
2 CHRONICLES 12:13

NAAMAN 17
Pleasantness

1) A son of Benjamin and a descendant of Abraham.

ONLY REFERENCE
GENESIS 46:21

2) A descendant of Abraham through Jacob's son Benjamin.

FIRST REFERENCE
NUMBERS 26:40
LAST REFERENCE
I CHRONICLES 8:4

3) Another descendant of Abraham through Jacob's son Benjamin.

ONLY REFERENCE
I CHRONICLES 8:7

4) Leprous captain of the Syrian army who came to the prophet Elisha for healing. Angered that Elisha told him to wash seven times in the Jordan River, he had to be persuaded to obey. When he did, he was healed.

FIRST REFERENCE
2 KINGS 5:1
LAST REFERENCE
LUKE 4:27

NAARAH 3
Girl

Wife of Ashur, who was a descendant of Abraham through Jacob's son Judah.

FIRST REFERENCE
I CHRONICLES 4:5
LAST REFERENCE
I CHRONICLES 4:6

NAARAI 1
Youthful

One of King David's valiant warriors.

ONLY REFERENCE
I CHRONICLES 11:37

NAASHON 1
Enchanter

Brother of Elisheba, Aaron's wife.

ONLY REFERENCE
EXODUS 6:23

NAASSON 3
A descendant of Abraham through Isaac; forebear of Jesus' earthly father, Joseph.

FIRST REFERENCE
MATTHEW 1:4
LAST REFERENCE
LUKE 3:32
GENEALOGY OF JESUS
LUKE 3:32

NABAL 22
Dolt

The churlish first husband of Abigail. Nabal refused to give David and his men anything in return for their protection of his lands during David's battles with Saul. Nabal's wife stepped in and generously provided them with food. When her husband heard what she had done, "his heart died within him" (1 Samuel 25:37). Ten days later, he died.

FIRST REFERENCE
I SAMUEL 25:3
LAST REFERENCE
2 SAMUEL 3:3
KEY REFERENCES
I SAMUEL 25:5–11, 37–38

NABOTH 22
Fruits

Owner of a vineyard that was coveted by King Ahab of Israel. When Naboth refused to trade his inheritance for another vineyard, Ahab became sulky. Discovering her husband in this mood, Queen Jezebel conspired to get Naboth's property. She ordered the leaders of Naboth's town to get two men to accuse Naboth of blasphemy. After the innocent man had been stoned, Ahab took possession of his land.

FIRST REFERENCE
I KINGS 21:1
LAST REFERENCE
2 KINGS 9:26
KEY REFERENCES
I KINGS 21:2–4, 7–16

NACHON
Prepared

Owner of the threshing floor at which Uzzah died for touching the ark of the covenant.

ONLY REFERENCE
2 SAMUEL 6:6

NACHOR
Snorer

1) Brother of Abraham. Same as Nahor (2).

ONLY REFERENCE
JOSHUA 24:2

2) A descendant of Abraham through Isaac; forebear of Jesus' earthly father, Joseph.

ONLY REFERENCE
LUKE 3:34
GENEALOGY OF JESUS
LUKE 3:34

NADAB
Liberal

1) A son of Aaron who, along with his brother Abihu, offered strange fire before the Lord. God sent fire from His presence to consume them, and they died.

FIRST REFERENCE
EXODUS 6:23
LAST REFERENCE
I CHRONICLES 24:2
KEY REFERENCE
NUMBERS 3:4

2) Son of Jeroboam, king of Israel, who inherited Jeroboam's throne. Nadab did evil and made his country sin. Baasha conspired against Nadab and killed him at Gibbethon before usurping his throne.

FIRST REFERENCE
I KINGS 14:20
LAST REFERENCE
I KINGS 15:31

3) A descendant of Abraham through Jacob's son Judah.

FIRST REFERENCE
I CHRONICLES 2:28
LAST REFERENCE
I CHRONICLES 2:30

4) A descendant of Abraham through Jacob's son Benjamin.

FIRST REFERENCE
I CHRONICLES 8:30
LAST REFERENCE
I CHRONICLES 9:36

NAGGE

A descendant of Abraham through Isaac; forebear of Jesus' earthly father, Joseph.

ONLY REFERENCE
LUKE 3:25
GENEALOGY OF JESUS
LUKE 3:25

NAHAM

A descendant of Jacob through his son Judah.

ONLY REFERENCE
1 CHRONICLES 4:19

NAHAMANI

Consolatory

Forefather of an exiled family that returned to Judah under Zerubbabel.

ONLY REFERENCE
NEHEMIAH 7:7

NAHARAI

Snorer

One of King David's valiant warriors. Same as Nahari.

ONLY REFERENCE
1 CHRONICLES 11:39

NAHARI

Snorer

One of King David's valiant warriors. Same as Naharai.

ONLY REFERENCE
2 SAMUEL 23:37

NAHASH 9

1) King of the Ammonites. Saul raised an army against him, won, and was made king over Gilgal.

FIRST REFERENCE
1 SAMUEL 11:1
LAST REFERENCE
1 SAMUEL 12:12

2) Father of a man who brought food and supplies to King David and his soldiers as they fled from the army of David's son Absalom.

FIRST REFERENCE
2 SAMUEL 10:2
LAST REFERENCE
1 CHRONICLES 19:2

3) Grandfather of Absalom's commander Amasa.

ONLY REFERENCE
2 SAMUEL 17:25

NAHATH 5

Quiet

1) A descendant of Abraham's grandson Esau, whose blessing as older brother was taken by the scheming Jacob.

FIRST REFERENCE
GENESIS 36:13
LAST REFERENCE
1 CHRONICLES 1:37

2) A descendant of Abraham through Jacob's son Levi.

ONLY REFERENCE
1 CHRONICLES 6:26

3) A temple overseer during the reign of King Hezekiah of Judah.

ONLY REFERENCE
2 CHRONICLES 31:13

NAHBI

Occult

One of the twelve spies sent by Moses to spy out the land of Canaan.

ONLY REFERENCE
NUMBERS 13:14

NAHOR 17
Snorer

1) Grandfather of Abram (Abraham).

FIRST REFERENCE
GENESIS 11:22
LAST REFERENCE
I CHRONICLES 1:26

2) Brother of Abram (Abraham) and son of Terah. He married Milcah. When Abram left Haran, Nahor stayed behind. He had eight sons with Milcah and four with his concubine. His son Laban became Jacob's father-in-law. Same as Nachor (1).

FIRST REFERENCE
GENESIS 11:26
LAST REFERENCE
GENESIS 31:53
KEY REFERENCES
GENESIS 22:20; 24:15

NAHSHON 9
Enchanter

Captain and prince of the tribe of Judah, he was appointed by God, through Moses. Nahshon was a forefather of Boaz.

FIRST REFERENCE
NUMBERS 1:7
LAST REFERENCE
I CHRONICLES 2:11

NAHUM 1
Comfortable

An Old Testament minor prophet who came from Elkosh. He preached to Judah after Assyria had captured Israel.

ONLY REFERENCE
NAHUM 1:1

NAOMI 21
Pleasant

Elimelech's wife, Naomi and her family moved to Moab during a famine. Following the deaths of her husband and two sons, Naomi and her daughter-in-law Ruth returned to Bethlehem. Ruth supported them by gleaning fields until Boaz, Elimelech's relative, became their kinsman-redeemer, buying Elimelech's inherited land and marrying Ruth. Naomi became nurse to their son, Obed, who was considered her grandson.

FIRST REFERENCE
RUTH 1:2
LAST REFERENCE
RUTH 4:17
KEY REFERENCES
RUTH 1:6, 20–22; 2:1–2; 4:3–6, 14–17

NAPHISH 2
Refreshed

A son of Ishmael.

FIRST REFERENCE
GENESIS 25:15
LAST REFERENCE
I CHRONICLES 1:31

NAPHTALI 8
My wrestling

A son of Jacob and founder of one of Israel's twelve tribes. Naphtali was the second son of Bilhah, Rachel's maid. When his father blessed him, he called Napthali "a hind let loose; he giveth godly words" (Genesis 49:21).

NARCISSUS

Narcissus (flower)

Head of a household of believers, Narcissus was greeted by Paul in his letter to the Romans.

ONLY REFERENCE
ROMANS 16:11

NATHAN   43

Given

1) A son of King David, born in Jerusalem.

FIRST REFERENCE
2 SAMUEL 5:14
LAST REFERENCE
LUKE 3:31
GENEALOGY OF JESUS
LUKE 3:31

2) The prophet who confronted King David about his sin with Bath-sheba. Though Nathan had encouraged David to build the temple, he had to tell the king that his son would build it at God's command. When David sinned with Bath-sheba, the prophet told him a parable that described his sin against her husband, Uriah. As the king became angry about the wrong, Nathan revealed it as David's own, and the king repented. Nathan warned Bathsheba when her son Solomon's claim to the throne was endangered by his brother Adonijah.

Together the prophet and Bath-sheba told David of the threat.

FIRST REFERENCE
2 SAMUEL 7:2
LAST REFERENCE
PSALM 51 (TITLE)
KEY REFERENCES
2 SAMUEL 7:3–12; 12:1–15; 1 KINGS 1:11–14, 23–27

3) Father of Igal, one of David's mighty men.

ONLY REFERENCE
2 SAMUEL 23:36

4) Father of a prince who commanded King Solomon's officers.

ONLY REFERENCE
1 KINGS 4:5

5) Father of an officer under King Solomon who was also the king's friend.

ONLY REFERENCE
1 KINGS 4:5

6) A descendant of Abraham through Jacob's son Judah. Nathan descended from the line of an unnamed Israelite woman and her Egyptian husband, Jarha.

ONLY REFERENCE
1 CHRONICLES 2:36

7) Brother of a valiant man in King David's army.

ONLY REFERENCE
1 CHRONICLES 11:38

8) A Jewish exile charged with finding Levites and temple servants to travel to Jerusalem with Ezra.

ONLY REFERENCE
EZRA 8:16

277

9) An exiled Israelite who married a "strange" (foreign) woman.

ONLY REFERENCE
EZRA 10:39

10) One who will mourn at the piercing of the Messiah when God defends Jerusalem.

ONLY REFERENCE
ZECHARIAH 12:12

NATHANAEL 6

A disciple from Cana who first heard of Jesus from His disciple Philip and wondered, "Can there be any good thing come out of Nazareth?" (John 1:46). Jesus described him as an Israelite in whom there was no guile. Quickly Nathanael recognized Jesus as Son of God and King of Israel and followed Him. Probably the same as Bartholomew.

FIRST REFERENCE
JOHN 1:45
LAST REFERENCE
JOHN 21:2

NATHAN-MELECH 1

Given of the king

A court official under King Josiah of Judah.

ONLY REFERENCE
2 KINGS 23:11

NAUM 1

A descendant of Abraham through Isaac; forebear of Jesus' earthly father, Joseph.

ONLY REFERENCE
LUKE 3:25
GENEALOGY OF JESUS
LUKE 3:25

NEARIAH 3

Servant of God

1) A descendant of Abraham through Jacob's son Judah, in the line of the nation of Judah's second-to-last king, Jeconiah (also known as Jehoiachin).

FIRST REFERENCE
1 CHRONICLES 3:22
LAST REFERENCE
1 CHRONICLES 3:23

2) A captain over the sons of Simeon during the reign of King Hezekiah of Judah.

ONLY REFERENCE
1 CHRONICLES 4:42

NEBAI 1

Fruitful

An Israelite who signed an agreement declaring that the exiles from Babylon would repent and obey God.

ONLY REFERENCE
NEHEMIAH 10:19

NEBAIOTH 1

Fruitfulness

A variant spelling of *Nebajoth*.

ONLY REFERENCE
1 CHRONICLES 1:29

NEBAJOTH 3

Fruitfulness

Ishmael's firstborn son. Nebajoth's sister married Esau. Same as Nebaioth.

FIRST REFERENCE
GENESIS 25:13
LAST REFERENCE
GENESIS 36:3

NEBAT 25

Regard

Father of King Jeroboam (1). Jeroboam was King Solomon's servant, a mighty man of valor, and king over Israel after Solomon's death and the division of his kingdom.

FIRST REFERENCE
I KINGS 11:26
LAST REFERENCE
2 CHRONICLES 13:6

NEBO 1

Father of several exiled Israelites who married "strange" (foreign) women.

ONLY REFERENCE
EZRA 10:43

NEBUCHAD-NEZZAR 60

Twice this king of Babylon besieged Jerusalem, took its king, and brought Judah's people into exile. King Jehoiakim of Judah had been Nebuchadnezzar's vassal for three years when he rebelled. Nebuchadnezzar attacked Jerusalem and took him, his family, and his servants, princes, and officers. He left only the poorest people in the nation's capital. Babylon's king also took the treasures of the palace and temple. Zedekiah, made king by Nebuchadnezzar, also rebelled. When his city was starving, the king and his soldiers fled. Nebuchadnezzar pursued, captured Zedekiah, killed his sons before him, put out his eyes, and carried him to Babylon. The prophet Daniel was one of Nebuchadnezzar's captives. He received a vision of the king's dream and interpreted it. Nebuchadnezzar made him a great man in Babylon. When Daniel's three friends, Shadrach, Meshach, and Abednego, refused to worship an idol, Nebuchadnezzar had them thrown into a fiery furnace, but they were not consumed. Amazed, the king declared that no one should speak anything amiss about their God and then promoted the three men to higher positions. Daniel prophesied that Nebuchadnezzar would be driven out from among people and eat grass until he recognized the Lord as the supreme God. Same as Nebuchadrezzar.

FIRST REFERENCE
2 KINGS 24:1
LAST REFERENCE
DANIEL 5:18
KEY REFERENCES
2 KINGS 24:1, 10, 12–14; 2 KINGS 25:1, 6–7,
9–10; DANIEL 2:28–48; 3:13–30; 4:25–36

NEBUCHAD-REZZAR 31 👤

King of Babylon. A variant spelling of *Nebuchadnezzar*.

FIRST REFERENCE
JEREMIAH 21:2
LAST REFERENCE
EZEKIEL 30:10
KEY REFERENCES
JEREMIAH 21:7; 39:1; 52:12; EZEKIEL 26:7

NEBUSHASBAN 1 👤

A Babylonian official who, at King Nebuchadnezzar's command, showed kindness to the prophet Jeremiah.

ONLY REFERENCE
JEREMIAH 39:13

NEBUZAR-ADAN 👤 15

Captain of the guard for King Nebuchadnezzar of Babylon. He burned Jerusalem when Nebuchadnezzar attacked King Zedekiah of Judah. Nebuzar-adan carried the Israelite captives to Babylon. He brought some important prisoners to his king, who killed them. Before he left Israel, Nebuzar-adan commanded the captain of the guard there not to harm the prophet Jeremiah, and Jeremiah was freed into Gedaliah's care.

FIRST REFERENCE
2 KINGS 25:8
LAST REFERENCE
JEREMIAH 52:30
KEY REFERENCES
2 KINGS 25:8–12, 18–21; JEREMIAH 39:11–12

NECHO 3 👤

A king of Egypt who attacked Carchemish. King Josiah of Judah fought him and was killed in the battle. Necho made Jehoiakim king in Josiah's place.

FIRST REFERENCE
2 CHRONICLES 35:20
LAST REFERENCE
2 CHRONICLES 36:4

NEDABIAH 1 👤
Largess of God

A descendant of Abraham through Jacob's son Judah, in the line of the nation of Judah's second-to-last king, Jeconiah (also known as Jehoiachin).

ONLY REFERENCE
1 CHRONICLES 3:18

NEHEMIAH 8 👤 3
Consolation of God

1) Forefather of an exiled family that returned to Judah under Zerubbabel.

FIRST REFERENCE
EZRA 2:2
LAST REFERENCE
NEHEMIAH 7:7

2) Sent at his own request, by the Persian king Artaxerxes, to rebuild Jerusalem, Nehemiah became the governor of Jerusalem. Under his rule, Jerusalem's walls were rebuilt.

FIRST REFERENCE
NEHEMIAH 1:1
LAST REFERENCE
NEHEMIAH 12:47

3) A man who repaired Jerusalem's walls under Nehemiah.

ONLY REFERENCE
NEHEMIAH 3:16

NEHUM 1

Comforted

Forefather of an exiled family that returned to Judah under Zerubbabel.

ONLY REFERENCE
NEHEMIAH 7:7

NEHUSHTA 1

Copper

Mother of King Jehoiachin of Judah.

ONLY REFERENCE
2 KINGS 24:8

NEKODA 4

Distinction, marked

1) Forefather of an exiled family that returned to Judah under Zerubbabel.

FIRST REFERENCE
EZRA 2:48
LAST REFERENCE
NEHEMIAH 7:50

2) Another forefather of an exiled family that returned to Judah under Zerubbabel.

FIRST REFERENCE
EZRA 2:60
LAST REFERENCE
NEHEMIAH 7:62

NEMUEL 3

Day of God

1) A Reubenite counted in the census taken by Moses and Aaron.

ONLY REFERENCE
NUMBERS 26:9

2) A descendant of Abraham through Jacob's son Simeon. Same as Jemuel.

FIRST REFERENCE
NUMBERS 26:12
LAST REFERENCE
1 CHRONICLES 4:24

NEPHEG 4

To spring forth, a sprout

1) A descendant of Abraham through Jacob's son Levi.

ONLY REFERENCE
EXODUS 6:21

2) A son of King David, born in Jerusalem.

FIRST REFERENCE
2 SAMUEL 5:15
LAST REFERENCE
1 CHRONICLES 14:6

NEPHISHESIM 1

To scatter, expansions

Forefather of an exiled family that returned to Judah under Zerubbabel.

ONLY REFERENCE
NEHEMIAH 7:52

NEPHUSIM 1

To scatter, expansions

Forefather of an exiled family that returned to Judah under Zerubbabel.

ONLY REFERENCE
EZRA 2:50

NER 16

Lamp

Grandfather of King Saul and father of Abner, Saul's army commander, who was called Abner son of Ner.

FIRST REFERENCE
1 SAMUEL 14:50
LAST REFERENCE
1 CHRONICLES 26:28

NEREUS
Wet

A Christian whom Paul greeted in his letter to the church at Rome.

ONLY REFERENCE
ROMANS 16:15

NERGAL-SHAREZER

1) A prince of Babylon who besieged Jerusalem during the reign of King Zedekiah of Judah.

ONLY REFERENCE
JEREMIAH 39:3

2) Another Babylonian prince who took part in the destruction of Jerusalem under King Nebuchadnezzar. Nergal-sharezer was an official who, at Nebuchadnezzar's command, showed kindness to the prophet Jeremiah.

FIRST REFERENCE
JEREMIAH 39:3
LAST REFERENCE
JEREMIAH 39:13

NERI

A descendant of Abraham through Isaac; forebear of Jesus' earthly father, Joseph.

ONLY REFERENCE
LUKE 3:27
GENEALOGY OF JESUS
LUKE 3:27

NERIAH
Light of God

Father of Baruch, the scribe of the prophet Jeremiah.

FIRST REFERENCE
JEREMIAH 32:12
LAST REFERENCE
JEREMIAH 51:59

NETHANEEL
Given of God

1) Head of the tribe of Issachar during Israel's wandering after the people failed to enter the Promised Land.

FIRST REFERENCE
NUMBERS 1:8
LAST REFERENCE
NUMBERS 10:15

2) A descendant of Abraham through Jacob's son Judah.

ONLY REFERENCE
I CHRONICLES 2:14

3) A priest who blew a trumpet before the ark of the covenant when David brought it to Jerusalem.

ONLY REFERENCE
I CHRONICLES 15:24

4) A descendant of Abraham through Jacob's son Levi.

ONLY REFERENCE
I CHRONICLES 24:6

5) A Levite "porter" (doorkeeper) in the house of the Lord.

ONLY REFERENCE
I CHRONICLES 26:4

6) A prince of Judah sent by King Jehoshaphat to teach the law of the Lord throughout the nation.

ONLY REFERENCE
2 CHRONICLES 17:7

7) A chief Levite who provided for the first Passover celebration under King Josiah of Judah.

ONLY REFERENCE
2 CHRONICLES 35:9

8) An exiled Israelite priest who married a "strange" (foreign) woman.

ONLY REFERENCE
EZRA 10:22

9) Forefather of a priest who returned to Jerusalem under Zerubbabel.

ONLY REFERENCE
NEHEMIAH 12:21

10) A priest who helped to dedicate the rebuilt walls of Jerusalem by playing a musical instrument.

ONLY REFERENCE
NEHEMIAH 12:36

NETHANIAH 20
Given of God

1) The father of a man named Ishmael, who killed the Judean governor placed over the land by the Babylonian king Nebuchadnezzar.

FIRST REFERENCE
2 KINGS 25:23
LAST REFERENCE
JEREMIAH 41:18
KEY REFERENCE
JEREMIAH 41:1–2

2) A son of King David's musician Asaph, who "prophesied according to the order of the king" (1 Chronicles 25:2).

FIRST REFERENCE
1 CHRONICLES 25:2
LAST REFERENCE
1 CHRONICLES 25:12

3) A Levite sent by King Jehoshaphat to teach the law of the Lord throughout the nation of Judah.

ONLY REFERENCE
2 CHRONICLES 17:8

4) Father of Jehudi. His son carried a message from King Josiah's court to Jeremiah's scribe, commanding him to read to Judah's princes the word that God sent through the prophet.

ONLY REFERENCE
JEREMIAH 36:14

NEZIAH 2
Conspicuous

Forefather of an exiled family that returned to Judah under Zerubbabel.

FIRST REFERENCE
EZRA 2:54
LAST REFERENCE
NEHEMIAH 7:56

NICANOR 1
Victorious

One of seven men, "full of the Holy Ghost and wisdom," selected to serve needy Christians in Jerusalem while the twelve disciples devoted themselves "to prayer, and to the ministry of the word" (Acts 6:3–4).

ONLY REFERENCE
ACTS 6:5

NICODEMUS 5

Victorious among his people

A member of the Jewish Sanhedrin who came to Jesus by night to question Him about His miracles. Jesus told Nicodemus that he had to be born again. When the Pharisees wanted to arrest Jesus, Nicodemus stood up for Him. He provided the spices with which Jesus' body was wrapped after His death.

FIRST REFERENCE
JOHN 3:1
LAST REFERENCE
JOHN 19:39

NICOLAS 1

Victorious over the people

One of seven men, "full of the Holy Ghost and wisdom," selected to serve needy Christians in Jerusalem while the twelve disciples devoted themselves "to prayer, and to the ministry of the word" (Acts 6:3–4).

ONLY REFERENCE
ACTS 6:5

NIGER 1

Black

A prophet and teacher in the church at Antioch in the time of the apostle Paul. Also called Simeon (4).

ONLY REFERENCE
ACTS 13:1

NIMROD 4

A descendant of Noah through his son Ham. Nimrod was "mighty upon the earth" (1 Chronicles 1:10), and he built the city of Nineveh.

FIRST REFERENCE
GENESIS 10:8
LAST REFERENCE
MICAH 5:6

NIMSHI 5

Extricated

Father of King Jehu of Israel, whom God anointed to kill off the line of King Ahab of Israel.

FIRST REFERENCE
1 KINGS 19:16
LAST REFERENCE
2 CHRONICLES 22:7

NOADIAH 2

Convened of God

1) A Levite who weighed the temple vessels after the Babylonian Exile.

ONLY REFERENCE
EZRA 8:33

2) A prophetess who opposed Nehemiah as he rebuilt Jerusalem's walls.

ONLY REFERENCE
NEHEMIAH 6:14

NOAH 53

Rest

1) The man God chose to build an ark that would save both animals and people. God gave Noah specific building directions. When his

boat-building project was finished, he and his family entered the ark and brought in seven of every clean animal and two of the unclean. God caused it to rain for forty days and nights until the world was flooded and everything else on earth was destroyed. For 150 days the ark floated, until the waters abated and the vessel rested on the mountains of Ararat. Noah tested the land by sending out a raven and then a dove. When the dove did not return, he knew that dry land had appeared. God commanded Noah and his family to leave the ark, and they went out. Noah made a sacrifice. Then God promised Noah and his sons that He would never curse the earth by flood again. Same as Noe.

FIRST REFERENCE
GENESIS 5:29
LAST REFERENCE
2 PETER 2:5
KEY REFERENCES
GENESIS 6:8–9, 14–16; 7:2–5, 24; 8:6–12, 20; 9:11–17

2) One of Zelophehad's five daughters who received his inheritance because he had no sons. Each had to marry within their tribe, which was Manasseh.

FIRST REFERENCE
NUMBERS 26:33
LAST REFERENCE
JOSHUA 17:3

NOBAH 2
A bark

A man who took Kenath and its villages for his inheritance when Moses divided the Promised Land between the tribes.

ONLY REFERENCE
NUMBERS 32:42

NOE 5
Noah

Greek spelling of *Noah*, used in the New Testament.

FIRST REFERENCE
MATTHEW 24:37
LAST REFERENCE
LUKE 17:27

NOGAH 2
Brilliancy

A son of King David, born in Jerusalem.

FIRST REFERENCE
I CHRONICLES 3:7
LAST REFERENCE
I CHRONICLES 14:6

NOHAH 1
Quietude

A descendant of Abraham through Jacob's son Benjamin. Nohah was Benjamin's fourth son.

ONLY REFERENCE
I CHRONICLES 8:2

NON   I

Perpetuity

A variant spelling of *Nun*; father of the Israelite leader Joshua.

ONLY REFERENCE
I CHRONICLES 7:27

NUN   29

Perpetuity

A descendant of Abraham through Joseph's son Ephraim and father of the Israelite leader Joshua. Same as Non.

FIRST REFERENCE
EXODUS 33:11
LAST REFERENCE
NEHEMIAH 8:17

NYMPHAS   I

Nymph given

A Colossian Christian who had a house church in her home.

ONLY REFERENCE
COLOSSIANS 4:15

OBADIAH   20 13

Serving God

1) "Governor" of the household of King Ahab of Israel and a man who feared God. Obadiah hid one hundred prophets in a cave when Queen Jezebel sought to kill them. Looking for water for Ahab's cattle, he met Elijah, who sent him to the king with the news that he had returned to Israel.

FIRST REFERENCE
I KINGS 18:3
LAST REFERENCE
I KINGS 18:16

2) A descendant of Abraham through Jacob's son Judah, in the line of the nation of Judah's second-to-last king, Jeconiah (also known as Jehoiachin).

ONLY REFERENCE
I CHRONICLES 3:21

3) A descendant of Abraham through Jacob's son Issachar.

ONLY REFERENCE
I CHRONICLES 7:3

4) A descendant of Abraham through Jacob's son Benjamin, in the line of King Saul and his son Jonathan.

FIRST REFERENCE
I CHRONICLES 8:38
LAST REFERENCE
I CHRONICLES 9:44

5) A Jewish exile from the tribe of Levi who resettled Jerusalem.

ONLY REFERENCE
I CHRONICLES 9:16

6) One of several warriors from the tribe of Gad who left Saul to join David during his conflict with the king. Obadiah and his companions were "men of might. . .whose faces were like the faces of lions" (1 Chronicles 12:8).

ONLY REFERENCE
I CHRONICLES 12:9

7) Ruler of the tribe of Zebulun in the days of King David.

ONLY REFERENCE
I CHRONICLES 27:19

8) A prince of Judah sent by King Jehoshaphat to teach the law of the Lord throughout the nation.

ONLY REFERENCE
2 CHRONICLES 17:7

9) An overseer of the men who repaired the temple under King Josiah of Judah.

ONLY REFERENCE
2 CHRONICLES 34:12

10) A Jewish exile who returned from Babylon to Judah under Ezra.

ONLY REFERENCE
EZRA 8:9

11) A priest who renewed the covenant under Nehemiah.

ONLY REFERENCE
NEHEMIAH 10:5

12) A Levite "porter" (doorkeeper) in the house of the Lord.

ONLY REFERENCE
NEHEMIAH 12:25

13) An Old Testament minor prophet who spoke God's words against Edom.

ONLY REFERENCE
OBADIAH 1:1

OBAL 1

A descendant of Noah through his son Shem.

ONLY REFERENCE
GENESIS 10:28

OBED 13 5

Serving

1) A descendant of Abraham through Isaac; forebear of Jesus' earthly father, Joseph.

FIRST REFERENCE
RUTH 4:17
LAST REFERENCE
LUKE 3:32
GENEALOGY OF JESUS
LUKE 3:32

2) A descendant of Abraham through Jacob's son Judah. Obed descended from the line of an unnamed Israelite woman and her Egyptian husband, Jarha.

FIRST REFERENCE
I CHRONICLES 2:37
LAST REFERENCE
I CHRONICLES 2:38

3) One of King David's warriors known as the "mighty men."

ONLY REFERENCE
I CHRONICLES 11:47

4) A Levite "porter" (doorkeeper) in the house of the Lord.

ONLY REFERENCE
I CHRONICLES 26:7

5) Father of a captain of hundreds under the priest Jehoiada.

ONLY REFERENCE
2 CHRONICLES 23:1

OBED-EDOM 20

Worker of Edom

1) Owner of a house where the ark of the covenant was kept for three months before David brought it to Jerusalem. God blessed Obed-edom's household while it held the ark.

FIRST REFERENCE
2 SAMUEL 6:10
LAST REFERENCE
I CHRONICLES 15:25

2) A Levite musician who performed in celebration when King David brought the ark of the covenant to Jerusalem. He was also gatekeeper at Jerusalem's South Gate.

FIRST REFERENCE
I CHRONICLES 15:18
LAST REFERENCE
I CHRONICLES 26:15

3) A man who worked in the temple treasury when Joash, king of Israel, invaded and looted the temple.

ONLY REFERENCE
2 CHRONICLES 25:24

OBIL

Mournful

A servant of King David who was in charge of the royal camels.

ONLY REFERENCE
I CHRONICLES 27:30

OCRAN 5

Muddler

Father of Pagiel, a chief of the tribe of Asher who helped Moses take a census of Israel.

FIRST REFERENCE
NUMBERS 1:13
LAST REFERENCE
NUMBERS 10:26

ODED 3

Reiteration

1) Father of Azariah (10) the prophet.

FIRST REFERENCE
2 CHRONICLES 15:1
LAST REFERENCE
2 CHRONICLES 15:8

2) A prophet who warned the Israelites not to enslave their fellow Jewish citizens whom they had captured when King Pekah led them into battle.

ONLY REFERENCE
2 CHRONICLES 28:9

OG 22

Round

The Amorite king of Bashan, whom Moses defeated after Israel failed to enter the Promised Land. Israel took sixty cities from him. News of Og's destruction spread to Rahab and the Gibeonites, who feared Israel's power.

FIRST REFERENCE
NUMBERS 21:33
LAST REFERENCE
PSALM 136:20
KEY REFERENCES
DEUTERONOMY 3:1–4; JOSHUA 2:10; 9:10

OHAD 2
Unity

A son of Simeon and descendant of Abraham.

FIRST REFERENCE
GENESIS 46:10
LAST REFERENCE
EXODUS 6:15

OHEL 1
A tent

A descendant of Abraham through Jacob's son Judah, in the line of the nation of Judah's second-to-last king, Jeconiah (also known as Jehoiachin).

ONLY REFERENCE
1 CHRONICLES 3:20

OLYMPAS 1
Olympian bestowed or heaven descended

A Christian whom Paul greeted in his letter to the church at Rome.

ONLY REFERENCE
ROMANS 16:15

OMAR 3
Talkative

A descendant of Abraham's grandson Esau, whose blessing as older brother was taken by the scheming Jacob.

FIRST REFERENCE
GENESIS 36:11
LAST REFERENCE
1 CHRONICLES 1:36

OMRI 18
Heaping

1) Commander of Israel's army under King Elah. After Zimri killed Elah, the people made Omri king. Omri and his army besieged Zimri at Tirzah and took the city. Omri overcame those who supported Tibni for king. He did evil and made Israel sin.

FIRST REFERENCE
1 KINGS 16:16
LAST REFERENCE
MICAH 6:16
KEY REFERENCE
1 KINGS 16:16–22

2) A descendant of Abraham through Jacob's son Benjamin. A son of Beker.

ONLY REFERENCE
1 CHRONICLES 7:8

3) Father of a returned exile, Uthai, who was head of his father's household.

ONLY REFERENCE
1 CHRONICLES 9:4

4) A ruler of the tribe of Issachar under David.

ONLY REFERENCE
1 CHRONICLES 27:18

ON 1

Ability, power, wealth

Forefather of Korah (3).

ONLY REFERENCE
NUMBERS 16:1

ONAM 4
Strong

1) A descendant of Seir, who lived in Esau's "land of Edom."

FIRST REFERENCE
GENESIS 36:23
LAST REFERENCE
I CHRONICLES 1:40

2) A descendant of Abraham through Jacob's son Judah.

FIRST REFERENCE
I CHRONICLES 2:26
LAST REFERENCE
I CHRONICLES 2:28

ONAN 8
Strong

Second son of Jacob's son Judah and his Canaanite wife. Onan refused to sire a son with his brother's widow, whom he had married, because the boy would be considered his brother's child. God put Onan to death for this.

FIRST REFERENCE
GENESIS 38:4
LAST REFERENCE
I CHRONICLES 2:3

ONESIMUS 2
Profitable

A slave of Philemon, Onesimus fled his master and met Paul, who led him to Christ. In his epistle to Philemon, Paul interceded for Onesimus.

FIRST REFERENCE
COLOSSIANS 4:9
LAST REFERENCE
PHILEMON 1:10

ONESIPHORUS 2
Profit bearer

An Ephesian Christian whose household refreshed Paul. Onesiphorus visited Paul while he was imprisoned in Rome.

FIRST REFERENCE
2 TIMOTHY 1:16
LAST REFERENCE
2 TIMOTHY 4:19

OPHIR 2

A descendant of Noah through his son Shem.

FIRST REFERENCE
GENESIS 10:29
LAST REFERENCE
I CHRONICLES 1:23

OPHRAH 1
Female fawn

A descendant of Abraham through Jacob's son Judah.

ONLY REFERENCE
I CHRONICLES 4:14

OREB 5
Mosquito

A prince of Midian who was killed by the tribe of Ephraim when Gideon called the tribe to fight that nation.

FIRST REFERENCE
JUDGES 7:25
LAST REFERENCE
PSALM 83:11

OREN 1

A descendant of Abraham through Jacob's son Judah.

ONLY REFERENCE
1 CHRONICLES 2:25

ORNAN 12

Strong

The owner of a threshing floor where King David saw the angel of the Lord after he had sinned by taking a census. The angel commanded David to build an altar there, so David tried to buy the land from Ornan. Ornan refused his money, but David insisted and paid him 600 shekels for the land. Same as Araunah.

FIRST REFERENCE
1 CHRONICLES 21:15
LAST REFERENCE
2 CHRONICLES 3:1

ORPAH 2

Mane

Naomi's daughter-in-law who did not follow her to Bethlehem.

FIRST REFERENCE
RUTH 1:4
LAST REFERENCE
RUTH 1:14

OSEE 1

Greek form of the name *Hoshea*.

ONLY REFERENCE
ROMANS 9:25

OSHEA 2

Deliverer

A variant spelling of the name *Joshua*. Same as Joshua (1).

FIRST REFERENCE
NUMBERS 13:8
LAST REFERENCE
NUMBERS 13:16

OTHNI 1

To force, forcible

A Levite "porter" (doorkeeper) in the house of the Lord whose father was Shemiah.

ONLY REFERENCE
1 CHRONICLES 26:7

OTHNIEL 6

Force of God

Caleb's brother, who by capturing Kirjath-sepher won the hand of Caleb's daughter, Achsah, in marriage. Othniel delivered Israel from the king of Mesopotamia and judged Israel for forty years.

FIRST REFERENCE
JOSHUA 15:17
LAST REFERENCE
1 CHRONICLES 4:13

OZEM 2

To be strong, strength

1) Sixth son of jesse and brother of King David.

ONLY REFERENCE
1 CHRONICLES 2:15

2) A descendant of Abraham through Jacob's son Judah.

ONLY REFERENCE
1 CHRONICLES 2:25

OZIAS 2

A descendant of Abraham through Isaac; forebear of Jesus' earthly father, Joseph.

FIRST REFERENCE
MATTHEW 1:8
LAST REFERENCE
MATTHEW 1:9
GENEALOGY OF JESUS
MATTHEW 1:8–9

OZNI 1

Having quick ears

A descendant of Abraham through Jacob's son Gad.

ONLY REFERENCE
NUMBERS 26:16

PAARAI 1

Yawning

One of King David's warriors known as the "mighty men."

ONLY REFERENCE
2 SAMUEL 23:35

PADON 2

Ransom

Forefather of an exiled family that returned to Judah under Zerubbabel.

FIRST REFERENCE
EZRA 2:44
LAST REFERENCE
NEHEMIAH 7:47

PAGIEL 5

Accident of God

A chief of the tribe of Asher who helped Moses take a census of Israel.

FIRST REFERENCE
NUMBERS 1:13
LAST REFERENCE
NUMBERS 10:26

PAHATH-MOAB 6

Pit of Moab

1) Father of a man who repaired Jerusalem's walls under Nehemiah. Some of his descendants married "strange" (foreign) women.

FIRST REFERENCE
EZRA 2:6
LAST REFERENCE
NEHEMIAH 7:11

2) Forefather of a Jewish exile who returned from Babylon to Judah under Ezra.

ONLY REFERENCE
EZRA 8:4

3) A Jewish leader who renewed the covenant under Nehemiah.

ONLY REFERENCE
NEHEMIAH 10:14

PALAL
Judge

A man who repaired Jerusalem's walls under Nehemiah.

ONLY REFERENCE
NEHEMIAH 3:25

PALLU 4
Distinguished

A descendant of Abraham through Jacob's son Reuben.

FIRST REFERENCE
EXODUS 6:14
LAST REFERENCE
I CHRONICLES 5:3

PALTI
Delivered

A spy from the tribe of Benjamin who reported that Israel could not take the Promised Land.

ONLY REFERENCE
NUMBERS 13:9

PALTIEL
Deliverance of God

Prince of the tribe of Issachar when the Israelites entered the Promised Land.

ONLY REFERENCE
NUMBERS 34:26

PARMASHTA

One of ten sons of Haman, the villain of the story of Esther.

ONLY REFERENCE
ESTHER 9:9

PARMENAS
Constant

One of seven men, "full of the Holy Ghost and wisdom," selected to serve needy Christians in Jerusalem while the twelve disciples devoted themselves "to prayer, and to the ministry of the word" (Acts 6:3–4).

ONLY REFERENCE
ACTS 6:5

PARNACH

Forefather of Elizaphan, prince of the tribe of Zebulun when the Israelites entered the Promised Land.

ONLY REFERENCE
NUMBERS 34:25

PAROSH 5
A flea

1) Forefather of an exiled family that returned to Judah under Zerubbabel.

FIRST REFERENCE
EZRA 2:3
LAST REFERENCE
NEHEMIAH 7:8

2) An exiled Israelite who married a "strange" (foreign) woman.

ONLY REFERENCE
EZRA 10:25

3) Father of a man who repaired Jerusalem's walls under Nehemiah.

ONLY REFERENCE
NEHEMIAH 3:25

4) A Jewish leader who renewed the covenant under Nehemiah.

ONLY REFERENCE
NEHEMIAH 10:14

PARSHAN-DATHA   I

One of ten sons of Haman, the villain of the story of Esther.

ONLY REFERENCE
ESTHER 9:7

PARUAH   I

Blossomed

Father of one of King Solomon's officers who provided food for the royal household.

ONLY REFERENCE
I KINGS 4:17

PASACH   I

Divider

A descendant of Abraham through Jacob's son Asher.

ONLY REFERENCE
I CHRONICLES 7:33

PASEAH   3

Limping

1) A descendant of Abraham through Jacob's son Judah.

ONLY REFERENCE
I CHRONICLES 4:12

2) Forefather of an exiled family that returned to Judah under Zerubbabel.

ONLY REFERENCE
EZRA 2:49

3) Father of a man who repaired Jerusalem's walls under Nehemiah.

ONLY REFERENCE
NEHEMIAH 3:6

PASHUR   14

Liberation

1) Forefather of a priest who resettled Jerusalem after the Babylonian Exile.

FIRST REFERENCE
I CHRONICLES 9:12
LAST REFERENCE
NEHEMIAH 11:12

2) A priest who renewed the covenant under Nehemiah.

ONLY REFERENCE
NEHEMIAH 10:3

3) A priest and "chief governor" of the temple who responded to Jeremiah's prophecies by hitting him and putting him in the stocks near the temple. When Pashur removed him from the stocks, the prophet gave him a new name, Magor-missabib, meaning "afright from around," because he would become a terror to himself and others as God gave Judah over to Babylon.

FIRST REFERENCE
JEREMIAH 20:1
LAST REFERENCE
JEREMIAH 38:1

4) A prince of Judah who sought to have King Zedekiah kill Jeremiah because of his negative prophecy.

FIRST REFERENCE
JEREMIAH 21:1
LAST REFERENCE
JEREMIAH 38:1

PATROBAS

Father's life

A Christian whom Paul greeted in his letter to the church at Rome.

ONLY REFERENCE
ROMANS 16:14

PAUL   157

Little

Latin form of the name *Saul*; God's chosen apostle to the Gentiles. Paul zealously persecuted Christians until he became one himself as he traveled to Damascus and was confronted by Jesus. Scripture begins calling him Paul when he and Barnabas set out on Paul's first missionary journey, to Galatia. Paul and Barnabas disagreed over bringing John Mark on a second missionary venture and split up. Paul brought Silas and Timothy on his next journey and later added Luke to the group. After Paul received a vision, they traveled to Macedonia. The apostle and his disciples made two more missionary journeys to the churches of Asia and Greece. He communicated with the churches through his epistles to the Romans, Corinthians, Galatians, Colossians, and Thessalonians and a letter to Titus. These form part of his contribution to the New Testament. Constrained by the Spirit, Paul went to Jerusalem. In the temple he was rescued from a riot by the Roman tribune, who arrested him. Following a plot to kill him, Paul was sent to Caesarea, where he stayed two years while Felix delayed making a decision on his case. Paul appealed to Caesar but on his way to Rome was shipwrecked. He finally arrived in Rome, where he lived for two years. He may have been released but then rearrested. During his time in prison, he wrote additional epistles that became scripture: Ephesians, probably Philippians, the letters to Timothy, and Philemon. Church tradition records that the emperor Nero martyred Paul. Same as Saul (3).

FIRST REFERENCE
ACTS 13:9
LAST REFERENCE
2 PETER 3:15
KEY REFERENCES
ACTS 15:1–21; 17:22–33; 21:27–35; 25:8;
28:30–31

PAULUS

Little

Sergius Paulus was a proconsul of Cyprus who called on Barnabas and Saul to share their faith with him.

ONLY REFERENCE
ACTS 13:7

295

PEDAHEL
God has ransomed

Prince of the tribe of Naphtali when the Israelites entered the Promised Land.

ONLY REFERENCE
NUMBERS 34:28

PEDAHZUR 5
A rock [God] has ransomed

Father of a chief of the tribe of Benjamin who helped Moses take a census.

FIRST REFERENCE
NUMBERS 1:10
LAST REFERENCE
NUMBERS 10:23

PEDAIAH 8 6
God has ransomed

1) Grandfather of King Jehoiakim of Judah.

ONLY REFERENCE
2 KINGS 23:36

2) A descendant of Abraham through Jacob's son Judah, in the line of the nation of Judah's second-to-last king, Jeconiah (also known as Jehoiachin).

FIRST REFERENCE
I CHRONICLES 3:18
LAST REFERENCE
I CHRONICLES 3:19

3) Father of a leader of the half tribe of Manasseh under King David.

ONLY REFERENCE
I CHRONICLES 27:20

4) A man who repaired Jerusalem's walls under Nehemiah.

ONLY REFERENCE
NEHEMIAH 3:25

5) A priest who assisted Ezra in reading the book of the law to the people of Jerusalem. Nehemiah also appointed him one of the temple treasurers.

FIRST REFERENCE
NEHEMIAH 8:4
LAST REFERENCE
NEHEMIAH 13:13

6) An exile of Benjamin's line who returned to Jerusalem and lived there.

ONLY REFERENCE
NEHEMIAH 11:7

PEKAH 11
Watch

Captain of King Pekahiah of Israel, Pekah conspired against his king, killed him, and usurped his throne. Pekah was an evil king. The Assyrian king Tiglath-Pileser conquered portions of Israel during Pekah's reign.

FIRST REFERENCE
2 KINGS 15:25
LAST REFERENCE
ISAIAH 7:1

PEKAHIAH 3
God has answered

An evil ruler of Israel who succeeded his father, Menahem, as king. Pekah conspired against Pekahiah and usurped his throne.

FIRST REFERENCE
2 KINGS 15:22
LAST REFERENCE
2 KINGS 15:26

PELAIAH 3
God has distinguished

1) A descendant of Abraham through Jacob's son Judah, in the line of the nation of Judah's second-to-last king, Jeconiah (also known as Jehoiachin).

ONLY REFERENCE
I CHRONICLES 3:24

2) A Levite who helped Israel to understand the law after Ezra read it to them.

ONLY REFERENCE
NEHEMIAH 8:7

3) A Levite who helped Ezra to explain the law to exiles returned to Jerusalem.

ONLY REFERENCE
NEHEMIAH 10:10

PELALIAH 1
God has judged

Forefather of a priest who returned to Jerusalem after the Babylonian Exile.

ONLY REFERENCE
NEHEMIAH 11:12

PELATIAH 5
God has delivered

1) A descendant of Abraham through Jacob's son Judah, in the line of the nation of Judah's second-to-last king, Jeconiah (also known as Jehoiachin).

ONLY REFERENCE
I CHRONICLES 3:21

2) A descendant of King David through David's son Solomon.

ONLY REFERENCE
I CHRONICLES 4:42

3) A Jewish leader who renewed the covenant under Nehemiah.

ONLY REFERENCE
NEHEMIAH 10:22

4) A prince of Judah and a wicked counselor who died as Ezekiel prophesied against Jerusalem.

FIRST REFERENCE
EZEKIEL 11:1
LAST REFERENCE
EZEKIEL 11:13

PELEG 7
Earthquake

A descendant of Noah through his son Ham. Same as Phalec.

FIRST REFERENCE
GENESIS 10:25
LAST REFERENCE
I CHRONICLES 1:25

PELET 2
Escape

1) A descendant of Abraham through Jacob's son Judah.

ONLY REFERENCE
I CHRONICLES 2:47

2) A "mighty man" who supported the future king David during his conflict with Saul.

ONLY REFERENCE
I CHRONICLES 12:3

PELETH 2
To flee, swiftness

Forefather of a Reubenite who joined Korah in rebellion against Moses.

FIRST REFERENCE
NUMBERS 16:1
LAST REFERENCE
I CHRONICLES 2:33

PENINNAH 3
A pearl, round

Elkanah's wife who had children and provoked his other wife, Hannah, who was barren.

FIRST REFERENCE
I SAMUEL 1:2
LAST REFERENCE
I SAMUEL 1:4

PENUEL 2
Face of God

1) A descendant of Abraham through Jacob's son Judah.

ONLY REFERENCE
I CHRONICLES 4:4

2) A descendant of Abraham through Jacob's son Benjamin.

ONLY REFERENCE
I CHRONICLES 8:25

PERESH 1

A descendant of Abraham through Joseph's son Manasseh.

ONLY REFERENCE
I CHRONICLES 7:16

PEREZ 3
A break

1) Forefather of a commander in David's army. Same as Pharez and Phares.

ONLY REFERENCE
I CHRONICLES 27:3

2) A Jewish exile from the tribe of Judah who resettled Jerusalem. Same as Pharez.

FIRST REFERENCE
NEHEMIAH 11:4
LAST REFERENCE
NEHEMIAH 11:6

PERIDA 1
Dispersion

Forefather of an exiled family— former servants of Solomon—who returned to Judah under Zerubbabel. Same as Peruda.

ONLY REFERENCE
NEHEMIAH 7:57

PERSIS 1

A Christian whom Paul greeted and commended in his letter to the church at Rome.

ONLY REFERENCE
ROMANS 16:12

PERUDA 1
Dispersions

Forefather of an exiled family that returned to Judah under Zerubbabel. Same as Perida.

ONLY REFERENCE
EZRA 2:55

PETER 162

A piece of rock

FIRST REFERENCE
MATTHEW 4:18
LAST REFERENCE
2 PETER 1:1
KEY REFERENCES
MATTHEW 14:28–33; 16:16; 17:1–8; JOHN
18:10; 20:1–7; 21:15–19; ACTS 2:14–41; 3:1–8;
4:13–20; 10:1–11:18

Jesus' disciple, also called Simon Peter and Simon Bar-Jonah, who was called from his fishing, along with his brother Andrew, to become a fisher of men. The brothers were among Jesus' most intimate disciples. Peter walked on water to meet Jesus after the feeding of the five thousand. He was the first to call Jesus "the Christ." With James and John, he witnessed the transfiguration of Jesus. In the Garden of Gethsemane, Peter fell asleep while Jesus prayed. As Jesus was arrested, Peter cut off the ear of the high priest's servant. While Jesus stood before Caiaphas in an illegal trial, three times Peter denied being His disciple. After the resurrection of Jesus, Peter and John checked the empty tomb. Later Jesus confronted Peter about his love for Him and reconfirmed his ministry. Following the giving of the Great Commission, Peter spoke out boldly in his Pentecost sermon. He healed the lame beggar at the temple gate and refused to stop preaching when the Jewish council arrested him. He had a vision about the acceptance of Gentile believers in the church but later failed to support them. He wrote the books of 1 and 2 Peter. Same as Cephas.

PETHAHIAH 4

God has opened

1) One of twenty-four priests in David's time who was chosen by lot to serve in the tabernacle.

ONLY REFERENCE
1 CHRONICLES 24:16

2) An exiled Levite who married a "strange" (foreign) woman.

ONLY REFERENCE
EZRA 10:23

3) One of a group of Levites who led a revival among the Israelites in the time of Nehemiah.

ONLY REFERENCE
NEHEMIAH 9:5

4) A man of the tribe of Judah who was Israel's representative with King Artaxerxes of Persia.

ONLY REFERENCE
NEHEMIAH 11:24

PETHUEL 1

Enlarged of God

Father of the Old Testament minor prophet Joel.

ONLY REFERENCE
JOEL 1:1

PEULTHAI
Laborious

A Levite "porter" (doorkeeper) in the house of the Lord.

ONLY REFERENCE
I CHRONICLES 26:5

PHALEC

A descendant of Abraham through Isaac; forebear of Jesus' earthly father, Joseph. Same as Peleg.

ONLY REFERENCE
LUKE 3:35
GENEALOGY OF JESUS
LUKE 3:35

PHALLU
Distinguished

A descendant of Abraham and grandson of Jacob through his son Reuben.

ONLY REFERENCE
GENESIS 46:9

PHALTI
Delivered

Michal's second husband, to whom Saul married her after David fled. Same as Phaltiel.

ONLY REFERENCE
I SAMUEL 25:44

PHALTIEL
Deliverance of God

Michal's second husband, from whom King David claimed her. Same as Phalti.

ONLY REFERENCE
2 SAMUEL 3:15

PHANUEL

Father of the prophetess Anna, who saw the baby Jesus in the temple.

ONLY REFERENCE
LUKE 2:36

PHARAOH-HOPHRA

The king of Egypt who Jeremiah prophesied would be given into the hands of his enemies.

ONLY REFERENCE
JEREMIAH 44:30

PHARAOH-NECHO

The king of Egypt aganist whom Jeremiah prophesied God would take vengeance. Same as Pharaoh-nechoh.

ONLY REFERENCE
JEREMIAH 46:2

PHARAOH-NECHOH

The king of Egypt who fought Assyria and King Josiah of Judah. Josiah was killed, and Pharaoh-nechoh made Jehoiakim king in his place. Same as Pharaoh-necho.

FIRST REFERENCE
2 KINGS 23:29
LAST REFERENCE
2 KINGS 23:35

PHARES 3

A descendant of Abraham through Isaac; forebear of Jesus' earthly father, Joseph. Same as Pharez and Perez.

FIRST REFERENCE
MATTHEW 1:3
LAST REFERENCE
LUKE 3:33
GENEALOGY OF JESUS
MATTHEW 1:3

PHAREZ 12

A grandson of Jacob, born to Jacob's son Judah and Judah's daughter-in-law Tamar. Same as Phares and Perez.

FIRST REFERENCE
GENESIS 38:29
LAST REFERENCE
1 CHRONICLES 9:4

PHAROSH 1
A flea

Forefather of a family of exiles who returned to Jerusalem under Ezra.

ONLY REFERENCE
EZRA 8:3

PHASEAH 1
Limping

Forefather of an exiled family that returned to Judah under Zerubbabel.

ONLY REFERENCE
NEHEMIAH 7:51

PHEBE 1
Bright

A believer whom Paul recommended that the Roman church assist.

ONLY REFERENCE
ROMANS 16:1

PHICHOL 3
Mouth of all

Commander of the Philistine king Abimelech's army in the time of Abraham and Isaac.

FIRST REFERENCE
GENESIS 21:22
LAST REFERENCE
GENESIS 26:26

PHILEMON 1
Friendly

Christian owner of the escaped slave Onesimus. Paul wrote Philemon an epistle appealing for the slave.

ONLY REFERENCE:
PHILEMON 1:1

PHILETUS 1
Amiable

A false teacher who opposed Paul, teaching that Christians would not be physically resurrected.

ONLY REFERENCE
2 TIMOTHY 2:17

PHILIP 36 [3]
Fond of horses

1) A disciple of Jesus who introduced the soon-to-be-disciple Nathanael to Him. Jesus asked Philip where they could buy bread to feed the five thousand, and Philip was at a loss. In Jerusalem, some Greeks who wanted to see Jesus came to Philip for an introduction. When Jesus told the disciples, "If ye had known me, ye should have known my Father also" (John 14:7), Philip wanted Him to show them the Father.

FIRST REFERENCE
MATTHEW 10:3
LAST REFERENCE
ACTS 1:13
KEY REFERENCES
JOHN 1:43–48; 6:5–7; 12:21–22; 14:8–9

2) Also called Herod Philip I, this tetrarch of Iturea and Trachonitis was a son of Herod the Great. His wife, Herodias, left him and married his half brother, Herod.

FIRST REFERENCE
MATTHEW 14:3
LAST REFERENCE
LUKE 3:1

3) One of seven men, "full of the Holy Ghost and wisdom," selected to serve needy Christians in Jerusalem while the twelve disciples devoted themselves "to prayer, and to the ministry of the word" (Acts 6:3–4). He preached to the Ethiopian eunuch and baptized him. Also called Philip the evangelist.

FIRST REFERENCE
ACTS 6:5
LAST REFERENCE
ACTS 21:8
KEY REFERENCES
ACTS 8:5–8, 26–39

PHILOLOGUS 1 [♂]
Fond of words

A Christian whom Paul greeted in his letter to the church at Rome.

ONLY REFERENCE
ROMANS 16:15

PHINEHAS 25 [3]
Mouth of a serpent

1) Son of the high priest Eleazar and grandson of Aaron. He killed Zimri (1), who brought a Midianite woman before Moses while God was judging those who had fallen into idolatry. Because of Phinehas's act, God turned His wrath from Israel.

FIRST REFERENCE
EXODUS 6:25
LAST REFERENCE
PSALM 106:30
KEY REFERENCE
NUMBERS 25:6–9

2) Son of the high priest Eli, who honored Phinehas and his brother, Hophni, more than the Lord. The brothers did not know the Lord, misused their priestly office, and disobeyed the law. A man of God prophesied that they would die in the same day. When the Philistines attacked and took the ark of the covenant, both were killed.

FIRST REFERENCE
I SAMUEL 1:3
LAST REFERENCE
I SAMUEL 14:3

3) Father of a Levite who weighed the temple vessels after the Babylonian Exile

ONLY REFERENCE
EZRA 8:33

PHLEGON

Blazing

A Christian whom Paul greeted in his letter to the church at Rome.

ONLY REFERENCE
ROMANS 16:14

PHURAH 2

Foliage

Gideon's servant who, before Israel attacked the enemy, went with Gideon to the Midianite camp to hear what the soldiers said about him.

FIRST REFERENCE
JUDGES 7:10
LAST REFERENCE
JUDGES 7:11

PHUT 2

A grandson of Noah through his son Ham.

FIRST REFERENCE
GENESIS 10:6
LAST REFERENCE
EZRA 27:10

PHUVAH 1

A blast

A descendant of Abraham through Jacob's son Issachar.

ONLY REFERENCE
GENESIS 46:13

PHYGELLUS 1

Fugitive

An Asian Christian who turned away from Paul.

ONLY REFERENCE
2 TIMOTHY 1:15

PILATE 56

Close pressed

Procurator (governor) of Judea before whom Jesus appeared after His trial before the Jewish religious authorities. When Pilate heard Jesus was a Galilean, he sent Jesus to Herod, who had his soldiers mock Him and return Him to Pilate. Pilate questioned Jesus briefly and understood He was innocent. Though Pilate knew envy had spurred the Jewish leaders to condemn Jesus, fearing these leaders, he gave the crowd a choice of prisoners to be released: Jesus or Barabbas. His wife warned him against condemning Jesus, but Pilate still gave Him over to be crucified. Same as Pontius Pilate.

FIRST REFERENCE
MATTHEW 27:2
LAST REFERENCE
I TIMOTHY 6:13
KEY REFERENCES
MATTHEW 27:11–26; LUKE 23:6–11;
JOHN 18:29–19:15

PILDASH

Son of Nahor and nephew of Abraham.

ONLY REFERENCE
GENESIS 22:22

PILEHA
Slicing

A Jewish leader who renewed the covenant under Nehemiah.

ONLY REFERENCE
NEHEMIAH 10:24

PILTAI
A Paltite or descendant of Palti

A chief priest under Joiakim in the days of Zerubbabel.

ONLY REFERENCE
NEHEMIAH 12:17

PINON 2
Perplexity

Forefather of a priest who returned to Jerusalem under Zerubbabel.

FIRST REFERENCE
GENESIS 36:41
LAST REFERENCE
I CHRONICLES 1:52

PIRAM
Wildly

A "duke of Edom," a leader in the family line of Esau.

ONLY REFERENCE
JOSHUA 10:3

PISPAH
Dispersion

A descendant of Abraham through Jacob's son Asher.

ONLY REFERENCE
I CHRONICLES 7:38

PITHON 2
Expansive

A descendant of Abraham through Jacob's son Benjamin, in the line of King Saul and his son Jonathan.

FIRST REFERENCE
I CHRONICLES 8:35
LAST REFERENCE
I CHRONICLES 9:41

POCHERETH 2
To entrap

An Israelite who returned to Jerusalem under Zerubbabel.

FIRST REFERENCE
EZRA 2:57
LAST REFERENCE
NEHEMIAH 7:59

PONTIUS PILATE 4
Pontius, "bridged"; Pilate, "close pressed"

Pilate's family name and first name. Same as Pilate.

FIRST REFERENCE
MATTHEW 27:2
LAST REFERENCE
I TIMOTHY 6:13

PORATHA

One of ten sons of Haman, the villain of the story of Esther.

ONLY REFERENCE
ESTHER 9:8

PORCIUS FESTUS 1

Porcius, "swinish"; Festus, "festal"

The governor of Judea who heard Paul's case and sent him to Caesar. Also called Festus.

ONLY REFERENCE
ACTS 24:27

POTIPHAR 2

The officer of Pharaoh and captain of Pharaoh's guard, Potiphar became master to the enslaved Joseph (1).

FIRST REFERENCE
GENESIS 37:36
LAST REFERENCE
GENESIS 39:1

POTIPHERAH 3

Egyptian priest of On and father-in-law of Joseph (1).

FIRST REFERENCE
GENESIS 41:45
LAST REFERENCE
GENESIS 46:20

PRISCA 1

With her husband, Aquila, she was a coworker of Paul. Same as Priscilla.

ONLY REFERENCE
2 TIMOTHY 4:19

PRISCILLA 5

Wife of Aquila. This tent-making couple worked with the apostle Paul in their craft and in spreading the gospel. They founded a house church in their home. Same as Prisca.

FIRST REFERENCE
ACTS 18:2
LAST REFERENCE
1 CORINTHIANS 16:19

PROCHORUS 1

Before the dance

One of seven men, "full of the Holy Ghost and wisdom," selected to serve needy Christians in Jerusalem while the twelve disciples devoted themselves "to prayer, and to the ministry of the word" (Acts 6:3–4).

ONLY REFERENCE
ACTS 6:5

PUA 1

A blast

A descendant of Abraham through Jacob's son Issachar. Same as Puah (1).

ONLY REFERENCE
NUMBERS 26:23

PUAH 3

A blast

1) A descendant of Abraham through Jacob's son Issachar. Same as Pua.

ONLY REFERENCE
1 CHRONICLES 7:1

2) Father of Israel's sixth judge, Tola.

ONLY REFERENCE
JUDGES 10:1

3) A Hebrew midwife who did not obey the king of Egypt's command to kill all male Israelite babies.

ONLY REFERENCE
EXODUS 1:15

PUBLIUS 2
Popular

The chief official of Melita who housed Paul and his companions after they were shipwrecked on their way to Rome.

FIRST REFERENCE
ACTS 28:7
LAST REFERENCE
ACTS 28:8

PUDENS 1
Modest

A Christian to whom Paul sent greetings when he wrote Timothy.

ONLY REFERENCE
2 TIMOTHY 4:21

PUL 3

The king of Assyria who extracted tribute from Israel then brought the nation into exile. Possibly the same as Tiglath-pileser.

FIRST REFERENCE
2 KINGS 15:19
LAST REFERENCE
1 CHRONICLES 5:26

PUT 1

A grandson of Noah through his son Ham.

ONLY REFERENCE
1 CHRONICLES 1:8

PUTIEL 1
Contempt of God

Father-in-law of Aaron's son Eleazar.

ONLY REFERENCE
EXODUS 6:25

QUARTUS 1
Fourth

A Christian in Corinth who sent his greetings to fellow believers in Paul's letter to Rome.

ONLY REFERENCE
ROMANS 16:23

-R-

RAAMAH 4

Mane

A descendant of Noah through his son Ham.

FIRST REFERENCE
GENESIS 10:7
LAST REFERENCE
1 CHRONICLES 1:9

RAAMIAH 1

God has shaken

A Jewish exile who returned to Judah under Zerubbabel.

ONLY REFERENCE
NEHEMIAH 7:7

RABMAG 2

Chief magician

A Babylonian prince who took part in the destruction of Jerusalem under King Nebuchadnezzar. Rabmag was an official who also, at Nebuchadnezzar's command, showed kindness to the prophet Jeremiah.

FIRST REFERENCE
JEREMIAH 39:3
LAST REFERENCE
JEREMIAH 39:13

RABSARIS 3 2

Chief eunuch

1) A Babylonian prince who took part in the destruction of Jerusalem under King Nebuchadnezzar. Rabsaris was an official who also, at Nebuchadnezzar's command, showed kindness to the prophet Jeremiah.

FIRST REFERENCE
JEREMIAH 39:3
LAST REFERENCE
JEREMIAH 39:13

2) An Assyrian military commander who participated in King Sennacherib's failed attempt to take Jerusalem in the days of King Hezekiah and the prophet Isaiah.

ONLY REFERENCE
2 KINGS 18:17

RAB-SHAKEH 16

Chief butler

An Assyrian field commander sent by King Sennacherib to attack King Hezekiah at Jerusalem. He attempted to get Hezekiah and his people to surrender to Assyria and fight with that nation. Same as Rabshakeh.

FIRST REFERENCE
2 KINGS 18:17
LAST REFERENCE
2 KINGS 19:8

RABSHAKEH 16
Chief butler

A variant spelling of the name of the Assyrian military commander Rab-shakeh.

FIRST REFERENCE
ISAIAH 36:2
LAST REFERENCE
ISAIAH 37:8

RACHAB 1
Proud

Greek form of the name *Rahab*, used in the New Testament.

ONLY REFERENCE
MATTHEW 1:5
GENEALOGY OF JESUS
MATTHEW 1:5

RACHEL 47
Ewe

Daughter of Laban and wife of Jacob. When Jacob came to Haran, he fell in love with the beautiful Rachel. He agreed to work for Laban for seven years to win her. But when it was time for the marriage, Laban fooled him by putting her sister, Leah, in Rachel's place. Jacob agreed to work seven more years to gain Rachel and finally received her as his bride. While Leah had children, Rachel remained barren, so Rachel gave her maid, Bilhah, to Jacob, to bear children for her. Finally God enabled Rachel to conceive, and she bore Joseph. Jacob decided to move his family back to his own homeland. When Laban discovered they had left secretly, he followed, partly in search of the idols Rachel had stolen and partly to make sure all would be well with his daughters. When they planned to meet Jacob's brother, Esau, whom he had wronged, Jacob put Rachel in the safest part of the caravan. As they traveled to Ephrath (Bethlehem), Rachel gave birth to her second son, whom she called Ben-oni, but Jacob renamed him Benjamin. Rachel died following this difficult childbirth and was buried there. Same as Rahel.

FIRST REFERENCE
GENESIS 29:6
LAST REFERENCE
MATTHEW 2:18
KEY REFERENCES
GENESIS 29:16–30; 30:1–8; 31:34; 33:2; 35:16–19

RADDAI 1
Domineering

Fifth son of Jesse and older brother of King David.

ONLY REFERENCE
1 CHRONICLES 2:14

RAGAU 1
Friend

Greek form of the name *Reu*, used in the New Testament.

ONLY REFERENCE
LUKE 3:35
GENEALOGY OF JESUS
LUKE 3:35

RAGUEL
Friend of God

Father-in-law of Moses. Same as Reuel and Jethro.

ONLY REFERENCE
NUMBERS 10:29

RAHAB 7
Proud

A prostitute of Jericho who hid the two spies whom Joshua sent to look over the city before Israel attacked it. When the king of Jericho was warned of their presence, Rahab hid the men on her roof and informed the king they had left. Rahab told the spies that she feared Israel and asked them to be kind to her family. The men promised she and her family would be spared if she hung a scarlet cord from her window when Israel attacked. When Jericho fell to Joshua's troops, he kept the spies' promise. Same as Rachab.

FIRST REFERENCE
JOSHUA 2:1
LAST REFERENCE
JAMES 2:25

RAHAM 1
Pity

A descendant of Abraham through Jacob's son Judah.

ONLY REFERENCE
1 CHRONICLES 2:44

RAHEL 1
Ewe

A variant spelling of the name of Jacob's wife Rachel.

ONLY REFERENCE
JEREMIAH 31:15

RAKEM 1
Parti-colored

A descendant of Abraham through Joseph's son Manasseh.

ONLY REFERENCE
1 CHRONICLES 7:16

RAM 7
High

1) Forefather of Boaz, Jesse, and David.

FIRST REFERENCE
RUTH 4:19
LAST REFERENCE
1 CHRONICLES 2:10

2) A descendant of Abraham through Jacob's son Judah.

FIRST REFERENCE
1 CHRONICLES 2:25
LAST REFERENCE
1 CHRONICLES 2:27

3) Family head of Job's accusing "friend," Elihu.

ONLY REFERENCE
JOB 32:2

RAMIAH 1
God has raised

An exiled Israelite who married a "strange" (foreign) woman.

ONLY REFERENCE
EZRA 10:25

RAMOTH
Elevations

An exiled Israelite who married a "strange" (foreign) woman.

ONLY REFERENCE
EZRA 10:29

RAPHA
Giant

1) A descendant of Abraham through Jacob's son Benjamin. Rapha was Benjamin's fifth son.

ONLY REFERENCE
I CHRONICLES 8:2

2) A descendant of Abraham through Jacob's son Benjamin, in the line of King Saul and his son Jonathan.

ONLY REFERENCE
I CHRONICLES 8:37

RAPHU
Cured

Father of one of the twelve spies sent by Moses to spy out the land of Canaan.

ONLY REFERENCE
NUMBERS 13:9

REAIA
God has seen

A descendant of Abraham through Jacob's son Reuben.

ONLY REFERENCE
I CHRONICLES 5:5

REAIAH
God has seen

1) A descendant of Abraham through Jacob's son Judah.

ONLY REFERENCE
I CHRONICLES 4:2

2) Forefather of an exiled family that returned to Judah under Zerubbabel.

FIRST REFERENCE
EZRA 2:47
LAST REFERENCE
NEHEMIAH 7:50

REBA
A fourth

A Midianite king killed by the Israelites at God's command.

FIRST REFERENCE
NUMBERS 31:8
LAST REFERENCE
JOSHUA 13:21

REBECCA
Fettering by beauty

Greek form of the name *Rebekah*, used in the New Testament.

ONLY REFERENCE
ROMANS 9:10

REBEKAH
Fettering by beauty

When Abraham's servant came to Nahor, seeking a wife for Abraham's son Isaac, Rebekah watered his camels, proving she was God's choice as the bride. She agreed to marry Isaac and traveled to her new home, where Isaac loved and married her. At first barren, when Rebekah conceived, she had the twins Esau and Jacob. Because she loved her second son best, she conspired with Jacob to get him the eldest son's blessing from his father. When Esau discovered what Jacob had done, he became so angry that Rebekah arranged for Jacob to leave before his brother killed him. Same as Rebecca.

FIRST REFERENCE
GENESIS 22:23
LAST REFERENCE
GENESIS 49:31
KEY REFERENCES
GENESIS 24:15–25, 62–67; 25:21–26;
27:5–10, 41–46

RECHAB 13
Rider

1) A leader of one of the raiding bands of Saul's son Ish-bosheth. Rechab and his brother, Baanah, killed Ish-bosheth. In turn, David had the brothers killed.

FIRST REFERENCE
2 SAMUEL 4:2
LAST REFERENCE
2 SAMUEL 4:9

2) Father of Jonadab, who commanded his descendants not to drink wine.

FIRST REFERENCE
2 KINGS 10:15
LAST REFERENCE
JEREMIAH 35:19

3) Father of a man who repaired Jerusalem's walls under Nehemiah.

ONLY REFERENCE
NEHEMIAH 3:14

REELAIAH 1
Fearful of God

A Jewish exile who returned to Judah under Zerubbabel.

ONLY REFERENCE
EZRA 2:2

REGEM 1
Stone heap

A descendant of Abraham through Jacob's son Judah.

ONLY REFERENCE
1 CHRONICLES 2:47

REGEM-MELECH 1
King's heap

A messenger sent to the prophet Zechariah to ask if the Jews should fast over their exile in Babylon.

ONLY REFERENCE
ZECHARIAH 7:2

REHABIAH 5
God has enlarged

A descendant of Abraham through Jacob's son Levi, through the line of Moses.

FIRST REFERENCE
1 CHRONICLES 23:17
LAST REFERENCE
1 CHRONICLES 26:25

REHOB 3
Width

1) Father of Hadadezer, king of Zobah, whom King David conquered.

FIRST REFERENCE
2 SAMUEL 8:3
LAST REFERENCE
2 SAMUEL 8:12

2) A Jewish leader who renewed the covenant under Nehemiah.

ONLY REFERENCE
NEHEMIAH 10:11

REHOBOAM 50
A people has enlarged

A son of King Solomon, Rehoboam inherited the kingdom of Israel. But his proud attitude toward his subjects' request for lower taxes made Israel rebel against him and set up Jeroboam as their king. When Rehoboam wanted to fight Jeroboam, God spoke through the prophet Shemiah and ordered Rehoboam not to. Only the southern kingdom of Judah remained under Rehoboam's rule, and he built up its defenses. The priests and Levites sided with Rehoboam, even moving into Judah, because Jeroboam had set up idols in his nation and rejected God's spiritual leaders. But once Rehoboam had established his power, "he forsook the law of the LORD, and all Israel with him" (2 Chronicles 12:1). In the fifth year of Rehoboam's reign, Shishak, king of Egypt, attacked Jerusalem. When Shemiah told Judah that God had abandoned their nation because it had abandoned Him, its leaders repented. But God did not free them from Shishak's rule, and he looted all the temple treasures. Yet Rehoboam was not destroyed and Judah became somewhat prosperous. Same as Roboam.

FIRST REFERENCE
I KINGS 11:43
LAST REFERENCE
2 CHRONICLES 13:7
KEY REFERENCES
I KINGS 12:1–24; 14:25–28;
2 CHRONICLES 11:5–14; 12:1–12

REHUM 8
Compassionate

1) An exiled priest who returned to Judah under Zerubbabel.

FIRST REFERENCE
EZRA 2:2
LAST REFERENCE
NEHEMIAH 12:3

2) An officer of the Persian king Artaxerxes who joined in opposition to Zerubbabel's rebuilding of the temple in Jerusalem. Rehum wrote a letter to the king calling Jerusalem "a rebellious city" (Ezra 4:15) and causing Artaxerxes to suspend the work.

FIRST REFERENCE
EZRA 4:8
LAST REFERENCE
EZRA 4:23

3) A Levite who repaired the walls of Jerusalem under Nehemiah.

ONLY REFERENCE
NEHEMIAH 3:17

4) A Jewish leader who renewed the covenant under Nehemiah.

ONLY REFERENCE
NEHEMIAH 10:25

REI

Social

A friend of King David who did not join in the attempted coup of David's son Adonijah.

ONLY REFERENCE
I KINGS 1:8

REKEM

Parti-colored

1) A Midianite king killed by the Israelites at God's command to Moses.

FIRST REFERENCE
NUMBERS 31:8
LAST REFERENCE
JOSHUA 13:21

2) A descendant of Abraham through Jacob's son Judah.

FIRST REFERENCE
I CHRONICLES 2:43
LAST REFERENCE
I CHRONICLES 2:44

REMALIAH

God has bedecked

Father of King Pekah of Israel.

FIRST REFERENCE
2 KINGS 15:25
LAST REFERENCE
ISAIAH 8:6

REPHAEL

God has cured

A Levite "porter" (doorkeeper) in the house of the Lord.

ONLY REFERENCE
I CHRONICLES 26:7

REPHAH

To sustain

A descendant of Abraham through Joseph's son Ephraim.

ONLY REFERENCE
I CHRONICLES 7:25

REPHAIAH

God has cured

1) A descendant of Abraham through Jacob's son Judah, in the line of the nation of Judah's second-to-last king, Jeconiah (also known as Jehoiachin).

ONLY REFERENCE
I CHRONICLES 3:21

2) One of Simeon's descendants who fought the Amalekites and won their lands.

ONLY REFERENCE
I CHRONICLES 4:42

3) A descendant of Abraham through Jacob's son Issachar.

ONLY REFERENCE
I CHRONICLES 7:2

4) A descendant of Jehiel, father of the Gibeonites.

ONLY REFERENCE
I CHRONICLES 9:43

5) A city official of Jerusalem and rebuilder of the walls under Nehemiah.

ONLY REFERENCE
NEHEMIAH 3:9

RESHEPH
Lightning

A descendant of Abraham through Joseph's son Ephraim.

ONLY REFERENCE
I CHRONICLES 7:25

REU
Friend

A descendant of Noah through his son Shem. Same as Ragau.

FIRST REFERENCE
GENESIS 11:18
LAST REFERENCE
I CHRONICLES 1:25

REUBEN
See ye a son

Jacob and Leah's first son. Reuben slept with his father's concubine Bilhah, and Jacob heard of it. When his brothers wanted to kill Joseph, Reuben balked at it. He was sorrowful when he learned his brothers had sold Joseph as a slave, since he had hoped to return him to their father. When Joseph commanded them to bring Benjamin to Egypt in order to buy food, Reuben offered his sons as hostages to his father. When Jacob blessed his sons, he did not forget Reuben's sin with Bilhah and prophesied that because he was unstable, Reuben would not excel.

FIRST REFERENCE
GENESIS 29:32
LAST REFERENCE
I CHRONICLES 5:3
KEY REFERENCES
GENESIS 37:21–22, 29; 49:3–4

REUEL
Friend of God

1) A son of Esau.

FIRST REFERENCE
GENESIS 36:4
LAST REFERENCE
I CHRONICLES 1:37

2) Father-in-law of Moses. Same as Raguel and Jethro.

ONLY REFERENCE
EXODUS 2:18

3) Father of Eliasaph, captain of the tribe of Gad under Moses.

ONLY REFERENCE
NUMBERS 2:14

4) A descendant of Abraham through Jacob's son Benjamin.

ONLY REFERENCE
I CHRONICLES 9:8

REUMAH
Raised

Concubine of Abraham's brother Nahor.

ONLY REFERENCE
GENESIS 22:24

REZIA
Delight

A descendant of Abraham through Jacob's son Asher.

ONLY REFERENCE
I CHRONICLES 7:39

REZIN
Delight

1) A king of Syria who attacked Judah during the reigns of kings Jotham and Ahaz. Rezin was killed in battle with King Tigleth-

pileser's troops after Ahaz asked the Assyrian king to come to his aid.

FIRST REFERENCE
2 KINGS 15:37
LAST REFERENCE
ISAIAH 9:11

2) Forefather of an exiled family that returned to Judah under Zerubbabel.

FIRST REFERENCE
EZRA 2:48
LAST REFERENCE
NEHEMIAH 7:50

REZON 1
Prince

A rebel leader in Damascus who became King Solomon's adversary.

ONLY REFERENCE
1 KINGS 11:23

RHESA 1
God has cured

A descendant of Abraham through Isaac; forebear of Jesus' earthly father, Joseph.

ONLY REFERENCE
LUKE 3:27
GENEALOGY OF JESUS
LUKE 3:27

RHODA 1
Rose

A young woman serving in the Jerusalem home of Mary, mother of John Mark. Responding to a knock at the gate, Rhoda heard the voice of Peter, who had just been miraculously freed from prison while Christians in Mary's home prayed for him. In her excitement, she forgot to let Peter in—and had a hard time convincing those praying that their request had been answered.

ONLY REFERENCE
ACTS 12:13

RIBAI 2
Contentious

Father of one of King David's valiant warriors.

FIRST REFERENCE
2 SAMUEL 23:29
LAST REFERENCE
1 CHRONICLES 11:31

RIMMON 3
Pomegranate

Father of two men who led raiding bands for Ish-bosheth, king of Israel.

FIRST REFERENCE
2 SAMUEL 4:2
LAST REFERENCE
2 SAMUEL 4:9

RINNAH 1
Creaking

A descendant of Abraham through Jacob's son Judah.

ONLY REFERENCE
1 CHRONICLES 4:20

RIPHATH 2

A descendant of Noah through his son Japheth.

FIRST REFERENCE
GENESIS 10:3
LAST REFERENCE
1 CHRONICLES 1:6

RIZPAH 4
Hot stone

A concubine of Saul who, after the king's death, was romanced by Saul's military commander, Abner. When Saul's son Ish-bosheth, king of ten of Israel's tribes, confronted Abner about the liaison with Rizpah, the commander switched his allegiance to David, king of the tribe of Judah. Later, when David ruled all Israel, he allowed men of Gibeon to kill two of Rizpah's sons by Saul in retaliation for an atrocity Saul had committed. The grieving Rizpah spent days outdoors protecting the bodies of her sons from birds and wild animals.

FIRST REFERENCE
2 SAMUEL 3:7
LAST REFERENCE
2 SAMUEL 21:11

ROBOAM 2
A people has enlarged

Greek form of the name *Rehoboam*, used in the New Testament. Rehoboam was a son of Solomon and the first king of Judah, the southern portion of divided Israel.

ONLY REFERENCE
MATTHEW 1:7
GENEALOGY OF JESUS
MATTHEW 1:7

ROHGAH 1
Outcry

A descendant of Abraham through Jacob's son Asher.

ONLY REFERENCE
1 CHRONICLES 7:34

ROMAMTI-EZER 2
I have raised up a help

A son of King David's musician Heman, who was "under the hands of [his] father for song in the house of the LORD" (1 Chronicles 25:6).

FIRST REFERENCE
1 CHRONICLES 25:4
LAST REFERENCE
1 CHRONICLES 25:31

ROSH 1
To shake the head

A descendant of Abraham through Jacob's son Benjamin.

ONLY REFERENCE
GENESIS 46:21

RUFUS 2
Red

1) One of two sons of Simon, a man from Cyrene forced by Roman soldiers to carry Jesus' cross to Golgotha, the crucifixion site.

ONLY REFERENCE
MARK 15:21

2) An acquaintance, "chosen in the Lord," whom the apostle Paul greeted in his letter to the Romans.

ONLY REFERENCE
ROMANS 16:13

RUTH 13
Friend

The Moabite daughter-in-law of Naomi, Ruth married Naomi's son Mahlon while the family lived in Moab during a famine. When Ruth's husband, brother-in-law, and father-in-law died, Naomi decided to move back to Bethlehem. Though her daughter-in-law Orpah went back to her family, Ruth refused to leave Naomi. Together they went to Bethlehem, and there Ruth gleaned the barley harvest to provide food for them. Boaz became aware of Ruth and became kinsman-redeemer for her and Naomi. Ruth married Boaz and had a son, Obed, who was considered Naomi's grandson.

FIRST REFERENCE
RUTH 1:4
LAST REFERENCE
MATTHEW 1:5
KEY REFERENCES
RUTH 1:14–19; 4:1–10, 13–14
GENEALOGY OF JESUS
MATTHEW 1:5

SABTA 1

A descendant of Noah through his son Ham. Same as Sabtah.

ONLY REFERENCE
I CHRONICLES 1:9

SABTAH 1

A descendant of Noah through his son Ham. Same as Sabta.

ONLY REFERENCE
GENESIS 10:7

SABTECHA 1

A descendant of Noah through his son Ham. Same as Sabtechah.

ONLY REFERENCE
I CHRONICLES 1:9

SABTECHAH 1

A descendant of Noah through his son Ham. Same as Sabtecha.

ONLY REFERENCE
GENESIS 10:7

SACAR 2
Recompense

1) Father of one of King David's valiant warriors.

ONLY REFERENCE
I CHRONICLES 11:35

317

2) A Levite "porter" (doorkeeper) in the house of the Lord.

ONLY REFERENCE
I CHRONICLES 26:4

SADOC 2
Just

A descendant of Abraham through Isaac; forebear of Jesus' earthly father, Joseph.

ONLY REFERENCE
MATTHEW 1:14
GENEALOGY OF JESUS
MATTHEW 1:14

SALA 1
Spear

Greek form of the name *Salah*, used in the New Testament.

ONLY REFERENCE
LUKE 3:35
GENEALOGY OF JESUS
LUKE 3:35

SALAH 6
Spear

A descendant of Noah through his son Shem. Same as Sala.

FIRST REFERENCE
GENESIS 10:24
LAST REFERENCE
GENESIS 11:15

SALATHIEL 4
I have asked God

A descendant of Abraham through Jacob's son Judah, in the line of the nation of Judah's second-to-last king, Jeconiah (also known as Jehoiachin).

FIRST REFERENCE
I CHRONICLES 3:17
LAST REFERENCE
LUKE 3:27
GENEALOGY OF JESUS
MATTHEW 1:2; LUKE 3:27

SALLAI 2
Weighed

1) A descendant of Benjamin who was chosen by lot to resettle Jerusalem after the Babylonian Exile.

ONLY REFERENCE
NEHEMIAH 11:8

2) A priest who returned to Jerusalem with Zerubbabel.

ONLY REFERENCE
NEHEMIAH 12:20

SALLU 3
Weighed

1) A descendant of Benjamin who was chosen by lot to resettle Jerusalem after the Babylonian Exile.

FIRST REFERENCE
I CHRONICLES 9:7
LAST REFERENCE
NEHEMIAH 11:7

2) An exiled priest who returned to Judah under Zerubbabel.

ONLY REFERENCE:
NEHEMIAH 12:7

SALMA 4
Clothing

Father of Boaz and a descendant of Abraham through Jacob's son Judah. He is called "the father of Bethlehem" (1 Chronicles 2:51). Same as Salmon.

FIRST REFERENCE
I CHRONICLES 2:11
LAST REFERENCE
I CHRONICLES 2:54

SALMON 5 ♔
Clothing

Father of Boaz, who was Ruth's second husband, and a forefather of Jesus. Same as Salma.

FIRST REFERENCE
RUTH 4:20
LAST REFERENCE
LUKE 3:32
GENEALOGY OF JESUS
LUKE 3:32

SALOME 2 ♀
Welfare

A follower of Jesus who witnessed His death on the cross and later brought spices to anoint His body—only to find it gone due to His resurrection.

FIRST REFERENCE
MARK 15:40
LAST REFERENCE
MARK 16:1

SALU 1 ♙
Weighed

Father of Zimri (1).

ONLY REFERENCE
NUMBERS 25:14

SAMGAR-NEBO 1 ♙

A Babylonian prince who took part in the destruction of Jerusalem under King Nebuchadnezzar.

ONLY REFERENCE
JEREMIAH 39:3

SAMLAH 4 ♙
Dress

A king of Edom, "before there reigned any king over the children of Israel" (Genesis 36:31).

FIRST REFERENCE
GENESIS 36:36
LAST REFERENCE
I CHRONICLES 1:48

SAMSON 39 ♙
Sunlight

The twelfth judge of Israel, from the time of his conception he was supposed to follow a Nazarite vow, which meant he could not eat or drink anything from a grapevine, drink alcohol, cut his hair, or eat anything unclean. Samson performed amazing feats of strength. When he married, Samson chose a Philistine woman. God used the union to confront the Philistines, who ruled over Israel. Betrayed by his wife, Samson took out his anger on her people, burning their grain and performing more feats of strength. When he fell in love with Delilah, her fellow Philistines offered her money to find out the source of Samson's strength. Though Samson lied to her several times, he finally admitted that if she shaved his head, he would become weak. She did this, and he lost his strength because God had left him. The Philistines captured Samson, blinded him, and made him a slave. But as his hair grew, his strength returned. Brought to the Philistine temple to perform during their celebration, Samson leaned on the pillars of the temple and brought it down, killing the worshippers and himself.

FIRST REFERENCE
JUDGES 13:24
LAST REFERENCE
HEBREWS 11:32
KEY REFERENCES
JUDGES 13:13; 14:4; 16:4–30

SAMUEL 142

Heard of God

Prophet and judge of Israel. Samuel was born after his mother, Hannah, petitioned God to give her a child and promised to give him up to God's service in return. After Samuel was weaned, Hannah brought him to the priest Eli to live at the temple and serve the Lord. Eli realized that God had spoken to Samuel and encouraged the boy to listen and respond. In his first prophecy, Samuel spoke out against the wickedness of Eli's sons. Samuel led the Israelites to repent of their idolatry, and he judged Israel during his entire life. But when he became old, his sons were not faithful, and the people of Israel asked for a king. Though Samuel warned them against it, Israel insisted on a king, so God had the prophet anoint Saul. Samuel turned his authority over to Saul and encouraged the people to obey him, though their choice of Saul as a leader was evil. When Saul disobeyed God, attacking the Amalekites but not destroying them and their cattle, Samuel informed Saul that God had rejected him as king. Samuel anointed David king in Saul's place. The prophet died and was buried in his home at Ramah. Same as Shemuel.

FIRST REFERENCE
1 SAMUEL 1:20
LAST REFERENCE
HEBREWS 11:32
KEY REFERENCES
1 SAMUEL 1:11, 19–20, 24–28; 3:1–18; 7:3–6,
15–17; 10:1, 20–25; 12:1–25; 15:26; 16:13

SANBALLAT 10

One of Nehemiah's opponents as he rebuilt Jerusalem, Sanballat plotted to fight against Jerusalem, forcing the Israelites to guard the uncompleted walls. Sanballat then accused Nehemiah of fomenting a revolt. When that came to nothing, he hired a man to report that men were coming to kill Nehemiah.

FIRST REFERENCE
NEHEMIAH 2:10
LAST REFERENCE
NEHEMIAH 13:28

SAPH 1

Containing

A son of a Philistine giant killed in battle by one of King David's warriors, Sibbechai.

ONLY REFERENCE
2 SAMUEL 21:18

SAPPHIRA 1 👤
Sapphire

Wife of Ananias (1). The couple agreed to sell property and give only a portion of their gains to the church, while claiming they gave the whole price. When she lied to the apostle Peter, Sapphira died.

ONLY REFERENCE
ACTS 5:1

SARA 2 👤
Female noble

Greek form of the name *Sarah*, used in the New Testament.

FIRST REFERENCE
HEBREWS 11:1
LAST REFERENCE
I PETER 3:6

SARAH 41
Female noble

1) The name God gave Sarai, wife of Abram (Abraham), after He promised she would bear a child. Though she was ninety years old, God repeated the promise to give Abraham a son by her. When Sarah heard this, she laughed. A year later she bore Isaac. When Abraham's son Ishmael—child of Sarah's maid, Hagar—mocked Isaac, Sarah feared for her own son and had Hagar and Ishmael sent out of Abraham's camp. When Sarah died, Abraham bought land from the Hittites and buried her in the cave of Machpelah.

FIRST REFERENCE
GENESIS 17:15
LAST REFERENCE
ROMANS 9:9
KEY REFERENCES
GENESIS 18:10–15; 21:1–10; 23:1–20

2) A daughter of Asher and granddaughter of Jacob.

ONLY REFERENCE
NUMBERS 26:46

SARAI 17
Controlling

The barren wife of Abram, Sarai traveled with her husband to Canaan at God's calling. Following a famine, they moved to Egypt, where Abram called her his sister, because he feared he would be killed so that an Egyptian could have her. She was taken by Pharaoh, but God revealed her marriage to him, and he returned her to Abram, sending them away. When Sarai had no children, she gave her maid, Hagar, to Abram to bear children for her. But Hagar despised Sarai and fled. God kept His promise to Abraham that He would give Sarai a son who would be the father of a multitude. He changed her name to Sarah. Same as Sarah.

FIRST REFERENCE
GENESIS 11:29
LAST REFERENCE
GENESIS 17:15
KEY REFERENCES
GENESIS 12:5, 10–20; 16:1–10; 17:15

SARAPH
Burning

A descendant of Abraham through Jacob's son Judah. Saraph was a potter.

ONLY REFERENCE
I CHRONICLES 4:22

SARGON

A king of Assyria in the days of the prophet Isaiah.

ONLY REFERENCE
ISAIAH 20:1

SARSECHIM

A Babylonian prince who took part in the destruction of Jerusalem under King Nebuchadnezzar.

ONLY REFERENCE
JEREMIAH 39:3

SARUCH
Tendril

A descendant of Abraham through Isaac; forebear of Jesus' earthly father, Joseph.

ONLY REFERENCE
LUKE 3:35
GENEALOGY OF JESUS
LUKE 3:35

SAUL 422
Asked

1) Anointed king of Israel by the prophet Samuel, Saul fought the Philistines throughout his reign. But after the king wrongly made a burnt offering to God at Michmash, Samuel told Saul that because of his sin, his kingdom would not be established forever, and God would seek a man after his own heart. When God ordered Saul to fight the Amalekites and kill all the people and cattle, Saul did not kill their king or cattle. God rejected him as Israel's king, and Samuel anointed David king. After David killed the giant Goliath, Saul brought him into his court. Though his son Jonathan loved David, Saul became increasingly jealous of the young man and sought to kill him. Eventually David fled the court and began a series of battles with Saul. When Saul gathered an army to fend off the Philistines, fearful, he sought out a witch at Endor. The king asked her to call up the dead Samuel, from whom he received a disconcerting answer. When Saul went into battle, three of his sons were killed, and he seemed to be losing. Saul's armor bearer refused to kill him, so he fell on his own sword.

FIRST REFERENCE
I SAMUEL 9:2
LAST REFERENCE
ACTS 13:21
KEY REFERENCES
I SAMUEL 10:1, 17–24; 13:8–14; 15:1–3, 8–14, 35;
18:1–2, 5–11; 28:7–19; 31:1–4

2) A king of Edom, "before there reigned any king over the children of Israel" (Genesis 36:31).

FIRST REFERENCE
GENESIS 36:37
LAST REFERENCE
GENESIS 36:38

3) A zealous Jew who witnessed the martyrdom of Stephen and persecuted Christians. As Saul traveled to Damascus, planning to imprison Christians there, Jesus met him and temporarily blinded him. At Damascus, God sent Ananias (2) to restore his sight. After becoming a Christian and being baptized, Saul began to preach the message of Christ in the synagogues. Learning of a conspiracy to kill him, he left Damascus and returned to Jerusalem. Only Barnabas's testimony about his preaching made the disciples believe that he was not plotting against them. Saul was chosen by the Holy Spirit for a missionary journey. At that time scripture begins to call him Paul.

FIRST REFERENCE
ACTS 7:58
LAST REFERENCE
ACTS 26:14
KEY REFERENCES
ACTS 8:1, 3; 9:1–20, 23–27; 13:1–3, 9

SCEVA 1
Left-handed

A Jewish chief priest in Ephesus whose seven sons were beaten by a demon-possessed man during an attempted exorcism.

ONLY REFERENCE
ACTS 19:14

SEBA 2

A descendant of Noah through his son Ham.

FIRST REFERENCE
GENESIS 10:7
LAST REFERENCE
I CHRONICLES 1:9

SECUNDUS 1
Second

A man from Thessalonica who was a traveling companion of the apostle Paul.

ONLY REFERENCE
ACTS 20:4

SEGUB 3
Aloft

1) A son of Hiel of Bethel who died when his father set up Jericho's gates.

ONLY REFERENCE
I KINGS 16:34

2) A descendant of Abraham through Jacob's son Judah.

FIRST REFERENCE
I CHRONICLES 2:21
LAST REFERENCE
I CHRONICLES 2:22

SEIR 2
Rough

Forefather of an Edomite family whose sons were Horite chiefs.

FIRST REFERENCE
GENESIS 36:20
LAST REFERENCE
I CHRONICLES 1:38

SELED 2
Exultation

A descendant of Abraham through Jacob's son Judah.

ONLY REFERENCE
1 CHRONICLES 2:30

SEM 1

Greek form of the name *Shem*, used in the New Testament.

ONLY REFERENCE
LUKE 3:36
GENEALOGY OF JESUS
LUKE 3:36

SEMACHIAH 1
Supported of God

A Levite "porter" (doorkeeper) in the house of the Lord.

ONLY REFERENCE
1 CHRONICLES 26:7

SEMEI 1
Famous

A descendant of Abraham through Isaac; forebear of Jesus' earthly father, Joseph.

ONLY REFERENCE
LUKE 3:26
GENEALOGY OF JESUS
LUKE 3:26

SENNACHERIB 13

The king of Assyria who attacked and captured Judah's fortified cities during King Hezekiah's reign. Hezekiah paid him tribute to withdraw, but Sennacherib sent his commanders to threaten Jerusalem's people and force them to capitulate. Because the commanders spoke against the Lord, the angel of death killed 185,000 Assyrian soldiers, and Sennacherib withdrew to Nineveh.

FIRST REFERENCE
2 KINGS 18:13
LAST REFERENCE
ISAIAH 37:37
KEY REFERENCES
2 CHRONICLES 32:1, 9–19; ISAIAH 37:36–37

SENUAH 1
Pointed

Father of a Benjamite who was chosen by lot to resettle Jerusalem after returning from the Babylonian Exile.

ONLY REFERENCE
NEHEMIAH 11:9

SEORIM 1
Barley

One of twenty-four priests in David's time who was chosen by lot to serve in the tabernacle.

ONLY REFERENCE
1 CHRONICLES 24:8

SERAH 2
Superfluity

Daughter of Asher, a descendant of Abraham through Jacob.

FIRST REFERENCE
GENESIS 46:17
LAST REFERENCE
1 CHRONICLES 7:30

SERAIAH 20

God has prevailed

1) The scribe in King David's court.

ONLY REFERENCE
2 SAMUEL 8:17

2) The high priest during King Zedekiah's reign. He was killed following Nebuchadnezzar's invasion of Jerusalem.

FIRST REFERENCE
2 KINGS 25:18
LAST REFERENCE
JEREMIAH 52:24

3) A captain of Judah's troops whom Nebuchadnezzar's governor Gedaliah tried to sway to support him.

FIRST REFERENCE
2 KINGS 25:23
LAST REFERENCE
JEREMIAH 40:8

4) A descendant of Abraham through Jacob's son Judah.

FIRST REFERENCE
I CHRONICLES 4:13
LAST REFERENCE
I CHRONICLES 4:14

5) A descendant of Abraham through Jacob's son Simeon.

ONLY REFERENCE
I CHRONICLES 4:35

6) A priest who renewed the covenant under Nehemiah.

FIRST REFERENCE
EZRA 2:2
LAST REFERENCE
NEHEMIAH 12:12

7) A priest who resettled Jerusalem following the Babylonian Exile.

ONLY REFERENCE
NEHEMIAH 11:11

8) A man whom King Jehoiakim ordered to imprison the prophet Jeremiah and his scribe.

ONLY REFERENCE
JEREMIAH 36:26

9) A "quiet prince" who went into exile with King Zedekiah of Judah. At Jeremiah's command, he spoke a prophecy against Babylon.

FIRST REFERENCE
JEREMIAH 51:59
LAST REFERENCE
JEREMIAH 51:61

SERED 2

Trembling

A son of Zebulun and descendant of Abraham through Jacob.

FIRST REFERENCE
GENESIS 46:14
LAST REFERENCE
NUMBERS 26:26

SERGIUS I

Roman ruler of Cyprus during the apostle Paul's first missionary journey. Sergius Paulus, "a prudent man" (Acts 13:7), asked Paul and Barnabas to share the word of God with him, but a false prophet named Bar-jesus (also known as Elymas) interfered. After Paul pronounced blindness on Bar-jesus, Sergius came to faith.

ONLY REFERENCE
ACTS 13:7

SERUG 5
Tendril

A descendant of Noah through his son Shem. Serug was the great-grandfather of Abraham. He lived 230 years.

FIRST REFERENCE
GENESIS 11:20
LAST REFERENCE
I CHRONICLES 1:26

SETH 8
Substituted

Adam and Eve's third son, whom Eve bore after Abel was killed by his brother, Cain. He became a forefather of Jesus. Same as Sheth (2).

FIRST REFERENCE
GENESIS 4:25
LAST REFERENCE
LUKE 3:38
KEY REFERENCE
GENESIS 4:25–26
GENEALOGY OF JESUS
LUKE 3:38

SETHUR 1
Hidden

One of twelve spies sent by Moses to spy out the land of Canaan.

ONLY REFERENCE
NUMBERS 13:13

SHAAPH 2
Fluctuation

A descendant of Abraham through Jacob's son Judah.

FIRST REFERENCE
I CHRONICLES 2:47
LAST REFERENCE
I CHRONICLES 2:49

SHAASHGAZ 1

A eunuch serving the Persian king Ahasuerus. Shaashgaz oversaw the king's harem, including the future queen Esther.

ONLY REFERENCE
ESTHER 2:14

SHABBETHAI 3
Restful

1) A Levite who urged the Israelites to give up their "strange" (foreign) wives.

ONLY REFERENCE
EZRA 10:15

2) A Levite who helped Ezra to explain the law to exiles returned to Jerusalem.

ONLY REFERENCE
NEHEMIAH 8:7

3) A Levite who oversaw the outside of the Jerusalem temple in the time of Nehemiah.

ONLY REFERENCE
NEHEMIAH 11:16

SHACHIA 1
Captivation

A descendant of Abraham through Jacob's son Benjamin.

ONLY REFERENCE
I CHRONICLES 8:10

SHADRACH 15

The Babylonian name for Hananiah, one of Daniel's companions in exile. Daniel had King Nebuchadnezzar make Shadrach a ruler in Babylon. When Chaldeans accused Shadrach and his fellow Jews, Meshach and Abed-nego, of not worshipping the king's golden idol, the three faithful men were thrown into a furnace. God protected them, and they were not even singed. Recognizing the power of their God, the king promoted them in his service.

FIRST REFERENCE
DANIEL 1:7
LAST REFERENCE
DANIEL 3:30
KEY REFERENCE
DANIEL 3:16–18

SHAGE 1

Father of one of King David's valiant warriors.

ONLY REFERENCE
1 CHRONICLES 11:34

SHAHARAIM 1

Double dawn

A descendant of Abraham through Jacob's son Benjamin. Shaharaim divorced two wives then had children by other wives in the land of Moab.

ONLY REFERENCE
1 CHRONICLES 8:8

SHALLUM 27

Retribution

1) The fifth-to-last king of the northern kingdom of Israel. Shallum obtained the throne by assassinating King Zachariah. Shallum was himself assassinated only one month later.

FIRST REFERENCE
2 KINGS 15:10
LAST REFERENCE
2 KINGS 15:15

2) Husband of the prophetess Huldah during the reign of King Josiah of Judah.

FIRST REFERENCE
2 KINGS 22:14
LAST REFERENCE
2 CHRONICLES 34:22

3) A descendant of Abraham through Jacob's son Judah. Shallum descended from the line of an unnamed Israelite woman and her Egyptian husband, Jarha.

FIRST REFERENCE
1 CHRONICLES 2:40
LAST REFERENCE
1 CHRONICLES 2:41

4) Fourth son of Judah's king Josiah who inherited the throne from his father. Same as Jehoahaz (2).

FIRST REFERENCE
1 CHRONICLES 3:15
LAST REFERENCE
JEREMIAH 22:11

5) A descendant of Abraham through Jacob's son Simeon.

ONLY REFERENCE
1 CHRONICLES 4:25

6) A descendant of Abraham

through Jacob's son Levi, and a priest through the line of Aaron. Shallum was a forefather of Ezra (2).

FIRST REFERENCE
I CHRONICLES 6:12
LAST REFERENCE
EZRA 7:2

7) A descendant of Abraham through Jacob's son Naphtali.

ONLY REFERENCE
I CHRONICLES 7:13

8) A Jewish exile from the tribe of Levi who resettled Jerusalem.

FIRST REFERENCE
I CHRONICLES 9:17
LAST REFERENCE
NEHEMIAH 7:45

9) A man of the tribe of Ephraim whose son Jehizkiah counseled his nation of Israel against enslaving fellow Jews from Judah who were captured in a civil war.

ONLY REFERENCE
2 CHRONICLES 28:12

10) An exiled Levite who married a "strange" (foreign) woman.

ONLY REFERENCE
EZRA 10:24

11) Another exiled Israelite who married a foreign woman.

ONLY REFERENCE
EZRA 10:42

12) A city official, who, with the aid of his daughters, helped to rebuild the walls of Jerusalem under Nehemiah.

ONLY REFERENCE
NEHEMIAH 3:12

13) The prophet Jeremiah's uncle.

ONLY REFERENCE
JEREMIAH 32:7

14) Father of Maaseiah, a temple doorkeeper during Jeremiah's ministry.

ONLY REFERENCE
JEREMIAH 35:4

SHALLUN
Retribution

A rebuilder of the walls of Jerusalem under Nehemiah. Shallun repaired the Fountain Gate, with its locks and bars, as well as the wall near the Pool of Siloam.

ONLY REFERENCE
NEHEMIAH 3:15

SHALMAI 2
Clothed

Forefather of an exiled family that returned to Judah under Zerubbabel.

FIRST REFERENCE
EZRA 2:46
LAST REFERENCE
NEHEMIAH 7:48

SHALMAN I

A variant spelling of the name *Shalmaneser*, king of Assyria. The prophet Hosea described Shalman's viciousness in battle: "The mother was dashed in pieces upon her children" (Hosea 10:14).

ONLY REFERENCE
HOSEA 10:14

SHALMANESER 2

The king of Assyria who imprisoned King Hoshea of Israel and besieged, then captured, Samaria. He brought Israel into exile. Same as Shalman.

FIRST REFERENCE
2 KINGS 17:3
LAST REFERENCE
2 KINGS 18:9

SHAMA 1
Obedient

One of King David's valiant warriors.

ONLY REFERENCE
1 CHRONICLES 11:44

SHAMARIAH 1

A son of Judah's king Rehoboam and a grandson of Solomon.

ONLY REFERENCE
2 CHRONICLES 11:19

SHAMED 1
Preserved

A descendant of Abraham through Jacob's son Benjamin.

ONLY REFERENCE
1 CHRONICLES 8:12

SHAMER 2
Preserved

1) A descendant of Abraham through Jacob's son Levi.

ONLY REFERENCE
1 CHRONICLES 6:46

2) A descendant of Abraham through Jacob's son Asher.

ONLY REFERENCE
1 CHRONICLES 7:34

SHAMGAR 2

The third judge of Israel. Shamgar killed six hundred Philistines with an ox goad.

FIRST REFERENCE
JUDGES 3:31
LAST REFERENCE
JUDGES 5:6

SHAMHUTH 1
Desolation

A commander in King David's army overseeing twenty-four thousand men in the fifth month of each year.

ONLY REFERENCE
1 CHRONICLES 27:8

SHAMIR 1
Observed

A descendant of Abraham through Jacob's son Levi.

ONLY REFERENCE
1 CHRONICLES 24:24

SHAMMA 1
Desolation

A descendant of Abraham through Jacob's son Asher.

ONLY REFERENCE
1 CHRONICLES 7:37

SHAMMAH 8
Consternation

1) A descendant of Abraham's grandson Esau, whose blessing as older brother was taken by the scheming Jacob.

FIRST REFERENCE
GENESIS 36:13
LAST REFERENCE
I CHRONICLES 1:37

2) Third son of Jesse and an older brother of King David. Shammah served as a soldier in King Saul's army. Same as Shimea (1) and Shimeah (1).

FIRST REFERENCE
I SAMUEL 16:9
LAST REFERENCE
I SAMUEL 17:13

3) One of King David's warriors known as the "mighty men." Shammah defeated a troop of Philistines in a lentil field.

FIRST REFERENCE
2 SAMUEL 23:11
LAST REFERENCE
2 SAMUEL 23:33

4) One of King David's valiant warriors.

ONLY REFERENCE
2 SAMUEL 23:25

SHAMMAI 6
Destructive

1) A descendant of Abraham through Jacob's son Judah.

FIRST REFERENCE
I CHRONICLES 2:28
LAST REFERENCE
I CHRONICLES 2:32

2) Another descendant of Abraham through Jacob's son Judah.

FIRST REFERENCE
I CHRONICLES 2:44
LAST REFERENCE
I CHRONICLES 2:45

3) Yet another descendant of Abraham through Jacob's son Judah.

ONLY REFERENCE
I CHRONICLES 4:17

SHAMMOTH I
Ruins

One of King David's valiant warriors.

ONLY REFERENCE
I CHRONICLES 11:27

SHAMMUA 4
Renowned

1) One of twelve spies sent by Moses to spy out the land of Canaan.

ONLY REFERENCE
NUMBERS 13:4

2) A son of King David, born in Jerusalem. Same as Shammuah.

ONLY REFERENCE
I CHRONICLES 14:4

3) Forefather of a Jewish exile from the tribe of Levi who resettled Jerusalem.

ONLY REFERENCE
NEHEMIAH 11:17

4) Forefather of a priest who returned to Jerusalem under Zerubbabel.

ONLY REFERENCE
NEHEMIAH 12:18

SHAMMUAH

Renowned

A son of King David, born in Jerusalem. Same as Shammua (2).

ONLY REFERENCE
2 SAMUEL 5:14

SHAMSHERAI

Sun-like

A descendant of Abraham through Jacob's son Benjamin.

ONLY REFERENCE
1 CHRONICLES 8:26

SHAPHAM

Baldly

A descendant of Abraham through Jacob's son Gad.

ONLY REFERENCE
1 CHRONICLES 5:12

SHAPHAN

Rock-rabbit

1) Scribe for King Josiah of Judah, Shaphan brought the high priest Hilkiah the money the Levites collected to refurbish the temple. The priest reported that he had found the book of the law in the temple. Following the king's orders, Shaphan consulted with Huldah the prophetess.

FIRST REFERENCE
2 KINGS 22:3
LAST REFERENCE
JEREMIAH 36:12

2) Father of Ahikam, who consulted the prophetess Huldah at King Josiah's command.

FIRST REFERENCE
2 KINGS 22:12
LAST REFERENCE
JEREMIAH 43:6

3) Father of Elasah, a messenger whom Jeremiah sent to Babylon.

ONLY REFERENCE
JEREMIAH 29:3

4) Father of Jaazaniah, who burned incense, though he was not a priest. Possibly the same as Shaphan (1).

ONLY REFERENCE
EZEKIEL 8:11

SHAPHAT

Judge

1) One of twelve spies sent by Moses to spy out the land of Canaan.

ONLY REFERENCE
NUMBERS 13:5

2) Father of the prophet Elisha.

FIRST REFERENCE
1 KINGS 19:16
LAST REFERENCE
2 KINGS 6:31

3) A descendant of Abraham through Jacob's son Judah, in the line of the nation of Judah's second-to-last king, Jeconiah (also known as Jehoiachin).

ONLY REFERENCE
1 CHRONICLES 3:22

4) A descendant of Abraham through Jacob's son Gad.

ONLY REFERENCE
1 CHRONICLES 5:12

5) King David's chief shepherd over herds in the valleys.

ONLY REFERENCE
1 CHRONICLES 27:29

SHARAI

Hostile

An exiled Israelite who married a "strange" (foreign) woman.

ONLY REFERENCE
EZRA 10:40

SHARAR

Hostile

Father of one of King David's valiant warriors.

ONLY REFERENCE
2 SAMUEL 23:33

SHAREZER

Son of the Assyrian king Sennacherib, who, with his brother Adrammelech, killed his father with a sword. After the assassination, Sharezer fled to Armenia.

FIRST REFERENCE
2 KINGS 19:37
LAST REFERENCE
ISAIAH 37:38

SHASHAI

Whitish

An exiled Israelite who married a "strange" (foreign) woman.

ONLY REFERENCE
EZRA 10:40

SHASHAK

Pedestrian

A descendant of Abraham through Jacob's son Benjamin.

FIRST REFERENCE
I CHRONICLES 8:14
LAST REFERENCE
I CHRONICLES 8:25

SHAUL

Asked

1) A descendant of Abraham through Jacob's son Simeon. Shaul was born to Simeon and a "Canaanitish" woman.

FIRST REFERENCE
GENESIS 46:10
LAST REFERENCE
I CHRONICLES 4:24

2) A king of Edom in the days before Israel had a king.

FIRST REFERENCE
I CHRONICLES 1:48
LAST REFERENCE
I CHRONICLES 1:49

3) A descendant of Abraham through Jacob's son Levi.

ONLY REFERENCE
I CHRONICLES 6:24

SHAVSHA

Joyful

A scribe serving in the government of King David.

ONLY REFERENCE
I CHRONICLES 18:16

SHEAL

Request

An exiled Israelite who married a "strange" (foreign) woman.

ONLY REFERENCE
EZRA 10:29

SHEALTIEL

I have asked God

Father of Zerubbabel, governor of Judah after the Babylonian Exile.

FIRST REFERENCE
EZRA 3:2
LAST REFERENCE
HAGGAI 2:23

SHEARIAH 2

God has stormed

A descendant of Abraham through Jacob's son Benjamin, in the line of King Saul and his son Jonathan.

FIRST REFERENCE
I CHRONICLES 8:38
LAST REFERENCE
I CHRONICLES 9:44

SHEAR-JASHUB 1

A remnant will return

Son of Isaiah who joined the prophet in delivering a message to Judah's king Ahaz.

ONLY REFERENCE
ISAIAH 7:3

SHEBA 15

1) A descendant of Noah through his son Ham.

FIRST REFERENCE
GENESIS 10:7
LAST REFERENCE
I CHRONICLES 1:9

2) A descendant of Noah through his son Shem.

FIRST REFERENCE
GENESIS 10:28
LAST REFERENCE
I CHRONICLES 1:22

3) A descendant of Abraham by his second wife, Keturah.

FIRST REFERENCE
GENESIS 25:3
LAST REFERENCE
I CHRONICLES 1:32

4) An Israelite who rebelled against King David.

FIRST REFERENCE
2 SAMUEL 20:1
LAST REFERENCE
2 SAMUEL 20:22

5) A descendant of Abraham through Jacob's son Gad.

ONLY REFERENCE
I CHRONICLES 5:13

SHEBANIAH 7

God has grown

1) A priest who blew a trumpet before the ark of the covenant when David brought it to Jerusalem.

ONLY REFERENCE
I CHRONICLES 15:24

2) One of a group of Levites who led a revival among the Israelites in the time of Nehemiah.

FIRST REFERENCE
NEHEMIAH 9:4
LAST REFERENCE
NEHEMIAH 10:10

3) A priest who renewed the covenant under Nehemiah.

FIRST REFERENCE
NEHEMIAH 10:4
LAST REFERENCE
NEHEMIAH 12:14

4) A Levite who renewed the covenant under Nehemiah.

ONLY REFERENCE
NEHEMIAH 10:12

SHEBER 1
Fracture

A descendant of Abraham through Jacob's son Judah.

ONLY REFERENCE
1 CHRONICLES 2:48

SHEBNA 9
Growth

1) Scribe for King Hezekiah of Judah, Shebna represented Hezekiah and spoke to King Sennacherib's representative, Rab-shakeh, when the Assyrians attacked Jerusalem. Afterward, Shebna took a message to the prophet Isaiah.

FIRST REFERENCE
2 KINGS 18:18
LAST REFERENCE
ISAIAH 37:2

2) A treasurer (steward) Isaiah prophesied against for building himself a kingly tomb.

ONLY REFERENCE
ISAIAH 22:15

SHEBUEL 3
Captive of God

1) A descendant of Abraham through Jacob's son Levi and the line of Moses.

FIRST REFERENCE
1 CHRONICLES 23:16
LAST REFERENCE
1 CHRONICLES 26:24

2) A son of King David's musician Heman, who was "under the hands of [his] father for song in the house of the LORD" (1 Chronicles 25:6).

ONLY REFERENCE
1 CHRONICLES 25:4

SHECANIAH 2
God has dwelt

1) One of twenty-four priests in David's time who was chosen by lot to serve in the tabernacle.

ONLY REFERENCE
1 CHRONICLES 24:11

2) A priest in the time of King Hezekiah who helped to distribute freewill offerings to his fellow priests.

ONLY REFERENCE
2 CHRONICLES 31:15

SHECHANIAH 8
God has dwelt

1) A descendant of Abraham through Jacob's son Judah, in the line of the nation of Judah's second-to-last king, Jeconiah (also known as Jehoiachin).

FIRST REFERENCE
1 CHRONICLES 3:21
LAST REFERENCE
1 CHRONICLES 3:22

2) Forefather of a Jewish exile who returned from Babylon to Judah under Ezra.

ONLY REFERENCE
EZRA 8:3

3) Forefather of another Jewish exile who returned from Babylon to Judah under Ezra.

ONLY REFERENCE
EZRA 8:5

4) An exiled Israelite who married a "strange" (foreign) woman. Shechaniah suggested to Ezra

that he and his fellow offenders "make a covenant with our God to put away all the wives, and such as are born of them" (Ezra 10:3).

ONLY REFERENCE
EZRA 10:2

5) Father of a man who repaired Jerusalem's walls under Nehemiah.

ONLY REFERENCE
NEHEMIAH 3:29

6) Father-in-law of Tobiah (2).

ONLY REFERENCE
NEHEMIAH 6:18

7) A priest who returned to Jerusalem under Zerubbabel.

ONLY REFERENCE
NEHEMIAH 12:3

SHECHEM 19
Neck

1) Prince of the city of Shechem who raped Jacob's daughter, Dinah, then wanted to marry her. Dinah's brothers insisted that all males in Shechem be circumcised. While they recovered, Simeon and Levi attacked the city; killed Shechem, his father, and all the males of the city; and brought Dinah home.

FIRST REFERENCE
GENESIS 34:2
LAST REFERENCE
JUDGES 9:28
KEY REFERENCES
GENESIS 34:2–7, 11–12, 25–26

2) A descendant of Abraham through Jacob's son Joseph; founder of the Shechemite clan.

FIRST REFERENCE
NUMBERS 26:31
LAST REFERENCE
JOSHUA 17:2

3) A descendant of Abraham through Joseph's son Manasseh.

ONLY REFERENCE
I CHRONICLES 7:19

SHEDEUR 5
Spreader of light

Forefather of a prince of the tribe of Reuben who helped Moses take a census.

FIRST REFERENCE
NUMBERS 1:5
LAST REFERENCE
NUMBERS 10:18

SHEHARIAH 1
God has sought

A descendant of Abraham through Jacob's son Benjamin.

ONLY REFERENCE
I CHRONICLES 8:26

SHELAH 11
Request

1) Son of Jacob's son Judah. Judah refused to marry Shelah to Tamar, the widow of his first two sons.

FIRST REFERENCE
GENESIS 38:5
LAST REFERENCE
I CHRONICLES 4:21

2) A descendant of Noah through his son Shem.

FIRST REFERENCE
I CHRONICLES 1:18
LAST REFERENCE
I CHRONICLES 1:24

SHELEMIAH 10

Thank-offering of God

1) A Levite who was chosen by lot to guard the east side of the house of the Lord.

ONLY REFERENCE
I CHRONICLES 26:14

2) An exiled Israelite who married a "strange" (foreign) woman.

ONLY REFERENCE
EZRA 10:39

3) Another exiled Israelite who married a foreign woman.

ONLY REFERENCE
EZRA 10:41

4) Father of a man who repaired Jerusalem's walls under Nehemiah.

ONLY REFERENCE
NEHEMIAH 3:30

5) A priest whom Nehemiah made a treasurer to distribute the portions of the Levites.

ONLY REFERENCE
NEHEMIAH 13:13

6) Father of Jehudi, who took a message from Judah's princes to the prophet Jeremiah's scribe.

ONLY REFERENCE
JEREMIAH 36:14

7) A man whom King Jehoiakim ordered to imprison the prophet Jeremiah and his scribe.

ONLY REFERENCE
JEREMIAH 36:26

8) Father of Jehucal, a messenger from King Hezekiah to the prophet Jeremiah.

FIRST REFERENCE
JEREMIAH 37:3
LAST REFERENCE
JEREMIAH 38:1

9) Father of Irijah, who accused the prophet Jeremiah of siding with the Chaldeans.

ONLY REFERENCE
JEREMIAH 37:13

SHELEPH 2

Extract

A descendant of Noah through his son Shem.

FIRST REFERENCE
GENESIS 10:26
LAST REFERENCE
I CHRONICLES 1:20

SHELESH 1

Triplet

A descendant of Abraham through Jacob's son Asher.

ONLY REFERENCE
I CHRONICLES 7:35

SHELOMI 1

Peaceable

Forefather of Ahihud, prince of the tribe of Asher when the Israelites entered the Promised Land.

ONLY REFERENCE
NUMBERS 34:27

SHELOMITH 9

Peaceableness, pacification

1) Mother of a man who was stoned for blaspheming the Lord.

ONLY REFERENCE
LEVITICUS 24:11

2) Daughter of Zerubbabel and a descendant of Abraham through Jacob's son Judah, in the line of the nation of Judah's second-to-last king, Jeconiah (also known as Jehoiachin).

ONLY REFERENCE
I CHRONICLES 3:19

3) A Levite chief appointed under King David.

ONLY REFERENCE
I CHRONICLES 23:9

4) A descendant of Abraham through Jacob's son Levi. Same as Shelomoth.

ONLY REFERENCE
I CHRONICLES 23:18

5) In David's reign, a Levite in charge of the treasures that were dedicated to the temple.

FIRST REFERENCE
I CHRONICLES 26:25
LAST REFERENCE
I CHRONICLES 26:28

6) A son of Judah's king Rehoboam and a grandson of Solomon.

ONLY REFERENCE
2 CHRONICLES 11:20

7) Forefather of a Jewish exile who returned from Babylon to Judah under Ezra.

ONLY REFERENCE
EZRA 8:10

SHELOMOTH 1

Pacification

A descendant of Abraham through Jacob's son Levi. Same as Shelomith (4).

ONLY REFERENCE
I CHRONICLES 24:22

SHELUMIEL 5

Peace of God

A man of the tribe of Simeon who helped Aaron take a census.

FIRST REFERENCE
NUMBERS 1:6
LAST REFERENCE
NUMBERS 10:19

SHEM 17

Name

The eldest son of Noah, he joined Noah in the ark. After leaving the ark, Noah became drunk and lay unclothed in his tent. With his brother Japheth, Shem covered their father without looking at him. For this Noah blessed Shem. Same as Sem.

FIRST REFERENCE
GENESIS 5:32
LAST REFERENCE
I CHRONICLES 1:24
KEY REFERENCES
GENESIS 7:13; 9:18, 24–26

SHEMA 5

Heard

1) A descendant of Abraham through Jacob's son Judah.

FIRST REFERENCE
I CHRONICLES 2:43
LAST REFERENCE
I CHRONICLES 2:44

2) A descendant of Abraham through Jacob's son Reuben.

ONLY REFERENCE
I CHRONICLES 5:8

3) A descendant of Abraham through Jacob's son Benjamin. Shema drove the original inhabitants out of the town of Gath.

ONLY REFERENCE
I CHRONICLES 8:13

4) A priest who assisted Ezra in reading the book of the law to the people of Jerusalem.

ONLY REFERENCE
NEHEMIAH 8:4

SHEMAAH 1

Annunciation

Father of two of King David's valiant warriors.

ONLY REFERENCE
I CHRONICLES 12:3

SHEMAIAH 41

God has heard

1) A prophet who told King Rehoboam not to fight Israel when it revolted against him.

FIRST REFERENCE
I KINGS 12:22
LAST REFERENCE
2 CHRONICLES 12:15

2) A descendant of Abraham through Jacob's son Judah, in the line of the nation of Judah's second-to-last king, Jeconiah (also known as Jehoiachin).

ONLY REFERENCE
I CHRONICLES 3:22

3) A descendant of Abraham through Jacob's son Simeon.

ONLY REFERENCE
I CHRONICLES 4:37

4) A descendant of Abraham through Jacob's son Reuben.

ONLY REFERENCE
I CHRONICLES 5:4

5) A Jewish exile from the tribe of Levi who resettled Jerusalem.

FIRST REFERENCE
I CHRONICLES 9:14
LAST REFERENCE
NEHEMIAH 11:15

6) Forefather of a Jewish exile from the tribe of Levi who resettled Jerusalem.

ONLY REFERENCE
I CHRONICLES 9:16

7) A descendant of Abraham through Jacob's son Levi. Shemaiah was among a group of Levites appointed by King David to bring the ark of the covenant from the house of Obed-edom to Jerusalem.

FIRST REFERENCE
I CHRONICLES 15:8
LAST REFERENCE
I CHRONICLES 15:11

8) A Levite scribe who transcribed King David's divisions of the priests.

ONLY REFERENCE
I CHRONICLES 24:6

9) A Levite "porter" (doorkeeper)

in the house of the Lord.

FIRST REFERENCE
1 CHRONICLES 26:4
LAST REFERENCE
1 CHRONICLES 26:7

10) A Levite sent by King Jehoshaphat to teach the law of the Lord throughout the nation of Judah.

ONLY REFERENCE
2 CHRONICLES 17:8

11) A descendant of Abraham through Jacob's son Levi. Shemaiah was among the Levites who cleansed the Jerusalem temple during the revival in King Hezekiah's reign.

ONLY REFERENCE
2 CHRONICLES 29:14

12) A priest in the reign of King Hezekiah, Shemaiah helped to distribute the freewill offerings to his fellow priests.

ONLY REFERENCE
2 CHRONICLES 31:15

13) A descendant of Abraham through Jacob's son Levi. Shemaiah was among those who distributed sacrificial animals to fellow Levites preparing to celebrate the Passover under King Josiah.

ONLY REFERENCE
2 CHRONICLES 35:9

14) A Jewish exile who returned from Babylon to Judah under Ezra.

ONLY REFERENCE
EZRA 8:13

15) A Jewish exile charged with finding Levites and temple servants to travel to Jerusalem with Ezra.

ONLY REFERENCE
EZRA 8:16

16) An exiled Israelite priest who married a "strange" (foreign) woman.

ONLY REFERENCE
EZRA 10:21

17) Another exiled Israelite who married a foreign woman.

ONLY REFERENCE
EZRA 10:31

18) A man who repaired Jerusalem's walls under Nehemiah.

ONLY REFERENCE
NEHEMIAH 3:29

19) A false prophet who encouraged Nehemiah to flee from Jerusalem.

ONLY REFERENCE
NEHEMIAH 6:10

20) A priest who renewed the covenant under Nehemiah.

FIRST REFERENCE
NEHEMIAH 10:8
LAST REFERENCE
NEHEMIAH 12:35

21) A priest who helped to dedicate the rebuilt walls of Jerusalem by playing a musical instrument.

ONLY REFERENCE
NEHEMIAH 12:36

22) A priest who helped to dedicate the rebuilt wall of Jerusalem by giving thanks.

ONLY REFERENCE
NEHEMIAH 12:42

23) Father of a prophet who ministered according to Jeremiah's words.

24) A false prophet who opposed the high priest Jehoiada and the prophet Jeremiah.

FIRST REFERENCE
JEREMIAH 29:24
LAST REFERENCE
JEREMIAH 29:32

25) Father of a prince of Judah who heard Jeremiah's book of prophecies.

ONLY REFERENCE
JEREMIAH 36:12

SHEMARIAH 3
God has guarded

1) A "mighty man" who supported the future king David during his conflict with Saul.

ONLY REFERENCE
I CHRONICLES 12:5

2) An exiled Israelite who married a "strange" (foreign) woman.

ONLY REFERENCE
EZRA 10:32

3) Another exiled Israelite who married a foreign woman.

ONLY REFERENCE
EZRA 10:41

SHEMEBER 1
Illustrious

The king of Zeboiim in the days of Abram.

ONLY REFERENCE
GENESIS 14:2

SHEMER 2
Preserved

The owner of the hill of Samaria, which he sold to King Omri of Israel.

ONLY REFERENCE
I KINGS 16:24

SHEMIDA 2
Name of knowing

A descendant of Abraham through Joseph's son Manasseh. Same as Shemidah.

FIRST REFERENCE
NUMBERS 26:32
LAST REFERENCE
JOSHUA 17:2

SHEMIDAH 1
Name of knowing

A descendant of Abraham through Joseph's son Manasseh. Same as Shemida.

ONLY REFERENCE
I CHRONICLES 7:19

SHEMIRAMOTH 4
Name of heights

1) A Levite musician who performed in celebration when King David brought the ark of the covenant to Jerusalem.

FIRST REFERENCE
I CHRONICLES 15:18
LAST REFERENCE
I CHRONICLES 16:5

2) A Levite sent by King Jehoshaphat to teach the law of the Lord throughout the nation of Judah.

FIRST REFERENCE
2 CHRONICLES 17:8

SHEMUEL 3

Heard of God

1) Prince of the tribe of Simeon when the Israelites entered the Promised Land.

ONLY REFERENCE
NUMBERS 34:20

2) An alternative name for the prophet Samuel.

ONLY REFERENCE
I CHRONICLES 6:33

3) A descendant of Abraham through Jacob's son Issachar.

ONLY REFERENCE
I CHRONICLES 7:2

SHENAZAR I

A descendant of Abraham through Jacob's son Judah, in the line of the nation of Judah's second-to-last king, Jeconiah (also known as Jehoiachin).

ONLY REFERENCE
I CHRONICLES 3:18

SHEPHATHIAH I

God has judged

Father of Meshullam, a Benjamite who resettled Jerusalem after the Babylonian captivity.

ONLY REFERENCE
I CHRONICLES 9:8

SHEPHATIAH 12

God has judged

1) Fifth son of David, born to his wife Abital in Hebron.

FIRST REFERENCE
2 SAMUEL 3:4
LAST REFERENCE
I CHRONICLES 3:3

2) A "mighty man" who supported the future king David during his conflict with Saul.

ONLY REFERENCE
I CHRONICLES 12:5

3) Leader of the tribe of Simeon in the days of King David.

ONLY REFERENCE
I CHRONICLES 27:16

4) A son of Judah's king Jehoshaphat, given "great gifts of silver, and of gold, and of precious things" by his father (2 Chronicles 21:3).

ONLY REFERENCE
2 CHRONICLES 21:2

5) Forefather of an exiled family that returned to Judah under Zerubbabel.

FIRST REFERENCE
EZRA 2:4
LAST REFERENCE
NEHEMIAH 7:9

6) Forefather of an exiled family— former servants of Solomon—that returned to Judah under Zerubbabel.

FIRST REFERENCE
EZRA 2:57
LAST REFERENCE
NEHEMIAH 7:59

7) Forefather of exiles who returned from Babylon to Judah under Ezra.

ONLY REFERENCE
EZRA 8:8

8) A Jewish exile from the tribe of Judah who resettled Jerusalem.

ONLY REFERENCE
NEHEMIAH 11:4

9) A prince of Judah who sought to have King Zedekiah kill Jeremiah for his negative prophecy.

ONLY REFERENCE
JEREMIAH 38:1

SHEPHI
Baldness

A descendant of Seir, who lived in Esau's "land of Edom." Same as Shepho.

ONLY REFERENCE
1 CHRONICLES 1:40

SHEPHO
Baldness

A descendant of Seir, who lived in Esau's "land of Edom." Same as Shephi.

ONLY REFERENCE
GENESIS 36:23

SHEPHUPHAN
Serpent-like

A descendant of Abraham through Jacob's son Benjamin.

ONLY REFERENCE
1 CHRONICLES 8:5

SHERAH
Kindred

A descendant of Abraham through Joseph's son Ephraim. She built the city of Beth-horon.

ONLY REFERENCE
1 CHRONICLES 7:24

SHEREBIAH
God has brought heat

1) A Levite whom Ezra called to serve in the temple upon his return to Jerusalem. Sherebiah was among a group of Levites who led a revival among the Israelites in the time of Nehemiah.

FIRST REFERENCE
EZRA 8:18
LAST REFERENCE
NEHEMIAH 9:5

2) A Levite who renewed the covenant under Nehemiah.

FIRST REFERENCE
NEHEMIAH 10:12
LAST REFERENCE
NEHEMIAH 12:24

SHERESH
Root

A descendant of Abraham through Joseph's son Manasseh.

ONLY REFERENCE
1 CHRONICLES 7:16

SHEREZER

A man sent by the people of Bethel to the prophet Zechariah to seek God's favor.

ONLY REFERENCE
ZECHARIAH 7:2

SHESHAI
Whitish

One of the gigantic children of Anak, who was killed after Joshua's death when Judah battled the Canaanites.

FIRST REFERENCE
NUMBERS 13:22
LAST REFERENCE
JUDGES 1:10

SHESHAN 4
Lily

A descendant of Abraham through Jacob's son Judah. Sheshan had only daughters and gave one in marriage to his Egyptian servant, Jarha.

FIRST REFERENCE
I CHRONICLES 2:31
LAST REFERENCE
I CHRONICLES 2:35

SHESHBAZZAR 4

Another name for Zerubbabel, the leader of exiles who returned from Babylon to Judah.

FIRST REFERENCE
EZRA 1:8
LAST REFERENCE
EZRA 5:16

SHETH 2
Substituted

1) A leader of Moab mentioned in one of Balaam's prophecies.

ONLY REFERENCE
NUMBERS 24:17

2) A variant spelling of the name *Seth*; Adam's third son.

ONLY REFERENCE
I CHRONICLES 1:1

SHETHAR 1

One of seven Persian princes serving under King Ahasuerus.

ONLY REFERENCE
ESTHER 1:14

SHETHAR-BOZNAI 4

A Persian official who objected to the rebuilding of the Jewish temple.

FIRST REFERENCE
EZRA 5:3
LAST REFERENCE
EZRA 6:13

SHEVA 2
False

1) A scribe serving in the government of King David.

ONLY REFERENCE
2 SAMUEL 20:25

2) A descendant of Abraham through Jacob's son Judah.

ONLY REFERENCE
I CHRONICLES 2:49

SHILHI 2
Armed

Grandfather of Judah's king Jehoshaphat.

FIRST REFERENCE
I KINGS 22:42
LAST REFERENCE
2 CHRONICLES 20:31

SHILLEM 2
Requital

A descendant of Abraham through Jacob's son Naphtali.

FIRST REFERENCE
GENESIS 46:24
LAST REFERENCE
NUMBERS 26:49

SHILONI

Inhabitant of Shiloh

A Jewish exile from the tribe of Judah who resettled Jerusalem.

ONLY REFERENCE
NEHEMIAH 11:5

SHILSHAH

Triplication

A descendant of Abraham through Jacob's son Asher.

ONLY REFERENCE
I CHRONICLES 7:37

SHIMEA

Annunciation

1) A brother of King David. Same as Shimeah (1), Shammah (2), and Shimma.

ONLY REFERENCE
I CHRONICLES 20:7

2) A son of King David, born in Jerusalem to Bath-sheba (also known as Bath-shua).

ONLY REFERENCE
I CHRONICLES 3:5

3) A descendant of Abraham through Jacob's son Levi.

ONLY REFERENCE
I CHRONICLES 6:30

4) Another descendant of Abraham through Jacob's son Levi.

ONLY REFERENCE
I CHRONICLES 6:39

SHIMEAH

Annunciation

1) A brother of King David. Same as Shimea (1), Shammah (2), and Shimma.

FIRST REFERENCE
2 SAMUEL 13:3
LAST REFERENCE
2 SAMUEL 21:21

2) A descendant of Abraham through Jacob's son Benjamin.

ONLY REFERENCE
I CHRONICLES 8:32

SHIMEAM

Annunciation

A cousin of King Saul and a descendant of Abraham through Jacob's son Benjamin.

ONLY REFERENCE
I CHRONICLES 9:38

SHIMEATH

Annunciation

Mother of Zabad, a royal official who conspired to kill Judah's king Joash.

FIRST REFERENCE
2 KINGS 12:21
LAST REFERENCE
2 CHRONICLES 24:26

SHIMEI

Famous

1) A descendant of Abraham through Jacob's son Levi. Same as Shimi.

FIRST REFERENCE
NUMBERS 3:18
LAST REFERENCE
I CHRONICLES 23:10

2) A relative of King Saul who cursed King David when he fled Jerusalem. Later Shimei apologized to David, who pardoned him. But before he died, David warned Solomon about Shimei. Solomon told Shimei not to leave Jerusalem, or he would die. When two of Shimei's servants ran away, he left Jerusalem, so Solomon had him killed.

FIRST REFERENCE
2 SAMUEL 16:5
LAST REFERENCE
I KINGS 2:44
KEY REFERENCES
2 SAMUEL 16:5–8; 19:18–23;
I KINGS 2:8–9, 36–46

3) An official who did not support Adonijah as king. Possibly the same as Shimei (4).

ONLY REFERENCE
I KINGS 1:8

4) One of King Solomon's twelve officials over provisions.

ONLY REFERENCE
I KINGS 4:18

5) A descendant of Abraham through Jacob's son Judah, in the line of the nation of Judah's second-to-last king, Jeconiah (also known as Jehoiachin).

ONLY REFERENCE
I CHRONICLES 3:19

6) A descendant of Abraham through Jacob's son Simeon. He fathered sixteen sons and six daughters.

FIRST REFERENCE
I CHRONICLES 4:26
LAST REFERENCE
I CHRONICLES 4:27

7) A descendant of Abraham through Jacob's son Reuben.

ONLY REFERENCE
I CHRONICLES 5:4

8) A descendant of Abraham through Jacob's son Levi.

ONLY REFERENCE
I CHRONICLES 6:29

9) Another descendant of Abraham through Jacob's son Levi.

ONLY REFERENCE
I CHRONICLES 23:9

10) One of twenty-four Levite musicians who was chosen by lot to serve in the house of the Lord.

ONLY REFERENCE
I CHRONICLES 25:17

11) King David's official who was in charge of the vineyards.

ONLY REFERENCE
I CHRONICLES 27:27

12) A descendant of Abraham through Jacob's son Levi. Shimei was among the Levites who cleansed the Jerusalem temple during the revival in King Hezekiah's reign.

ONLY REFERENCE
2 CHRONICLES 29:14

13) A Levite appointed by King Hezekiah to care for the temple contributions.

FIRST REFERENCE
2 CHRONICLES 31:12
LAST REFERENCE
2 CHRONICLES 31:13

14) An exiled Levite who married a "strange" (foreign) woman.

ONLY REFERENCE
EZRA 10:23

15) Another exiled Israelite who married a foreign woman.

ONLY REFERENCE
EZRA 10:33

16) Another exiled Israelite who married a foreign woman.

ONLY REFERENCE
EZRA 10:38

17) Grandfather of Mordecai, one of the heroes of the story of Esther.

ONLY REFERENCE
ESTHER 2:5

18) Head of a household whom Zechariah prophesied would be set apart before the day of the Lord.

ONLY REFERENCE
ZECHARIAH 12:13

SHIMEON
Hearing

An exiled Israelite who married a "strange" (foreign) woman.

ONLY REFERENCE
EZRA 10:31

SHIMHI
Famous

A descendant of Abraham through Jacob's son Benjamin.

ONLY REFERENCE
I CHRONICLES 8:21

SHIMI
Famous

A descendant of Abraham through Jacob's son Levi. Same as Shimei (1).

ONLY REFERENCE
EXODUS 6:17

SHIMMA
Annunciation

Third son of Jesse and an older brother of David. Same as Shammah (2), Shimea (1) and Shimeah (1).

ONLY REFERENCE
I CHRONICLES 2:13

SHIMON
Desert

A descendant of Abraham through Jacob's son Judah.

ONLY REFERENCE
I CHRONICLES 4:20

SHIMRATH
Guardship

A descendant of Abraham through Jacob's son Benjamin.

ONLY REFERENCE
I CHRONICLES 8:21

SHIMRI
Watchful

1) A descendant of Abraham through Jacob's son Simeon.

ONLY REFERENCE
I CHRONICLES 4:37

2) Father of one of King David's valiant warriors.

ONLY REFERENCE
I CHRONICLES 11:45

3) A descendant of Abraham through Jacob's son Levi. Shimri was among the Levites who cleansed the Jerusalem temple during the revival in King Hezekiah's reign.

ONLY REFERENCE
2 CHRONICLES 29:13

SHIMRITH

Female guard

Mother of Jehozabad, a royal official who conspired to kill Judah's king Joash. Same as Shomer (1).

ONLY REFERENCE
2 CHRONICLES 24:26

SHIMROM

Guardianship

A descendant of Abraham through Jacob's son Issachar. Same as Shimron.

ONLY REFERENCE
1 CHRONICLES 7:1

SHIMRON 4

Guardianship

A descendant of Abraham through Jacob's son Issachar. Same as Shimrom.

FIRST REFERENCE
GENESIS 46:13
LAST REFERENCE
JOSHUA 19:15

SHIMSHAI 4

Sunny

A scribe who wrote King Artaxerxes a letter objecting to the rebuilding of Jerusalem. As a result, the king temporarily stopped the rebuilding.

FIRST REFERENCE
EZRA 4:8
LAST REFERENCE
EZRA 4:23

SHINAB

Father has turned

The king of Admah in the days of Abraham.

ONLY REFERENCE
GENESIS 14:2

SHIPHI

Copious

A descendant of Abraham through Jacob's son Simeon.

ONLY REFERENCE
1 CHRONICLES 4:37

SHIPHRAH

Brightness

A Hebrew midwife who did not obey the king of Egypt's command to kill all male Israelite babies.

ONLY REFERENCE
EXODUS 1:15

347

SHIPHTAN
Judge-like

Forefather of Kemuel, prince of the tribe of Ephraim when the Israelites entered the Promised Land.

ONLY REFERENCE
NUMBERS 34:24

SHISHA
Whiteness

Father of two scribes who served King Solomon.

ONLY REFERENCE
I KINGS 4:3

SHISHAK 7

The king of Egypt to whom Jeroboam fled when Solomon discovered he had been anointed king over the northern ten tribes. During the reign of Solomon's son Rehoboam, Shishak attacked Judah, captured Jerusalem, and took the treasures of the temple and palace.

FIRST REFERENCE
I KINGS 11:40
LAST REFERENCE
2 CHRONICLES 12:9

SHITRAI I
Magisterial

King David's chief shepherd over herds in Sharon.

ONLY REFERENCE
I CHRONICLES 27:29

SHIZA I

Father of one of King David's valiant warriors.

ONLY REFERENCE
I CHRONICLES 11:42

SHOBAB 4
Rebellious

1) A son of King David, born in Jerusalem.

FIRST REFERENCE
2 SAMUEL 5:14
LAST REFERENCE
I CHRONICLES 4:14

2) A descendant of Abraham through Jacob's son Judah.

ONLY REFERENCE
I CHRONICLES 2:18

SHOBACH 2
Thicket

A captain in the Syrian army of King Hadarezer. Shobach was defeated in battle by King David and his Israelite warriors. Same as Shophach.

FIRST REFERENCE
2 SAMUEL 10:16
LAST REFERENCE
2 SAMUEL 10:18

SHOBAI 2
Captor

Forefather of an exiled family that returned to Judah under Zerubbabel.

FIRST REFERENCE
EZRA 2:42
LAST REFERENCE
NEHEMIAH 7:45

SHOBAL   9

Overflowing

1) A descendant of Seir, who lived in Esau's "land of Edom."

FIRST REFERENCE
GENESIS 36:20
LAST REFERENCE
I CHRONICLES 1:40

2) A descendant of Abraham through Jacob's son Judah.

FIRST REFERENCE
I CHRONICLES 2:50
LAST REFERENCE
I CHRONICLES 2:52

3) Another descendant of Abraham through Jacob's son Judah.

FIRST REFERENCE
I CHRONICLES 4:1
LAST REFERENCE
I CHRONICLES 4:2

SHOBEK   I

Forsaking

A Jewish leader who renewed the covenant under Nehemiah.

ONLY REFERENCE
NEHEMIAH 10:24

SHOBI   I

Captor

A man who brought food and supplies to King David and his soldiers as they fled from the army of David's son Absalom, who was staging a coup.

ONLY REFERENCE
2 SAMUEL 17:27

SHOHAM   I

To blanch

A descendant of Abraham through Jacob's son Levi.

ONLY REFERENCE
I CHRONICLES 24:27

SHOMER   2

Keeper

1) Mother of one of two royal officials who conspired to kill Judah's king Joash. Same as Shimrith.

ONLY REFERENCE
2 KINGS 12:21

2) A descendant of Abraham through Jacob's son Asher.

ONLY REFERENCE
I CHRONICLES 7:32

SHOPHACH   2

Poured

A captain in the Syrian army of King Hadarezer. Shophach was defeated in battle by King David and his Israelite warriors. Same as Shobach.

FIRST REFERENCE
I CHRONICLES 19:16
LAST REFERENCE
I CHRONICLES 19:18

SHUA   2

A cry

1) Mother-in-law of Judah, the son of Jacob. Same as Shuah (2).

ONLY REFERENCE
I CHRONICLES 2:3

2) Daughter of Heber and a descendant of Abraham through Jacob's son Asher.

ONLY REFERENCE
I CHRONICLES 7:32

SHUAH 5
Dell

1) A son of Abraham by his second wife, Keturah.

FIRST REFERENCE
GENESIS 25:2
LAST REFERENCE
I CHRONICLES 1:32

2) Mother-in-law of Judah, the son of Jacob. Same as Shua (1).

FIRST REFERENCE
GENESIS 38:2
LAST REFERENCE
GENESIS 38:12

3) A descendant of Abraham through Jacob's son Judah.

ONLY REFERENCE
I CHRONICLES 4:11

SHUAL 1
Jackal

A descendant of Abraham through Jacob's son Asher.

ONLY REFERENCE
I CHRONICLES 7:36

SHUBAEL 3
God has favored

1) A descendant of Abraham through Jacob's son Levi.

ONLY REFERENCE
I CHRONICLES 24:20

2) One of twenty-four Levite musicians who was chosen by lot to serve in the house of the Lord.

ONLY REFERENCE
I CHRONICLES 25:20

SHUHAM 1
Humbly

A descendant of Abraham through Jacob's son Dan.

ONLY REFERENCE
NUMBERS 26:42

SHUNI 2
Rest

A descendant of Abraham through Jacob's son Gad.

FIRST REFERENCE
GENESIS 46:16
LAST REFERENCE
NUMBERS 26:15

SHUPHAM 1
Serpent-like

A descendant of Abraham through Jacob's son Benjamin.

ONLY REFERENCE
NUMBERS 26:39

SHUPPIM 3
Serpents

1) A descendant of Abraham through Jacob's son Benjamin.

FIRST REFERENCE
I CHRONICLES 7:12
LAST REFERENCE
I CHRONICLES 7:15

2) A Levite who was chosen by lot to guard the west side of the house of the Lord.

ONLY REFERENCE
I CHRONICLES 26:16

SHUTHELAH 4
Crash of breakage

1) A descendant of Abraham through Joseph's son Ephraim.

FIRST REFERENCE
NUMBERS 26:35
LAST REFERENCE
I CHRONICLES 7:20

2) Another descendant of Abraham through Joseph's son Ephraim.

ONLY REFERENCE
I CHRONICLES 7:21

SIA 1
Converse

Forefather of an exiled family that returned to Judah under Zerubbabel. Same as Siaha.

ONLY REFERENCE
NEHEMIAH 7:47

SIAHA 1
Converse

Forefather of an exiled family that returned to Judah under Zerubbabel. Same as Sia.

ONLY REFERENCE
EZRA 2:44

SIBBECAI 2
Corpse-like

A commander in King David's army overseeing twenty-four thousand men in the eighth month of each year. Same as Sibbechai.

FIRST REFERENCE
I CHRONICLES 11:29
LAST REFERENCE
I CHRONICLES 27:11

SIBBECHAI 2

One of King David's valiant warriors, Sibbechai killed Sippai, who "was of the children of the giant" (1 Chronicles 20:4). Same as Sibbecai.

FIRST REFERENCE
2 SAMUEL 21:18
LAST REFERENCE
I CHRONICLES 20:4

SIDON 1
Fishery

A descendant of Noah though his son Ham.

ONLY REFERENCE
GENESIS 10:15

SIHON 37
Tempestuous

An Amorite king whom the Israelites defeated when he would not let them pass through his land as they turned back before the Promised Land. Israel conquered Sihon's capital, Heshbon, and all his cities. After killing all his people, they settled there, taking their livestock for themselves. Their success in the conquest of Sihon and his land became a repeated reminder of God's leading as Israel moved into the Promised Land. Rahab and the Gibeonites feared Israel because of their victory.

FIRST REFERENCE
NUMBERS 21:21
LAST REFERENCE
JEREMIAH 48:45
KEY REFERENCES
NUMBERS 21:21–25; DEUTERONOMY 2:26–35;
JOSHUA 2:10; PSALM 135:10–11

SILAS 13
Sylvan

A prophet chosen by the Jerusalem Council to accompany Paul and Barnabas to the Gentiles. After Barnabas and Paul separated, Paul took Silas on a new journey. Together they were imprisoned in Philippi after Paul freed a slave girl of an evil spirit. They led the jailer and his family to Christ and continued their mission in Greece. Same as Silvanus (1).

FIRST REFERENCE
ACTS 15:22
LAST REFERENCE
ACTS 18:5
KEY REFERENCES
ACTS 15:38–41; 16:16–40

SILVANUS 4
Sylvan

1) Latin name for Silas, who accompanied Paul on his missionary journeys. Paul included Silvanus's name in his greetings to the churches at Corinth and Thessalonica.

FIRST REFERENCE
2 CORINTHIANS 1:19
LAST REFERENCE
2 THESSALONIANS 1:1

2) A "faithful brother" by whom Peter wrote the epistle of 1 Peter. Possibly the same as Silvanus (1).

ONLY REFERENCE
1 PETER 5:12

SIMEON 18
Hearing

1) Second son of Jacob and Leah. With his full brother Levi, Simeon killed the men of Shechem because the prince of that city raped their sister, Dinah. In Egypt, Joseph held Simeon ransom until their nine brothers brought Benjamin to Egypt with them. When Jacob blessed his sons, he remembered Simeon's and Levi's anger at Shechem and cursed them for it.

FIRST REFERENCE
GENESIS 29:33
LAST REFERENCE
EXODUS 6:15
KEY REFERENCES
GENESIS 29:32–33; 34:25; 42:18–20, 24; 49:5–7

2) A devout man at the Jerusalem temple who held the eight-day-old Jesus and prophesied, "This child is set for the fall and rising again of many in Israel" (Luke 2:34). Simeon, who had been "waiting for the consolation of Israel" (Luke 2:25), said he could die in peace after having seen God's salvation.

FIRST REFERENCE
LUKE 2:25
LAST REFERENCE
LUKE 2:34

3) A descendant of Abraham through Isaac; forebear of Jesus' earthly father, Joseph.

ONLY REFERENCE
LUKE 3:30
GENEALOGY OF JESUS
LUKE 3:30

4) A prophet and teacher in the church at Antioch during the apostle Paul's ministry. Also called Niger.

ONLY REFERENCE
ACTS 13:1

5) A variant name for the apostle Simon Peter.

ONLY REFERENCE
ACTS 15:14

SIMON 76
Hearing

1) The disciple whom Jesus surnamed Peter, also called Simon Bar-jona.

FIRST REFERENCE
MATTHEW 4:18
LAST REFERENCE
2 PETER 1:1
KEY REFERENCES
MATTHEW 16:16–17; MARK 3:16

2) One of Jesus' twelve disciples, called "the Canaanite" and "Zelotes" (the Zealot).

FIRST REFERENCE
MATTHEW 10:4
LAST REFERENCE
ACTS 1:13

3) One of four brothers of Jesus, as recorded by Matthew's and Mark's Gospels.

FIRST REFERENCE
MATTHEW 13:55
LAST REFERENCE
MARK 6:3

4) Called Simon the Leper, he lived in Bethany. In his home a woman anointed Jesus before His crucifixion.

FIRST REFERENCE
MATTHEW 26:6
LAST REFERENCE
MARK 14:3

5) A man from Cyrene whom the Romans forced to carry Jesus' cross to the crucifixion site.

FIRST REFERENCE
MATTHEW 27:32
LAST REFERENCE
LUKE 23:26

6) A Pharisee who invited Jesus to eat in his home and thought Jesus should have known that the woman who anointed him with oil was a sinner.

FIRST REFERENCE
LUKE 7:40
LAST REFERENCE
LUKE 7:44

7) Father of Judas Iscariot, the disciple who betrayed Jesus.

FIRST REFERENCE
JOHN 6:71
LAST REFERENCE
JOHN 13:26

8) A sorcerer who became a Christian. Simon offered the apostles money to be able to use the laying on of hands to fill people with the Holy Spirit.

FIRST REFERENCE
ACTS 8:9
LAST REFERENCE
ACTS 8:24

9) A tanner of Joppa who lived by the sea and lodged Peter.

FIRST REFERENCE
ACTS 9:43
LAST REFERENCE
ACTS 10:32

SIMRI
Watchful

A Levite "porter" (doorkeeper) in the house of the Lord.

ONLY REFERENCE
I CHRONICLES 26:10

SIPPAI
Basin-like

A Philistine warrior, "of the children of the giant," killed by one of King David's soldiers.

ONLY REFERENCE
I CHRONICLES 20:4

SISAMAI 2
A descendant of Abraham through Jacob's son Judah. Sisamai descended from the line of an unnamed Israelite woman and her Egyptian husband, Jarha.

ONLY REFERENCE
I CHRONICLES 2:40

SISERA 21
1) Captain under Jabin, king of Canaan. He fought with Barak, Israel's captain, and lost. Sisera fled on foot to the tent of Jael, the wife of Heber the Kenite. She encouraged him to come in then killed him by nailing a tent peg into his temple.

FIRST REFERENCE
JUDGES 4:2
LAST REFERENCE
PSALM 83:9
KEY REFERENCE
JUDGES 4:13–21

2) Forefather of an exiled family that returned to Judah under Zerubbabel.

FIRST REFERENCE
EZRA 2:53
LAST REFERENCE
NEHEMIAH 7:55

SO
A king of Egypt approached by Israel's last king, Hoshea, for aid against the Assyrian Empire. News of the attempted alliance caused Assyria to overrun Israel and carry its people into captivity.

ONLY REFERENCE
2 KINGS 17:4

SOCHO
Entwine

A descendant of Abraham through Jacob's son Judah.

ONLY REFERENCE
I CHRONICLES 4:18

SODI
Confidant

Father of one of the twelve spies sent by Moses to spy out the land of Canaan.

ONLY REFERENCE
NUMBERS 13:10

SOLOMON 306
Peaceful

Son of King David and Bath-she-ba, Solomon was loved by God. Despite the efforts of his half brother Adonijah to take the throne, Solomon became king over Israel with the support of his father, David. When God came to Solomon in a vision and asked what he wanted, the king requested "an understanding heart" to rule His people (1 Kings 3:9). Because Solomon asked wisely, God gave him wisdom, understanding, and the wealth and honor he had not requested. The queen of Sheba heard of Solomon and came to ask him hard questions, and he proved his wisdom before her.

Solomon built the Lord's temple with the aid of Hiram, Tyre's king. At the high point of his reign, Solomon dedicated the temple with a prayer and benediction. Though Solomon loved God, he also worshipped at pagan altars and married many "strange" (foreign) women, including the daughter of Pharaoh. Solomon had seven hundred wives and three hundred concubines. When he was old, his wives turned his heart away from God and he did evil, building pagan altars and worshipping there. So God promised that the throne of all Israel would be taken from his son, who would only rule over Judah.

FIRST REFERENCE
2 SAMUEL 5:14
LAST REFERENCE
ACTS 7:47
KEY REFERENCES
2 SAMUEL 12:24; 1 KINGS 3:1–14; 5:1–6; 6:1;
8:22–61; 10:1–3; 11:1–8, 11–13
GENEALOGY OF JESUS
MATTHEW 1:6–7

SOPATER 1
Of a safe father

A man from Berea and a traveling companion of the apostle Paul.

ONLY REFERENCE
ACTS 20:4

SOPHERETH 2
Scribe

Forefather of an exiled family—former servants of Solomon—that returned to Judah under Zerubbabel.

FIRST REFERENCE
EZRA 2:55
LAST REFERENCE
NEHEMIAH 7:57

SOSIPATER 1
Of a safe father

A relative of Paul who lived in Rome. He was greeted in the apostle's letter to the Romans.

ONLY REFERENCE
ROMANS 16:21

SOSTHENES 2
Of safe strength

1) Chief ruler of the synagogue at Corinth. Sosthenes was beaten by a mob stirred up by Jewish leaders who opposed the apostle Paul.

ONLY REFERENCE
ACTS 18:17

2) A coworker of Paul, named in the greeting of the apostle's first letter to the Corinthians.

ONLY REFERENCE
1 CORINTHIANS 1:1

SOTAI 2

Roving

Forefather of an exiled family—former servants of Solomon—that returned to Judah under Zerubbabel.

FIRST REFERENCE
EZRA 2:55
LAST REFERENCE
NEHEMIAH 7:57

STACHYS 1

Head of grain

A Christian acquaintance of the apostle Paul in Rome, called "my beloved."

ONLY REFERENCE
ROMANS 16:9

STEPHANAS 3

A Corinthian Christian whose household, the first converts in Achaia, was baptized by Paul. The apostle commended the family for its ministry to believers.

FIRST REFERENCE
I CORINTHIANS 1:16
LAST REFERENCE
I CORINTHIANS 16:17

STEPHEN 7

Wreathe

A man of the Jewish church, "full of faith and of the Holy Ghost," Stephen was ordained to care for the physical needs of church members. He became involved in a disagreement with Jews who accused him of blasphemy. After witnessing to the Jewish council, Stephen was stoned by an angry mob that included Saul.

FIRST REFERENCE
ACTS 6:5
LAST REFERENCE
ACTS 22:20

SUAH 1

Wipe away

A descendant of Abraham through Jacob's son Asher.

ONLY REFERENCE
I CHRONICLES 7:36

SUSANNA 1

Lily

A woman who followed Jesus and provided for his financial needs.

ONLY REFERENCE
LUKE 8:3

SUSI 1

Horselike

Father of one of the twelve spies sent by Moses to spy out the land of Canaan.

ONLY REFERENCE
NUMBERS 13:11

SYNTYCHE 1

Accident

A Christian woman of Philippi who had "laboured with [Paul] in the gospel" but who had conflict with another church member, Euodias. Paul begged them to "be of the same mind in the Lord."

ONLY REFERENCE
PHILIPPIANS 4:2

-T-

TABBAOTH 2
Rings

Forefather of an exiled family that returned to Judah under Zerubbabel.

FIRST REFERENCE
EZRA 2:43
LAST REFERENCE
NEHEMIAH 7:46

TABEAL 1
Pleasing to God

Father of a man whom Syria and Israel wanted to make king over Judah in Ahaz's place.

ONLY REFERENCE
ISAIAH 7:6

TABEEL 1
Pleasing to God

A man who tried to stop the rebuilding of Jerusalem's wall.

ONLY REFERENCE
EZRA 4:7

TABITHA 2
The gazelle

A Christian of Joppa who did many good works. When she died, her friends called Peter, who raised her back to life. Same as Dorcas.

FIRST REFERENCE
ACTS 9:36
LAST REFERENCE
ACTS 9:40

TABRIMON 1
Pleasing to Rimmon

Father of Ben-Hadad, king of Syria in the time of Judah's king Asa.

ONLY REFERENCE
I KINGS 15:18

TAHAN 2
Station

1) A descendant of Abraham through Joseph's son Ephraim.

ONLY REFERENCE
NUMBERS 26:35

2) Another descendant of Abraham through Joseph's son Ephraim.

ONLY REFERENCE
I CHRONICLES 7:25

TAHATH 4
Bottom

1) A descendant of Abraham through Jacob's son Levi.

FIRST REFERENCE
I CHRONICLES 6:24
LAST REFERENCE
I CHRONICLES 6:37

2) A descendant of Abraham through Joseph's son Ephraim.

ONLY REFERENCE
I CHRONICLES 7:20

3) Another descendant of Abraham through Joseph's son Ephraim.

ONLY REFERENCE
I CHRONICLES 7:20

TAHPENES 3 👤

Queen of Egypt during the rule of Solomon and sister-in-law of Solomon's adversary Hadad the Edomite.

FIRST REFERENCE
I KINGS 11:19
LAST REFERENCE
I KINGS 11:20

TAHREA 1 👤
Earth

Great-grandson of Jonathan (2).

ONLY REFERENCE
I CHRONICLES 9:41

TALMAI 6 👤2
Ridged

1) One of the gigantic children of Anak who was killed after Joshua's death when Judah battled the Canaanites.

FIRST REFERENCE
NUMBERS 13:22
LAST REFERENCE
JUDGES 1:10

2) King of Geshur and grandfather of King David's son Absalom.

FIRST REFERENCE
2 SAMUEL 3:3
LAST REFERENCE
I CHRONICLES 3:2

TALMON 5 👤
Oppressive

A Jewish exile from the tribe of Levi who resettled Jerusalem.

FIRST REFERENCE
I CHRONICLES 9:17
LAST REFERENCE
NEHEMIAH 12:25

TAMAH 1 👤

Forefather of an exiled family that returned to Judah under Nehemiah.

ONLY REFERENCE
NEHEMIAH 7:55

TAMAR 22 👤3
Palm tree

1) Daughter-in-law of Jacob's son Judah. She married Judah's eldest two sons, whom God killed for wickedness. Judah refused to marry her to his third son, so she pretended to be a harlot, lay with Judah, and had twins by him. Same as Thamar.

FIRST REFERENCE
GENESIS 38:6
LAST REFERENCE
I CHRONICLES 2:4

2) Daughter of King David and half sister of Amnon. Amnon fell in love with her and pretended to be sick so David would send Tamar to him. He raped Tamar and threw her out of his house. Her full brother Absalom heard of this and later had his servants kill Amnon.

FIRST REFERENCE
2 SAMUEL 13:1
LAST REFERENCE
I CHRONICLES 3:9

3) The beautiful only daughter of the very handsome Absalom, son of King David.

ONLY REFERENCE
2 SAMUEL 14:27

TANHUMETH 2
Compassion

Father of one of Judah's captains at the time of the Babylonian Exile.

FIRST REFERENCE
2 KINGS 25:23
LAST REFERENCE
JEREMIAH 40:8

TAPHATH I
Drop of ointment

A daughter of Solomon and the wife of one of the king's commissary officers.

ONLY REFERENCE
I KINGS 4:11

TAPPUAH I
Apple

A descendant of Abraham through Jacob's son Judah.

ONLY REFERENCE
I CHRONICLES 2:43

TAREA I
Earth

A descendant of Abraham through Jacob's son Benjamin, in the line of King Saul and his son Jonathan.

ONLY REFERENCE
I CHRONICLES 8:35

TARSHISH 3
Topaz

1) A descendant of Noah through his son Japheth.

FIRST REFERENCE
GENESIS 10:4
LAST REFERENCE
I CHRONICLES 1:7

2) One of seven Persian princes serving under King Ahasuerus.

ONLY REFERENCE
ESTHER 1:14

TARTAN 2

An Assyrian military commander who conquered the city of Ashdod and participated in King Sennacherib's failed attempt to take Jerusalem in the days of King Hezekiah and the prophet Isaiah.

FIRST REFERENCE
2 KINGS 18:17
LAST REFERENCE
ISAIAH 20:1

TATNAI 4

A governor who objected to the rebuilding of Jerusalem's temple and wrote the Persian king Darius. Darius commanded Tatnai to let the work continue.

FIRST REFERENCE
EZRA 5:3
LAST REFERENCE
EZRA 6:13

TEBAH   I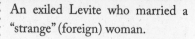
Massacre

A nephew of Abraham, born to his brother Nahor's concubine, Reumah.

ONLY REFERENCE
GENESIS 22:24

TEBALIAH   I
God has dipped

A Levite "porter" (doorkeeper) in the house of the Lord.

ONLY REFERENCE
I CHRONICLES 26:11

TEHINNAH   I
Graciousness

A descendant of Abraham through Jacob's son Judah.

ONLY REFERENCE
I CHRONICLES 4:12

TEKOA   2
Trumpet

A descendant of Abraham through Jacob's son Judah.

FIRST REFERENCE
I CHRONICLES 2:24
LAST REFERENCE
I CHRONICLES 4:5

TELAH   I
Breach

A descendant of Abraham through Joseph's son Ephraim.

ONLY REFERENCE
I CHRONICLES 7:25

TELEM   I
Oppression

An exiled Levite who married a "strange" (foreign) woman.

ONLY REFERENCE
EZRA 10:24

TEMA   4

A descendant of Abraham through Ishmael, Abraham's son with his surrogate wife, Hagar.

FIRST REFERENCE
GENESIS 25:15
LAST REFERENCE
I CHRONICLES 1:30

TEMAN   5
South

A "duke of Edom," a leader in the family line of Esau.

FIRST REFERENCE
GENESIS 36:11
LAST REFERENCE
I CHRONICLES 1:53

TEMENI   I
South

A descendant of Abraham through Jacob's son Judah.

ONLY REFERENCE
I CHRONICLES 4:6

TERAH   11

Father of Abram (Abraham), Nahor, and Haran. With Abram and Nahor and their families, he left Ur of the Chaldees and headed for Canaan. But when they came to Haran, they stayed there. Terah died in Haran.

TERESH 2

One of two palace doorkeepers who conspired to kill their king, Ahasuerus of Persia. Their plot was uncovered by Mordecai, and both were hanged.

FIRST REFERENCE
ESTHER 2:21
LAST REFERENCE
ESTHER 6:2

TERTIUS 1

Third

An assistant of Paul who wrote down the apostle's message to the Romans.

ONLY REFERENCE
ROMANS 16:22

TERTULLUS 2

An orator from Jerusalem who accused the apostle Paul before the Roman governor in Caesarea. Tertullus called Paul "a pestilent fellow," charging him with profaning God's temple as "a ringleader in the sect of the Nazarenes" (Acts 24:5).

FIRST REFERENCE
ACTS 24:1
LAST REFERENCE
ACTS 24:2

THADDAEUS 2

One of Jesus' twelve disciples, as listed by Matthew and Mark. Matthew mentions that Thaddaeus's surname was Lebbaeus. Apparently called "Judas, the brother of James" in Luke's Gospel and the book of Acts. Same as Judas (3) and Jude.

FIRST REFERENCE
MATTHEW 10:3
LAST REFERENCE
MARK 3:18

THAHASH 1

Antelope

A nephew of Abraham, born to his brother Nahor's concubine, Reumah.

ONLY REFERENCE
GENESIS 22:24

THAMAH 1

Forefather of an exiled family that returned to Judah under Zerubbabel.

ONLY REFERENCE
EZRA 2:53

THAMAR 1

Palm tree

Greek form of the name *Tamar*, used in the New Testament. Same as Tamar (1).

ONLY REFERENCE
MATTHEW 1:3
GENEALOGY OF JESUS
MATTHEW 1:3

THARA 1

Greek form of the name *Terah*, used in the New Testament.

ONLY REFERENCE
LUKE 3:34

THARSHISH 1
Topaz

A descendant of Abraham through Jacob's son Benjamin.

ONLY REFERENCE
1 CHRONICLES 7:10

THEOPHILUS 2
Friend of God

An otherwise unknown person for whom Luke wrote his Gospel and the book of Acts, "that thou mightest know the certainty of those things, wherein thou hast been instructed" (Luke 1:4).

FIRST REFERENCE
LUKE 1:3
LAST REFERENCE
ACTS 1:1

THEUDAS 1

A false Jewish messiah who attracted four hundred people. They scattered when he was killed.

ONLY REFERENCE
ACTS 5:36

THOMAS 12
The twin

Jesus' disciple whom people often call "Doubting Thomas." When Jesus wanted to go to Lazarus, courageous Thomas said, "Let us also go, that we may die with him" (John 11:16). But when Jesus appeared to the others, Thomas doubted their story until he saw the Master himself.

FIRST REFERENCE
MATTHEW 10:3
LAST REFERENCE
ACTS 1:13
KEY REFERENCES
JOHN 11:16; 20:24–29

TIBERIUS 1
Pertaining to the Tiber River

The Roman emperor who was ruling when John the Baptist and Jesus began their ministries.

ONLY REFERENCE
LUKE 3:1

TIBNI 3
Straw-like

The losing contender for the throne of Israel after Zimri killed King Elah.

FIRST REFERENCE
1 KINGS 16:21
LAST REFERENCE
1 KINGS 16:22

TIDAL 2
Fearfulness

The "king of nations" in the days of Abraham. Tidal was part of a battle alliance that kidnapped Abram's nephew Lot.

FIRST REFERENCE
GENESIS 14:1
LAST REFERENCE
GENESIS 14:9

TIGLATH-PILESER 3

The king of Assyria who conquered the land of Naphtali and Galilee and took the Israelites captive. When Syria and Israel attacked Judah, King Ahaz sought Tiglath-pileser's help. Same as Tilgath-pilneser and possibly Pul.

FIRST REFERENCE
2 KINGS 15:29
LAST REFERENCE
2 KINGS 16:10

TIKVAH 2
Cord

1) Father-in-law of the prophetess Huldah, who served during the reign of Judah's king Josiah. Same as Tikvath.

ONLY REFERENCE
2 KINGS 22:14

2) Forefather of a man who encouraged the Israelites to give up their "strange" (foreign) wives.

ONLY REFERENCE
EZRA 10:15

TIKVATH 1
Cord

Father-in-law of the prophetess Huldah, who served during the reign of Judah's king Josiah. Same as Tikvah (1).

ONLY REFERENCE
2 CHRONICLES 34:22

TILGATH-PILNESER 3

A variant spelling of the name of the Assyrian king Tiglath-pileser.

FIRST REFERENCE
1 CHRONICLES 5:6
LAST REFERENCE
2 CHRONICLES 28:20

TILON 1
Suspension

A descendant of Abraham through Jacob's son Judah.

ONLY REFERENCE
1 CHRONICLES 4:20

TIMAEUS 1
Foul

Father of a blind man of Jericho who was healed by Jesus.

ONLY REFERENCE
MARK 10:46

TIMNA 4
Restraint

1) Concubine of Esau's son Eliphaz.

ONLY REFERENCE
GENESIS 36:12

2) A daughter of Seir, who lived in Esau's "land of Edom."

FIRST REFERENCE
GENESIS 36:22
LAST REFERENCE
1 CHRONICLES 1:39

3) A descendant of Abraham's grandson Esau.

ONLY REFERENCE
1 CHRONICLES 1:36

TIMNAH 2

Restraint

A "duke of Edom," a leader in the family line of Esau.

FIRST REFERENCE
GENESIS 36:40
LAST REFERENCE
1 CHRONICLES 1:51

TIMON 1

Valuable

One of seven men, "full of the Holy Ghost and wisdom," selected to serve needy Christians in Jerusalem while the twelve disciples devoted themselves "to prayer, and to the ministry of the word" (Acts 6:3–4).

ONLY REFERENCE
ACTS 6:5

TIMOTHEUS 18

Dear to God

An alternative name for Timothy, the apostle Paul's coworker and "son in the faith" (1 Timothy 1:2).

FIRST REFERENCE
ACTS 16:1
LAST REFERENCE
2 THESSALONIANS 1:1
KEY REFERENCE
1 CORINTHIANS 4:17

TIMOTHY 8

Dear to God

Coworker of the apostle Paul, his name is joined with Paul's in the introductory greetings of 2 Corinthians and Philemon. Paul also wrote two epistles of guidance to this young pastor who was like a son to him. Same as Timotheus.

FIRST REFERENCE
2 CORINTHIANS 1:1
LAST REFERENCE
HEBREWS 13:23
KEY REFERENCES
1 TIMOTHY 1:2; 6:20–21

TIRAS 2

Fearful

A descendant of Noah through his son Japheth.

FIRST REFERENCE
GENESIS 10:2
LAST REFERENCE
1 CHRONICLES 1:5

TIRHAKAH 2

The king of Ethiopia in the time of Judah's king Hezekiah.

FIRST REFERENCE
2 KINGS 19:9
LAST REFERENCE
ISAIAH 37:9

TIRHANAH 1

A descendant of Abraham through Jacob's son Judah.

ONLY REFERENCE
1 CHRONICLES 2:48

TIRIA 1

Fearful

A descendant of Abraham through Jacob's son Judah.

ONLY REFERENCE
1 CHRONICLES 4:16

TIRSHATHA 5 👤

Title of the governor of Judea, used to describe Nehemiah.

FIRST REFERENCE
EZRA 2:63
LAST REFERENCE
NEHEMIAH 10:1

TIRZAH 4 👤
Delightsomeness

One of five daughters of Zelophehad, an Israelite who died during the wilderness wanderings. The women asked Moses if they could inherit their father's property in the Promised Land (a right normally reserved for sons), and God ruled that they should, since Zelophehad had no sons.

FIRST REFERENCE
NUMBERS 26:33
LAST REFERENCE
JOSHUA 17:3

TITUS 14 👤

The apostle Paul's highly trusted Greek coworker who traveled with him and whom Paul sent to Corinth with a letter of rebuke for the church. Titus had a successful mission, so Paul sent him again to the Corinthians. When Titus was in Crete, Paul wrote him an epistle on church leadership.

FIRST REFERENCE
2 CORINTHIANS 2:13
LAST REFERENCE
TITUS 1:4
KEY REFERENCES
2 CORINTHIANS 7:6–9, 13–15;
GALATIANS 2:1, 3

TOAH 1 👤
To depress

An ancestor of the prophet Samuel. Same as Tohu.

ONLY REFERENCE
1 CHRONICLES 6:34

TOB-ADONIJAH 1 👤
Pleasing to Adonijah

A Levite sent by King Jehoshaphat to teach the law of the Lord throughout the nation of Judah.

ONLY REFERENCE
2 CHRONICLES 17:8

TOBIAH 15 👤2
Goodness of Jehovah

1) Forefather of an exiled family that returned to Judah under Zerubbabel.

FIRST REFERENCE
EZRA 2:60
LAST REFERENCE
NEHEMIAH 7:62

2) An Ammonite who resisted the rebuilding of Jerusalem under Governor Nehemiah. With Sanballat the Horonite he interfered and tried to distract Nehemiah from his work. The two hired a man to warn Nehemiah that he would be killed, and Tobiah sent threatening letters to scare Nehemiah.

FIRST REFERENCE
NEHEMIAH 2:10
LAST REFERENCE
NEHEMIAH 13:8
KEY REFERENCES:
NEHEMIAH 4:3, 7–8; 6:10–12, 17–19

TOBIJAH 3
Goodness of Jehovah

1) A Levite sent by King Jehoshaphat to teach the law of the Lord throughout the nation of Judah.

ONLY REFERENCE
2 CHRONICLES 17:8

2) Forefather of a family of Jewish exiles in Babylon who participated in a symbolic crowning of the Messiah by the prophet Zechariah.

FIRST REFERENCE
ZECHARIAH 6:10
LAST REFERENCE
ZECHARIAH 6:14

TOGARMAH 4
A descendant of Noah through his son Japheth.

FIRST REFERENCE
GENESIS 10:3
LAST REFERENCE
EZEKIEL 38:6

TOHU 1
Abasement

An ancestor of the prophet Samuel. Same as Toah.

ONLY REFERENCE
1 SAMUEL 1:1

TOI 3
Error

The king of Hamath who sent congratulations and gifts to King David for defeating Toi's enemy Hadadezer. Same as Tou.

FIRST REFERENCE
2 SAMUEL 8:9
LAST REFERENCE
2 SAMUEL 8:10

TOLA 6
Worm

1) A descendant of Abraham through Jacob's son Issachar.

FIRST REFERENCE
GENESIS 46:13
LAST REFERENCE
1 CHRONICLES 7:2

2) The seventh judge of Israel who led the nation for twenty-three years.

ONLY REFERENCE
JUDGES 10:1

TOU 2
Error

A variant spelling of the name of the Assyrian king Toi, who sent congratulations and gifts to King David for defeating Toi's enemy Hadadezer.

FIRST REFERENCE
1 CHRONICLES 18:9
LAST REFERENCE
1 CHRONICLES 18:10

TROPHIMUS 3
Nutritive

A Gentile believer and coworker of the apostle Paul. Trophimus was falsely accused of defiling the Jewish temple, which caused an uproar in Jerusalem. He traveled with Paul on his missionary journeys but was left ill in the city of Miletum near Ephesus.

FIRST REFERENCE
ACTS 20:4
LAST REFERENCE
2 TIMOTHY 4:20

TRYPHENA

Luxurious

A Christian woman in Rome commended by the apostle Paul for her "labour in the Lord."

ONLY REFERENCE
ROMANS 16:12

TRYPHOSA

Luxuriating

A Christian woman in Rome commended by the apostle Paul for her "labour in the Lord."

ONLY REFERENCE
ROMANS 16:12

TUBAL

A descendant of Noah through his son Japheth.

FIRST REFERENCE
GENESIS 10:2
LAST REFERENCE
1 CHRONICLES 1:5

TUBAL-CAIN

Offspring of Cain

A descendant of Cain through Lamech and his wife Zillah. Tubal-cain was the first recorded metalworker in the Bible.

ONLY REFERENCE
GENESIS 4:22

TYCHICUS

Fortunate

An Asian coworker of Paul who accompanied him to Macedonia. Paul also sent him on missions to the Ephesians and Colossians and perhaps to Crete.

FIRST REFERENCE
ACTS 20:4
LAST REFERENCE
TITUS 3:12

TYRANNUS

Tyrant

An Ephesian teacher who allowed the apostle Paul to debate Christianity in his school "daily" for two years.

ONLY REFERENCE
ACTS 19:9

-U-

UCAL
Devoured

A man to whom Agur spoke the words of Proverbs 30.

ONLY REFERENCE
PROVERBS 30:1

UEL
Wish of God

An exiled Israelite who married a "strange" (foreign) woman.

ONLY REFERENCE
EZRA 10:34

ULAM 4
Solitary

1) A descendant of Abraham through Joseph's son Manasseh.

FIRST REFERENCE
I CHRONICLES 7:16
LAST REFERENCE
I CHRONICLES 7:17

2) A descendant of Abraham through Jacob's son Benjamin, in the line of King Saul and his son Jonathan.

FIRST REFERENCE
I CHRONICLES 8:39
LAST REFERENCE
I CHRONICLES 8:40

ULLA 1
Burden

A descendant of Abraham through Jacob's son Asher.

ONLY REFERENCE
I CHRONICLES 7:39

UNNI 3
Afflicted

1) A Levite musician who performed in celebration when King David brought the ark of the covenant to Jerusalem.

FIRST REFERENCE
I CHRONICLES 15:18
LAST REFERENCE
I CHRONICLES 15:20

2) A Jewish exile from the tribe of Levi who returned from Babylon to Judah under Zerubbabel.

ONLY REFERENCE
NEHEMIAH 12:9

UR 1
Flame

Father of one of King David's valiant warriors.

ONLY REFERENCE
I CHRONICLES 11:35

URBANE 1
Of the city

A Christian acquaintance of the apostle Paul in Rome who was called "our helper in Christ."

ONLY REFERENCE
ROMANS 16:9

URI 8
Fiery

1) Father of Bezaleel, a craftsman in the construction of the tabernacle.

FIRST REFERENCE
EXODUS 31:2
LAST REFERENCE
2 CHRONICLES 1:5

2) Father of one of King Solomon's officials over provisions.

ONLY REFERENCE
1 KINGS 4:19

3) An exiled Levite who married a "strange" (foreign) woman.

ONLY REFERENCE
EZRA 10:24

URIAH 28
Flame of God

1) Called Uriah the Hittite, he was Bath-sheba's first husband and a warrior in King David's army. When Bath-sheba discovered she was pregnant by the king, David called Uriah home and tried to make him go to his wife, but the faithful soldier would not do so while his fellow soldiers were in the field. So David ordered his commander, Joab, to put Uriah in the heaviest fighting so he would be killed. After Uriah's death, the prophet Nathan confronted David with this murder and prophesied that Israel would not live in peace during David's reign. Same as Urias.

FIRST REFERENCE
2 SAMUEL 11:3
LAST REFERENCE
1 CHRONICLES 11:41
KEY REFERENCES
2 SAMUEL 11:6–17; 12:9–10

2) Father of a man who weighed the temple vessels after the Babylonian Exile.

ONLY REFERENCE
EZRA 8:33

3) A priest who witnessed Isaiah's prophecy about Maher-shalal-hash-baz.

ONLY REFERENCE
ISAIAH 8:2

URIAS 1
Flame of God

Greek form of the name *Uriah*, used in the New Testament. Same as Uriah (1).

ONLY REFERENCE
MATTHEW 1:6

URIEL 4
Flame of God

1) A descendant of Abraham through Jacob's son Levi. Uriel was among a group of Levites appointed by King David to bring the ark of the covenant from the house of Obed-edom to Jerusalem.

FIRST REFERENCE
1 CHRONICLES 6:24
LAST REFERENCE
1 CHRONICLES 15:11

2) Grandfather of Judah's second king, Abijah. Uriel was the father of Abijah's mother, Michaiah.

ONLY REFERENCE
2 CHRONICLES 13:2

URIJAH 11
Flame of God

1) The priest who followed King Ahaz's command to build a pagan altar as a place of worship. When Ahaz moved the Jewish temple altars and told Urijah how to worship, the priest obeyed him.

FIRST REFERENCE
2 KINGS 16:10
LAST REFERENCE
2 KINGS 16:16

2) Father of a man who repaired Jerusalem's walls under Nehemiah.

FIRST REFERENCE
NEHEMIAH 3:4
LAST REFERENCE
NEHEMIAH 3:21

3) A priest who assisted Ezra in reading the book of the law to the people of Jerusalem.

ONLY REFERENCE
NEHEMIAH 8:4

4) A faithful prophet executed by King Jehoiakim of Judah.

FIRST REFERENCE
JEREMIAH 26:20
LAST REFERENCE
JEREMIAH 26:23

UTHAI 2
Succoring

1) A descendant of Judah who returned to Jerusalem after the Babylonian Exile.

ONLY REFERENCE
1 CHRONICLES 9:4

2) A leader of Judah who returned from exile with Ezra.

ONLY REFERENCE
EZRA 8:14

UZ 4
Consultation

1) A descendant of Noah through his son Shem. He possibly lent his name to Job's home territory, "the land of Uz" (Job 1:1).

FIRST REFERENCE
GENESIS 10:23
LAST REFERENCE
1 CHRONICLES 1:17

2) A descendant of Seir, who lived in Esau's "land of Edom."

FIRST REFERENCE
GENESIS 36:28
LAST REFERENCE
1 CHRONICLES 1:42

UZAI 1
Strong

Father of a man who repaired Jerusalem's walls under Nehemiah.

ONLY REFERENCE
NEHEMIAH 3:25

UZAL 2
A descendant of Noah through his son Shem.

FIRST REFERENCE
GENESIS 10:27
LAST REFERENCE
1 CHRONICLES 1:21

UZZA 8
Strength

1) A descendant of Abraham through Jacob's son Levi.

ONLY REFERENCE
1 CHRONICLES 6:29

2) A descendant of Abraham through Jacob's son Benjamin.

ONLY REFERENCE
1 CHRONICLES 8:7

3) A man who drove the cart in which the ark of the covenant was transported from Kirjath-jearim. When the oxen stumbled, Uzza reached out to steady the ark. God killed him for daring to touch the holy object. Same as Uzzah.

FIRST REFERENCE
I CHRONICLES 13:7
LAST REFERENCE
I CHRONICLES 13:11

4) Forefather of an exiled family that returned to Judah under Zerubbabel.

FIRST REFERENCE
EZRA 2:49
LAST REFERENCE
NEHEMIAH 7:51

UZZAH 4

Strength

A variant spelling of the name *Uzza*. Same as Uzza (3).

FIRST REFERENCE
2 SAMUEL 6:3
LAST REFERENCE
2 SAMUEL 6:8

UZZI 11

Forceful

1) A descendant of Abraham through Jacob's son Levi, and a priest through the line of Aaron.

FIRST REFERENCE
I CHRONICLES 6:5
LAST REFERENCE
EZRA 7:4

2) A descendant of Abraham through Jacob's son Issachar.

FIRST REFERENCE
I CHRONICLES 7:2
LAST REFERENCE
I CHRONICLES 7:3

3) A descendant of Abraham through Jacob's son Benjamin.

ONLY REFERENCE
I CHRONICLES 7:7

4) A Jewish exile from the tribe of Benjamin who resettled Jerusalem.

ONLY REFERENCE
I CHRONICLES 9:8

5) Overseer of the Levites after their return from exile.

ONLY REFERENCE
NEHEMIAH 11:22

6) A priest who helped to dedicate the rebuilt walls of Jerusalem by giving thanks.

FIRST REFERENCE
NEHEMIAH 12:19
LAST REFERENCE
NEHEMIAH 12:42

UZZIA 1

Strength of God

One of King David's valiant warriors.

ONLY REFERENCE
I CHRONICLES 11:44

UZZIAH 27

Strength of God

1) Son of Amaziah, king of Judah. Uzziah obeyed God, and the Lord helped him fight the Philistines and other enemies. The king fortified Jerusalem and built a powerful army. But in his power, Uzziah became proud and wrongly burned incense on the temple's incense altar. Confronted by the priests, he became angry.

God immediately made him a leper. Thereafter Uzziah was cut off from the temple, and his son Jotham ruled in his name. Same as Azariah (3).

FIRST REFERENCE
2 KINGS 15:13
LAST REFERENCE
ZECHARIAH 14:5
KEY REFERENCES
2 CHRONICLES 26:1–23

2) A descendant of Abraham through Jacob's son Levi.

ONLY REFERENCE
I CHRONICLES 6:24

3) Father of Jehonathan, who was in charge of King David's storehouses.

ONLY REFERENCE
I CHRONICLES 27:25

4) An exiled Israelite priest who married a "strange" (foreign) woman.

ONLY REFERENCE
EZRA 10:21

5) A Jewish exile from the tribe of Judah who resettled Jerusalem.

ONLY REFERENCE
NEHEMIAH 11:4

UZZIEL 16
Strength of God

1) A descendant of Abraham through Jacob's son Levi.

FIRST REFERENCE
EXODUS 6:18
LAST REFERENCE
I CHRONICLES 24:24

2) An army captain under King Hezekiah of Judah.

ONLY REFERENCE
I CHRONICLES 4:42

3) A descendant of Abraham through Jacob's son Benjamin.

ONLY REFERENCE
I CHRONICLES 7:7

4) A son of King David's musician Heman, who was "under the hands of [his] father for song in the house of the LORD" (1 Chronicles 25:6).

ONLY REFERENCE
I CHRONICLES 25:4

5) A descendant of Abraham through Jacob's son Levi. Uzziel was among the Levites who cleansed the Jerusalem temple during the revival in King Hezekiah's reign.

ONLY REFERENCE
2 CHRONICLES 29:14

6) Son of a goldsmith and a repairer of Jerusalem's walls under Nehemiah.

ONLY REFERENCE
NEHEMIAH 3:8

-V-

VOPHSI | 👤
Additional

Father of one of the twelve spies sent by Moses to spy out the land of Canaan.

ONLY REFERENCE
NUMBERS 13:14

VAJEZATHA | 👤

One of ten sons of Haman, the villain of the story of Esther.

ONLY REFERENCE
ESTHER 9:9

VANIAH | 👤
God has answered

An exiled Israelite who married a "strange" (foreign) woman.

ONLY REFERENCE
EZRA 10:36

VASHNI | 👤
Weak

The firstborn son of the prophet Samuel. Vashni and his brother, Abiah, served as judges in Beersheba, but their poor character caused Israel's leaders to ask Samuel for a king to rule over them. Same as Joel (1).

ONLY REFERENCE
I CHRONICLES 6:28

VASHTI | 10 👤

Queen of the Persian king Ahasuerus, Vashti refused to appear at his banquet. The king revoked her position and had no more to do with her.

-Z-

ZAAVAN
Disquiet

A descendant of Seir, who lived in Esau's "land of Edom."

ONLY REFERENCE
GENESIS 36:27

ZABAD 8
Giver

1) A descendant of Abraham through Jacob's son Judah. Zabad descended from the line of an unnamed Israelite woman and her Egyptian husband, Jarha.

FIRST REFERENCE
I CHRONICLES 2:36
LAST REFERENCE
I CHRONICLES 2:37

2) A descendant of Abraham through Joseph's son Ephraim.

ONLY REFERENCE
I CHRONICLES 7:21

3) One of King David's valiant warriors.

ONLY REFERENCE
I CHRONICLES 11:41

4) One of two royal officials who conspired to kill Judah's king Joash.

ONLY REFERENCE
2 CHRONICLES 24:26

5) An exiled Israelite who married a "strange" (foreign) woman.

ONLY REFERENCE
EZRA 10:27

6) Another exiled Israelite who married a foreign woman.

ONLY REFERENCE
EZRA 10:33

7) Yet another exiled Israelite who married a foreign woman.

ONLY REFERENCE
EZRA 10:43

ZABBAI 2
Pure

1) An exiled Israelite who married a "strange" (foreign) woman.

ONLY REFERENCE
EZRA 10:28

2) Father of a man who repaired Jerusalem's walls under Nehemiah.

ONLY REFERENCE
NEHEMIAH 3:20

ZABBUD 1
Given

An exiled Israelite who returned to Judah with Ezra.

ONLY REFERENCE
EZRA 8:14

ZABDI 6
Giving

1) Father of Achan. Achan disobeyed Joshua and took goods from Jericho when Israel conquered the city.

FIRST REFERENCE
JOSHUA 7:1
LAST REFERENCE
JOSHUA 7:18

2) A descendant of Abraham through Jacob's son Benjamin.

ONLY REFERENCE
1 CHRONICLES 8:19

3) A man in charge of the grapes for King David's wine cellars.

ONLY REFERENCE
1 CHRONICLES 27:27

4) Forefather of a Levite who re-settled Jerusalem after the Babylonian Exile.

ONLY REFERENCE
NEHEMIAH 11:17

ZABDIEL 2

Gift of God

1) Forefather of a captain of thousands under King David.

ONLY REFERENCE
1 CHRONICLES 27:2

2) An overseer of the priests who served following the exiles' return to Jerusalem.

ONLY REFERENCE
NEHEMIAH 11:14

ZABUD 1

Given

A principle officer of King Solomon's court and a friend of the king.

ONLY REFERENCE
1 KINGS 4:5

ZACCAI 2

Pure

Forefather of an exiled family that returned to Judah under Zerubbabel.

FIRST REFERENCE
EZRA 2:9
LAST REFERENCE
NEHEMIAH 7:14

ZACCHAEUS 3

Pure

A wealthy chief tax collector. Zacchaeus climbed a tree so he could see Jesus. The Master called him down, saying He would stay with him. Zacchaeus repented and promised Jesus he would give half his goods to the poor and repay fourfold anyone he had wronged.

FIRST REFERENCE
LUKE 19:2
LAST REFERENCE
LUKE 19:8

ZACCHUR 1

Mindful

A descendant of Abraham through Jacob's son Simeon.

ONLY REFERENCE
1 CHRONICLES 4:26

ZACCUR 8

Mindful

1) Father of one of the twelve spies sent by Moses to spy out the land of Canaan.

ONLY REFERENCE
NUMBERS 13:4

2) A descendant of Abraham through Jacob's son Levi.

ONLY REFERENCE
1 CHRONICLES 24:27

3) A son of King David's musician Asaph, who "prophesied according to the order of the king" (1 Chronicles 25:2).

FIRST REFERENCE
1 CHRONICLES 25:2
LAST REFERENCE
NEHEMIAH 12:35

4) A rebuilder of the walls of Jerusalem under Nehemiah.

ONLY REFERENCE
NEHEMIAH 3:2

5) A Levite who renewed the covenant under Nehemiah.

ONLY REFERENCE
NEHEMIAH 10:12

6) One of the temple treasurers appointed by Nehemiah.

ONLY REFERENCE
NEHEMIAH 13:13

ZACHARIAH   4
God has remembered

1) Son of King Jeroboam of Israel, Zachariah reigned over Israel for six months before he was killed by the conspirator Shallum.

FIRST REFERENCE
2 KINGS 14:29
LAST REFERENCE
2 KINGS 15:11

2) Grandfather of Hoshea, king of Israel.

ONLY REFERENCE
2 KINGS 18:2

ZACHARIAS   11
God has remembered

1) A man, possibly a prophet, mentioned by Jesus. Zacharias was killed between the sanctuary and the altar.

FIRST REFERENCE
MATTHEW 23:35
LAST REFERENCE
LUKE 11:51

2) A priest who received a vision that his barren wife would bear a child who would be great before the Lord. Because Zacharias doubted, God struck him dumb until the birth of the child. When he agreed with his wife to name the child John, Zacharias could suddenly speak. His son was John the Baptist.

FIRST REFERENCE
LUKE 1:5
LAST REFERENCE
LUKE 3:2

ZACHER   1
Memento

A chief of the tribe of Benjamin who lived in Jerusalem.

ONLY REFERENCE
1 CHRONICLES 8:31

ZADOK   53
Just

1) A priest during King David's reign. Zadok and the priest Abiathar consecrated Levites to bring the ark of the covenant into Jerusalem. With Zadok's help, David

reorganized the priesthood. As David fled Jerusalem, attacked by his son Absalom, Zadok brought out the ark, planning to go with him. Instead, David left him behind to support him in the city. Following Absalom's death, Zadok helped to persuade Judah to take David back as king. When David was old, his son Adonijah tried to set himself up as king. But Zadok would not support him. Instead, at David's command, he anointed Solomon king. Solomon later made Zadok high priest.

FIRST REFERENCE
2 SAMUEL 8:17
LAST REFERENCE
EZEKIEL 48:11
KEY REFERENCES
2 SAMUEL 15:24–29; 19:11; 1 KINGS 1:8, 32–39;
2:35; 1 CHRONICLES 15:11–12; 24:3

2) Grandfather of King Jotham of Judah.

FIRST REFERENCE
2 KINGS 15:33
LAST REFERENCE
2 CHRONICLES 27:1

3) A descendant of Abraham through Jacob's son Levi, and a priest through the line of Aaron.

FIRST REFERENCE
1 CHRONICLES 6:12
LAST REFERENCE
1 CHRONICLES 9:11

4) A young soldier, "mighty of valour," who helped to crown David king of Judah in Hebron.

ONLY REFERENCE
1 CHRONICLES 12:28

5) A man who repaired Jerusalem's walls under Nehemiah.

ONLY REFERENCE
NEHEMIAH 3:4

6) Another man who repaired Jerusalem's walls under Nehemiah.

ONLY REFERENCE
NEHEMIAH 3:29

7) A Jewish leader who renewed the covenant under Nehemiah.

ONLY REFERENCE
NEHEMIAH 10:21

8) A priest who resettled Jerusalem following the Babylonian Exile.

ONLY REFERENCE
NEHEMIAH 11:11

9) One of the temple treasurers appointed by Nehemiah.

ONLY REFERENCE
NEHEMIAH 13:13

ZAHAM
Loathing

A son of Judah's king Rehoboam and a grandson of Solomon.

ONLY REFERENCE
2 CHRONICLES 11:19

ZALAPH

Father of a man who repaired Jerusalem's walls under Nehemiah.

ONLY REFERENCE
NEHEMIAH 3:30

ZALMON 1
Shady

One of King David's mightiest warriors known as "the thirty."

ONLY REFERENCE
2 SAMUEL 23:28

ZALMUNNA 12
Shade has been denied

A Midianite king whom Gideon pursued after Zalmunna killed Gideon's brothers at Tabor. Gideon killed Zalmunna.

FIRST REFERENCE
JUDGES 8:5
LAST REFERENCE
PSALM 83:11

ZANOAH 1
Rejected

A descendant of Abraham through Jacob's son Judah.

ONLY REFERENCE
1 CHRONICLES 4:18

ZAPHNATH-PAANEAH 1

A name the Egyptian pharaoh gave to Joseph, the revealer of dreams.

ONLY REFERENCE
GENESIS 41:45

ZARA 1
Rising

Greek form of the name *Zarah*, used in the New Testament.

ONLY REFERENCE
MATTHEW 1:3
GENEALOGY OF JESUS
MATTHEW 1:3

ZARAH 2
Rising

A twin born to Jacob's son Judah and Judah's daughter-in-law, Tamar.

FIRST REFERENCE
GENESIS 38:30
LAST REFERENCE
GENESIS 46:12

ZATTHU 1

A Jewish leader who renewed the covenant under Nehemiah.

ONLY REFERENCE
NEHEMIAH 10:14

ZATTU 3

Forefather of an exiled family that returned to Judah under Zerubbabel.

FIRST REFERENCE
EZRA 2:8
LAST REFERENCE
NEHEMIAH 7:13

ZAVAN 1
Disquiet

A descendant of Seir, who lived in Esau's "land of Edom."

ONLY REFERENCE
1 CHRONICLES 1:42

ZAZA 1
Prominent

A descendant of Abraham through Jacob's son Judah.

ONLY REFERENCE
1 CHRONICLES 2:33

ZEBADIAH 9

God has given

1) A descendant of Abraham through Jacob's son Benjamin.

ONLY REFERENCE
I CHRONICLES 8:15

2) Another descendant of Abraham through Jacob's son Benjamin.

ONLY REFERENCE
I CHRONICLES 8:17

3) A "mighty man" who supported the future king David during his conflict with Saul.

ONLY REFERENCE
I CHRONICLES 12:7

4) A Levite "porter" (doorkeeper) in the house of the Lord.

ONLY REFERENCE
I CHRONICLES 26:2

5) One of King David's captains of thousands.

ONLY REFERENCE
I CHRONICLES 27:7

6) A Levite sent by King Jehoshaphat to teach the law of the Lord throughout the nation of Judah.

ONLY REFERENCE
2 CHRONICLES 17:8

7) "Ruler of the house of Judah" who was in charge of King Jehoshaphat's houeshold.

ONLY REFERENCE
2 CHRONICLES 19:11

8) A Jewish exile who returned from Babylon to Judah under Ezra.

ONLY REFERENCE
EZRA 8:8

9) An exiled Israelite priest who married a "strange" (foreign) woman.

ONLY REFERENCE
EZRA 10:20

ZEBAH 12

Sacrifice

A Midianite king whom Gideon pursued with three hundred men after Zebah killed Gideon's brothers at Tabor. Gideon killed Zebah.

FIRST REFERENCE
JUDGES 8:5
LAST REFERENCE
PSALM 83:11

ZEBEDEE 12

Giving

Father of Jesus' disciples James and John and a fisherman on the Sea of Galilee. Zebedee's sons worked with him until they left to follow Jesus. James and John are frequently referred to as "the sons of Zebedee."

FIRST REFERENCE
MATTHEW 4:21
LAST REFERENCE
JOHN 21:2

ZEBINA 1

Gainfulness

An exiled Israelite who married a "strange" (foreign) woman.

ONLY REFERENCE
EZRA 10:43

ZEBUDAH 1

Gainfulness

Mother of the evil Jehoiakim, the third-to-last king of Judah.

ONLY REFERENCE
2 KINGS 23:36

ZEBUL 6
Dwelling

Ruler of the city of Shechem under King Abimelech. He encouraged the conspirator Gaal to fight Abimelech's army and pushed him and his men out of the city.

FIRST REFERENCE
JUDGES 9:28
LAST REFERENCE
JUDGES 9:41

ZEBULUN 6
Habitation

Sixth and last son of Jacob and Leah. Jacob foretold that Zebulun would dwell "at the haven of the sea" (Genesis 49:13), bordering on Zidon.

FIRST REFERENCE
GENESIS 30:20
LAST REFERENCE
I CHRONICLES 2:1

ZECHARIAH 39 27
God has remembered

1) A descendant of Abraham through Jacob's son Reuben.

ONLY REFERENCE
I CHRONICLES 5:7

2) A Levite, known as "a wise counsellor," who was chosen by lot to guard the west side of the house of the Lord.

FIRST REFERENCE
I CHRONICLES 9:21
LAST REFERENCE
2 CHRONICLES 29:1

3) A descendant of Jehiel, the founder of the land of Gibeon.

ONLY REFERENCE
I CHRONICLES 9:37

4) A Levite musician who performed in celebration when King David brought the ark of the covenant to Jerusalem.

FIRST REFERENCE
I CHRONICLES 15:18
LAST REFERENCE
I CHRONICLES 16:5

5) A priest who blew a trumpet before the ark of the covenant when David brought it to Jerusalem.

ONLY REFERENCE
I CHRONICLES 15:24

6) A Levite worship leader during David's reign. Lots were cast to determine his duties.

ONLY REFERENCE
I CHRONICLES 24:25

7) A Levite "porter" (doorkeeper) in the house of the Lord.

ONLY REFERENCE
I CHRONICLES 26:11

8) Father of a ruler of the half tribe of Manasseh under King David.

ONLY REFERENCE
I CHRONICLES 27:21

9) A prince of Judah sent by King Jehoshaphat to teach the law of the Lord throughout the nation.

ONLY REFERENCE
2 CHRONICLES 17:7

10) Father of Jahaziel, a Levite worship leader of the order of the sons of Asaph.

ONLY REFERENCE
2 CHRONICLES 20:14

11) A son of Judah's king Jeho-shaphat, given "great gifts of silver, and of gold, and of precious things" by his father (2 Chronicles 21:3).

ONLY REFERENCE
2 CHRONICLES 21:2

12) Son of Jehoiada the priest who was killed for telling Judah's people they had forsaken God.

ONLY REFERENCE
2 CHRONICLES 24:20

13) A prophet who influenced King Uzziah of Judah and "had under-standing in the visions of God."

ONLY REFERENCE
2 CHRONICLES 26:5

14) A descendant of Abraham through Jacob's son Levi. Zechariah was among the Levites who cleansed the Jerusalem temple during the revival in King Hezekiah's reign.

ONLY REFERENCE
2 CHRONICLES 29:13

15) An overseer of temple repairs under King Josiah of Judah.

ONLY REFERENCE
2 CHRONICLES 34:12

16) A temple ruler during the reign of King Josiah of Judah.

ONLY REFERENCE
2 CHRONICLES 35:8

17) An Old Testament minor prophet who ministered in Jerusa-lem following the return from exile. Judah prospered under his ministry as the people rebuilt the temple.

FIRST REFERENCE
EZRA 5:1
LAST REFERENCE
ZECHARIAH 7:8

18) A Jewish exile who returned from Babylon to Judah under Ezra.

ONLY REFERENCE
EZRA 8:3

19) A Jewish exile charged with finding Levites and temple ser-vants to travel to Jerusalem with Ezra.

FIRST REFERENCE
EZRA 8:11
LAST REFERENCE
EZRA 8:16

20) An exiled Israelite who mar-ried a "strange" (foreign) woman.

ONLY REFERENCE
EZRA 10:26

21) A priest who assisted Ezra in reading the book of the law to the people of Jerusalem.

ONLY REFERENCE
NEHEMIAH 8:4

22) A Jewish exile from the tribe of Judah who resettled Jerusalem.

ONLY REFERENCE
NEHEMIAH 11:4

23) Another Jewish exile from the tribe of Judah who resettled Jerusalem.

ONLY REFERENCE
NEHEMIAH 11:5

24) Forefather of an exiled family that resettled Jerusalem.

ONLY REFERENCE
NEHEMIAH 11:12

25) Forefather of a priest who returned to Jerusalem under Zerubbabel.

ONLY REFERENCE
NEHEMIAH 12:16

26) A priest who helped to dedicate the rebuilt walls of Jerusalem by playing a musical instrument.

FIRST REFERENCE
NEHEMIAH 12:35
LAST REFERENCE
NEHEMIAH 12:41

27) A witness of Isaiah to his prophecy about Maher-shalal-hash-baz.

ONLY REFERENCE
ISAIAH 8:2

ZEDEKIAH 62 5
Right of God

1) A false prophet who predicted that King Jehoshaphat of Judah would win over the Syrians. Zedekiah struck and mocked the faithful prophet Micaiah.

FIRST REFERENCE
I KINGS 22:11
LAST REFERENCE
2 CHRONICLES 18:23

2) Originally named Mattaniah, Zedekiah was a brother of King Jehoiachin of Judah. Nebuchadnezzar, king of Babylon, conquered Judah, deposed Jehoiachin, renamed Mattaniah as Zedekiah, and made him king. Like his brother, Zedekiah rebelled against Babylon. Zedekiah did not heed the prophet Jeremiah and imprisoned him. Nebuchadnezzar besieged Jerusalem. When the city no longer had food, Zedekiah and his troops sought to escape. The Chaldean army caught Zedekiah, killed his sons before him, and put out his eyes. They bound him and carried him to Babylon.

FIRST REFERENCE
2 KINGS 24:17
LAST REFERENCE
JEREMIAH 52:11
KEY REFERENCES
2 KINGS 24:17–20; JEREMIAH 39:4–7

3) A son of King Jehoiakim of Judah.

ONLY REFERENCE
I CHRONICLES 3:16

4) A false prophet aganist whom Jeremiah spoke after Judah went into captivity.

FIRST REFERENCE
JEREMIAH 29:21
LAST REFERENCE
JEREMIAH 29:22

5) A prince of Judah who heard Jeremiah's prophecy from Micaiah (5).

ONLY REFERENCE
JEREMIAH 36:12

ZEEB 6
Wolf

A Midianite prince captured and killed by the men of Ephraim under Gideon's command.

FIRST REFERENCE
JUDGES 7:25
LAST REFERENCE
PSALM 83:11

ZELEK 2
Fissure

One of King David's valiant warriors.

FIRST REFERENCE
2 SAMUEL 23:37
LAST REFERENCE
I CHRONICLES 11:39

ZELOPHEHAD 11
United

A descendant of Joseph through Manasseh who died during the wilderness wanderings. Zelophehad's five daughters asked Moses if they could inherit their father's property in the Promised Land (a right normally reserved for sons). God ruled that they should, since Zelophehad had no sons.

FIRST REFERENCE
NUMBERS 26:33
LAST REFERENCE
I CHRONICLES 7:15

ZELOTES 2
Zealot

Surname of Simon, one of Jesus' twelve disciples.

FIRST REFERENCE
LUKE 6:15
LAST REFERENCE
ACTS 1:13

ZEMIRA 1
Song

A descendant of Abraham through Jacob's son Benjamin.

ONLY REFERENCE
I CHRONICLES 7:8

ZENAS 1
Jove-given

A lawyer whom the apostle Paul encouraged Titus to help on a journey.

ONLY REFERENCE
TITUS 3:13

ZEPHANIAH 10
God has secreted

1) The second priest in the temple whom King Zedekiah sent to the prophet Jeremiah, asking him to pray for Israel. When King Nebuchadnezzar of Babylon captured Jerusalem, Zephaniah was taken to Riblah, where Nebuchadnezzar killed him.

FIRST REFERENCE
2 KINGS 25:18
LAST REFERENCE
JEREMIAH 52:24

2) Forefather of a Levite worship leader who served in the tabernacle during David's reign.

ONLY REFERENCE
I CHRONICLES 6:36

3) A descendant of Abraham through Jacob's son Levi.

ONLY REFERENCE
ZEPHANIAH 1:1

4) Forefather of Josiah (2), in whose house the high priest Joshua received a prophecy from Zechariah.

FIRST REFERENCE
ZECHARIAH 6:10
LAST REFERENCE
ZECHARIAH 6:14

ZEPHI 1
Observant

A descendant of Abraham's grandson Esau.

ONLY REFERENCE
I CHRONICLES 1:36

ZEPHO 2

Observant

A grandson of Isaac's son Esau.

FIRST REFERENCE
GENESIS 36:11
LAST REFERENCE
GENESIS 36:15

ZEPHON 1

Watchtower

A descendant of Abraham through Jacob's son Gad.

ONLY REFERENCE
NUMBERS 26:15

ZERAH 19 7

Rising

1) A descendant of Abraham's grandson Esau.

FIRST REFERENCE
GENESIS 36:13
LAST REFERENCE
1 CHRONICLES 1:37

2) Father of a king of Edom, "before there reigned any king over the children of Israel" (Genesis 36:31).

FIRST REFERENCE
GENESIS 36:33
LAST REFERENCE
1 CHRONICLES 1:44

3) A grandson of Jacob, born to Jacob's son Judah and Judah's daughter-in-law, Tamar.

FIRST REFERENCE
NUMBERS 26:20
LAST REFERENCE
NEHEMIAH 11:24

4) A descendant of Abraham through Jacob's son Simeon.

FIRST REFERENCE
NUMBERS 26:13
LAST REFERENCE
1 CHRONICLES 4:24

5) A descendant of Abraham through Jacob's son Levi.

ONLY REFERENCE
1 CHRONICLES 6:21

6) Another descendant of Abraham through Jacob's son Levi.

ONLY REFERENCE
1 CHRONICLES 6:41

7) An Ethiopian commander whose army fled before King Asa of Judah.

ONLY REFERENCE
2 CHRONICLES 14:9

ZERAHIAH 5 2

God has risen

1) A descendant of Abraham through Jacob's son Levi, and a priest through the line of Aaron.

FIRST REFERENCE
1 CHRONICLES 6:6
LAST REFERENCE
EZRA 7:4

2) Forefather of a Jewish exile who returned from Babylon to Judah under Ezra.

ONLY REFERENCE
EZRA 8:4

ZERESH 4

Wife of Haman, the villain of the story of Esther. Zeresh, along with friends, encouraged Haman to build a gallows on which to hang Esther's cousin Mordecai—the gallows that Haman himself would later die on.

FIRST REFERENCE
ESTHER 5:10
LAST REFERENCE
ESTHER 6:13

ZERETH
Splendor

A descendant of Abraham through Jacob's son Judah.

ONLY REFERENCE
1 CHRONICLES 4:7

ZERI
Distillation

A son of King David's musician Jeduthun, "who prophesied with a harp, to give thanks and to praise the LORD" (1 Chronicles 25:3).

ONLY REFERENCE
1 CHRONICLES 25:3

ZEROR
Parcel

An ancestor of Israel's first king, Saul.

ONLY REFERENCE
1 SAMUEL 9:1

ZERUAH

A widow and the mother of Jeroboam, who became the first king of the northern Jewish nation of Israel.

ONLY REFERENCE
1 KINGS 11:26

ZERUBBABEL 22
Descended of Babylon

Governor of Judah, Zerubbabel returned from the Babylonian Exile with many Israelites in his train. He began by rebuilding an altar so Judah could worship for the Feast of Tabernacles. When God spoke through the prophet Haggai, Zerubbabel and the high priest Jeshua obeyed, organizing workers to rebuild the temple. When Israel's enemies came to offer their help, Zerubbabel refused and tried to forestall trouble by telling them that Israel was following the Persian king Cyrus's command. God told the prophet Zechariah that Zerubbabel would finish his task.

FIRST REFERENCE
1 CHRONICLES 3:19
LAST REFERENCE
ZECHARIAH 4:10
KEY REFERENCES
EZRA 3:2–5; 3:8; 4:1–3; 5:2; HAGGAI 1:1–2, 12;
ZECHARIAH 4:9

ZERUIAH 26
Wounded

Sister of King David and mother of David's battle commander, Joab, and his brothers, Abishai and Asahel.

FIRST REFERENCE
1 SAMUEL 26:6
LAST REFERENCE
1 CHRONICLES 27:24
KEY REFERENCES
2 SAMUEL 2:18; 1 CHRONICLES 2:15–16

ZETHAM 2

Olive

A chief Levite during King David's reign, Zetham was in charge of the temple treasures.

FIRST REFERENCE
I CHRONICLES 23:8
LAST REFERENCE
I CHRONICLES 26:22

ZETHAN 1

Olive

A descendant of Abraham through Jacob's son Benjamin.

ONLY REFERENCE
I CHRONICLES 7:10

ZETHAR 1

A eunuch serving the Persian king Ahasuerus in Esther's time.

ONLY REFERENCE
ESTHER 1:10

ZIA 1

Agitation

A descendant of Abraham through Jacob's son Gad.

ONLY REFERENCE
I CHRONICLES 5:13

ZIBA 16

Station

A servant of King Saul who told King David where Mephibosheth lived after David took the throne. When David fled Jerusalem, Ziba brought him food and the news that his master sought to take David's throne. David gave him everything Mephibosheth owned. When David returned to Jerusalem as king, Mephibosheth claimed his servant had lied.

FIRST REFERENCE
2 SAMUEL 9:2
LAST REFERENCE
2 SAMUEL 19:29
KEY REFERENCES
2 SAMUEL 9:2–3; 16:1–4; 19:24–30

ZIBEON 8 2

Variegated

1) Grandfather of Anah, a wife of Esau.

FIRST REFERENCE
GENESIS 36:2
LAST REFERENCE
GENESIS 36:14

2) A descendant of Seir, who lived in Esau's "land of Edom."

FIRST REFERENCE
GENESIS 36:20
LAST REFERENCE
I CHRONICLES 1:40

ZIBIA 1

Gazelle

A descendant of Abraham through Jacob's son Benjamin.

ONLY REFERENCE
I CHRONICLES 8:9

ZIBIAH 2

Gazelle

Mother of Joash, one of the good kings of Judah.

FIRST REFERENCE
2 KINGS 12:1
LAST REFERENCE
2 CHRONICLES 24:1

ZICHRI 12
Memorable

1) A brother of Korah (3), who rebelled against Moses and was killed by God.

ONLY REFERENCE
EXODUS 6:21

2) A descendant of Abraham through Jacob's son Benjamin.

ONLY REFERENCE
I CHRONICLES 8:19

3) Another descendant of Abraham through Jacob's son Benjamin.

ONLY REFERENCE
I CHRONICLES 8:23

4) A chief of the tribe of Benjamin who lived in Jerusalem.

ONLY REFERENCE
I CHRONICLES 8:27

5) Forefather of a chief Levite and a son of Asaph (2).

ONLY REFERENCE
I CHRONICLES 9:15

6) A Levite worship leader who was part of King David's reorganization of the Levites.

ONLY REFERENCE
I CHRONICLES 26:25

7) Forefather of a ruler over the Reubenites under King David.

ONLY REFERENCE
I CHRONICLES 27:16

8) A mighty man of valor who served King Jehoshaphat of Judah.

ONLY REFERENCE
2 CHRONICLES 17:16

9) A captain of hundreds who made a covenant with the priest Jehoiada.

ONLY REFERENCE
2 CHRONICLES 23:1

10) "A mighty man of Ephraim" who killed a son of King Ahaz and two of his officers.

ONLY REFERENCE
2 CHRONICLES 28:7

11) Father of a Benjamite who was chosen by lot to resettle Jerusalem after returning from the Babylonian Exile.

ONLY REFERENCE
NEHEMIAH 11:9

12) Forefather of a priest who returned to Jerusalem under Zerubbabel.

ONLY REFERENCE
NEHEMIAH 12:17

ZIDKIJAH 1
Right of God

An Israelite who renewed the covenant under Nehemiah.

ONLY REFERENCE
NEHEMIAH 10:1

ZIDON 1
Fishery

A descendant of Noah through his son Ham.

ONLY REFERENCE
I CHRONICLES 1:13

ZIHA 3

Drought

1) Forefather of a family of temple servants who returned from exile.

FIRST REFERENCE
EZRA 2:43
LAST REFERENCE
NEHEMIAH 7:46

2) An official over the temple servants after the Babylonian Exile. Possibly the same as Ziha (1).

ONLY REFERENCE
NEHEMIAH 11:21

ZILLAH 3

Shade

Second wife of Lamech, a descendant of Cain. Her son was Tubal-cain.

FIRST REFERENCE
GENESIS 4:19
LAST REFERENCE
GENESIS 4:23

ZILPAH 7

Trickle

Servant of Leah. Leah gave Zilpah to her husband, Jacob, as a wife because she thought her own childbearing days were ended. Zilpah had two sons, Gad and Asher.

FIRST REFERENCE
GENESIS 29:24
LAST REFERENCE
GENESIS 46:18

ZILTHAI 2

Shady

1) A descendant of Abraham through Jacob's son Benjamin.

ONLY REFERENCE
I CHRONICLES 8:20

2) One of a group of "mighty men of valour" who fought for King David.

ONLY REFERENCE
I CHRONICLES 12:20

ZIMMAH 3

Lewdness

1) A descendant of Abraham through Jacob's son Levi.

ONLY REFERENCE
I CHRONICLES 6:20

2) A descendant of Abraham through Jacob's son Levi.

ONLY REFERENCE
I CHRONICLES 6:42

3) Forefather of a Levite worship leader who helped to consecrate the temple during King Hezekiah's reign.

ONLY REFERENCE
2 CHRONICLES 29:12

ZIMRAN 2

Musical

A son of Abraham by his second wife, Keturah.

FIRST REFERENCE
GENESIS 25:2
LAST REFERENCE
I CHRONICLES 1:32

ZIMRI 14
Musical

1) A man killed by Phinehas (1) for blatant sexual sin.

ONLY REFERENCE
NUMBERS 25:14

2) The king of Israel who conspired against King Elah and killed him. After usurping Elah's throne, Zimri killed Elah's male relatives, fulfilling the prophecy of Jehu (1). Zimri reigned for seven days before Israel made Omri king in his place. When the capital was taken, Zimri burned down the king's house with himself inside it.

FIRST REFERENCE
I KINGS 16:9
LAST REFERENCE
2 KINGS 9:31

3) A descendant of Abraham through Jacob's son Judah.

ONLY REFERENCE
I CHRONICLES 2:6

4) A descendant of Abraham through Jacob's son Benjamin, in the line of King Saul and his son Jonathan.

FIRST REFERENCE
I CHRONICLES 8:36
LAST REFERENCE
I CHRONICLES 9:42

ZINA 1
Well fed

A Levite who was part of David's reorganization of the Levites. Same as Zizah.

ONLY REFERENCE
I CHRONICLES 23:10

ZIPH 2
Flowing

1) A descendant of Abraham through Jacob's son Judah.

ONLY REFERENCE
I CHRONICLES 2:42

2) Another descendant of Abraham through Jacob's son Judah.

ONLY REFERENCE
I CHRONICLES 4:16

ZIPHAH 1
Flowing

A descendant of Abraham through Jacob's son Judah.

ONLY REFERENCE
I CHRONICLES 4:16

ZIPHION 1
Watchtower

A descendant of Abraham through Jacob's son Gad.

ONLY REFERENCE
GENESIS 46:16

ZIPPOR 7
Little bird

Father of the Moabite king Balak, who consulted the false prophet Balaam.

FIRST REFERENCE
NUMBERS 22:2
LAST REFERENCE
JUDGES 11:25

ZIPPORAH 3
Bird

Daughter of the Midianite priest Reuel (also known as Jethro) and wife of Moses. She had a disagreement with her husband over the circumcision of their firstborn son.

FIRST REFERENCE
EXODUS 2:21
LAST REFERENCE
EXODUS 18:2

ZITHRI 1
Protective

A descendant of Abraham through Jacob's son Levi.

ONLY REFERENCE
EXODUS 6:22

ZIZA 2
Prominence

1) A descendant of Abraham through Jacob's son Simeon.

ONLY REFERENCE
1 CHRONICLES 4:37

2) A son of Judah's king Rehoboam and a grandson of Solomon.

ONLY REFERENCE
2 CHRONICLES 11:20

ZIZAH 1
Prominence

A Levite who was part of David's reorganization of the Levites. Same as Zina.

ONLY REFERENCE
1 CHRONICLES 23:11

ZOBEBAH 1
Canopy

Daughter of Coz, a descendant of Abraham through Jacob's son Judah.

ONLY REFERENCE
1 CHRONICLES 4:8

ZOHAR 4
Whiteness

1) Father of Ephron, who sold Abraham a burial place.

FIRST REFERENCE
GENESIS 23:8
LAST REFERENCE
GENESIS 25:9

2) A grandson of Jacob through his son Simeon.

FIRST REFERENCE
GENESIS 46:10
LAST REFERENCE
EXODUS 6:15

ZOHETH 1

A descendant of Abraham through Jacob's son Judah.

ONLY REFERENCE
1 CHRONICLES 4:20

ZOPHAH 2
Breadth

A descendant of Abraham through Jacob's son Asher.

FIRST REFERENCE
1 CHRONICLES 7:35
LAST REFERENCE
1 CHRONICLES 7:36

ZOPHAI 1

Honeycomb

A descendant of Abraham through Jacob's son Levi.

ONLY REFERENCE
I CHRONICLES 6:26

ZOPHAR 4

Departing

One of three friends of Job who mourned his losses for a week and then accused him of wrongdoing. God ultimately chastised the three for their criticism of Job, commanding them to sacrifice burnt offerings while Job prayed for them.

FIRST REFERENCE
JOB 2:11
LAST REFERENCE
JOB 42:9

ZOROBABEL 3

Descended of Babylon

A descendant of Abraham through Isaac; forebear of Jesus' earthly father, Joseph.

FIRST REFERENCE
MATTHEW 1:12
LAST REFERENCE
LUKE 3:27
GENEALOGY OF JESUS
MATTHEW 1:12

ZUAR 5

Small

Father of a prince of the tribe of Issachar in Moses' day.

FIRST REFERENCE
NUMBERS 1:8
LAST REFERENCE
NUMBERS 10:15

ZUPH 2

Honeycomb

An ancestor of the prophet Samuel.

FIRST REFERENCE
I SAMUEL 1:1
LAST REFERENCE
I CHRONICLES 6:35

ZUR 5

Rock

1) A Midianite king killed by the Israelites at God's command.

FIRST REFERENCE
NUMBERS 25:15
LAST REFERENCE
JOSHUA 13:21

2) A descendant of Abraham through Jacob's son Benjamin, and a relative of King Saul.

FIRST REFERENCE
I CHRONICLES 8:30
LAST REFERENCE
I CHRONICLES 9:36

ZURIEL 1

Rock of God

A chief of the Levites under Eleazar (1).

ONLY REFERENCE
NUMBERS 3:35

ZURISHADDAI 5

Rock of the Almighty

Father of a prince of Simeon in Moses' day.

FIRST REFERENCE
NUMBERS 1:6
LAST REFERENCE
NUMBERS 10:19

_____

_____

_____

_____

_____

_____

_____

_____

_____

_____

_____

_____

_____

_____

_____

_____

NOTES

Other popular Bible reference books from Barbour Publishing

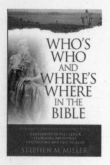

Who's Who and Where's Where in the Bible
6" x 9" / Paperback / 400 pages / $14.97
ISBN 978-1-59310-111-4

Here's a Bible dictionary that's actually fun to read! Dig deeply into the stories of 500 people and places that make the Bible such a fascinating book.

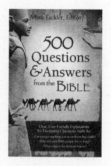

500 Questions & Answers from the Bible
6" x 9" / Paperback / 256 pages / $9.97
ISBN 978-1-59789-473-9

For inquisitive readers of any age—adults and students alike—here's a book to shed light on the Bible's great questions. And it's fully illustrated in color!

The Complete Guide to the Bible
7" x 9½" / Paperback / 528 pages / $19.97
ISBN 978-1-59789-374-9

A reliable, jargon-free handbook for average people who want to better understand the entire Bible. Beautifully illustrated in full color, with photos, paintings, and maps.

Available wherever Christian books are sold.